John Henry Newman, Anne Mozley

Letters and Correspondence During His Life in the English Church

Vol. 1

John Henry Newman, Anne Mozley

Letters and Correspondence During His Life in the English Church
Vol. 1

ISBN/EAN: 9783744687393

Printed in Europe, USA, Canada, Australia, Japan

Cover: Foto ©Thomas Meinert / pixelio.de

More available books at **www.hansebooks.com**

LETTERS AND CORRESPONDENCE

OF

JOHN HENRY NEWMAN

DURING HIS LIFE IN THE ENGLISH CHURCH

WITH A BRIEF AUTOBIOGRAPHY

EDITED, AT CARDINAL NEWMAN'S REQUEST, BY

ANNE MOZLEY

EDITOR OF 'LETTERS OF THE REV. J. B. MOZLEY, D.D.
REGIUS PROFESSOR OF DIVINITY IN THE UNIVERSITY OF OXFORD'

IN TWO VOLUMES—VOL. I.

LONDON
LONGMANS, GREEN, AND CO.
AND NEW YORK: 15 EAST 16th STREET
1890

All rights reserved

ADVERTISEMENT

MATERIALS for the present work were placed in the Editor's hands towards the close of 1884. The selection from them was made, and the papers returned to Cardinal Newman, in the summer of 1887. Since the return of these papers, other and important collections of letters have been placed at the Editor's disposal, and much has been added—indeed, such a work can never be said to be finished, till every page has passed through the printer's hands.

In obedience to the original intention and lately expressed wish of the Cardinal, no time is lost in placing the volumes before the public.

One passage in the Introduction makes it necessary to explain that it was in print before the deeply regretted death of Dr. Liddon.

ORIEL LODGE, DERBY:
   Nov. 1890.

PORTRAIT

JOHN HENRY NEWMAN . . . . . *Frontispiece*

Engraved from a photograph by Messrs. Hills & Saunders of the bust made in 1841 by T. WESTMACOTT, *now in the possession of* Mr. H. W. MOZLEY.

INTRODUCTION

'It has ever been a hobby of mine, though perhaps it is a truism, not a hobby, that the true life of a man is in his letters. . . . Not only for the interest of a biography, but for arriving at the inside of things, the publication of letters is the true method. Biographers varnish, they assign motives, they conjecture feelings, they interpret Lord Burleigh's nods; but contemporary letters are facts.'—*Dr. Newman to his Sister, Mrs. John Mozley, May* 18, 1863.

THESE words, addressed to his sister by Cardinal Newman—to anticipate the title with which the reader is familiar—may explain the purpose of the present work, which is, through the medium of his letters, to place John Henry Newman before the reader as he was to his family, to his friends, to his correspondents; as he was in early youth and in manhood; in public and in private; and in his action in, and for, the English Church, while he remained in her communion. With his secession the Editor's task—as being a member of that communion—is ended. Under the total change of circumstances the work, if pursued, must be carried on by another hand. Yet because only half a life furnishes the material and matter of these volumes, the reader need not imagine that the letters of a later date may or must contain intimations of a changed character. Perhaps no man, passing through a course of change, ever remained more substantially the same through the lapse of years and revolution of circumstances and opinions.

His high estimate of letters as records and custodians of the truth of things made him from early youth a preserver of letters; though his esteem for his correspondent might be the more prominent motive. In early days a postscript often speaks of arranging letters as one of the tasks of the closing year. The task, as he would perform it, would help to fill in the details of that map of the past which in its outline was so vividly marked in his memory.[1] The habits of his life, as being congenial to his nature, were early formed; just as the turn of thought, the tastes, the more powerful bents of his mind, may all be traced to an early dawn.

Few persons preserve their letters; it is, indeed, a rare habit; but there was in Newman's letters to his friends, as in his character, a weight and distinctiveness, whether of subject or mode of treatment, which secured them an exemption from the common fate after perusal; and, once escaping this, their value increased with years, and, in fact, as time went on, they were felt to be history.

Thus, in the hurry of collecting material for his 'Apologia pro Vita sua,' Dr. Newman could rely on his friends having preserved his letters with method; so that, on a hasty appeal, he could be supplied with the true record of his thoughts, motives and actions, at critical periods. Eventually, as is now seen, he commits to his letters, when he shall have passed away, the task of placing himself, his course of thought and action, in their true light—as he believed it—before the world. But the facts and early circumstances of a life cannot be given through this medium. To supply a true record of these the Cardinal committed to those entrusted with his papers what he calls a Memoir, written in the third person, not to conceal the hand that penned it, but better to show the simplicity of style in which he desired that all told about himself should be composed. One motive impelling him to this effort would certainly be, to tell in his own words, without the possibility of error, his earliest history, and what he felt towards his earliest benefactors: whether his parents, so dear to him, and for whom he felt such sensitive devotion; or his

---

[1] In a note to the present writer, received shortly after the death of his sister, Mrs. Mozley, Cardinal Newman writes: 'I miss, and shall miss, in Jemima this—she alone, with me, had a memory of dates. I knew quite well, as anniversaries of all kinds came round, she was recollecting them as well as I—*e.g.* my getting into Oriel. Now I am the only one in the world who know a hundred things most interesting to me. Yesterday was the anniversary of Mary's death—my mind turned at once to Jemima, but she was away.'

schoolmaster, whose boast he was; or 'the excellent man,' whose deeper teaching influenced his life; or the tutors at Trinity, who encouraged him in his prosperous start and consoled him in defeat—all, according to their several claims, held a lasting, ever-present place in his affections. To all his heart had opened with a grateful effusion which no time cooled, and which never lost its freshness.

In the private paper which precedes the account of his early years, dated June 1, 1874, he writes:

I am forced to forebode that some one or other who knows little or nothing about me, whether well or ill disposed towards me, will have something to say about my history, if my friends are silent, and in consequence, that they who have known me well and who have been in my intimate confidence, will find it their duty to meet by some sort of biographical notice vague and random ideas and accounts of me, derived from the ephemeral literature and controversy of the last forty years. This necessity, I am aware, has been in a measure obviated by myself in my 'Apologia pro Vita sua.' Nevertheless, the anticipation of it has led me to leave behind, in addition, for the inspection of my friends, portions of my private memoranda by way of assisting and supplementing their recollections of me, leaving to their affection for me and their discretion, to deal tenderly with what in the first instance is confidential and sacred.

These words were written during the lifetime of Father St. John, who died May 24, 1875, and may be said to have been especially addressed to him; but before this date Dr. Newman had come to the conclusion that, to use his own words, 'If a memoir was to be published of me, a Protestant Editor must take the Protestant part.'

Certainly when once the question was faced no other conclusion could be arrived at. It would not have been just, either to the names with which his own is associated or to the English Church, for which the friends worked together, to leave the stirring period of their joint labours in other than Anglican hands. But the longer men live the more difficult it becomes to assign such tasks to adequate hands. The honours of biography have fallen, as is fitting, to the two leaders of the movement who died in the communion of the Church of England ; the life of Keble being undertaken by an early friend, distinguished both by name and office ; and Dr. Pusey's being still [1] in the charge of one whose own work in and for the Church is recognised as so important that his strength and energies can scarcely be spared even for the task of commemorating, as no other could, the name to whose memory he shows such sincerity of devotion.

Dr. Pusey continued a living influence in his Church to the last. But among the band of early workers or youthful sympathisers in the start of the movement, how few remain qualified at once in themselves and by circumstances for the task now proposed ! From 'Who would do it best ?'—a question which, in Dr. Pusey's case, would find a ready answer in Dr. Liddon—it changes to, 'Who among the friends he parted from some forty years ago remains in a position to do it at all ?' Each year some fit or possible chronicler passes away ; some memory which lived in the Oxford movement, and recognised in its chief mover, the quickener of a life. Some who remember and shared the enthusiasm of the hour have turned away to new interests ; some have elevated duties which render such a task at once neither fitting nor possible.

It must be considered that the task could not be self-chosen ; it must be imposed, and the materials for its execution placed at hand. The years pass ; old age—vigorous, but still old age—is reached ; and in old age (such as it ought to be), carrying its youth with it, and living its whole life in retrospect, men are thrown perforce upon the ties of family, its friendships and associations. In the instance now before the reader—in Newman—such ties never lost their hold. To him, then, it seemed natural to propose the task of editing the letters of the first half of his life to one who, as he knew, was allowed free access to family records and correspondence, from earliest years down to the time when his last surviving sister —the guardian of them—passed away. His choice of an editor possessing these advantages may have been strengthened by a volume recently published, 'The Letters of the Rev. J. B. Mozley,' which answered in its form and plan to his idea of a biography. In acknowledging his copy he concludes :

[1] Written in 1886.

James would have reason to say with Queen Katharine, 'After my death I wish no other herald but such an honest chronicler as Griffith,' and that because you have let him speak for himself.

The letter continues (November 20, 1884):

This leads me to speak of myself. Many years ago, at two independent times, I came to the conclusion that if a memoir was to be published of me, a Protestant Editor must take the Protestant part. ... What I thought would be done, and what only, was a sketch of my life up to 1833, which, with the 'Apologia' from 1833, would finish my Protestant years. With this view, in 1874 I wrote a brief memoir of my life up to 1833. ... I have a number of letters of my own and of my Mother's and sisters', and while I know they afford illustration of my memoir, yet in a matter so personal I cannot go by my own judgment. What I ask of you is to read the memoir.

Such a task—the task of placing one of the foremost men of his day before the world—when thus hinted at, was too strange and undreamt of to be understood. The Memoir was read and returned at once with the reader's comments. But when the proposed task was explained and thought over, it lost its more startling aspects. The work must depend absolutely on the letters and the Memoir for its interest and value; and though the letters—whether Mr. Newman's own or his correspondents'—should extend beyond the date first assigned, and treat of matters of the deepest public interest, facts and dates for the 'running notices' would be furnished by contemporary records; and there were Anglican friends of Cardinal Newman who might be consulted on questions, whether of fact or opinion, whose testimony would carry weight with all readers if their names might with propriety be given here; while the very requirement that the Editor must be a Protestant implied that no agreement with views as views was exacted on the one hand, or need be assumed on the other. One qualification essential to the task, without tacit belief in which the request could not have been made, the Editor may claim; and that is an absolute trust, under all changes of thought and circumstances, in the truth, sincerity, and disinterestedness of the one subject of the work. And, recognising and bearing in mind these qualities, the Anglican reader may surely acknowledge John Henry Newman's work for the Church of England as having been blessed to her, and believe that to those zealous services she owes much of the strength of her present position, and her greater fitness to meet the trials which may lie before her.

In the question of selection of letters Mr. Newman happens to have given his own rule quite apart from the point as a personal one. Writing to a friend (1836) on the letters in Hurrell Froude's 'Remains,' he says, 'I am conscious that even those who know me will say, What *could* he mean by putting this in ? What is the use of that ? What in the world if so and so ? How injudicious ! But, on the whole, I trust it will present, as far as it goes, the picture of a mind. And that being gained as the scope, the details may be left to take their chance.'

By this rule, 'to give the picture of a mind,' the Editor, while using the letters as records of a busy life, has desired to be guided ; and for this purpose it is necessary to show the subject of it in every relation that furnishes examples—thus, in his domestic and private character as a son, as a brother, as a pupil, as a friend, as a teacher, as a pastor ; in his inner religious life, as far as can be done without outraging privacy ; in his energy and devotion to his work, in his political capacity, in his temperament, his subtilty and candour, his sweetness and severity, his impetuosity and tenderness ; in all that constitutes his distinct and marked individuality.

In the execution of such a task the Editor cannot be bound by any formal pre-arranged plan, nor go by any strict rules. Nor was any rule imposed. What may be assumed as Cardinal Newman's motive for giving his letters publicity, was to give his share to the private history of the movement, and to show the line of his thought in it ; and, above all, to show himself sincere and honest in the course of it. And thus to defend himself—that is, his name—from the charges that had been levelled in the heat of conflict or under strong personal feeling ; though, in truth, he has long outlived them.

The reader will have gathered that the first suggestion,

that of illustrating the Memoir by family letters up to 1833, when the 'Apologia' continues the history, grew necessarily into a more comprehensive plan. To carry it out the Editor has been allowed to select material from the body of correspondence between Mr. Newman and his intimate friends, and others, whose letters illustrate the first stir and awakening of the movement. For this purpose, as interesting in themselves and as contributing to the history, whether of the leader or of the movement, many letters from correspondents are given; some most material, in fact as coming from a joint leader of high name and distinction, forming a very important contribution; while others are given for the sake of some name still dear to living memories, and which they would not willingly let die.

Mr. Newman's correspondence with his intimates, whether selected by himself or gathered from private sources, bears out what he has said of himself in the 'Apologia' and of the title of leader as applied to him.

For myself, I was not a person to take the lead of a party. I had lived for ten years among my personal friends : at no time have I acted on others without their acting upon me. I had lived with my private, nay, with some of my public, pupils, and with the junior Fellows of my college, without form or distance, on a footing of equality. I had a lounging, free-and-easy way of carrying things on.[1]

The correspondence which has been placed before the Editor, and now before the reader, is in marked confirmation of this picture of past intimacies as they would appear to the writer in looking back. Nothing can be more free and confiding than the tone or more entirely opposed to donnishness.

But, busy as Mr. Newman's life was, and, as it were, public, his home and family letters are at least as essential to the proper fulfilment of the task—to give the picture of a mind. We do not know 'Newman' as a letter-writer without being admitted to his home intimacies, his frank expressions of feelings and emotions which belong only to that inner circle.

As for style, it is always his own; the subject dictates the

[1] *Apologia*, p. 58.

choice of words best for the purpose. It may be observed that his letters are instinct with the consciousness of the person he addresses. There is a distinct tone to each of his familiar correspondents. Intimate as his letters are, there is a separate tone of intimacy, as there would be in conversing with friends. Where something unexpected occurs, and he feels to have miscalculated, it is a new experience. For example, writing on a hot July day from his college rooms, he says to the correspondent he is engaged with, that to such an one (a mutual friend), 'good fellow as he is,' it does not do to write with perfect unrestraint. 'Now, don't you see that for his good and comfort one must put on one's company coat before him; he cannot bear one's shirt sleeves.' He had been made conscious of a mistake in character or temper; but, as a rule, every circumstance of person and surrounding is present with him—all the traits that distinguish one from another. To all he is open, candid, confiding; but there is distinction in his confidences. Thus to his Mother he writes what it would not occur to him to say to anyone else: experiences, sensations, and odd encounters, dreams, fancies, passing speculations; while to Hurrell Froude, on another field altogether, there is the same absolute trust and unlocking of the heart.

The entire trust that he felt in his correspondent infused into his style a tone of simplicity. A correspondent of his sister's, on returning a letter of her brother's, written by him with a full heart on the death of a friend, applies this word 'simplicity' to his directness of tone.

It is a relief to see your brother so absolutely himself in his power of writing. This is quite an example of his nature and his gift of what is called *simplicity*—that power of saying exactly what he means, and going straight at his subject, putting a state of things directly before one, feelings as well as facts. I hope it all shows that he has the natural relief that the expression of natural feeling always brings.

His letters on business, whether of a public nature or on his literary work, show another side of character in their aim at thoroughness, in their keeping close to their subject and showing fixed principles and aims, in the management alike of time and of his personal gifts. The point of some letters is rather to show the amount and variety of his labours, than the effect these labours had on the course of events or public opinion. One does not seem to know Mr. Newman without the opportunity they furnish for realising the extent and variety of his occupations—his work of mind and pen.

Here and there a letter is given that might be considered to have done its work when read by the person addressed; but it has either seemed to help towards a picture or history of the time in some way or on some slight point as characteristic of the writer. Mr. Newman's character comes out by indirect touches. Not that he had the thought how he would show to any reader beyond the person addressed; but it is clear he felt pleasure in saying what he had to say, in his own way and with some touch which would bring reader and writer together, beyond the slight matter in question.

Now and then a note or seemingly insignificant sentence is given as showing how constant his thoughts were, to persons and things far removed from the busy world, whether of thought or action, in which he lived and acted with such intense activity of mind and pen. The present, with all its interests and responsibilities, did not put out of sight the absent and the past, and the workers and interests of that past.

It is not the Editor's part to make comments on views and principles found in the letters. They speak for themselves, and are given to the reader for his judgment. Of course the Anglican reader must keep his judgment in exercise. A looker-on sees things (and such a looker-on the reader may feel himself at certain periods) of which the actor is not conscious. Mr. Newman, on looking back on his past career, sometimes shows himself alive to this. 'He knew me better than I knew myself.'

Now and then, where circumstances have given the Editor especial opportunities, an opinion is expressed, but generally the reader is left to his unassisted judgment, having fully as much opportunity as the Editor to arrive at a right conclusion. It is the Editor's part to put facts before the reader —such may be called the historical letters contained in the correspondence—but in no sense to assume the historical tone.

The task was finally, on February 19, 1885, committed to the Editor in these words : 'I wish you to keep steadily in mind, and when you publish to make it known, that I am cognisant of no part of your work.' A rule which has been steadily adhered to. And again on March 13 of the same year Cardinal Newman quotes the Editor's own words as accepting them : 'Your own letters to be brought into use with every document you send me, all to be as true and simple as I can make it.'

JOHN HENRY NEWMAN

HIS CHILDHOOD AND SCHOOL LIFE

Mr. Newman's Autobiographical Memoir, after a few brief statements, may be said to begin with his college life, probably because he has touched upon his school life in the 'Apologia pro Vita sua.' It may be well, then, for the Editor to devote some preliminary pages to his life from infancy up to his entrance into Trinity, deriving information from records preserved amongst his papers, and from the recollections of his family and early friends. But there are also passages in Mr. Newman's works which seem to take us back into the past, and to throw light on his earliest childhood, passages that could only be inspired by memory; important as giving an early picture of his mind, in harmony with its subsequent development. And as such a few extracts may be given.

Thus:

At first children do not know that they are responsible beings, but by degrees they not only feel that they are, but reflect on the great truth and on what it implies. Some persons recollect a time as children when it fell on them to reflect what they were, whence they came, whither they tended, why they lived, what was required of them. The thought fell upon them long after they had heard and spoken of God; but at length they began to realise what they had heard, and they began to muse about themselves.[1]

Again:

Such are the feelings with which men often look back on their childhood when any accident brings it vividly before

[1] *Parochial Sermons*, vol. vi. p. 98.

them. Some relic or token of that early time ; some spot or some book, or a word, or a scent, or a sound, brings them back in memory to the first years of their discipleship, and they then see, what they could not know at the time, that God's presence went up with them and gave them rest. Nay, even now, perhaps, they are unable to discern fully what it was that made that time so bright and glorious. They are full of tender, affectionate thoughts towards those first years, but they do not know. why. They think it is those very years which they yearn after, whereas it is the presence of God, which they now see was then over them, which attracts them.[1]

Again :

We may have a sense of the presence of a Supreme Being which never has been dimmed by even a passing shadow : which has inhabited us ever since we can recollect anything, and which we cannot imagine our losing.[2]

Again :

It is my wish to take an ordinary child, but still one who is safe from influences destructive of his religious instincts. Supposing he has offended his parents, he will all alone and without effort, as if it were the most natural of acts, place himself in the presence of God and beg of Him to set him right with them. Let us consider how much is contained in this simple act. First, it involves the impression on his mind of an unseen Being with whom he is in immediate relation, and that relation so familiar that he can address Him whenever he himself chooses ; next, of One whose goodwill towards him he is assured of, and can take for granted—nay, who loves him better, and is nearer to him, than his parents ; further, of One who can hear him, wherever he happens to be, and who can read his thoughts, for his prayer need not be vocal ; lastly, of One who can effect a critical change in the state of feeling of others towards him. That is, we shall not be wrong in holding that this child has in his mind the image of an invisible Being, who exercises a particular providence among us, who is present everywhere, who is heart-reading, heart-changing, ever-accessible, open to impetration. What a strong and intimate vision of God must he have already attained if, as I have supposed, an ordinary trouble of mind

---

[1] *Parochial Sermons*, vol. iv. p. 262.
[2] *Grammar of Assent*, p. 178.

has the spontaneous effect of leading him for consolation and aid to an Invisible Personal Power! Such is the apprehension which even a child may have of his sovereign Lawgiver and Judge, which is possible in the case of children, because at least some children possess it, whether others possess it or no; and which, when it is found in children, is found to act promptly and keenly by reason of the paucity of their ideas. It is an image of the good God, good in Himself, good relatively towards the child with whatever incompleteness; an image before it has been reflected on, and before it is recognised by him as a notion. Though he cannot explain or define the word 'God' when told to use it, his acts show that to him it is far more than a word. He listens, indeed, with wonder and interest to fables or tales; he has a dim shadowy sense of what he hears about persons and matters of this world; but he has that within him which actually vibrates, responds, and gives a deep meaning to the lessons of his first teachers about the will and the providence of God.[1]

In the 'Apologia' we read:

I was brought up from a child to take great delight in reading the Bible; but I had no formed religious convictions till I was fifteen. Of course I had perfect knowledge of my Catechism.

After I was grown up I put on paper my recollections of the thoughts and feelings on religious subjects which I had at the time that I was a child and a boy; such as had remained in my mind with sufficient prominence to make me then consider them worth recording. Out of these, written in the Long Vacation of 1820, and transcribed with additions in 1823, I select two.

I used to wish the Arabian Tales were true. My imagination ran on unknown influences, on magical powers, and talismans. I thought life might be a dream, or I an angel, and all this world a deception, my fellow-angels, by a playful device, concealing themselves from me, and deceiving me with the semblance of a material world.

The other remark is this:

I was very superstitious, and for some time previous to my conversion (when I was fifteen) used constantly to cross myself on going into the dark.[2]

[1] *Grammar of Assent*, p. 112.   [2] *Apologia*, p. 2.

These unspoken memories—however in place here—must give way to such recollections of early boyhood as fell from him in conversation, or to notices remaining amongst his early papers. One anecdote of a very early date, told to the present writer by Dr. Newman's sister in her last illness, has provoked a smile in those who knew him in later days. After an infantile struggle for mastery between mother and son— the loving mother and her strong-willed child—she reminded him, 'You see, John, you did not get your own way.' 'No,' was his answer, 'but I tried very hard.'

There is a letter from his Father, Nov. 1806, which shows an early estimate. It begins: 'This is the first letter your Father ever wrote to his son'; and, after bidding him 'read it to his Mother and Charles to show how well he could read writing,' goes on, 'but you will observe that you must learn something new every day, or you will no longer be called a clever boy.'[1]

Another characteristic shows itself in one of his earliest recollections of school life, recalled to his memory as a friend led him to look back to that time. After his Father's and Mother's first visit to him, the child of seven was found, after their departure, by Dr. Nicholas, crying by himself, who, to cheer him up, proposed that he should go to the big room where the boys were. To this he objected; his tears had no doubt been observed and excited derision. 'O sir! they will say such things! I can't help crying.' On his master making light of it: 'O sir! but they will; they will say all sorts of things,' and, taking his master's hand, 'Come and see for yourself!' and led him into the crowded room, where, of course, under the circumstances, there was no teasing.

On hearing that the letters which compose these volumes

---

[1] Writing to a friend in after years, he says, 'I have been going about seeing once again, and taking leave for good of, the places I saw as a child. I have been looking at the windows of our house at Ham, near Richmond, where I lay, aged five, looking at the candles stuck in them in celebration of the victory of Trafalgar. I have never seen the house since September 1807. I know more about it than any house I have been in since, and could pass an examination in it. It has ever been in my dreams.'

were to be published, an early Oriel friend and pupil of Mr. Newman's said that he remembered his once telling him of having in his childhood seen Cumberland, 'the perfect man of his day,' who impressed upon his childish memory the interview as one to be remembered. To get at the truth of this story the Editor applied to the Cardinal for his recollections. The following was his answer :

Lord Blachford is substantially right about Cumberland. I think he came to an evening party at our house. My Father's partial love for me led to my reciting something or other in the presence of a literary man. I wish I could think it was 'Here Cumberland lies,' from Goldsmith's 'Retaliation,' which I knew really well as a boy. The interview ended by his putting his hand on my head and saying, 'Young gentleman, when you are old you can say that you have had on your head the hand of Richard Cumberland.'

A recollection of a similar class is mentioned by a friend, who writes :

Ealing school at that date had a great name. It was conducted on the Eton lines ; everybody sent his sons there ; they got on. Once a year the school had a great day—a *speech day*—and the Duke of Kent used to come to it. One year Newman had to make a speech before him. Unfortunately his voice had just begun to break, yet for all that he went through his speech. He must have done it very well so far as his voice would let him ; for, on Dr. Nicholas apologising to the Duke, 'His voice is breaking,' the Duke immediately replied, 'But the *action* was so good.'

One recollection of his childhood is given in a letter to Hope-Scott, 1871, in thanking him for a copy of the abridged Life of Walter Scott.

In one sense [he writes] I deserve it ; I have ever had such a devotion, I may call it, to Walter Scott. As a boy, in the early summer mornings I read 'Waverley' and 'Guy Mannering' in bed when they first came out, before it was time to get up ; and long before that—I think, when I was eight years old—I listened eagerly to the 'Lay of the Last Minstrel,' which my mother and aunt were reading aloud.[1]

---
[1] *Memoirs of J. R. Hope-Scott*, vol. ii. p. 243.

All through his school course [1] his letters from home show the high estimate his parents formed of him, and that he inspired those about him with respect and confidence. His Mother writes, ' I feel great comfort in the conviction that you will always act to the best of your knowledge.' His tastes were borne in mind. ' We were at the concert,' she writes, ' and fascinated with the Dutchman ' (the name he had given to Beethoven to tease his music-master, because of the *Van* to his name), 'and thought of you and your musical party frequently.' Music was a family taste and pursuit ; Mr. Newman, the father, encouraged it in his children. In those early days they could get up performances among themselves, operatic or simply dramatic. Thus in a book recalling memories he writes :

In the year 1812 I think I wrote a mock drama of some kind ; also, whether included in it or not I cannot recollect, a satire on the Prince Regent. And at one time I wrote a dramatic piece in which Augustus comes on. Again I wrote a burlesque opera in 1815, composing tunes for the songs.

At the age of fourteen a sort of passion for writing seems to have possessed him.

In 1815 I wrote two periodicals—that is, papers called the ' Spy ' and ' Anti-Spy.' They were written against each other. The former ran to thirty numbers from May 8 to October 27, the latter ran to twenty-seven numbers from August 8 to October 31. There is not a sentence in either worth preserving. Still, I am rescuing from the flames the commencing lines of each and the last words of the latter.

---

[1] At nine years old he kept a pocket-book Diary, which remains —*e.g.*:
    1810, *May* 4.—Heard for the first time the cuckoo.
        Dreamed that Mary was dead.

Then follow ' Lines on Nelson ' ; moral axioms ; verses on the death of a beggar :—' When the rude winter's blast blew keen.' But he is not satisfied, and concludes : ' I think I shall burn it.'

In an old diary he records his early school course.
        1810, *May* 25.—Got into Ovid and Greek.
        1811, *February* 11.—Began verses.
        1812, *March* 5.—Got into Diatessaron.
           May 25.—Began Homer.
        1813, *May* 3.—Herodotus.

'The Portfolio'—the name being given by G. Adams, the eldest of the three sons of the American Minister to the British Court—was written by the club of senior boys nicknamed the Spy Club. The American Minister himself contributed to it. It began November 6, 1815, ran through twenty numbers; ended May 16, 1816. There is nothing in it worth preserving. I have kept, however, Mr. Adams' lines on 'The Grasshopper and the Ant.' 'The Beholder' was all my own writing; it ran through forty numbers and 160 octavo pages closely written.[1] The first number is dated February 22, 1816, but I rather think some of the later numbers were written in 1817, after I had left school. It is far superior in composition to my others; but nothing worth keeping but some verses in No. 23 and No. 24, to the doctrine of which I hold fast now.

The copybook which contains the Beads and Cross spoken of in the 'Apologia' has a coloured sketch, a half-involuntary caricature, probably by one of themselves, of a party of boys of fifteen or sixteen sitting round a table, addressed by a member standing on his chair, whose marked features make it clear who was the leading spirit of the company. Is this the Spy Club?

Certain rough notes, written not very long after, touch upon what proved to be the beginning of a great family trial—the stoppage of the bank in which Mr. Newman's father was partner—and connect the close of his school-days with what he always considered the event of his life—his conversion.

On my conversion how the wisdom and goodness of God is discerned! I was going from school half a year sooner than I did. My staying arose from the 8th of March. Thereby I was left at school by myself, my friends gone away.

To explain this sentence a few words from a private paper may be given. Writing March 17, 1874, Dr. Newman says:

I fell in with the following important letter a day or two ago while looking through and destroying papers connected with our 'School Portfolio.' It was written à propos of some contribution my Father made to it; but it accidentally contains

---

[1] These MS. books contain essays with comments: 'This is a school theme in the style of Addison.' Again: one of the papers in *The Beholder* has a saying of Addison's on the love of fame.

a notice of a fact which I know very well myself because I, and we all, made much of it at the time, but of which I had, as far as I know, no record. I have kept the autograph.

MR. NEWMAN TO JOHN HENRY NEWMAN.

Your Mother will add something to this, which is principally to say that our Banking House has to-day paid every one in full. Tell this to Dr. Nicholas.

[The question arises why it should have stopped payment at all if it could pay in full at the end of a month? I recollect at the time hearing that it arose from the obstinacy of one individual.—J. H. N.]

Not to touch again on this subject, a letter may be given here, written by Mr. J. W. Bowden, a year or two later, in answer to a communication from his friend.

MR. J. W. BOWDEN TO JOHN HENRY NEWMAN.

Fulham: January 14, 1819.

. . . With regard to your Father's affairs I am much obliged to you for your communication, and will confess that I was acquainted with some of its leading features. I had heard of your Father's *failure* [It was not a failure; the house stopped payment, but paid in full; there was no bankruptcy.—J.H.N.], and I solemnly assure you that I had also heard of the highly honourable way in which all was settled. My information came principally from Mrs. Owen, to whom I once, before you came, mentioned your name as a person she might recollect; and, as on a subject like this I may speak without suspicion of flattery, I must say she lavished the highest possible encomiums on the manner in which the affairs of the house were arranged.

On the fact and the effects of his conversion Cardinal Newman's language remains the same throughout his life, from the words just recorded—'On my conversion how the wisdom and goodness of God is discerned!'—written probably in 1816; from those words in the 'Apologia' penned in 1864— 'Of the inward conversion of which I speak I am still more certain than that I have hands and feet'—down to 1885, when

Cardinal Newman writes, in answer to the Editor, who had spoken of possible early letters:

February 28, 1885.

Of course I cannot myself be the judge of myself; but, speaking with this reserve, I should say that it is difficult to realise or imagine the identity of the boy before and after August 1816 . . . I can look back at the end of seventy years as if on another person.

Recalling his state of mind at the age of fourteen, he wrote in a manuscript book of early date:

I recollect, in 1815 I believe, thinking that I should like to be virtuous, but not religious. There was something in the latter idea I did not like. Nor did I see the meaning of loving God. I recollect contending against Mr. Mayer in favour of Pope's 'Essay on Man.' What, I contended, can be more free from objection than it? Does it not expressly inculcate 'Virtue alone is happiness below'?

The conversion that succeeded this posture of mind produced in him as a necessary consequence a desire for some additional strictness of life in evidence of its reality. Some reflections, written probably in 1816, remain on the subject of recreations, in which he looked forward to the probability of a difference between himself and his parents, which show a freedom from the wilfulness of enthusiasm.

Although it is far from pleasant to give my reasons, inasmuch as I shall appear to set myself up, and to be censuring recreations and those who indulge in them, yet when I am urged to give them, I hope I shall never be ashamed of them; presenting my scruples with humility and a due obedience to my parents; open to conviction, and ready to obey in a matter so dubious as this is, and to act against my judgment if they command, thus satisfying at once my own conscience and them. . . . [but continuing the argument] I have too much sense of my own weakness to answer for myself. The beginnings of sin are small, and is it not better, say, to be too cautious than too negligent? Besides, I know myself in some things better than you do; I have hidden faults, and if you knew them, so serious a protest would not appear to you strange. . . . I think those things of importance to myself;

but I hope I am not so enthusiastic as to treat it as a concern of high religious importance. You may think this contradicts what I said just now about the beginning of sin; if so, I am sorry I cannot express myself with greater exactness and propriety.

After matriculation, but before residence, he wrote the fo'lowing letter to his late tutor, the Rev. Walter Mayer. It illustrates that passage in the 'Apologia' where, in speaking of his conversion, he says, 'I fell under the influence of a definite creed, and received into my intellect impressions of dogma.'

JOHN HENRY NEWMAN TO REV. W. MAYER.

January, 1817.

. . . I have not yet finished reading Bishop Beveridge, but it seems to me, as far as I have read it, an excellent work; and indeed I know it must be so, else you would not have given it me.

There is one passage in the first chapter of the second part that I do not quite comprehend: it is on the Sacrament of Baptism. I had, before I read it, debated with myself how it could be that baptized infants dying in their infancy could be saved unless the spirit of God was given them: which seems to contradict the opinion that baptism is not accompanied by the Holy Spirit. Dr. Beveridge's opinion seems to be that the seeds of grace are sown in baptism, though they often do not spring up. That baptism is the mean whereby we receive the Holy Spirit, although not the only mean; that infants when baptized receive the inward and spiritual grace, without the requisite repentance and faith: if this be his opinion, the sermon Mr. Milman preached on grace last year was exactly consonant with his sentiments. . . .

The texts of some dozen of sermons, so to call them, composed in 1817, which are all that remain of them, show his mind occupied on questions which were henceforth the subject of thought and speculation.[1] Looking over these

---

[1] 1. He that eateth and drinketh unworthily. 2. Great things doeth He which we cannot comprehend. 3. These shall go into everlasting punishment. 4. Man is like to vanity, his days are as a shadow. 5. Let no one despise thy youth. 6. Let not sin therefore reign in your mortal bodies. 7. Thou when thou fastest.

youthful efforts, Dr. Newman wrote : 'I was very fond of Beveridge's "Private Thoughts" at this time, and the above *quasi* sermons are, I think, in his style.' It is, perhaps, a greater proof of a youth of sixteen or seventeen being very gravely in earnest that he was 'very fond' of Beveridge's 'Private Thoughts' than that he could write sermons on his own account.

During his solitary first term at Trinity he was still meditating on mysteries. He hears a sermon (June 29, 1817) preached at St. Mary's by the Rev. W. Crowe. The line of the sermon led him to the question of predestination and efficacious grace, and to argue it out at full length.

From this date it may almost be said that the subjects which then filled his thoughts were the subjects that occupied his life. Theology proper at once filled his mind and never relaxed its hold; and also those cognate subjects, searching the heart and appealing to the conscience, which have been treated by him with such telling effect on his generation, are seen to be there in embryo. Thus in a MS. book of this date is this sentence :

The reality of conversion, as cutting at the root of doubt, providing a chain between God and the Soul, that is with every link complete; I know I am right. How do you know it? I know I know.[1]

There are many boyish anticipations or buddings of his after thoughts noted down at about this date. On reading these in later life, Dr. Newman is severe on his early style :

The unpleasant style in which it is written arises from my habit, from a boy, *to compose.* I seldom wrote without an eye to style, and since my taste was bad my style was bad. I wrote in style as another might write in verse, or sing instead of speaking, or dance instead of walking. Also my evangelical tone contributed to its bad taste.

May it not be said that so young a mind was weighted with thought beyond its power of easy expression? Deeply

[1] See *Grammar of Assent*, p. 197.

impressed with the solemn truth and vital importance of the subjects which occupied it, the mind could hardly avoid some formality of style. To be easy would seem to itself to be familiar. This question may be put to other early passages where the style is in contrast with that known to the reader.

The point is now reached for entering on the first chapter of the Memoir.

AUTOBIOGRAPHICAL MEMOIR

CHAPTER I

JOHN HENRY NEWMAN was born in Old Broad Street in the City of London on February 21, 1801, and was baptized in the church of St. Benet Fink on April 9 of the same year. His Father was a London banker, whose family came from Cambridgeshire. His Mother was of a French Protestant family, who left France for this country on the revocation of the Edict of Nantes. He was the eldest of six children, three boys and three girls.

On May 1, 1808, when he was seven years old, he was sent to a school of 200 boys, increasing to 300, at Ealing, near London, under the care of the Rev. George Nicholas, D.C.L., of Wadham College, Oxford. As a child he was of a studious turn and of a quick apprehension, and Dr. Nicholas, to whom he became greatly attached, was accustomed to say that no boy had run through the school, from the bottom to the top, as rapidly as John Newman. Though in no respect a precocious boy, he attempted original compositions in prose and verse from the age of eleven, and in prose showed a great sensibility, and took much pains in matter of style. He devoted to such literary exercises, and to such books as came in his way, a good portion of his playtime; and his schoolfellows have left on record that they never, or scarcely ever, saw him taking part in any game.

At Ealing he remained eight years and a half, his own entreaties aiding his Mother and his schoolmaster in hindering his removal to Winchester College. In the last half-year of his school life, from August to December 1816—accidentally out-staying his immediate school friends—he fell under the influence of an excellent man, the Rev. Walter Mayer, of Pembroke College, Oxford, one of the Classical masters, from whom he received deep religious impressions, at the time Calvinistic in character, which were to him the beginning of a new life. From school he went straight to Oxford, being entered at Trinity College on December 14, 1816, when he was as yet two months short of sixteen.

He (Newman) used to relate in illustration of the seeming accidents on which our course of life and personal history turn, that, even when the postchaise was at the door, his Father was in doubt whether to direct the postboy to make for Hounslow, or for the first stage on the road to Cambridge. He seems to have been decided in favour of Oxford by the Rev. John Mullins, curate of St. James's, Piccadilly, a man of ability and learning, who had for some years taken an interest in the boy's education. When they got to Oxford Mr. Mullins at first hoped to find a vacancy for him in his own college— Exeter. But, failing this, he took the advice of his Exeter friends to introduce him to Dr. Lee, President of Trinity, and at that time Vice-Chancellor, by whom Newman was matriculated as a commoner of that society. On his return to Ealing to inform his schoolmaster of the issue of his expedition, his timid mention of a college of which he himself had never heard before was met by Dr. Nicholas's reassuring reply : 'Trinity ? a most gentlemanlike college—I am much pleased to hear it.'

Newman was called into residence the following June, in his fourth term, and, for want of the vacancy of a room, not till the term was far advanced, the Commemoration close at hand, the college lectures over, and the young men on the point of leaving for the Long Vacation.

However, it was his good fortune, in the few days which remained before he was left to himself, to make the acquaintance of Mr. John William Bowden, a freshman also, afterwards one of His Majesty's Commissioners of Stamps and Taxes. The acquaintance ripened into a friendship so intimate, though Mr. Bowden was just by three years the elder of the two (the birthday of both being February 21), that the two youths lived simply with and for each other all through their undergraduate time, up to the term when they went into the schools for their B.A. examination, being recognised in college as inseparables—taking their meals together, reading, walking, boating together—nay, visiting each other's homes in the vacations ; and, though so close a companionship could not continue when at length they ceased to be in a state of pupilage, and had taken their several paths in life, yet the mutual attachment thus formed at the University was maintained between them unimpaired till Mr. Bowden's premature death in 1844, receiving an additional tie as time went on by their cordial agreement in ecclesiastical views and academical politics, and by the interest with which both entered into the Oxford movement of 1833. Mr. Bowden was one of the first writers in the 'Tracts for the Times,' and it was at Mr. Newman's suggestion that he wrote his history of Pope Gregory VII., the valuable work of his leisure hours and yearly vacation, when a Commissioner at the Stamps and Taxes. It may be added that Mr. Newman's first literary attempts in print were made in partnership with Mr. Bowden, when they were both of them undergraduates.

In May 1818 Mr. Newman gained one of the Trinity scholarships then lately thrown open to University competition ; and here it may be well to trace, from his own letters at the time, the steps by which he had already risen in the good opinion of his college, during the year since he was called up, an unknown youth of sixteen, for his solitary residence of three weeks. It is hoped that the details of his progress, though seemingly trifling, will not be uninteresting.

A letter of his remains which he wrote to his Father immediately upon his being left to himself on that occasion ; like a boy his first thought is about his outward appearance :

June 11, 1817.

The minute I had parted from you I went straight to the tailor's, who assured me that, if he made me twenty gowns, they would fit me no better. If he took it shorter—he would if I pleased—but I might grow, &c. &c. I then went *home* (!) and had hardly seated myself, when I heard a knock at the door, and opening it, one of the Commoners entered whom Mr Short[1] had sent to me, having before come himself with this said Commoner, when I was out. He came to explain to me some of the customs of the college, and accompany me into the Hall at dinner. I have learned from him something I am much rejoiced at. 'Mr. Ingram,' said he, 'was very much liked; he was very good-natured; he was presented with a piece of plate the other day by the members of the college. Mr. Short on the contrary is not liked; he is strict; all wish Mr. Ingram were tutor still.' Thus I think I have gained by the exchange, and that is a lucky thing. Some time after, on my remarking that Mr. Short must be very clever, having been second master at Rugby, he replied, 'Do you think so?' Another proof that he is a strict tutor.

At dinner I was much entertained with the novelty of the thing. Fish, flesh and fowl, beautiful salmon, haunches of mutton, lamb, &c., fine strong beer; served up in old pewter plates and misshapen earthenware jugs. Tell mamma there were gooseberry, raspberry, and apricot pies. And in all this the joint did not go round, but there was such a profusion that scarcely two ate of the same. Neither do they sit according to their rank, but as they happen to come in.

I learned from the same source whence I learned concerning Mr. Short, that there are a great many juniors to me. I hear also that there are no more lectures this term, this being the week for examinations, and next week most of them go. I shall try to get all the information I am able respecting what books I ought to study, and hope, if my eyes are good-natured to me, to fag.[2]

Tell Harriett [his sister] I have seen the fat cook. The wine has come; $8\frac{1}{3}$ per cent. is taken off for ready money. Two things I cannot get, milk and beer; so I am obliged to put up with cream for the one and ale for the other.

He writes again to his Father on the 16th:

June 16, 1817.

I was very uncomfortable the first day or two because my eyes were not well, so that I could not see to read, and whenever my eyes are bad I am low-spirited. Besides, I did not know anyone, and, after having been used to a number about

---

[1] The Rev. Thomas Short, for so many years the respected and popular tutor of the college.
[2] He suffered from weakness of the eyes at this time.

me, I felt very solitary. But now my eyes are better, and I can read without hurting them, and I have begun to fag pretty well.

I am not noticed at all except by being silently stared at. I am glad, not because I wish to be apart from them and ill-natured, but because I really do not think I should gain the least advantage from their company. For H. the other day asked me to take a glass of wine with two or three others, and they drank and drank all the time I was there. I was very glad that prayers came half an hour after I came to them, for I am sure I was not entertained with either their drinking or their conversation.

He (Newman) was very impatient to be directed in his reading, and as he understood he could not leave college without permission from the President, he resolved, in his simplicity, to 'take that opportunity,' as he says, 'of asking him what books he ought to read' in the vacation. On June 27, three days before his departure, he tells his Father the result of his experiment:

I went to-day to the President, and was shown into a parlour, the servant saying he would be ready to see me in a minute. I waited an hour and a half, and then rang the bell; when it proved to be a mistake, and he was not at home. I shall go again to-morrow morning.

He did go again, and was told by the President, who was a courteous gentlemanlike man, and afterwards very kind to him, that he left all such questions as Mr. Newman asked to be answered by the tutors.

In consequence, up to Sunday the 29th, the day before his departure, he had not gained any information on the point which lay so near his heart; but he persevered, and fortune favoured him. As in the evening of that day he was returning home from a walk along the Parks, he saw one of the tutors in topboots on horseback on his way into the country. Thinking it his last chance, he dashed into the road, and, abruptly accosting him, asked him what books he should read during the vacation. The person addressed answered him very kindly; explained that he was leaving Oxford for the vacation, and referred him to one of his colleagues still in college, who would give him the information he desired. On his return home he availed himself of this reference, and obtained a satisfactory answer to all his difficulties.

Such was his introduction to University life; not of a character to make him at home with it; but the prospect of things improved immediately on his return after the Long Vacation. He writes to his Mother thus, on October 28: 'Mr. Short has not examined me; but he has appointed me some lectures.' After naming them, he adds, 'This is little enough, but of course they begin with little to see what I can do.'

On November 13:

I have been fagging very hard, but not without benefit, and, I may add, not without recompense. The first day I attended my tutor [Mr. Short] for mathematics. I found I was in the second division of what at school is called a class. I own I was rather astonished at hearing them begin the Ass's Bridge, nor was my amazement in the least degree abated, when my turn came, to hear him say, with a condescending air, 'I believe, sir, you never saw Euclid before?' I answered I had. 'How far?' 'I had been over five books.' Then *he* looked surprised; but I added I could not say I knew them perfectly by any means. I am sure by his manner he then took it into his head that I was not well grounded, for he proceeded to ask me what a point was, and what a line, and what a plane angle. He concluded, however, by telling me that I might come in with the other gentlemen at 10 o'clock, with the 4th, 5th, and 6th books.

The next time I came he was not condescending, but it was 'sir,' very stiffly indeed.

The next time, after I had demonstrated, I saw him peep at my paper, to see if I had anything written down—a good sign.

The next time, he asked if I wanted anything explained—another good sign.

And to-day, after I had demonstrated a tough one out of the fifth book, he told me I had done it very correctly.

Nor is this all. I had a declamation to do last week, a Latin one. I took a great deal of pains with it. As I was going to lecture to-day, I was stopped by the Fellow who looks over the declamations [the Dean, Mr. Kinsey], and to whom we recite them, and told by him that mine did me much credit.

He adds on another subject :

The tailor entered my room the other day, and asked me if I wanted mourning. I told him no. ' Of course you have got some,' said he. ' No,' I answered with surprise. ' Everyone will be in mourning,' he returned. ' For whom ?' ' The Princess Charlotte.' You see what a hermit I am ; but the paper had been lying on my table the whole day, and I had not had time to take it up.

He continues the last subject in a letter to his Mother :

November 21.

The dismal figure Oxford makes from the deep mourning. Black coat, waistcoat, trousers, gloves, ribbon (no chain) to the watch ; no white except the neckcloth and unplaited frill. The Proctors will not suffer anyone to appear unless in black.[1]

I have not mentioned the conclusion of my approximation to Mr. Short. The next time I went to him he lent me a book on mathematics, being a dissertation &c. upon Euclid ; and the next morning invited me to breakfast. As to the book, I have made some extracts from it, and I know all about multiple, superparticular, submultiple, subsuperparticular, subsuperpartient of the lesser inequality, sesquilateral, sesquiquintal, supertriquartal, and subsuperbitertial. I am engaged at present in making a dissertation on the fifth book ; indeed, I even dream of four magnitudes being proportionals.

By November 28 he has risen still higher in the good opinion of Mr. Short. He writes to his Mother, and, after

[1] The original letter in the family collection goes on to say, ' And I believe [the Proctors] wish to make up by the universality of the mourning for the neglect of observing the day of the funeral, last Wednesday, in some particular manner; for the Master of Balliol [the Bishop of Peterborough] is said to have proposed in Convocation that the churches and chapels should be all hung with black, and that there should be sermons in all ; but some of the old Doctors conceived it would be introducing new customs (just like them), and consequently the motion was negatived.'

making some remarks on 'every one of his lectures being so childishly easy,' he continues:

These very thoughts suggested themselves to Mr. Short, and the other morning he said he was sorry I should not be attending lectures which would profit me more, and that next term he should take care to give me books which would give me more trouble.[1]

He adds that the higher class in mathematics into which he had been advanced fell off to two; in other words that he and another went on too fast for the rest to keep up with them; then of that other he says:

This one who remained is the one I was first introduced to last term [Mr. Bowden]; he is pretty assiduous. The consequence is, as he is much forwarder than myself, he spurns at the books of Euclid, and hurries to get through them. I disdain to say he goes too fast; so I am obliged to fag more

Then he adds in an exulting tone:

If anyone wishes to study much, I believe there can be no college that will encourage him more than Trinity. It is wishing to rise in the University, and is rising fast. The scholarships were formerly open only to members of the college; last year, for the first time, they were thrown open to the whole University. In discipline it has become one of the strictest of the colleges. There are lamentations in every corner of the increasing rigour; it is laughable, but it is delightful, to hear the groans of the oppressed.

Mr. Short seems to have taken an increased interest in Newman during the term which immediately followed. He it was who had the reputation of having led the authorities of the college to the step just mentioned of opening their scholarships to all comers, which in the event has been so great a benefit to Trinity. He was naturally anxious for the success of his important measure, and therefore it was a special token of his good opinion when he invited Mr. Newman to present

[1] In looking over old papers the Editor has come upon some words of Mr. Short's which show the high estimate he had formed of J. H. N. at this time. Meeting Mr. Newman (the father) he went up to him as an old friend, and holding out his hand, said 'O Mr. Newman! what have you given us in your son!'

himself as a candidate at the competitive examination which was to determine the election of a scholar on the ensuing Trinity Monday. This Mr. Short could do without impropriety, because, as he told Newman, the tutors had no votes in the election. As has been already said, Newman stood and was elected.

He relates the circumstances attendant on this, to him, happy event in a letter to his Mother of May 25:

> On Wednesday, April 29, about breakfast-time, Mr. Wilson [1] and Mr. Short called for me, and asked me whether I intended to stand for the scholarship. I answered that I intended next year. However, they wished me to stand this year, because they would wish to see me on the foundation. I said I would think of it. I wrote home that day. How often was my pen going to tell the secret! but I determined to surprise you. I told you in a letter written in the midst of the examination that there were five [candidates] of our own [men]; did you suspect that I was one of the five? A Worcester man was very near getting it.[2]
>
> They made me first do some verses; then Latin translation; then Latin theme; then chorus of Euripides; then an English theme; then some Plato; then some Lucretius; then some Xenophon; then some Livy. What is more distressing than suspense? At last I was called to the place where they had been voting; the Vice-Chancellor [the President] said some Latin over me; then made a speech. The electors then shook hands with me, and I immediately assumed the scholar's gown.
>
> First, as I was going out, before I had changed my gown, one of the candidates met me, and wanted to know if it was decided. What was I to say? 'It was.' 'And who has got it?' 'Oh, an in-college man,' I said; and I hurried away as fast as I could. On returning with my newly-earned gown, I met the whole set going to their respective homes. I did not know what to do; I held my eyes down.
>
> By this I am a scholar for nine years at 60l. a year. In which time, if there be no Fellow of my county (among the Fellows), I may be elected Fellow, as a regular thing, for five years without taking orders.

[1] Afterwards President.
[2] Afterwards Archdeacon Coxe. It was said that 'J. H. N.'s mathematics *decided* the question between the two.'

He adds the next day :

I am sure I felt the tortures of suspense so much that I wished and wished I had never attempted it. The idea of *turpis repulsa* haunted me. I tried to keep myself as cool as possible, but I could not help being sanguine. I constantly reverted to it in my thoughts, in spite of my endeavours to the contrary. Very few men thought I should get it, and my *reason* thought the same. My age was such a stumbling-block [that is, he could stand again, being only seventeen, others could not]. But I, when I heard the voice of the Dean summoning me before the electors, seemed to myself to feel no surprise. I am told I turned pale.

There is one other matter which should be mentioned in connexion with this May 18, 1818, a day which was ever so dear to the subject of this Memoir, though the matter in question is not of a very pleasant character. Trinity Monday was not only the election day of Fellows and scholars, but also the Gaudy of the year : and among other *vestigia ruris* [1] then remaining was the custom of keeping it throughout the college, with few exceptions, by a drinking bout.

Since Newman had not a grain in his composition of that temper of conviviality so natural to young men, it was no merit in him that the disgust of drink, which he showed in one of his first letters from Oxford, should have continued in him all through his course. For the most part he was let go his own way, as soon as it was discovered what that way was ; but Trinity Monday would come once a year, and then that way of his, whether he would or not, became a protest against those who took another way. Moreover, much as he might wish to keep his feelings to himself, which he did generally, and, as he afterwards thought on looking back, too much, he had very strong feelings on the point, as the following vehement letter, addressed to his friend Mr. Mayer in the following year, manifests clearly enough. It is quite out of keeping with his letters, as they have been quoted above, and as he generally wrote ; but, in spite of his gentleness of manner, there were in him at all times *ignes suppositi cineri doloso*

---

[1] 'Vestigia ruris,' Hor. *Ep.* ii. 1 160, or 'vestigia fraudis,' Virg. *Ecl.* iv. 31.

which, as the sequel of his life shows, had not always so much to justify them as they may be considered to have in the instance before us.

J. H. NEWMAN TO REV. W. MAYER.

Trinity Sunday, 1819.

To-morrow is our Gaudy. If there be one time of the year in which the glory of our college is humbled, and all appearance of goodness fades away, it is on Trinity Monday. Oh, how the angels must lament over a whole society throwing off the allegiance and service of their Maker, which they have pledged the day before at His table, and showing themselves the sons of Belial!

It is sickening to see what I might call the apostasies of many. This year it was supposed there would have been no such merry-making. A quarrel existed among us: the college was divided into two sets, and no proposition for the usual subscription for wine was set on foot. Unhappily, a day or two before the time a reconciliation takes place; the wine party is agreed upon, and this wicked union, to be sealed with drunkenness, is profanely joked upon with allusions to one of the expressions in the Athanasian Creed.

To see the secret eagerness with which many wished there would be no Gaudy; to see how they took hope, as time advanced and no mention was made of it; but they are all gone, there has been weakness and fear of ridicule. Those who resisted last year are going this. I fear even for myself, so great a delusion seems suddenly to have come over all.

Oh that the purpose of some may be changed before the time! I know not how to make myself of use. I am intimate with very few. The Gaudy has done more harm to the college than the whole year can compensate. An habitual negligence of the awfulness of the Holy Communion is introduced. How can we prosper?

It is necessary to observe here that Mr. Bowden was at this time away from Oxford for the vacation, having gone home a fortnight before to attend the death-bed of a sister. To return. The Trinity scholarship, thus unexpectedly gained, was the only academical distinction which fell to the lot of Mr. Newman during his undergraduate course; and as he had on this occasion the trial of success, so when the course was coming to its end he had to undergo the trial of failure. After passing with credit his first University examination, he settled down to read for honours in the final examination; but, standing for the highest honours, he suffered an utter breakdown and a seeming extinction of his prospects of a University career.

He had come to Oxford young. Apparently he had himself been impatient to get to college; but he recognised his disadvantage in consequence as soon as he began lectures. He writes to his Father in the first term of lectures—that term in which he was so successfully to make his way with Mr. Short: 'I now see the disadvantage of going too soon to Oxford, and before I had the great addition of time that two or three more years would have given me; for there are several who know more than I do in Latin and Greek, and I do not like that.' He was not twenty when he went in for final examination, whereas the usual age was twenty-two.

His youth was against him in another respect also. It was not only that he was short by two or three years of the full period marked out for the B.A. examination, but he had not that experience for shaping for himself his course of reading, or that maturity of mind for digesting it, which a longer time would have given him. He read books, made ample analyses and abstracts, and entered upon collateral questions and original essays which did him no service in the schools. In the Long Vacation of 1818 he was taken up with Gibbon and Locke. At another time he wrote a critique of the plays of Æschylus, on the principles of Aristotle's 'Poetics,' though original composition at that time had no place in school examinations, and he spent many weeks in reading and transcribing Larcher's 'Notes on Herodotus.' Moreover, though the examiners were conscientiously fair and considerate in their decisions, they would understand a candidate better, and follow his lead and line of thought more sympathetically, if they understood his position of mind and intellectual habits, than if these were new to them.[1]

---

[1] Mr. Newman in his old age recollected one instance in which the examiners had missed his meaning. When the tutors of Trinity inquired of the examiners how he came so utterly to fail, his having translated

It is also true that Mr. Newman had, in union with his friend Mr. Bowden, for a few months at the end of 1818 and the beginning of 1819, been tempted to dabble in matters foreign to academical objects. They had published a *poem*, their joint composition, and commenced a small periodical like Addison's 'Spectator'; but these excursive acts only occupied their leisure hours, and that for a very short time, and were not more than such a recreation as boating might be in the summer term. The memoranda which Mr. Newman has left behind him would show this abundantly were it worth while to quote them.

As to the literary efforts in question, the periodical was called 'The Undergraduate,' and it began and ended in February 1819. It sold well, but, to his great disgust, Newman's name got out, and this was its death-blow. They made it over to its publishers, who continued it with an editor of their own for some weeks; then it expired.

His and Bowden's poem was a romance founded on the Massacre of St. Bartholomew. The subject was the sequel of the unfortunate union of a Protestant gentleman with a Catholic lady, ending in the tragical death of both, through the machinations of a cruel fanatical priest, whose inappropriate name was Clement. Mr. Bowden did the historical and picturesque portions, Mr. Newman the theological. There were no love scenes, nor could there be; for, as it turned out, to the monk's surprise, the parties had been some time before the action husband and wife, by a clandestine marriage, known however to the father of the lady.

The following passage from Mr. Newman's pen will give an idea of the theology of the poem:

> In silent agony she shrank to feel
> How fierce his soul, how bigoted his zeal:
> For he had been to her, from early youth,
> From vice her guardian, and her guide to truth.

---

the word 'proprium' in Virgil by 'proper' instead of 'his own' was specified as a critical instance in point, but he knew the sense of the La in word perfectly well; only, as translating a poet, he had in mind *Cymbeline*, and again in *Measure for Measure* (in the Duke's speech, 'The mere effusion of thy proper loins'), and foolishly copied it on purpose, not considering how he might be misunderstood.

> Her memory told her that he once was kind,
> Ere the monk's cowl had changed his gentler mind;
> But now of late his holy call had thrown
> A haughty coldness o'er him not his own.
> Yet still she paid him reverence, tho' no more
> She told her bosom secrets as before.
> True he was stern, but they who knew him best,
> Said fast and penance steeled that holy breast;
> She knew him harsh avenge Heaven's injured laws,
> But deemed superior sanctity the cause;
> She knew him oft mysterious, wild and strange,
> But hoped that heavenly converse wrought the change.

This was in February 1819. In the summer term, in the absence of his friend Bowden, the Dean—Mr. Kinsey, who treated Newman with the familiar kindness of an elder brother —took him to Professor Buckland's Lectures on Geology, at that time a new and interesting science, but in no degree subserving the interest of candidates for a first class in the examination schools. But in the Long Vacation of 1819 he began to read hard for the honours of his final examination. He did a great deal of work, nor did a second study of Gibbon, in which he then indulged himself, take him away from the classics. He writes to Bowden in October 1819:

What books had we better read this time? We settled on Sophocles and Æschylus. We are to begin reading without let or hindrance,—on, on, like the Destroyer[1] in the mysterious boat, till we arrive at the ocean of great-goes.

He adds:

You must excuse my talking on book subjects; but, having been stationary all the vacation, I have no others to discourse upon; and Herodotus, Thucydides, and Gibbon have employed me nearly from morning to night. A second perusal of the last historian has raised him in my scale of merit. With all his faults, his want of simplicity, his affectation and his monotony, few can be put in comparison with him, and sometimes, when I reflect on his happy choice of expressions, his vigorous compression of ideas, and the life and significance of every word, I am prompted indignantly to exclaim that no style is left for historians of an after day. Oh, who is worthy to succeed our Gibbon? *Exoriare aliquis!* and may he be a better man!

[1] *Thalaba.*

In the same month he writes to his Mother :

I think I contemplate with brighter hopes the honours of the schools. We are reading between eleven and twelve hours a day, and have an hour for walking and an hour for dinner.

At the end of the term, December 18, he writes to her :

The Fellows have been very kind, have said we might stop up as long as we like, and have offered to do anything they can for us. This is to me an important year ; I heartily wish it over, though most probably I shall look back on it with regret when past.

The Long prospect is now before me. I anticipate that soothing, quiet, unostentatious pleasure which only an equable unvarying time of living can give. I look forward to it with great delight. I hope it will resemble the last Long Vacation. When I first went to college I could write long letters without effort, and lament when the full sheet refused additional matter; for everything then was novel, and I had not any dread of approaching examinations to awe me into silence. I have often remarked that the undergraduate residence [of three years] is a picture of a whole life—of youth, of manhood, and of old age—which could not be understood or felt without actual experience.

At this time he seems to have been half conscious of some mental or moral change within him, which he fully recognised in the following year, when he took a retrospect of his undergraduate experiences. 'In 1819 and the beginning of 1820,' he wrote in 1821, 'I hoped great things for myself. Not liking to go into the Church, but to the law, I attended Modern History lectures [professorial], hearing that the names were reported to the Minister.' These dreams of a secular ambition, which were quite foreign to his frame of mind in 1817, when he employed himself in writing sermons and sermonets as an exercise, seem now to have departed from him, never to return.

In the Long Vacation of 1820, which he was now entering, whenever Bowden was not with him he had Trinity College, its garden and library, all to himself; and in his solitude, pleasant as he found it, he became graver and graver. At first he says to his Mother, 'The prospect before me looks

alternately dark and bright, but when I divest my mind of
hurried fear, I think I may say I have advanced much more,
and much more quickly and easily, than I had expected.'
This was in July; in August he writes to his brother Frank :

August 1820.

Here at Oxford I am most comfortable. The quiet and
stillness of everything around me tends to calm and lull those
emotions which the near prospect of my grand examination,
and a heart too solicitous about fame and too fearful of failure,
are continually striving to excite. I read very much, certainly,
but God enables me to praise Him with joyful lips when I
rise, and when I lie down, and when I wake in the night.
For the calm happiness I enjoy I cannot feel thankful as I
ought. How in my future life, if I do live, shall I look back
with a sad smile at these days! It is my daily, and I hope
heartfelt, prayer that I may not get any honours here if they
are to be the least cause of sin to me. As the time approaches
and I have laboured more at my books, the trial is greater.

At the same date he writes to one of his sisters :

I try to keep myself as cool as I can, but find it very difficult. However it is my duty not to 'take thought for the
morrow.' I cannot think much of the schools without wishing
much to distinguish myself in them; and that wishing much
would make me discontented if I did not succeed; and that is
coveting, for then we covet when we desire a thing so earnestly
as to be discontented if we fail in getting it; I will not therefore ask for success, but for good.

Meanwhile his application to his books, which had recommenced with such vigour in the Long Vacation of 1819, was
now almost an absorption by them; he gives a retrospective
account of it in a letter to an Irish friend, written in 1821 :

During the Long Vacation of 1819 [he says], I read nearly
at the rate of nine hours a day. From that time to my
examination in November 1820 it was almost a continuous
mass of reading. I stayed in Oxford during the vacations,
got up in winter and summer at five or six, hardly allowed
myself time for my meals, and then ate, indeed, the bread of
carefulness. During twenty out of the twenty-four weeks
immediately preceding my examination, I fagged at an average

of more than twelve hours a day. If one day I read only nine, I read the next fifteen.

The termination of these 'laborious days' was now approaching, and he ushered it in with a long letter to his friend Mr. Mayer. In the course of it he says :

I am more happy here than I suppose I ever was yet . . . yet in truth I am in no common situation. The very few honours that have been taken by men of our college, the utter absence of first classes for the last ten years, the repeated failures which have occurred, and the late spirit of reading which has shown itself among us, render those who attempt this, objects of wonder, curiosity, speculation, and anxiety. Five of us were going up for first classes this term ; one has deferred his examination, one most likely goes up for no honours at all ; one is expected to fail ; one—whom I think most certain of success—may before the examination remove to another college ; one remains. ' Unless,' I am told, 'success at length attends on Trinity this examination, we have determined it is useless to read.'

The high expectations, too, that are formed of me ; the confidence with which those who know nothing of me put down two first classes to my name ; the monstrous notions they form of the closeness of my application, and, on the other hand, my consciousness of my own deficiencies—these things may create a smile, in my future life, to think I feared them, but they are sufficient to dismay me now. I fear much more from failure than I hope from success.

It was not strangers only who did not know him that felt so assured that Newman would succeed. His friend Bowden, who had read with him so long, and, having passed his own ordeal, had gone home before him, wrote thence to Newman, prophesying all good things of him, being confident that his examination would be brilliant. This was in November. 'I shall expect,' he said, 'to hear in your answer whether they put you on in any books besides those you took up.' And in a second letter : 'By the time you receive this, I conclude you will have completed your labours in the schools and covered yourself and the college with glory.' Bowden did but express the expectations of his friends generally, but fortune had gone against him. He had over-read himself, and being suddenly called up a day sooner than he expected, he lost his head, utterly broke down, and, after vain attempts for several days, had to retire, only first making sure of his B.A. degree. When the list came out, his name did not appear at all on the mathematical side of the paper, and in classics it was found in the lower division of the second class of honours, which at that time went by the contemptuous title of the 'Under-the-line,' there being as yet no third and fourth classes.

Though he never was able to satisfy himself how it came about that he did so little justice on that occasion to his long and assiduous toil, it must be borne in mind that a similar affection, after a severe course of reading, overtook him seven years later, on all but the same day (November 26, instead of November 25), when he was exercising his office of University examiner in the very same schools in which in 1820 he had failed as examinee, and that that attack came on with greater violence, for he was obliged to leave Oxford, and for a time relinquish his office.

During the long days of his ineffectual efforts in the schools he suffered severely; and again, with especial keenness, immediately on his having to give those efforts up; but he was not long in recovering his composure. His first letter home ran as follows:

TO HIS FATHER.

December 1, 1820.

It is all over, and I have not succeeded. The pain it gives me to be obliged to inform you and my mother of it, I cannot express. What I feel on my own account is indeed nothing at all, compared with the thought that I have disappointed you. And most willingly would I consent to a hundred times the sadness that now overshadows me, if so doing would save my mother and you from feeling vexation. I will not attempt to describe what I have gone through, but it is past away, and I feel quite lightened of a load. The examining masters were as kind as it was possible to be; but my nerves quite forsook me and I failed. I have done everything I could to attain my object; I have spared no labour, and my reputation in my college is as solid as before, if not so splendid. If a man falls in battle after a display of bravery, he is honoured as a hero;

ought not the same glory to attend him who falls in the field of literary conflict?

His parents answered him, as might be supposed, that they were more than satisfied with his exertions; that he must wait patiently and cheerfully the time appointed for his reaping the fruit of them. 'The only sorrow we feel,' they said, 'is for the keenness of your feelings.' By the time this letter came he had recovered himself, and in his answer to his Mother he was unwilling to allow that his distress was so great as she implied it to be:

December 3, 1820.

I am ashamed to think that anything I have said should have led you to suppose that I am at all pained on my own account. . . . I am perfectly convinced that there are few men in the college who do not feel for me more than I feel for myself. . . . A man has just left me, and his last words were, 'Well, Newman, I would rather have your philosophy than the high honours to which you have been aspiring.' I say this, not in vanity, but to prove the truth of my assertion. . . . I am sure success could not have made me happier than I am at present . . . very much *I have* gone through, but the clouds have passed away. . . . Since I have done my part I have gained what is good.[1]

Only a few words are necessary to complete the outline of this portion of Mr. Newman's career.

He had been destined by his Father's loving ambition for the Bar, and with that purpose had been sent to the University, and in 1819 had entered at Lincoln's Inn; but his failure in the schools making his prospect of rising in a difficult profession doubtful, and his religious views becoming more pronounced, he decided in the course of 1821, with his Father's

---

[1] The length of time and space Mr. Newman gives to his failure in the schools is only interesting to the reader as illustrating the indomitable resolution and industry of the young aspirant for honours. Of course the cause of his failure was overwork; he overtaxed his powers and broke down. There was a determination in him to work up to the point—just short of health and strength failing him. He overstepped this point on more than one subsequent occasion, as he did conspicuously here.

It may be noted that his confession of certain periods of *idleness* would represent the *industry* of the average undergraduate.—ED.

full acquiescence, on taking Orders. His scholarship at Trinity continuing for several years still, he was furnished with a sufficient plea for remaining at Oxford, though a B.A., and for taking private pupils as a means of support. He wished also to be of use to his youngest brother, whom he was desirous of bringing to the University; and, as the year drew to its close, and just at the time he began to take pupils, he conceived the audacious idea of standing for a fellowship at Oriel—at that time the object of ambition of all rising men at Oxford, and attainable only by those who had the highest academical pretensions. It may be called audacious for various reasons, and certainly would so seem to others; but, in truth, he had never himself accepted his failure in the schools as the measure of his intellectual merits, and in proportion as the relief of mind ceased to be felt, consequent at first upon his freedom from scholastic work and its anxieties, a reaction took place within him, and he began to think about retrieving his losses, and to aspire to some honourable and permanent place in his loved University, refusing tempting offers of tutorships in gentlemen's families which would call him away from Oxford, and applying in whispers to himself the line of Gray:

And hushed in grim repose expects his evening prey.

This change in his state of mind took place in him in the autumn of 1821, and he has described his feelings at that time in the following passage in 'Loss and Gain':

He recollected with what awe and transport he had at first come to the University, as to some sacred shrine; and how from time to time hopes had come over him that some day or other he should have gained a title to residence on one of its old foundations. One night in particular came across his memory: how a friend and he had ascended to the top of one of its many towers with the purpose of making observations on the stars; and how, while his friend was busily engaged with the pointers, he, earthly-minded youth, had been looking down into the deep gas-lit, dark-shadowed quadrangles, and wondering if he should ever be Fellow of this or that college, which he singled out from the mass of academical buildings.

It is scarcely necessary to say here that his attempt at Oriel, startling as it was to his friends and hopeless as it was in his own calm judgment, was successful. It follows next to draw out the circumstances under which it was made.

LETTERS AND EXTRACTS CONNECTING CHAPTERS I. AND II. OF THE MEMOIR

The close of the first chapter of the Autobiographical Memoir seems the proper occasion for introducing contemporary letters from the family correspondence, and such extracts from Mr. Newman's records of the period as throw further light on the Memoir.

More space may have been given to the mischance of a failure—due, in fact, to physical causes—than, considering the subsequent career and reputation of the narrator, may seem called for; but, after all, it illustrates the faith in taking pains which was a feature of his mind through life; and, in fact, the history throughout is characteristic. No subsequent intellectual triumph would efface this blow in a memory which held its whole being in so firm a grasp. The intense labour and capacity for work which later on were the wonder of his friends, the sensitive nerves, the keenness of pain in disappointing the hopes he had raised, all belonged to his mature nature, as did also the latent undisturbed consciousness of power—as shown in his next move—which no failure or reverse, whether in the schools or elsewhere, could disturb. At sixteen he wrote an essay on Fame, which shows him speculating on the question in the tone of his manhood:

. . . But this is not the fame I intend to discuss; I mean by fame the knowledge your contemporaries have of you while living, and posterity when dead. On this I will advance an assertion which may at first appear strange, but which has often struck me very forcibly—that is, that there is no such thing as a *person* being famed. Let it not be thought a quibble when I say it is his name that is celebrated, and not himself.[1]

It was one of the consequences of Mr. Newman beginning his Oxford career so early that he had no idea of husbanding his strength. He made his eyesight the test. So long as his eyes did not pain him he worked on, or, as he called it, fagged, till he could do no more. The following letter to his Mother, written early in his Oxford days, tells of a complete breakdown, clearly the consequence of overtaxing his strength :

October 28, 1817.

. . . Last Sunday, while in St. Mary's, a dizziness came over my eyes : I could see nothing, and to my surprise I found my head was on the shoulder of the gownsman who sat next to me. He took me out and brought me to my rooms, for my mind was alive and I could show him the way, so that while he was stumbling up the stairs, I, by recollection, did not miss a step. He brought me some water, and he bade me good morning, and neither his face, his name, nor his rank in the University (except that he must either be a bachelor or an undergraduate) have I an idea of. While I was sitting reading about eight in the evening I dropped asleep for an hour, and woke quite myself.

In fact, Mr. Newman never had robust health. The letters from home, even at this early period, show a constant solicitude on the score of overwork and its consequences. His constitution showed singular powers of continuous application all through his life, and even when this was pushed too far there was a recuperative energy in reserve which saved him from the ordinary consequences of an overtaxed brain ; but there was not even in early days the sense or aspect of exuberant health. In his busiest years toothache was a constant suffering and hindrance, and seems to have been something abnormal. His youth, indeed, was chequered by cares ; his Mother's tone shows him the sharer of all family anxieties, and him, indeed, solicitous to share them. Her early letters show an unbounded confidence in his 'well-regulated mind,' equal to all trials, whether prosperous or adverse. And how

[1] See this thought carried out in the sermon on the 'Vanity of Human Glory'—*Parochial Sermons*, vol. viii.

dear this trust was to him is almost pathetically apparent as time goes on.[1]

Answering his Mother's birthday letter of 1819 his memory goes far back :

February 24, 1819.

I woke on the morning of February 21, and, without recollecting it was my birthday, my mind involuntarily recurred to the day I was four years old, and said the 'Cat and the Cream Bowl' [to a party of little ones in Southampton Street], and the day I was five years old your telling me that now I was a big boy, and must behave myself accordingly ; to the day I was six years old, when I spoke Cowper's ' Faithful Friend ' at Ham [where his grandmother lived]. I have no doubt I shall look back with regret on the time I was at Oxford and on my birthday of 1819.

In the memoranda of this year 1819 there occurs this thought :

Sunday evening bells pealing. The pleasure of hearing them. It leads the mind to a longing after something, I know not what. It does not bring past years to remembrance ; it does not bring anything. What does it do ? We have a kind of longing after something dear to us, and well known to

---

[1] Mr. Newman's eyes, which troubled him so early, were not a permanent trouble. The rules prescribed by the oculist of the day may be given, as it were, to impress the fact upon the reader of the short-sightedness which made spectacles a necessity all through his active life.

' The following is the advice of Mr. Alexander concerning my eyes : " Those who have a disposition to be short-sighted, books, contracting as they do the muscles of the eye, are apt to make more so. They first feel it about twelve years of age; this short-sightedness increases until twenty-two. It then stops, and time will bring a longer sight. There is this consolation for you, you will never be blind. With respect to what is advisable for you to do, observe the following directions. Strain not your sight at distant objects, rather use a glass; when you read have your neckcloth loose, your head erect ; avoid everything like a stooping posture. In bed your head very high, your feet low, your bed an inclined plane, your head cool, your feet warm. In your diet avoid anything which may cause a sudden rush of blood to the head. Keep your temperature cool, and apply leeches to your temples once a fortnight. An observance of these directions will keep you from being worse, and may make you a shade better." Oh, consolation ! " may " !'

It does not appear that the last direction was ever followed ; the writer makes no comment on it.

us—very soothing. Such is my feeling at this minute as I hear them.

Music in his undergraduate days was a constant recreation. In 1820 he had found sympathisers, and a music club was formed.

To HIS SISTER, H. E. N.
February 26.

Our music club at St. John's has been offered and has accepted the music room for our weekly private concerts. [Again *June* 3 :] I was asked by a man yesterday to go to his rooms for a *little* music at seven o'clock. I went. An old Don—a very good-natured man, but too fond of music—played Bass ; and through his enthusiasm I was kept playing quartets on a heavy tenor from seven to twelve ! O my poor arm and eyes and head and back ! [Again he writes later :] I went to the R.'s to play the difficult first violin to Haydn, Mozart, &c.

He found time for lighter reading ; is enthusiastic to his Mother on 'Ivanhoe,' especially the second volume ; and writes to his Father of Crabbe's poems, for which he had a lasting admiration :

I also send Crabbe's 'Tales of the Hall,' a work of which I am excessively fond ; but the monotonous gloominess of which is so great an objection that I can hardly think he will ever have many admirers. Hardly one of his Tales has a fortunate ending ; hardly one of his Tales but has the same ending ; hardly one of his Tales but is disfigured by the most prosaic lines or degraded by familiar vulgarity. However, for all this, he seems to me one of the greatest poets of the present day. His 'Lady Barbara,' out of many beautiful ones, is the most uniformly elevated and animated.

A letter to his Father of this date mentions Dr. Routh. It is observable that no Oxford memory ever knew this name but as associated with the word Venerable. It was a remark of Mr. Rickards's, who had an early experience of Oxford, not only that Dr. Routh was old at any given date, but that he always had been old, and gave the world the impression of never having known any other stage of being.

One of our Dons is on the eve of marriage, the President

of Magdalen, noted for his learning, his strange appearance, his venerable age.[1]

A letter already quoted in the Memoir, 'The Long prospect is now before me, &c.,' excited its writer as he read it in after years to inscribe on it the following comments : 'This means that I was idle in the Long Vacation 1818,' after gaining the scholarship ; and on the whole letter is this notice : 'This is in very Gibbonian style.' It is difficult to connect the writing of this early date with what has been described as the short, sharp, terse fire of Mr. Newman's style some ten or a dozen years later, but at each date his subject mastered him, whether he leant upon a model for giving his thought adequate expression, or later on trusted the energy of his thought to take its course by the most direct road.

We read in the 'Apologia' that 'when I was fifteen [in the autumn of 1816] a great change of thought took place in me. I fell under the influences of a definite creed, and received into my intellect impressions of dogma, which through God's mercy have never been effaced or obscured.' The remarks noted down during the years of his undergraduateship illustrate this. The Memoir says, 'In the solitude of the Long I became graver and graver.' In evidence of this many records of thought remain, showing a mind set upon subjects far removed from the ordeal he was preparing for, with such excessive industry. Thus, in a memorandum dated August 20, 1820 :

It may be supposed that the greatest agony Christ endured was not that which He suffered in the body, but that inward horror and darkness which caused the drops of blood in the garden, and the mysterious exclamation on the Cross. May not this be stated in such a manner as to repel the objection, that His corporal sufferings could not cleanse us from sin which is spiritual ?[2]

A few months later the same MS. book contains the following reflection on mysteries (March 4, 1821) :

[1] Dean Burgon gives Dr. Routh's age on marriage as sixty-five. The marriage took place September 18, 1820.
[2] The reader of Mr. Newman's works will recognise in this passage the dawn of a thought subsequently most powerfully worked out.

The Second Person of the Trinity is called the Son of the Father, the Only Begotten. Not in a literal sense, but as the nearest analogy in human language to convey the idea of an incomprehensible relation between the Father and the Son. Nothing can show this more clearly than the other titles given to him in Scripture. If He were in every respect a Lamb, He would not be the Shepherd. If He were in every respect the Husband of the Church, He could not be the Father.

Again (June 1, 1821):

About a week ago I dreamed a spirit came to me and discoursed about the other world. I had several meetings with it. Dreams address themselves so immediately to the mind, that to express in any form of words the feelings produced by the speeches themselves of my mysterious visitant, were a fruitless endeavour. Among other things it said that it was absolutely impossible for the reason of man to understand the mystery of the Holy Trinity, and in vain to argue about it; but that everything in another world was so very, very plain that there was not the slightest difficulty about it. I cannot put into any sufficiently strong form of words the ideas that were conveyed to me. I thought I instantly fell on my knees overcome with gratitude to God for so kind a message.

It is not idle to make a memorandum of this, for out of dreams often much good can be extracted.

Again (June 1, 1821):

When I have heard or read that Horsley, Milner, &c., were adverse to the introduction of the doctrine of election, final perseverance, &c., into the pulpit, I have wondered, and been sorry for such an opinion. However, when I came to examine my own opinion on the subject, I have much the same sentiments. Do we see St. Paul or St. Peter in the Acts addressing the unconverted in this manner?

Some touches of his home life and its varying influences on his character may here be given. In the Long Vacation of 1821, when he was for a short time at home, there occurs this entry in his journal:

September 30, 1821. *Sunday.*—After dinner to-day I was suddenly called downstairs to give an opinion whether I thought it a sin to write a letter on a Sunday. I found dear F. had refused to copy one. A scene ensued more painful than any I have experienced. I have been sadly deficient in meekness, long-suffering, patience, and filial obedience. With God's assistance I will redeem my character.

Monday, October 1, 1821.—My Father was reconciled to us to day. When I think of the utter persuasion he must entertain of the justice of his views, of our apparent disobedience, the seeming folly of our opinions, and the way in which he is harassed by worldly cares, I think his forgiveness of us an example of very striking candour, forbearance and generosity.

On the question of his brother Francis going to read with him in Oxford, he writes to his Father :

June 21, 1821.

I am turned out of college in a little more than a fortnight, and for Trinity term I have engaged lodgings. The Dean tells me there is nothing extraordinary in a brother coming up to Oxford to study before entrance at any college. Tell Charles I cannot find in the Bodleian any work on the mathematical principles of chess. [Writing a day or two after :] I am glad to say that Mr. Short has been good enough to get me a man of our college for a private pupil. I am to begin with him after the Long Vacation. He is to give me a hundred a year. I am naturally much delighted to find you propose Francis should come to Oxford, and have been arranging things as well as I can.

J. H. N. TO HIS MOTHER.

October 26, 1821.

I am very glad to hear you say that yourself and my Father are both well ; of course whatever you say concerning him and his anxieties must interest me very much. There is no one who is on any side without cause of sorrow ; and, this being the case, it is a most happy thing to feel one's particular distress comes from without. When I look round, I see few families but what are disturbed from within. Many are wasted by death ; many distracted by disagreements ; many scattered. We have not had to weep over the death of those we love. We are not disquieted by internal variance ; we are not parted from each other by circumstances we cannot control. We have kind and indulgent parents, and our tastes, disposition, and pursuits are the same. How grateful ought we to be ! Surely it is a joyful thing that that distress, which must be, leaves unimpaired, or rather heightened, all domestic affection and love.

And then as to the very trial itself, there is nothing in any way to fear. 'All things work together for good to those who love God.' I am firmly and rootedly persuaded of this. Everything that happens to them is most certainly the very best, in every light, that could by any possibility have happened. God will give good. I will do as much as I can, and *then* I have nothing to apprehend. This is indeed a privilege, for it takes away all care as to the future.

> His other gifts
> All bear the royal stamp that speaks them His,
> And are august; but this transcends them all.

To his sister Harriett he tells of the end of a successful career, with what may be supposed a personal warning.

January 19, 1822.

I informed you in my last that Dr. Hodson was very ill. He died yesterday morning. Having attained the Headship of Brasenose, the Regius Chair of Divinity, and a Canonry of Ch. Ch.; when all men looked on in expectation of what would come next, in the height of his influence with Lord Grenville and Lord Buckingham, he is suddenly taken ill, and in a few days died.

I trust I ask sincerely, Give me nothing which will in any way delay me in my Christian course; and such prayers God is accustomed, and promises, to grant.

To his Mother he writes on attaining his majority:

March 6, 1822

Thank you for your very kind letter. When I turn to look at myself I feel quite ashamed of the praise it contains, so numerous and so great are the deficiencies that even I can see. There is an illusion in the words 'being of age' which is apt to convey the idea of some sudden and unknown change. That point, instead of being gained by the slow and silent progress of one and twenty years, seems to divide, by some strongly marked line, the past from the to-come. . . . Not that I am sorry so great a part of life is gone—would that all were over!—but I seem now more left to myself, and when I reflect upon my own weakness I have cause to shudder.

Not unnaturally, his Mother thinks the tone of the last line morbid. Out of the midst of troubles of her own—which, indeed, he shared with her—she writes anxiously on his account :

March 11, 1822.

. . . This subject I have been anxious to begin with, but another is equally pressing on my mind and your Father's ; that is the state of your health and spirits. We fear very much, from the tone of your letter, you are depressed ; and if imperious reasons did not forbid us, you would certainly *see* us. We fear you debar yourself a proper quantity of wine. . . . Take proper air and exercise ; accept all the invitations you receive ; and do not be over-anxious about anything. Nothing but your own over-anxiety can make you suppose we give a thought to Oriel. . . .

To show you I do not think you *too old* for a mother's correction and advice, I shall not hesitate to tell you I see one great fault in your character which alarms me, as I observe it grows upon you seriously ; and as all virtues may degenerate into vices, it is everyone's duty to have a strict guard over themselves to avoid extremes. Your fault is a want of self-confidence and a dissatisfaction with yourself. . . .

His answer comes by return of post. And first he assures his Mother his health is not at all in fault.

. . . I have hardly a moment to write, I am going out to a wine party, and to the music room in the evening. . . . I am very very much obliged to you for your anxiety, but never was anxiety so ill founded. I was only the other day congratulating myself on the great improvement of my health from what it was a year ago. . . .

As to my opinions, and the sentiments I expressed in my last letter, they remain fixed in my mind, and are repeated deliberately and confidently. If it were any new set of opinions I had lately adopted, they might be said to arise from nervousness, or over-study, or ill-health ; but no, my opinion has been exactly the same for these five years. . . . The only thing is, opportunities have occurred of late for my mentioning it more than before ; but believe me, those sentiments are neither new nor slightly founded. If they made me melancholy, morose, austere, distant, reserved, sullen, then indeed they might with justice be the subject of anxiety ; but if, as I think is the case, I am always cheerful, if at home I am always ready and eager to join in any merriment, if I am not clouded with sadness, if my meditations make me neither absent in mind nor deficient in action, then my principles may be gazed at and puzzle the gazer, but they cannot be accused of bad practical effects. Take me when I am most foolish at home, and extend mirth into childishness ; stop me short and ask me then what I think of myself, whether my opinions are less gloomy ; no, I think I should seriously return the same answer, that 'I shuddered at myself.' And what is to make me so ? Am I in the midst of persons of the same opinions ? Am I solitary ? Neither. However, I have no time to finish this ; so good-bye.

It is now time to return to Mr. Newman's own account of himself.

AUTOBIOGRAPHICAL MEMOIR

CHAPTER II

It did certainly startle Mr. Newman's friends at Trinity to find him contemplating an attempt upon an Oriel fellowship; and many of them it pained also, for they were sure it would end in a second miscarriage. They had not the shadow of a hope of his succeeding; they would have thought him wise if, instead of following an *ignis fatuus*, he had accepted one of the family tutorships offered for his acceptance. What would confirm them in this view was the grave fact, that he had lost almost the whole of the current year in recreations and diversions of his own, instead of devoting the time since he took his Bachelor's degree in preparation for a difficult competition. What his actual occupations had been appears accidentally from a series of passages in his letters home, and in his private memoranda, some of which shall now be given in the order in which they were written.

To his Father he writes on his return to Oxford in February 1821, after his failure in the schools:

I arrived here safe the day before yesterday, and have found a general welcome. Dr.[1] and Mrs. Lee have been very kind. I intend attending the lectures on anatomy and mineralogy.

To the same on March 20:

I have been with Mr. Kinsey to Abingdon, to the house of a gentleman who has a fine collection of minerals. We were employed in looking over them from one to four o'clock. Some of them are most beautiful. When I come home I shall make various excursions to the British Museum, if open, for the sake of the minerals.

[1] The President.

During this term he attended the course of lectures on mineralogy given by Professor Buckland, and made a careful analysis of them, which is to be found among his papers. To his Mother in the same month :

Thank Harriett for her skill in steaming away the superfluous water of the nitro-sulphate of copper. The mineralogical lectures were finished yesterday. . . .

I am glad to be able to inform you that Signor Giovanni Enrico Neandrini has finished his first composition. The melody is light and airy, and is well supported by the harmony.

To the same in June :

I have been very much to myself this term. Buckland's lectures [on geology] I had intended to have taken down, as I did last term, but several things prevented me—the time it takes, and the very desultory way in which he imparts his information : for, to tell the truth, the science is so in its infancy that no regular system is formed. Hence the lectures are rather an enumeration of facts from which probabilities are deduced, than a consistent and luminous theory of certainties, illustrated by occasional examples. It is, however, most entertaining, and opens an amazing field to imagination and to poetry.

To these accidental notices of his employment of his time after his B.A. degree, others may be added, more complete because in retrospect. He says in passages of his private memoranda that he had now 'more leisure for religious exercises and the study of the Scriptures than when he was a fagging drudge'; that 'mineralogy and chemistry were his chief studies, and the composition of music'; though, from the time he thought of standing at Oriel, he gave considerable time to Latin composition, to logic, and to natural philosophy; that, as an undergraduate, he used to say, 'When I have taken my degree I will do many things—compose a piece of music for instruments, experimentalise in chemistry, thirdly [on which he insisted much] get up the Persian language.' In consequence of this last design, his Mother bought him an Arabic and Persian vocabulary, now in the Oratory library, but nothing came of it. It does not appear from any papers he has left how this study came into his mind. Was it suggested by Henry Martyn's history?

These notices have, perhaps, a claim to be introduced into this Memoir for their own sake; but here they are simply meant to illustrate the surprise and discomposure with which his good friends at Trinity, nay, almost he himself, in spite of himself, contemplated his resolution to engage in so forlorn a hope as an attempt on an Oriel fellowship. None thought it possible that he could succeed in it; and, at his suggestion, Mr. Kinsey wrote to his father with the purpose, as far as might be, of putting before him the state of the case, and guarding him against disappointment. He, Kinsey, told him that in the competition at Oriel 'the struggles of the best have failed'; and that, ' knowing the many opponents which his son would have to encounter, men of celebrity for talent and reading, he, the writer, with all his eager desire for his friend's success, did not permit himself to be at all sanguine as to his beating the field.'

Mr. Short was as little inclined to look hopefully upon Newman's prospects at Oriel as the rest, but he took a larger view of the matter, and was not unwilling that he should stand. He knew enough of him to expect that he would do himself and his college credit, and he had strongly expressed this to friends of Newman in London, who, being sincerely interested in him, and anxious about his future, asked Mr. Short what he had to say on the subject, who answered them that Newman would not succeed, but that he would show what was in him, and thereby in a certain measure retrieve his unexpected failure the year before; he wished the Oriel men to have an opportunity of passing a judgment on him. In truth, it was, naturally and fairly, a matter of personal and collegiate interest with Mr. Short, over and above his goodwill towards Newman. The opening of the Trinity scholarships was Short's doing, and he had actually recommended him to stand in 1818. In the election, formidable out-college opponents had been put aside for him, and his failure in examination had been an untoward incident in the first start of a great reform. Mr. Short had brought out these feelings to him with the greatest delicacy, soon after his misfortune. On his asking

Short, in April 1821, whether he should write for one of the Chancellor's prizes, yearly given for the best English and Latin essays, Mr. Short answered in the affirmative, and went on to give the following reasons for wishing it: 'I have no doubt,' he said, 'of your producing something that either will succeed now or train you to certain success another year. In fact, the uppermost wish in my mind respecting you is that you may distinguish yourself in the rostrum, and prove to the world, what is already well known to ourselves, that the purity of our elections is unsullied. For should your old competitor at Worcester obtain high honours in the schools, sneerers will not be wanting to amuse themselves at your and our expense. Perhaps these reasons never occurred to you.' Short had said, in a former part of the letter, that he should himself have suggested to him to attempt the essay long before, but he had been anxious whether Mr. Newman's health allowed it.

By a singular coincidence Oriel College that same year, and at that very time, was subjecting itself, and even more directly and wittingly, to a criticism upon its impartiality in conducting its competitive examinations, fiercer and more public than this, which Mr. Short only feared for Trinity. Though in that day the acknowledged centre of Oxford intellectualism, Oriel had never professed, in its elections, simply to choose the candidate who passed the best examination; and, though on its foundation were for the most part men who had taken the highest honours in the schools, it never made the school standard its own. Religious, ethical, social considerations, as well as intellectual merits, external to the *curriculum* of the schools, all told in its decisions; the votes fell on the men whom each elector in his conscience thought best to answer to the standard of a Fellow of Oriel, as the statutes of Adam de Brome and King Edward II. determined it. In consequence, there was ever the chance of the election of a candidate of a nature to startle his competitors and the public at large, as being unexpected and unaccountable. Such an anomalous election, as many men thought it, had taken place in 1821, just three days before Newman's letter to Mr. Short above spoken of. A second-class man had been preferred to one whose name stood in the first class; and though the successful candidate did, as if in justification of his selection, gain the Chancellor's Latin essay prize a few months later, yet it so happened his rival, whom he had beaten, was able, at the annual Commemoration, to hurl defiance at him in the theatre from the opposite rostrum, as having been the successful competitor for the English essay. This essay, as being in English, gave opportunity for vigorous, brilliant, and popular writing, which was denied to a composition written in Latin; and judgment on the rival merits of the two men was thus shifted to a public opinion, external both to college and University, and in fact that judgment was passed in certain influential quarters to the disadvantage of the successful candidate and his electors. There was a Review of great name, then as now, which had for many years been in feud with Oxford, and especially with Dr. Copleston, Provost of Oriel, and his Society. An editor, whoever he be, taking human nature at the best, sometimes 'dormitat,' however 'bonus'; and an article against Oriel found its way into his July number, so exceptionable, to use a mild word, that in a second edition—according to the recollection of the present writer—sentences or expressions were erased from it.

The article is upon classical study; and after speaking of the English Universities generally in that connexion, it directs its attention to their open fellowships, and to the nature of the examination usual for determining the choice between the candidates, and to the proceedings and the result of the election. The allusion to Oriel, and to the election made at the preceding Easter, was unmistakable. The following is a portion of the writer's invective, for such it must be called.

[N.B.—Let it be observed I have concealed the really *bad* fact that the *writer* was the *unsuccessful candidate*. But Copleston has blabbed it.][1]

Let a young man only abdicate the privilege of thinking—to some no painful sacrifice—and devote his whole body and soul to the sordid ambition of success, and the way to win

---

[1] Wherever a note enclosed in brackets occurs in the text, it is to be understood that it comes from the pen of J. H. N., as writer or transcriber, whether these initials appear or not.

with such electors is no formidable problem. . . . After a dull examination in the schools—if a failure so much the better—he may begin to be the butt of Common-Rooms, circulate tutor's wit, and prose against the 'Edinburgh Review.' . . . Guiltless of fame, of originality, or humour, our tyro may then approach the scene of action, secure that the judges will take good care that 'the race shall not be to the swift nor the battle to the strong.' Hardy professions of impartiality are indeed held forth, to attract unwary merit; and selfish mediocrity finds the most exquisite of all its gratifications in the momentary chance of harassing the talent it would tremble to confront. The candidates are locked up to write themes, solve a sorites, discover the Latin for an earthquake, and perform other equally edifying tasks; and the close of this solemn farce is the annunciation of a choice that had been long before determined, in proportion to the scrapings, grins and genuflections of the several competitors. Who can be surprised if, under a system like this, genius and knowledge should so seldom strike a lasting root? or that maturity, which succeeds to a youth so prostituted, should produce, by its most vigorous efforts, nothing better than learned drivelling and marrowless inflation?

It is scarcely necessary to say that this tirade against Oxford and Oriel was as unjust as it was unmannerly; however, *diis aliter visum*. Such a spirited denunciation seems to have been considered in a high quarter just what was wanted to show the world what retribution was to descend, and what terrible examples would be made, if an Oxford college presumed to maintain a standard and exercise a judgment of its own, on the qualifications necessary in those who were to fill up vacant places on its foundation; and, though the Oriel Fellows were of too independent and manly a cast of mind, and had too high a repute and too haughty pretensions, to succumb to a self-appointed and angry censor, yet, in spite of their natural indignation at his language, the charge brought against them, as coming with so weighty a sanction, would necessarily tend to make them more wary of the steps they took in the ensuing election of 1822—more unwilling, if it could be helped, to run risks, and more anxious that their decisions should be justified by the event. This state of things, then, at Oriel cannot be said to have told in Mr. Newman's favour, when at length he resolved on submitting his talents and attainments, such as they were, to the inspection of Provost and Fellows. For they could not pronounce in his favour without repeating, in an exaggerated form, their offence of the foregoing year : that is, without passing over the first-class competitors, and electing instead of them one whose place in the paper of honours was ever taken, in popular estimation, as the token of a mistake or a misfortune; an intimation, known and understood by all men, that there had been an attempt at something higher and a failure in attaining it.

Such being the external view presented to us by Mr. Newman's venturous proceeding, let us trace *seriatim*, from his private memoranda, how it presented itself to his own mind.

The examination was to be in the first days of the ensuing April; it was now the middle of November; he had at least four good months before him. He notes down on November 15:

I passed this evening with the Dean—Mr. Kinsey—whose Oriel cousin was there. He said the principal thing in the examination for Fellows was writing Latin. I thought I ought to stand; and, indeed, since, I have nearly decided on so doing. How active still are the evil passions of vainglory, ambition, &c. within me! After my failure last November, I thought that they would never be unruly again. Alas! no sooner is any mention made of my standing for a fellowship than every barrier seems swept away; and they spread, and overflow, and deluge me: ὥσπερ ξὺν ἵπποις ἡνιοστροφῶ δρόμου, &c.[1]

He continues (December 1):

There is every reason for thinking I shall not succeed, and I seem to see it would not be good for me, but my heart boils over with vainglorious anticipations of success. It is not likely, because I am not equal to it in abilities or attainments; it seems probable that I shall fail once or twice, and get some fellowship somewhere at last.

Two months later, February 5, 1822, he writes:

To-day I called on the Provost of Oriel, and asked his permission to stand at the ensuing election. I cannot help

[1] *Choeph.* 1009.

thinking I shall one time or other get a fellowship there : most probably next year. I am glad I am going to stand now; I shall make myself known, and learn the nature of the examination. The principal thing seems to be Latin composition, and a metaphysical turn is a great advantage ; general mathematics are also required. . . . Last 5th of January [1821], I wrote to my aunt : 'I deprecate the day in which God gives me any repute, or any approach to wealth.' Alas, how I am changed! I am perpetually praying to get into Oriel, and to obtain the prize for my essay. O Lord ! dispose of me as will best promote Thy glory, but give me resignation and contentment.

On February 21 he came of age, and he writes to his Mother in answer to her congratulations : 'I thought of the years that are gone, and the expanse which lies before me, and quite shed tears to think I could no longer call myself a boy'; and then, after noticing his employments, he continues : ' What time I have left, I am glad—and, indeed, obliged—to devote to my attempt at Oriel, wishing to prepare myself for that which (after all) will not admit of preparation.'

Then he says, in corroboration of what Mr. Kinsey was saying in the letter above quoted :

I was very uneasy to find by something in my Father's and your letter, that you thought I had a chance of getting in this time. Do not think so, I entreat. You only hear, and cannot see the difficulties. Those on the spot think there is little or no chance ; and who, indeed, will not rightly wonder at the audacity of him who, being an under-the-line himself, presumes to contend with some of the first men in the University, for a seat by the side of names like Keble and Hawkins ?

He wished his home friends not to share his hopes, lest they should have to share his disappointment. The chances were much against him ; his hopes, nevertheless, were high, but while an avowal of this might mislead those who did not know Oxford, it would incur the ridicule of those who did. His hopes are recorded in a memorandum made the next day :

I have called on Tyler to-day [the then Dean of Oriel]. I do not know how it happens, but I certainly feel very confident with respect to Oriel, and seem to myself to have a great chance of success. Hope leads me on to fancy my confidence itself has something of success in it, and I seem to recollect something of the same kind of ardour when I stood at Trinity.

However, before many weeks were out, he was obliged to let out to his Father the hopes he had been so carefully concealing from him. Made anxious by the tone of his son's letter, written on occasion of his birthday, he wrote to warn him that, if he continued in the desponding temper which his letters home betokened, he certainly would not be able to do justice to his talents and attainments, and would be the cause of his own failure. This obliged him to answer on March 15 thus :

I assure you that they know very little of me, and judge very superficially of me, who think I do not put a value on myself *relatively* to others. I think (since I am forced to speak boastfully) few have attained the facility of comprehension which I have arrived at from the regularity and constancy of my reading, and the laborious and nerve-bracing and fancy-repressing study of mathematics, which has been my principal subject.

On the 18th he repeats in a private memorandum :

I fear I am treasuring up for myself great disappointment ; for I think I have a great chance of succeeding. I lay great stress on the attention I have given to mathematics, on account of the general strength it imparts to the mind. Besides, ever since my attempts at school, I have given great time to composition. As when I was going up for my degree examination every day made my hopes fainter, so now they seem to swell and ripen as the time approaches.

The examination was now close at hand, and he suffered some reaction of feeling when he plunged into it. On the close of it he thus writes :

I have several times been much comforted yesterday and to-day by a motto in Oriel hall [in a coat of arms in a window], *Pie repone te*. I am now going to bed, and have been very calm the whole evening. Before I look into this book again it will be decided.

Next day—the Friday in Easter week—he writes: 'I have this morning been elected Fellow of Oriel.'[1]

Some account of what passed in this, to him, memorable day is introduced in his 'Apologia'; other incidents of it are noted in his letters to members of his family, and others again he used to recount at a later date to his friends. When the examination had got as far as the third day, his papers had made that impression on Dr. Copleston and others of the electors, that three of them—James, Tyler, and Dornford—went over to Trinity to make inquiries of the Fellows about his antecedents and general character. This, of course, was done in confidence; nor did his kind tutor, Mr. Short, in any degree violate it; at the same time he was himself so excited by this visit, that he could not help sending for Mr. Newman on the pretext of inquiring of him what had been his work, and how he had done it; and by the encouraging tone in which he commented on his answers, he did him a great deal of good.[2]

Newman used to relate how, when sent for, he found Mr. Short at an early dinner in his rooms, being about to start from Oxford; and how Short made him sit down at table and partake of his lamb cutlets and fried parsley—a bodily refreshment which had some share in the reassurance with which Short's words inspired him. He wrote to his Mother in retrospect, some three weeks after, 'Short elevated me so much, and made me fancy I had done so well, that on Wednesday I construed some part of my [*viva voce*] passages with very great readiness and even accuracy.'

Mr. Newman used also to relate the mode in which the announcement of his success was made to him. The Provost's butler—to whom it fell by usage to take the news to the fortunate candidate—made his way to Mr. Newman's lodgings in Broad Street, and found him playing the violin. This in itself disconcerted the messenger, who did not associate such

---

[1] Writing to his Father, the words were, 'I am just made Fellow of Oriel. Thank God!'

[2] Mr. Short told him on February 27, 1878, when he was in Oxford on the occasion of his being elected Honorary Fellow of Trinity, that, on sending for him, he found him intending to retire from the examination, and that he persuaded him to continue the contest.

an accomplishment with a candidateship for the Oriel Common-Room; but his perplexity was increased when, on his delivering what may be supposed to have been his usual form of speech on such occasions, that 'he had, he feared, disagreeable news to announce, viz. that Mr. Newman was elected Fellow of Oriel, and that his immediate presence was required there,' the person addressed, thinking that such language savoured of impertinent familiarity, merely answered, 'Very well,' and went on fiddling. This led the man to ask whether, perhaps, he had not mistaken the rooms and gone to the wrong person, to which Mr. Newman replied that it was all right. But, as may be imagined, no sooner had the man left, than he flung down his instrument, and dashed down stairs with all speed to Oriel College. And he recollected, after fifty years, the eloquent faces and eager bows of the tradesmen and others whom he met on his way, who had heard the news, and well understood why he was crossing from St. Mary's to the lane opposite at so extraordinary a pace.

He repeats, in his letter to his Mother, a circumstance in his first interview, which followed, with the Provost and Fellows—which in his 'Apologia' he has quoted from his letter to Mr. Bowden : 'I could bear the congratulations of Copleston, but when Keble advanced to take my hand I quite shrank, and could have nearly shrunk into the floor, ashamed at so great an honour—however, I shall soon be used to this.' He pursues his history of the day thus :

. . . The news spread to Trinity with great rapidity. I had hardly been in Kinsey's room a minute when in rushe ! Ogle like one mad. Then I proceeded to the President's, and in rushed Ogle again. I find that Tomlinson rushed into Echalaz's room, nearly knocking down the door, to communicate the news. Echalaz in turn ran down stairs ; Tompson heard a noise and my name mentioned, and rushed out also ; and in the room opposite found Echalaz, Ogle, and Ward. Men hurried from all directions to Trinity to their acquaintance there, to congratulate them on the success of their college. The bells were set ringing from three towers (I had to pay for them). The men who were staying up at Trinity, reading for their degree, accuse me of having spoilt their day's reading.

There is a letter from him to his brother Charles, in which he says: 'I took my seat in chapel, and dined with a large party in the Common-Room. I sat next to Keble, and, as I had heard him represented, he is more like an undergraduate than the first man in Oxford; so perfectly unassuming and unaffected in his manner.'

And, lastly, he says in a letter to his Father: 'I am absolutely a member of the Common-Room; am called by them "Newman," and am abashed, and find I must soon learn to call them "Keble," "Hawkins," "Tyler."'

So ends the eventful day.

As to Mr. Newman, he ever felt this twelfth of April, 1822, to be the turning-point of his life, and of all days most memorable. It raised him from obscurity and need, to competency and reputation. He never wished anything better or higher than, in the words of the epitaph, 'to live and die a Fellow of Oriel.' Henceforth, his way was clear before him; and he was constant all through his life, as his intimate friends know, in his thankful remembrance year after year of this great mercy of Divine providence. Nor was it in its secular aspect only that it was so unique an event in his history; it opened upon him a theological career, placing him upon the high and broad platform of University society and intelligence, and bringing him across those various influences, personal and intellectual, and the teaching of those various schools of ecclesiastical thought, whereby the religious sentiment in his mind, which had been his blessing from the time he left school, was gradually developed and formed and brought on to its legitimate issues.

This narrative of his attempt and its success will be most suitably closed by the judgment on his examination, as given by the very man to whom, more than to anyone, the Oriel examinations owed their form and colour, and who specially on that account had to meet the stress of those Northern criticisms which, in their most concentrated and least defensible shape, have been exhibited above. 'That defect,' says Bishop Copleston, speaking of the qualifications of a Fellow, in a letter to Dr. Hawkins under date of May 2, 1843, 'which I always saw and lamented in examiners, and in vain endeavoured to remedy, still seems not only to exist but increases—the quackery of the schools. Every election to a fellowship which tends to discourage the narrow and almost the technical routine of public examinations, I consider as an important triumph. You remember Newman himself was an example. He was not even a good classical scholar, yet in mind and power of composition, and in taste and knowledge, he was decidedly superior to some competitors who were a class above him in the schools.'

As Mr. Newman held the important offices of tutor and public examiner in the years which followed, it may be right to observe here that immediately on his becoming Fellow of Oriel, he set himself to make up his deficiency in critical scholarship, and with very fair success. Whately, soon after his election, among his other kind offices, signified this to him, being what he said a little bird had told him.

LETTERS AND EXTRACTS CONNECTING CHAPTERS II. AND III. OF THE AUTOBIOGRAPHICAL MEMOIR

There remains a letter, from a schoofellow and University friend, which shows the popular estimate of an Oriel fellowship as well as the writer's sense of his friend's power :

F. R. THRESHER TO JOHN HENRY NEWMAN.

April 12, 1822.

Behold you now a Fellow of Oriel, the great object of the ambition of half the Bachelors of Oxford. Behold you (to take a peep into futurity) in Holy Orders, taking pupils in college, and having a curacy within a short distance; then Public Tutor, Vicar of ——, Provost, Regius Professor of Divinity, Bishop of ——, Archbishop of Canterbury ; or shall we say thus—Student-at-law, Barrister, Lord Chancellor, or at least Lord Chief Justice of the King's Bench? Which of these ladders is it your intention to climb? You now have it in your power to decide.

In a letter with some college details to his Father he speaks of Keble :

May 16, 1822.

... I shall only mention Keble. At eighteen he took two first classes. Soon after he gained the two essays in one year, and a fellowship at Oriel. He is the first man in Oxford.

TO HIS SISTER HARRIETT.

August 2, 1822.

... Whately sets off for his living, bidding adieu to the Towers of Oxford, after a residence of fifteen years, on Tuesday next. I dined with him last Monday. Some years back I found bound up in tracts an old number of the 'Quarterly Review,' and in it I found the review of a Latin work of Dr. Whitaker's. The criticisms I thought so judicious that I copied them out and nearly got them by heart. Indeed, for a long time, wandering as I was without a guide, wishing to write Latin and having no one to inform me how to set about it, those criticisms were my only comfort, the only remarks which seemed vigorous and certain, and on which I felt I could lean. How much was I surprised by Whately's incidentally mentioning that the article was written by Copleston ! He was surprised in his turn, saying he was sure the Provost would be much gratified at hearing I had copied them out, since he had written them for the very purpose of instructing those who were aiming at Latin composition. Whately tells me, if I have any desire ever to write in the ' Quarterly,' I have nothing to do but to mention it to the Provost [Copleston], and that the editor will quite jump at anyone recommended from so high a quarter ; but what if the Provost will not recommend me ? I should not think of writing yet.

The following lines speak of the fatigue to hand and wrist that continuous writing was to Mr. Newman through life :

TO HIS SISTER.

August 17, 1822.

Excuse my bad writing. You cannot tell how hurried I am and how tired my hand is with writing. [Again :] My hand is very tired . . . O my poor hand ! . . . My hand will not compose a flowing sentence.

Possibly the care and attention used to defy this weakness may have contributed to the beauty and precision which Mr. Newman's handwriting maintained to the end.

Mr. Newman spent the Long Vacation of 1822 in Oxford, where his youngest brother Francis, about to enter Worcester College, joined him. In expectation of his arrival he writes to his Mother :

September 25, 1822.

. . . Expecting to see Frank, I am in fact expecting to see you all. I shall require you to fill him full of all of you, that when he comes I may squeeze and wring him out as some sponge. . . .

The only way ultimately to succeed is to do things thoroughly. I lost much time by superficial reading during the whole Long Vacation this time two years. Francis shall not go such bad ways to work. *Liber sum* (my pupil having gone), and I have been humming, whistling, and laughing loud to myself all day.

At the end of the following letter a name occurs which was in the future to be closely connected with his own.

To his Father.

Dr. and Mrs. Lee were kind enough to call on me and ask me to dinner to meet Serjeant Frere, Head of Downing College. Mrs. Frere sings *finely*. Serjeant Frere seems to have a great veneration for Copleston, and asked me much about him. He did not know him. Directly he heard I was of Oriel he turned round, as if the name of the college was an old acquaintance.

I mentioned to you the names of Greswell, Pusey, and Churton, who are to stand next year. Surely I should have had no chance next year if I had not succeeded this.

Of his brother Francis, who was reading with him up to November 29 of this year, when he was entered at Worcester College, Mr. Newman writes to his Mother :

Oriel: *November* 5, 1822.

. . . My time has been so engaged that I have hardly had an opportunity of examining Frank as I could wish. As far as I have done so he seems to have much improved. To say that he knows more than most of those who take common degrees would be saying little. I am convinced that he knows much more of Greek as a language than most of those who take first classes, and to complete the climax, because it is I who say it, he certainly knows much more of Greek as a language, in fact is a much better Greek scholar, than I. Recollect I am not talking of history or anything which is the subject of Greek. Again he is a much better mathematician than I am. I mean he reads more mathematically, as Aristotle would say. . . .

It was a time of family anxieties, in which Mr. Newman eagerly took his part. To his Father he had written, Dec. 5, 1822 : 'Everything will—I see it will—be very right if only you will let me manage'; telling him in the same letter of his work lately undertaken for the 'Encyclopædia Metropolitana.' Mrs. Newman acknowledges his letter a few days after :

December 12, 1822.

Your Father forwarded to me your delightful letter, which I know it will gratify you to hear gave him so much pleasure, that I have not seen anything cheer and comfort him like it a long time. I am quite at a loss to say anything adequate to my feelings on the whole business. . . . I congratulate Francis on his matriculation, and am delighted to anticipate that he will, whenever opportunity occurs, do you credit, and reward all your labours and anxiety for him. I fully accord with you when you say, 'Let me alone, I shall do it all well. If you will let me manage, all will be right.' This is just the text I have preached from, whenever your Father and I have discussed the subject. For many months I always begin and end by saying, 'I have no fear, John will manage.'

And that he did manage may be gathered from indirect notices. Looking back in 1823 on the past year 1822, Mr. Newman writes in a private journal :

This year past (1822) has been a scene of laborious study from the commencement to the close. Let me praise that excessive mercy which has blessed me with so strong a frame. I have sometimes quite trembled on retiring to rest at my own exertions. Quite well, indeed, am I; free from headache and every pain.

Recalling this year later on, there is added:

For the Long Vacation of 1822 I took, for I do not know how long, only four hours' sleep.

The year 1823 begins busily. To his Mother Mr. Newman writes:

I have four pupils. I have since had an application from a Merton man, and this morning from a Wadham man. My fourth pupil is from Exeter, very docile and very *nice*. . . .

Mr. Mayer passed through Oxford on Tuesday, and dined with me in Hall. The President of Corpus died about ten days since. He was the father of the University, being entered in George II.'s time.

TO HIS SISTER HARRIETT.

July 23, 1823.

You are continually in my thoughts, and I should contrive to write to you oftener, perhaps, than I do, were I sure I was writing to you alone; not because there would be anything in my communications that I should mind the world knowing, but from that instinctive feeling in consequence of which, the smaller the company the freer and more intimate becomes our conversation, and those things which we should delight to impart to each individually, we cannot force ourselves to disclose to them all together. You are, as I said before, continually in my thoughts; need I add, continually in my prayers?

The Oriel election is coming on very soon. There are very strong men standing. Besides Mr. Pusey, whom I think you have heard me mention, there are two Queen's men (one a double first), a Brasenose, who has read (his friends are ready to depose) twelve hours a day ever since he came to Oxford; a Balliol; Mr. Proctor, of Jesus; an Oriel; and two Trinity. All are first classes except the two last.

In a book of private memoranda occur the following thoughts written in 1823:

April 6.—If a man speaks incoherently, as I think, on regeneration, if he speaks of the merit of works, if he speaks of man's natural free will, I may suppose I do not understand him, and that we differ in *terms*. But when he talks of our natural sin as an *infirmity* and I as a *disease*, he as an imperfection and I as a poison, he as making man imperfect, as tho angels may be, I as making him the foe of God, and an object of God's wrath, here we can come to no argument with each other, but one or other of us must fearfully mistake the Scriptures.

Again:

April 13.—We are apt to get censorious with respect to others as soon as we ourselves have adopted any new strictness. At least, that is the case with *me*. For a long time after God had vouchsafed His grace to me, I saw no harm in going to the play. [Till 1821. But I don't suppose I can have gone more than once or twice between 1816 and 1820.] Directly I changed I grew uncharitable towards those who went. While I was an undergraduate I profaned Sunday; for instance, I made no objection to reading newspapers on Sunday; yet the minute I leave off this practice, I can hardly bring myself to believe anyone to have a renewed mind who does so. Humility is the root of charity. Charity hopeth all things, even as regards those who outwardly appear offending.

The following letter, to a young man of sceptical opinions, is of the same date—1823:

. . . I cannot conclude this without adverting to the subject which engaged our attention on our last walk. We find one man of one opinion on religion, another of another; and thus may be led hastily to conclude that opinions diametrically opposed to each other, may be held without danger to one side or the other in a future state. But contradictions can be no more true in religion than in astronomy or chemistry; and there is this most important distinction between scientific and religious opinions, that, whereas errors in the former are unattended with danger to the person who maintains them, he who 'holdeth not the faith' (I am not now determining what that faith is), such a one is said to be incapable of true moral excellence, and so exposed to the displeasure of God. The first point, then, is to press upon the conscience that we are playing with edged tools; if, instead of endeavouring perseveringly to ascertain what the truth is, we consider the subject carelessly, captiously, or with indifference. Now it will be found, I presume, on a slight examination, that the generality of men have *not* made up their religious views in this sincere spirit. . . . This is not the frame of mind in which they can hope for success in any worldly pursuit; why then in that most difficult one of religious truth ?... I should be grieved if you thought I was desirous of affecting superior wisdom, or gaining converts to a set of opinions. In every one of us there is naturally a void, a restlessness, a hunger of the soul, a craving after some unknown and vague happiness, which we suppose seated in wealth, fame, knowledge, in fact any worldly good which we are not ourselves possessed of....

Mr. Newman's letters to his sisters about this date show an active sympathy and interest in their education, and progress in thought and accomplishments. They sent their verses to him for criticism, and his answers always show interest and a mind at work.

August 22, 1823, he writes to H. E. N. :

My first reason for not having been down to see you is that I wish to give you time for perfecting your translation of Tasso, and your Andante minor.

Again, speaking of his sister :

Harriett has been showing me what she has done of the passage of Gibbon ; of course it may be corrected, but it does her much credit. It is a harder thing to do than might at first be imagined.

In a postscript he writes :

Jemima is an ingenious girl, and has invented a very correct illustration of the generation of asymptotic curves.

In a letter to his Mother he sets his youngest sister of eleven a task :

For Mary I hang on the end of this letter a string of grammatical questions.[1]

The following advice was written about the time when, acting on his own precepts, he had committed the Epistle to the Ephesians to memory :

[1] Perhaps some reader may like to see these questions. 'Mary, supply the words omitted in the following elliptical expressions and phrases : Wake Duncan with the knocking—would thou couldst. The Duke, brave as he was, shuddered. So far from it that he fled the enemy. O well is thee, and happy shalt thou be ! You are as odd a girl as ever I saw. A thrill how sweet, who feels alone can know.'

TO HIS SISTER HARRIETT.
October 13, 1823.

If you have leisure time on Sunday, learn portions of Scripture by heart. The benefit seems to me incalculable. It imbues the mind with good and holy thoughts. It is a resource in solitude, on a journey, and in a sleepless night; and let me press most earnestly upon you and my other dear sisters, as well as on myself, the frequent exhortations in Scripture to prayer.

The following letter to his Mother lets the reader into the social habits, with regard to costume, of the Oxford of some seventy years ago:

November 1, 1823.

What a significant intimation yesterday's snow has given us of a severe winter! Trees have been torn up by the wind in all directions. And to-day the Cherwell is so swollen with the rains, that it nearly overflows Christ Church water walk. My lodgings are in the High Street, some way from Oriel, so you may fancy it is very inconvenient to paddle to dinner in thin shoes and silk stockings.

I am beginning to attend some private lectures in divinity by the Regius Professor, Dr. Charles Lloyd, which he has been kind enough to volunteer to about eight of us;[1] so you may fancy my time is much occupied. I have taken a ride or two, make it a practice to be in bed by eleven o'clock, and rise with the lark at half-past five. When I rise I sometimes think that you are lying awake and thinking—and only such apprehensions make me uncomfortable.

The year 1824 naturally brought reflections with it, such as are found among his memoranda:

February 21.—I quite tremble to think the age is now come when, as far as years go, the ministry is open to me. Is it possible? have twenty-three years gone over my head? The days and months fly past me, and I seem as if I would cling hold of them and hinder them from escaping. There they lie, entombed in the grave of Time, buried with faults and failings, and deeds of all sorts, never to appear till the sounding of

---

[1] Dr. Mozley's Old Testament Lectures, delivered to Masters of Arts, were undertaken by him as following the example of Dr. Lloyd.

the last trump. . . . Keep me from squandering time—it is irrevocable.

Writing to his sister Jemima, after telling of the prevalence of smallpox in Oxford, owing, it is said, to the poorer sort of persons persisting in having their children inoculated, and of his own re-vaccination, the letter goes on :

March 8, 1824.

Bishop Hobart, of New York, is in Oxford. I dined with him at the Provost's yesterday. He is an intelligent man, and gave us a good deal of information on the affairs of the American Episcopal Church. . . . W. Coleridge and Lipscombe are, I believe, to be the West Indian Bishops. . . .

Keble has declined one of the Archdeaconries. . . . The other day I had a letter from Bowden. He tells me that Sola, his sister's music master, brought Rossini to dine in Grosvenor Place not long since ; and that, as far as they could judge (for he does not speak English), he is as unassuming and obliging a man as ever breathed. He seemed highly pleased with everything and anxious to make himself agreeable. Labouring, indeed, under a very severe cold, he did not sing, but he accompanied two or three of his own songs in the most brilliant manner, giving the piano the effect of an orchestra. . . . As he came in a private not a professional way, Bowden called on him, and found him surrounded, in a low, dark room, by about eight or nine Italians, all talking as fast as possible, who, with the assistance of a great screaming *macaw*, and of Madame Rossini, in a dirty gown and her hair in curl papers, made such a clamour that he was glad to escape as fast as he could.

We are going through 'Prideaux's Connexion' with Dr. Charles Lloyd. A very fine class we are ! Eleven individuals and eight first-classes.

Mr. Newman was ordained deacon on Trinity Sunday, June 13, 1824. Amongst his papers is the following memorandum, written shortly before that event :

May 16, 1824.—St. Clement's Church is to be rebuilt ; but before beginning the subscription, it is proposed to provide a curate who shall be a kind of guarantee to the subscribers, that every exertion shall be made, when the church is built, to recover the parish from meeting-houses, and on the other hand ale-houses, into which they have been driven for want of convenient Sunday worship. . . . The only objection against my taking it is my weakness of voice. . . . Mr. Mayer advises me to take it, so do Tyler, Hawkins, Jelf, Pusey, Ottley. Through Pusey, indeed, it was offered.

Yesterday I went and subscribed to the Bible Society, thinking it better to do so before engaging in this undertaking.

To his Father he wrote when the matter was so far settled :

May 25, 1824.

I have delayed writing because I wished to tell you particulars. Directly I knew that I had got a curacy, I did let you know. I am convinced it is necessary to get used to parochial duty early, and that a Fellow of a college, after ten years' residence in Oxford, feels very awkward among poor and ignorant people. The rector of the parish, being infirm, wanted a curate, and applied to a Fellow of Balliol [C. Girdlestone], who, through a friend of mine [Pusey], offered the curacy to me. The parish consists of 2,000 inhabitants, and they wish to build a new church, since the present holds but 300.

I have much more business on my hands than I ought to have. . . .

Again he writes :

To HIS FATHER.

June 3, 1824.

. . . In the autumn of 1801 the parish of St. Clement's contained about 400 inhabitants ; in 1821 about 800. Since that time Oxford has become more commercial than before, owing to the new canals, &c., all which has tended to increase the population. But the increase of this particular period has been also owing to the improvements in the body of the town. Old houses which contained, perhaps, several families, have been pulled down to make way for collegiate buildings, to widen streets, to improve the views. This had made building a very profitable speculation on the outskirts of the place, and the poor families, once unpacked, have not been induced to dwell so thickly as before. The parish in which I am interested I find consists at present of 2,000, and it is still increasing. The living, I am told, is worth about 80*l.* ; I do not suppose the curacy will be more than 40*l.* or 50*l.*

As I shall be wanted as soon as possible, my present intention is to run away from Oxford by a night coach on Trinity Sunday night, or Monday morning, stopping an hour or two at Strand,[1] thence proceeding to London, and returning to Oxford Wednesday or Thursday. More time neither my pupils nor the duties of the curacy will allow, and I wish, if possible, to see you all before I am nailed down to Oxford.

I finished the Cicero on Friday last ; finished the corrections &c. by Tuesday, and despatched my parcel to town by a night coach. It will appear, I expect, in the course of a month or five weeks.[2]

To his Mother.

July 28, 1824.

You must have thought me very silent, but I have not had time to write. . . . I was at Cuddesdon yesterday ; at Warton, Saturday to Monday ;[3] at Deddington shortly before ; at Nuncham before that ; and expect to go to Pusey, which is fourteen miles off, in the course of next week.

About ten days ago I began my *visitation* of the whole parish, going from house to house, asking the names, numbers, trades, where they went to church, &c. I have got through, as yet, about a third (and the most respectable third) of the

---

[1] Where his aunt, Mrs. Elizabeth Newman, resided.

[2] When the edition of 1872 was brought out, the following prefatory notice was added, but finally cancelled by the author (*Historical Sketches*, vol. i. p. 245):

'If the following sketch of Cicero's life and writings be thought unworthy of so great a subject, the author must plead the circumstances under which it was made.

'In the spring of 1824, when his hands were so full of work, Dr. Whately paid him the compliment of asking him to write for the *Encyclopædia Metropolitana*, to which he was at that time contributing himself. Dr. Whately explained to him that the editor had suddenly been disappointed in the article on Cicero, which was to have appeared in the *Encyclopædia*, and that in consequence he could not allow more than two months for the composition of the paper which was to take its place ; also that it must contain such and such subjects. The author undertook to finish it under these conditions. It will serve to show how busy he was at the time, to say that one day, after working with his private pupils till the evening, he sat down to his article till four o'clock next morning, and then walked over from Oxford to Warton, a distance of eighteen miles, in order to appear punctually at the breakfast table of a friend, the Rev. Walter Mayer, who on quitting home had committed his pupils in his parsonage to the author's charge.'

[3] Mr. Newman preached his first sermon, June 23, at Warton.

population. In general they have been very civil; often expressed gratification that a clergyman should visit them; hoped to see me again, &c. &c. If in the habit of attending the dissenting meeting, they generally excused themselves on the plea of the rector being old, and they could not hear him; or the church too small, &c.; but expressed no unwillingness to come back. I rather dread the two-thirds of the parish which are to come; but trust (and do not doubt) I shall be carried through it well, and as I could wish. It will be a great thing done; I shall know my parishioners, and be known by them. I have taken care always to speak kindly of Mr. Hinton, the dissenting minister, expressed a wish to know him, &c.; said I thought he had done good—which he had—in the place.

Last Sunday I had it given out in church that there would be an afternoon sermon during the summer. From what I hear, on talking to various people about it, I doubt not, with God's blessing, it will answer very well. I am glad to say the church is so full in the morning that people go away; but that is not saying much. As you recollect, it only holds two hundred; however, there often used not (I am told) to be more than fifty at church. I wish very much to establish a Sunday School. The only Sunday I have been absent from St. Clement's was last Sunday, when I was at Warton. I had three services and sermons there in the day; but did not feel fatigue.

The sermons I send you were not intended for compositions: you will find them full of inaccuracies. I am aware they contain truths which are unpalatable to the generality of mankind; but the doctrine of Christ crucified is the only spring of real virtue and piety, and the only foundation of peace and comfort. I know I must do good. I may and shall meet with disappointments, much to distress me, much (I hope) to humble me; but as God is true, He will go with the doctrine: *magna est veritas et prævalebit.*

On the subject of preaching, a memorandum, written this year of his ordination, remains:

September 16.—Those who make comfort the great subject of their preaching seem to mistake the end of their ministry. *Holiness* is the great end. There must be a struggle and a toil here. Comfort is a cordial, but no one drinks cordials from morning to night.

The following letter seems to show that his Father had questioned the wisdom of house-to-house visitation—a feeling prevalent with lay Churchmen of that day, by many of whom these uninvited clerical calls were regarded as an infringement of the Englishman's privilege of feeling his house his castle.

TO HIS FATHER.

August 9, 1824.

So far from this invasion of an Englishman's castle being galling to the feelings of the poor, I am convinced by facts that it is very acceptable. In all places I have been received with civility, in most with cheerfulness and a kind of glad surprise, and in many with quite a cordiality and warmth of feeling. One person says, 'Aye, I was sure that one time or other we should have a proper minister.' Another, that she had understood from such a one that a 'nice young gentleman had come to the parish'; a third 'begged I would do him the favour to call on him, whenever it was convenient to me.' (This general invitation has been by no means uncommon.) Another, speaking of the parish she came from, said, 'The old man preached very good doctrine, but he did not come to visit the people at their houses as the new one did.' Singularly enough, I had written down as a memorandum a day or two before I received your letter, 'I am more convinced than ever of the necessity of frequently visiting the poorer classes—they seem so gratified at it, and praise it.' Nor do I visit the poor only; I mean to go all through the parish; and have already visited the shopkeepers and principal people. These, it is obvious, have facilities for educating their children, which the poor have not; and on that ground it is that a clergyman is more concerned with the children of the latter, though our Church certainly intended that, not only schoolmasters of the poorer children, but all schoolmasters high and low, should be under her jurisdiction. The plan was not completed, and we must make the best of what we have got. I have not tried to bring over any regular dissenters. Indeed, I have told them all 'I shall make no difference between you and church-goers. I count you all my flock, and shall be most happy to do you a service out of church if I cannot within it.' A good dissenter is, of course, incomparably better than a bad churchman, but a good churchman I think better than a good dissenter. There is too much irreligion in the place for me to be so mad as to drive away so active an ally as Mr. Hinton seems to be. Thank you for your letter and pardon my freedom of reply.

FROM HIS MOTHER.
August 30, 1824.

. . I thank you for your sermons. They arrived at the happy moment to be valuable to me . . . those I most particularly admire are 'Wait on the Lord'; and 'Man goeth forth to his work, and to his labour,'[1] and the one on prayer. I am very loth to part with them. . . .

Pray take care of your health. Your dear Father desires his love. Adieu, my dear—that the Almighty may guide and preserve you in all things is my earnest prayer.

TO HIS MOTHER.
August, 1824.

. . . Thank you for your kind hint about future sermons, which I shall attend to. At the same time I doubt whether I shall have occasion to preach on the texts you mention for some little time. My parish (I fear) wants to be taught the very principles of Christian doctrine. It has not got so far as to abuse them. Different places, of course, require different treatment. I shall certainly *always* strive in every pulpit *so* to preach the Christian doctrines as at the same time to warn people that it is quite idle to pretend to faith and holiness, unless they show forth their inward principles by a pure disinterested upright line of conduct.

My afternoon sermons have, thank God, succeeded very well, and I find myself much stronger in voice than when I began preaching.

Thank Charles for his two French letters. Tell him the article in the 'Quarterly' on pulpit eloquence is by Milman.

In the autumn of this year Mr. Newman was called home by grave accounts of his Father's illness, and found him on his death-bed.

[1] The Editor was once told, by Mr. Newman's sister, that this was the text of his first sermon.

FROM HIS MOTHER.
August 17, 1824.

My letters mentioned your dear Father's indisposition. I lament to say it has much increased in the last month. . . . He found it necessary to apply to some physician. . . . On Tuesday he told him that, as the best of such cases were serious, he should feel more satisfied to have a second opinion in consultation with him. . . . I thank God your Father has been much relieved from pain for the last three or four days. . . . I have postponed writing to you the last week, hoping to send you better news; but I think it would no longer be kind to keep you in ignorance of his sad illness.

In a private diary are some touching entries on his Father's last days, in which he ministered to him. The father and son were very dear to each other:

That dread event has happened. Is it possible? O my Father! I got to town on Sunday morning. He knew me; tried to put out his hand, and said 'God bless you!' Towards the evening of Monday he said his last words. He seemed in great peace of mind. He could, however, only articulate 'God bless you; thank my God, thank my God!' and, lastly, 'My dear.' Dr. C. came on Wednesday and pronounced him dying. Towards evening we joined in prayer, commending his soul to God. . . . Of late he had thought his end approaching. One day on the river he told my Mother, 'I shall never see another summer.' On Thursday he looked beautiful. Such calmness, sweetness, composure, and majesty were in his countenance. Can a man be a materialist who sees a dead body? I had never seen one before. His last words to me, or all but his last, were to bid me read to him the 53rd chapter of Isaiah.

Mr. Newman died on Wednesday, September 29, 1824. In the same diary is the following entry:

October 6.—Performed the last sad duties to my dear Father. When I die, shall I be followed to the grave by my children? My Mother said the other day, she hoped to live to see me married; but I think I shall either die within college walls, or as a missionary in a foreign land. No matter where, so that I die in Christ.¹

Shortly after the loss of his Father, Mr. Newman hears from his aunt, Mrs. Elizabeth Newman, of his grandmother's declining state.

MRS. E. NEWMAN TO J. H. N.

November 4, 1824.

My poor dear mother is much the same as when you saw her, but still weaker and in much pain; but when she does speak she talks more of you and Francis than of anybody.

She lived to the May of the following year, having attained the age of ninety-one. On the notice of her death occur these words : 'She was my earliest benefactor, and how she loved me!'²

Some private notes remain of Mr. Newman's visits to his sick parishioners. One of these experiences may be given, as telling something of the matter and manner of his pastoral visiting :

... *August*, 1824 [or possibly 1825].—John C. ..., perhaps thirty-five : had been a coachman, and all his life in the society of coachmen. ... For some months past, hearing he was in a declining way, I have called from time to time, and particularly

---

¹ In the *Apologia*, referring to an earlier date, we read : ' I am obliged to mention, though I do it with great reluctance, another deep imagination that at this time, the autumn of 1816, took possession of me. There can be no mistake about the fact, viz. that it would be the will of God that I should lead a single life. This anticipation, which has held its ground almost continuously ever since ... was more or less connected in my mind with the notion that my calling in life would require such a sacrifice as celibacy involved; as, for instance, missionary work among the heathen, to which I had a great drawing for some years. It also strengthened my feeling of separation from the visible world, of which I have spoken above.'—*Apologia pro Vita sua*, p. 7.

² See stanzas to his brother, F. W. N., in the volume of poems entitled *Verses*.
   In her affection all had share—
      All six, she loved them all;
      Yet on her early-chosen pair
         Did her full favour fall ;
      And we became her dearest theme,
      Her waking thought, her nightly dream.

left Doddridge's 'Rise and Progress.' At length, the day before yesterday, I was sent for. He seemed very near his end, and was very desirous of seeing me. He talked of sin being a heavy burden, of which he wished to be released. 'God was most merciful in having spared him ; and he ought to be most thankful' (and he said it with energy) 'that he was favoured with a clergyman to attend him.' Such is the substance of the conversation I had with him yesterday and the day before. To-day I found that he had suddenly declared the weight of sin was taken off him, and tears burst from him, and he said he was *so* rejoiced. He seems very humble and earnest, and willingly listened to what I said about the danger of deception. I was indeed much perplexed, fearing to speak against the mysterious working of God (if it was His working), yet equally fearing to make him satisfied with a partial repentance and with emotions, and should do harm to his wife, &c. I spoke *very* strongly on our being sinful and corrupt till death ; on the necessity of sin being found a burden *always*, on the fear of self-deception and of falling away even after the most vivid feelings ; and on the awful state of those who, *having* left religion for their death-bed, could give no *evidence* of their sincerity. All this he seemed to admit, and thanked me very fervently. I am thinking of the *cause* of this. His mother, I see, is a religious woman. She cannot be indiscreet? Doddridge *could not* mislead him—or is it the work of the Holy Spirit even in its suddenness?

The correspondence of this date shows that Mr. Newman's name was becoming known beyond his parish or the walls of his college. The Athenæum Club was formed in 1823 'for the association of persons of scientific and literary attainments, and artists; and noblemen and gentlemen, patrons of learning, &c.,' by the Earl of Aberdeen, Marquis of Lansdowne, Davy, Scott, Mackintosh, Faraday, Chantry, Lawrence and others.

MR. HEBER TO REV. J. H. NEWMAN.
November 29, 1824.

Mr. Heber presents his compliments to Mr. Newman, and encloses for his inspection a list of the Athenæum.

If Mr. Newman should wish to become a member, Mr. Heber will be happy to propose his name to the committee as a candidate for election *without ballot*.

[N.B. I declined.—J. H. N.]

To HIS MOTHER.
January 17, 1825.

I got down very safely on Saturday by half-past three. It was very cold on the journey, the wind blowing against us all the way. To my great mortification I was obliged, not merely to put on my cloak, but even to wrap myself in it. I had the satisfaction, however, of observing that the outside passengers in front had close box coats as well as cloaks; and on arriving at Oxford I had the additional gratification of hearing it was the coldest day we have had. I bathed the following morning [the cold bath at Holywell]—yesterday—and got through the duties of the day without fatigue. The waters have retired from the flat country about us, and have left effluvia which are neither agreeable nor wholesome.

The subscription for St. Clement's Church amounts to above 2,600*l*., and the colleges are yet to come. Mr. Peel has subscribed 100*l*., so has Mr. Heber. Lord Liverpool's carriage being at the Bishop's door, has collected a crowd: Mr. Canning is with him. I forgot to talk to you about your delightful plan for next Long Vacation.

In a note-book he writes:

As yet the church subscription flourishes greatly, and my Sunday school is in a good train for success. I find I am called a Methodist.

To HIS SISTER HARRIETT.
February 14, 1825.

Will you think me out of my senses when I tell you I have engaged to write in two publications in spite of my other occupations? and one of them the 'Encyclopædia'! But I must explain myself. I was conditionally engaged, as you know, to the 'Theological Review,' when Whately sent me a message that he wanted me to write some theological articles (ecclesiastical history, for instance) in the 'Encyclopædia.' And so firmly was his mind made up on the subject, that before he received my answer he wrote to Smedley about it, who, in sending me a draft for my Cicero article (14*l*.), expressed his hope in a civil way that I should comply with Whately's arrangement. I *had* made up my mind in the affirmative, and for the following reasons: (1) I am persuaded, as

Whately suggested, that sermon-writing by *itself* has a tendency to produce a loose, rambling kind of composition, nay even of thought. (2) The ecclesiastical articles at present are in the hands of a person whom a certain friend of mine [Whately] does not like, and wishes kindly to substitute me. Now I thought, in so important a work as an Encyclopædia, when an opportunity was there offered me of influencing the religious tone of the work, it was my duty to avail myself of it. (3) My *great* objection to writing a second time in the work was because I wished to devote my time to studies more connected with my profession. This is now removed; I do not, however, begin till June next.

To his Mother.
February 14, 1825

The subscription to the church amounts to 3,700*l*. We hope to get 500*l*. from the Society, and a liberal person has said he will subscribe whatever is finally wanted to the amount of 1,000*l*. I fear the church will cost 6,000*l*.

At last I have managed to begin a Sunday school. We could get no Room of any kind. So Pusey was kind enough to give the church a stove, and now we muster in the church, but there is no Room.

These words explain what follows. In order to use the church a temporary gallery was found necessary. The body of the old church, small as it was, being no doubt crowded with pews, and thus affording no proper standing or sitting room for scholars or teachers.

To his Mother.
March 4, 1825.

... The difficulty of warming has been overcome, and now to the more serious one of the erection of a gallery. It was estimated at 20*l*. An objection was anticipated on the score of its being likely to hurt the subscription to the new church. This made it necessary that not a shilling of the money should come from the parish, and that the subscription should be quite private. The bishop [Legge] was not against it. A friend of *mine* has subscribed 10*l*., his father or mother 5*l*., and various other friends 5*l*., besides my own subscription. After all difficulties it was begun on Monday and finished yesterday. It will contain ninety-four children. We are in some want of teachers, but get on better than we did.

I have undertaken for the 'Encyclopædia Metropolitana the memoir of Apollonius Tyanæus, and the argument on Miracles, as connected with it. It is a very difficult subject, and I hesitated before I accepted it. It requires a great deal of reading and much thought. No doubt it will improve me much, but it must be done by September, and cannot be begun till June. I trust God will carry me through it. I am in hopes the 'Theological Review' will not claim my promise. [This hope proved fallacious.]

TO HIS MOTHER.

March 29, 1825.

You have seen by the papers, perhaps. Dr. Elmsley's death, and Whately's appointment to the Headship of St. Alban Hall. He has done me the honour of appointing me Vice-Principal. This will not be a great addition to my income—perhaps 50*l.* a year; but it is a post of considerable authority and responsibility. I am Dean, Tutor, Bursar, and all—in his absence, indeed, Principal. I think I hinted something of the kind to you last summer as a possible thing. . . .

The following tender mother's letter needs perhaps an apology for its insertion; but hers was a troubled life, and such pleasure as the letter shows, would have been at any time the greatest reward that her son's successes could earn him:

MRS. NEWMAN TO HER DAUGHTER H. E. N.

March 31, 1825.

. . . Next, my dear, I have a very agreeable piece of news to tell you. On my return I was delightfully greeted by a letter from John, to say he can and will come here next Wednesday to stay till Saturday morning. Though short, it will be a delightful peep at him. Of course you will wish, if possible, to return to us on Wednesday evening. I look forward to Wednesday as a happy day, please God! Next, my dear, I must beg you to be prepared to treat John with the proper respect due to a real 'Don.' To be serious; Dr. Elmsley of St. Alban Hall is dead. John's friend Whately is appointed 'Principal,' and he has nominated John 'Vice-Principal.' . . . Were it anyone but John I should fear it would be too much for his *head* or his *heart* at so early an age; but in him I have the comforting anticipation that he will use his power for the benefit of those who entrust him with it; that he will not be high-minded; that he will be sedulous to avail himself of his talents and authority, to correct and improve a Hall. . . .

REV. DR. JENKYNS, VICE-CHANCELLOR, TO
REV. J. H. NEWMAN.
April 30, 1825.

Allow me to take the opportunity of requesting you to favour the University with a sermon at St. Mary's, either in the morning or afternoon of Whitsunday next.

REV. J. H. NEWMAN TO REV. DR. JENKYNS.
April 30, 1825.

Allow me to express my sense of the kindness with which you have honoured me, by the offer of a preacher's turn in the University pulpit. I am as yet, however, so inexperienced [N.B.—I was only a Deacon], and feel myself so insufficient for such an office that I must beg to decline it.

Accept my most sincere thanks for your kind liberality to the orphans of my parishioners, who, I can assure you, stand in need of every assistance.

On May 29, 1825, Mr. Newman was ordained Priest.

Mr. Newman seems to have been at this time in all but universal favour in his parish; but, if there must be an exception, his journal records what all experience will be prepared for as the obvious one: 'I had a dispute with my singers in May, which ended in their leaving the church, and we now sing *en masse*.'

To H. E. N.
June 10, 1825.

My singers are quite mute; and the business seems to have dropt. Pusey left London for Germany, Wednesday last. He will not, alas! assist me [in the St. Clement's curacy] till Christmas.

In the summer of this year it was arranged that on the Principal of St. Alban's (Whately) leaving Oxford with his family for the vacation, Mrs. Newman and her daughters should occupy the Principal's lodgings during two months of the Long Vacation.

TO HIS MOTHER.   *July*, 1825.

I need not say how glad I am you are coming. I intend to have a sacrament August 7, at St. Clement's, and it will be a great satisfaction to me, if two of my sisters for the first time partake of it the first time you hear me do duty. [I administered it as priest for the first time.]

His sisters Jemima and Mary had lately been confirmed.

TO J. C. N.   *July*, 1825.

. . . Pusey, by this time, I suppose, is near Göttingen, and Χυρτον (Churton) on his way to Rome; and Pope on his way to his curacy, which is near Bath.

The Provost [Copleston] has been so indisposed that he has been to Cheltenham, and goes again, I fancy. Dr. Burrows has called on me, and in very polite language pressed me to write a third article, which I declined; to which he gave a rebutter, and I a sur-rebutter; and there the matter dropped.

Tell Mary I sometimes think of her.

REV. JOHN KEBLE TO REV. J. H. NEWMAN.
July 19, 1825.

'Tis a shame to give the curate of St. Clement's any additional trouble this hot weather, but now you are a brick-and-mortar man [he was rebuilding St. Clement's Church] and must learn to bear the heat. I wish you joy of your grand work being begun; may it prosper in the best sense. . . . The leaves are beginning to shrink and fall as if they were frozen, and the corn is almost ready to cut. Wishing you a cool breeze and plenty of ice and lemonade, I remain very *warmly* and affectionately yours,   J. KEBLE, junr.

REV. E. HAWKINS TO REV. J. H. NEWMAN.
August, 1825.

I hope by this time your essay on Miracles *à priori* and *à posteriori* parts, and all the contents of all the books in the window-seat, are in a beautiful state of effervescence.

E. B. PUSEY, ESQ. (Fellow of Oriel) TO REV. J. H. NEWMAN.

Göttingen: August 19, 1825.

I have not at any time forgotten my engagement to read the part of Less [qy. Lessing] that relates to miracles, but I own I was disappointed with the result. Some single points seem well done, others are overstrained ; and though the whole work seems to be prized as the fullest and most satisfactory here, I did not seem to recognise the master who is seen in the translated piece. I will, however—not to do nothing—extract any points, illustrations, &c., which may furnish you with any matter for thought. . . . Of our books, Clarke and Ditton on the Resurrection seem to be very much prized, so Lord Lyttelton. I would have read Nosotti's 'Defence' for you also, but it is not in the library.

I have now been here six weeks, read not so much as I wish, attend three lectures a day for the sake of the German, see what society I can, and hope to be able, at the end of the time, to understand German pretty well, but have not yet read long enough and variety enough to know it. As to what I have seen of German inquiry in different subjects, it seems to be much more solid than usually among us.

I hope your church is rising rapidly, and that, without hurting your health, you feel the good you are doing.

REV. J. POPE TO REV. J. H. NEWMAN.

September 10, 1825.

I am extremely sorry to discover that, owing no doubt to the multiplicity of business in your hands, you are in a complete nervous fever. You certainly overwork yourself, and your epistle informed me, without your mentioning it, that you were in low spirits. Come down and pay me your promised visit. Country air, novelty, superb scenery, and relaxation from intense and overwhelming study ; a hearty welcome, with a beautiful pony, &c.

REV. DR. WHATELY TO REV. J. H. NEWMAN.

September 27, 1825.

As you so much admire my fallacy, I will honour you by communicating a very good way of classifying the errors of Romanists : namely, according to Aristotle's enumeration in the 'Poetics' of the manœuvres performed on words; some are *curtailed*, some *enlarged*, some *altered*, some *invented*, some borrowed from *foreigners*, some *transferred* from one sense to another, some *tacked* on where they are not wanted, and some *confounded* together.

I trust to come out the beginning of the term with a volume of essays made out of University sermons.

REV. E. HAWKINS TO REV. J. H. NEWMAN.

September 27, 1825.

.. I have also replaced forty volumes for you in the library, but I perceive you have still several in your keeping. Enjoy your holiday and return to your duty the better for it.

In the Long Vacation Mr. Newman takes a short holiday with his friend Bowden in the Isle of Wight, and writes of its beauties:

TO HIS SISTER HARRIETT.

Peartree, Southampton: September 29, 1825.

Bowden's is in a very fine situation; exquisite in scenery. Yesterday we made an expedition in a yacht to the Needles. The beauty of water and land only makes me regret that our language has not more adjectives of admiration.

TO HIS MOTHER.

Peartree: October 2, 1825.

I have tried to write, for I have little or no time, from a different reason, indeed, from my want of time at Oxford, for here it has been from drives, sailings, music, &c. I hope this recreation will quite set me up for the ensuing term. The weather, indeed, has been beautiful. I have been persuaded to stay my whole holiday here. Jelf takes my duty for me.

We have been round the Needles, made an excursion to Carisbrooke, dined with Mr. Ward; we breakfasted also with Judge Bailey. We have had music almost every evening; Bowden, you know, plays the bass. I saw Kinsey at Mr. Ward's. I have not been idle; I am reading Davison on Primitive Sacrifice, and have written much on other subjects, and thought about some sermons. I return Wednesday next to Oxford.

To His Mother.
Oxford: October 26, 1825.

My holiday was passed very pleasantly at Peartree. They wished me to come again in the course of the autumn, and when they found that impossible, pressed me to come at Christmas. I have promised, however, to make the visit annual. Pusey is just returned, after having been nearly lost at sea.

To His Mother.
Oriel: November 14, 1825.

I have taken bark according to Dr. Bailey's prescription for three weeks; and this, added to my excursion, has made me so strong that parish, hall, college and 'Encyclopædia,' go on together in perfect harmony. I have begun the essay on Miracles in earnest, and think I feel my footing better and grasp my subject more satisfactorily.

I can pursue two separate objects better than at first. It is a great thing to have pulled out my mind. I am sure I shall derive great benefit from it in after life.

I have joined in recommending Pusey not going into orders yet. He has so much to do in the theological way in Hebrew and Syriac.

Looking back in 1826 on the work done in 1825, there are again allusions to the clash of occupations pressing at this time. The refreshment of Mr. Newman's holiday had enabled him to return to the various calls on his energies with less sense of painful effort than he suffered from when such enforced breaks upon concentration of thought were for any length of time the rule.

I have been involved in work against my will. This time last year Smedley asked me to write an article in the 'Encyclopædia.' After undertaking it Whately offered me the Vice-Principalship. The Hall accounts, &c., being in disorder, have haunted me incessantly. Hence my parish has suffered. I have had a continual wear on my mind, mislaying memoranda, forgetting names, &c. . . . The succeeding to the tutorship at Oriel has occasioned my relinquishing my curacy to

Mr. Simcox, of Wadham, at Easter next; at the same time resigning the Vice-Principalship of St. Alban Hall, being succeeded by the Rev. Samuel Hinds.

The interval of a year and a half between Mr. Newman's election to Oriel and his ordination has been illustrated by his letters. It is now time to return to the Memoir, and its history of the influence of Oriel within that period on his mind and principles.

AUTOBIOGRAPHICAL MEMOIR

CHAPTER III

THE responsibility of becoming guarantee to the University, that Newman, in spite of his ill success in the schools, was deserving of academical distinction, was now transferred from Trinity to Oriel ; and, if it had required courage in him to offer himself to his electors in the latter college, it also required courage, as has been said, in them to take him Strong as they might be in their reliance on the independence and purity of their elections, and broad as were their shoulders if public opinion was invoked against them, still they had, in choosing him, taken on themselves a real onus, and a real anxiety in the prospect of his future ; and, if the sense of such generosity towards him had remained at all times present with him, he might have been saved from the hard thoughts and words, and the impatient acts to which in after times he was led to indulge at the expense of some of them. However true might be the principles and sacred the interests which, on the occasions referred to, he was defending, he had no call to forget the past, no license at an after date to forget, that if he was able to assert his own views in opposition to theirs it was, in truth, they who had put him into a position enabling him to do so.

As to their anxiety, upon his election, how he would turn out, there were certainly, on his first introduction to the Common-Room, definite points about him which made him somewhat a difficulty to those who brought him there. In the first place, they had to deal with his extreme shyness. It disconcerted them to find that, with their best efforts, they could not draw him out or get him to converse. He shrank into himself when his duty was to meet their advances. Easy and fluent as he was among his equals and near relatives, his very admiration of his new associates made a sudden intimacy with them impossible to him. An observant friend, who even at a later date saw him accidentally among strangers, not knowing the true account of his bearing, told him he considered he had had a near escape of being a stutterer. This untowardness in him was increased by a vivid self-consciousness, which sometimes inflicted on him days of acute suffering from the recollection of solecisms, whether actual or imagined, which he recognised in his conduct in society. And then there was, in addition, that real isolation of thought and spiritual solitariness which was the result of his Calvinistic beliefs. His electors, however, had not the key to the reserve which hung about him; and in default of it accounts of him of another kind began to assail their ears which increased their perplexity. With a half-malicious intent of frightening them, it was told them that Mr. Newman had for years belonged to a club of instrumental music, and had himself taken part in its public performances, a diversion innocent indeed in itself, but scarcely in keeping or in sympathy with an intellectual Common-Room, or promising a satisfactory career to a nascent Fellow of Oriel.

It was under the circumstance of misgivings such as these that Mr. Tyler, Mr. James, and other leading Fellows of the day took a step as successful in the event for their own relief as it was advantageous to Mr. Newman. Mr. Whately, afterwards Protestant Archbishop of Dublin, who had lately relinquished his fellowship by marriage, was just at that time residing in lodgings in Oxford previously to his taking possession of a Suffolk benefice, and they determined on putting their unformed probationer into his hands. If there was a man easy for a raw bashful youth to get on with it was Whately—a great talker, who endured very readily the silence of his company, original in his views, lively, forcible, witty in expressing them, brimful of information on a variety of subjects—so entertaining that, logician as he was, he is said sometimes to have fixed the attention of a party of ladies to his conversation, or rather discourse, for two or three hours at a stretch; free and easy in manners, rough indeed and dogmatic in his enunciation of opinion, but singularly gracious to undergraduates and young masters who, if they were worth anything, were only too happy to be knocked about in argument by such a man. And he on his part professed to be pleased at having cubs in hand whom he might lick into shape, and who, he said, like dogs of King Charles's breed, could be held up by one leg without yelling.

Mr. Newman brought with him the first of recommendations to Whately in being a good listener, and in his special facility of entering into ideas as soon as, or before, they were expressed. It was not long before Mr. Whately succeeded in drawing him out, and he paid him the compliment of saying that he was the clearest-headed man he knew. He took him out walking and riding, and was soon able to reassure the Oriel men that they had made no great mistake in their election. Mr. Newman, on his part, felt the warmest admiration for Whately, much gratitude and a deep affection. If his master was now and then sharp, rude and positive, this inflicted no pain on so young a man, when relieved by the kindness of heart, the real gentleness and generous spirit, which those who came near him well understood to be his characteristics. The worst that could be said of Whately was that, in his intercourse with his friends, he was a bright June sun tempered by a March north-easter.

During these months Whately was full of the subject of logic; which, in spite of the Aldrich read for his B.A. examination, was quite a novelty to Mr. Newman. He lent him the MS. of his 'Analytical Dialogues,' never printed and now very scarce, and allowed him to take copies of it, which are to be found among his (Mr. Newman's) papers. At length he went so far as to propose to him to cast these dialogues into the shape of a synthetical treatise. It was a peculiarity of Whately's to compose his books by the medium of other brains. This did not detract at all from the originality of what he wrote. Others did but stimulate his intellect into the activity necessary for carrying him through the drudgery of composition. He called his hearers his anvils. He expounded his views as he walked with them; he indoctrinated them; made them repeat him; and sometimes even to put him on paper, with the purpose of making use of such sketches when he should take in hand the work which was to be given to the public. He attempted to make, at one time, Mr. Rickards such an anvil, at another Mr. Woodgate; he succeeded best with Mr. Hinds, afterwards Bishop of Norwich; and it was in some such way that he began to write his well-known Treatise upon Logic through Mr. Newman—that is, under the start he gained by revising and recomposing the rude essays of a probationer Fellow of twenty-one.

This work, however—namely, his 'Elements of Logic'—was not actually published till four years later; and in his Preface to it he thus graciously speaks of Mr. Newman's infinitesimal share in its composition:

I have to acknowledge assistance received from several friends, who have at various times suggested remarks and alterations. But I cannot avoid particularising the Rev. J. Newman, Fellow of Oriel College, who actually composed a considerable portion of the work as it now stands, from manuscript not designed for publication, and who is the original author of several pages.

Newman, much gratified by this notice, thus acknowledged it to Whately:

November 14, 1826.

I cannot tell you the surprise I felt on seeing you had thought it worth while to mention my name as having contributed to the arrangement of the material [of the work]. Whatever I then wrote I am conscious was of little value, &c. &c. . . . Yet I cannot regret that you have introduced my name in some sort of connexion with your own. There are few things which I wish more sincerely than to be known as a friend of yours, and though I may be on the verge of propriety in the earnestness with which I am expressing myself, yet you must let me give way to feelings which never want much excitement to draw them out, and now will not be restrained. Much as I owe to Oriel in the way of mental improvement, to none, as I think, do I owe so much as to you. I know who it was that first gave me heart to look about me after my election, and taught me to think correctly, and (strange office for an instructor) to rely upon myself.

It was with reference to these first Oriel experiences of Newman, his bashfulness, awkwardness, and affectionate abandonment of himself to those who were so kind to him, as contrasted with his character as it showed to outsiders in succeeding years, that Bishop Copleston, after the notice of him quoted above, goes on to say: 'Alas, how little did we anticipate the fatal consequences!' and then applies to him the passage of Æschylus:

ἔθρεψεν δὲ λέοντα
σίνιν δόμοις ἀγάλακτον
. . . . . .
ἄμερον, εὐφιλόπαιδα, κ.τ.λ.—*Agam.* 717.

Whately's formal connexion with Oriel had closed before Newman was introduced to him; and he was but an occasional visitor at the University till the year 1825, when, on the death of Dr. Elmsley, he was preferred by Lord Grenville—the Chancellor—to the Headship of Alban Hall. On this occasion he showed his good opinion of the subject of this Memoir by at once making him his Vice-Principal, and though, to the sorrow of both parties, this connexion between them lasted only for a year—Mr. Newman succeeding in 1826 to the Tutor's place at Oriel vacated by Mr. R. W. Jelf—Whately continued on familiar terms with him down to the promotion of the former to the archbishopric of Dublin in 1831.

That when this great preferment came he manifested no such desire to gain Mr. Newman's co-operation in his new sphere of action, as had led him to ask his assistance at Alban Hall, was no surprise to Mr. Newman. Great changes had taken place in the interval in Mr. Newman's views and position at Oxford, and he sorrowfully recognised to the full, the gradual but steady diminution of intimacy and sympathy between himself and Dr. Whately, which had accompanied the successive events of those five years. In a correspondence which passed between them in 1834, and which has been published in part by the Archbishop's executors, and in full by Dr. Newman in his 'Apologia,' is traced the course of this mournful alienation. At length, in 1836, Mr. Newman incurred the Archbishop's deep displeasure on his taking part against Dr. Hampden's appointment to the chair of Divinity;

so much so that, on Dr. Whately's coming to Oxford in 1837, Mr. Newman felt it necessary to use the intervention of a friend before venturing to call on him; and twenty years later, when Mr. Newman—then a Catholic priest—was in Dublin, in the years 1854-1858, on his making a like application, he was informed in answer, from various quarters, that his visit would not be acceptable to the Archbishop.

Dr. Whately honoured Mr. Newman with his friendship for nearly ten years. During the year in which they were in close intimacy at Alban Hall, Mr. Newman served him with all his heart as his factotum—as tutor, chaplain, bursar, and dean; and he ever found in him a generous, confiding, and indulgent superior. Never was there the faintest shadow of a quarrel, or of even an accidental collision between them, though in their walks they often found themselves differing from each other on theological questions. As to theology, Mr. Newman was under the influence of Dr. Whately for four years, from 1822 to 1826; when, coincidently with his leaving Alban Hall, he began to know Mr. Hurrell Froude. On looking back he found that he had learned from Dr. Whately one momentous truth of Revelation, and that was the idea of the Christian Church as a Divine appointment, and as a substantive visible body, independent of the State, and endowed with rights, prerogatives and powers of its own.

There was another person, high in position, who, on Mr. Newman's becoming Fellow of Oriel, had a part in bringing him out of the shyness and reserve which had at first perplexed his electors. This was Dr. Charles Lloyd, Canon of Christ Church, and Regius Professor of Divinity. This eminent man, who had been the tutor, and was the intimate friend of Mr. Peel, was in an intellectual and academical point of view diametrically opposite to Dr. Whately, and it was a strange chance which brought Mr. Newman under the immediate notice of divines of such contrary schools. At that time there was a not unnatural rivalry between Christ Church and Oriel; Lloyd and Whately were the respective representatives of the two societies, and of their antagonism. Sharp words passed between them; they spoke scornfully of each other, and stories about them and the relation in which they stood towards each other were circulated in the Common-Rooms. Lloyd was a scholar, and Whately was not. Whately had the reputation specially of being an original thinker, of which Lloyd was not at all ambitious. Lloyd was one of the high-and-dry school, though with far larger views than were then common; while Whately looked down on both High and Low Church, calling the two parties respectively Sadducees and Pharisees. Lloyd professed to hold to theology, and laid great stress on a doctrinal standard, on authoritative and traditional teaching, and on ecclesiastical history; Whately called the Fathers 'certain old divines,' and, after Swift or some other wit, called orthodoxy 'one's own doxy,' and heterodoxy 'another's doxy.' Lloyd made much of books and reading, and, when preacher at Lincoln's Inn, considered he was to his lawyers the official expounder of the Christian religion and the Protestant faith, just as it was the office of his Majesty's Courts to lay down for him peremptorily the law of the land; whereas Whately's great satisfaction was to find a layman who had made a creed for himself, and he avowed that he was *prima facie* well inclined to a heretic, for his heresy at least showed that he had exercised his mind upon its subject-matter. It is obvious which of the two men was the more Catholic in his tone of mind. Indeed, at a later date Mr. Newman availed himself, when accused of Catholicity, of the distinctions which Dr. Lloyd in an article in a Review had introduced into a controversy with Rome; and others who came within his influence [I believe, Mr. Oakeley] have testified to that influence in their case having acted in a Catholic direction. But such men attended his lectures some years later than Mr. Newman, whose debt to him was of a different kind.

These lectures were an experiment which Dr. Lloyd made on becoming Regius Professor, with a view of advancing theological studies in the University. An annual set of public lectures had been usual, attendance on them being made a *sine qua non* for ordination; but Dr. Lloyd's new lectures were private and familiar. He began them in 1823, the year after Mr. Newman's election at Oriel, and the year of Mr. Pusey's. His initial class consisted of eight: four Fellows of

Oriel—Jelf, Ottley, Pusey and Newman—and four of Christ Church. Others were soon added, notably Mr. Richard Greswell, of Worcester, whose acquaintance with theological topics was, for a young man, wonderful. The subjects of the lectures betokened the characteristic tastes and sentiments of the lecturer. He had more liking for exegetical criticism, historical research and controversy, than for dogma or philosophy. He employed his mind upon the grounds of Christian faith rather than on the faith itself; and in his estimate of the grounds he made light of the internal evidence for revealed religion, in comparison with its external proofs. During the time that Mr. Newman attended his lectures, the years 1823 and 1824—when he left them on taking orders and a parochial charge—the class went through Sumner's 'Records of Creation'; 'Graves on the Pentateuch'; 'Carpzov on the Septuagint'; 'Prideaux's Connexion,' and other standard works, getting up the books thoroughly; for Dr. Lloyd made the lecture catechetical, taking very little part in it himself beyond asking questions, and requiring direct, full and minutely accurate answers. It is difficult to see how into a teaching such as this purely religious questions could have found their way; but Dr. Lloyd, who took a personal interest in those he came across, and who always had his eyes about him, certainly did soon make out that Mr. Newman held what are called Evangelical views of doctrine, then generally in disrepute in Oxford; and in consequence bestowed on him a notice, expressive of vexation and impatience on the one hand, and of a liking for him personally and a good opinion of his abilities on the other. He was free and easy in his ways and a bluff talker, with a rough, lively, good-natured manner, and a pretended pomposity, relieving itself by sudden bursts of laughter, and an indulgence of what is now called *chaffing* at the expense of his auditors; and, as he moved up and down his room, large in person beyond his years, asking them questions, gathering their answers, and taking snuff as he went along, he would sometimes stop before Mr. Newman, on his speaking in his turn, fix his eyes on him as if to look him through, with a satirical expression of countenance, and then make a feint to box his ears or kick his shins before he went on with his march to and fro. There was nothing offensive or ungracious in all this, and the attachment which Mr. Newman felt for him was shared by his pupils generally ; but he was not the man to exert an intellectual influence over Mr. Newman or to leave a mark upon his mind as Whately had done. To the last Lloyd was doubtful of Newman's outcome, and Newman felt constrained and awkward in the presence of Lloyd ; but this want of sympathy between them did not interfere with a mutual kind feeling. Lloyd used to ask him over to his living at Ewelme in the vacations, and Newman retained to old age an affectionate and grateful memory of Lloyd. Many of his pupils rose to eminence, some of them through his helping hand. Mr. Jelf was soon made preceptor to Prince George, the future King of Hanover ; Mr. Churton, who died prematurely, became chaplain to Howley, Bishop of London, afterwards Primate ; Mr. Pusey he recommended to the Minister for the Hebrew professorship, first sending him to Germany to study that language in the Universities there. As to Mr. Newman, before he had been in his lecture-room half a year, Lloyd paid him the compliment of proposing to him, young as he was, to undertake a work for students in divinity, containing such various information as is for the most part only to be found in Latin or in folios, such as the history of the Septuagint version, an account of the Talmud, &c. ; but nothing came of this design.

His attendance on Dr. Lloyd's lectures was at length broken off in 1824 by his accepting the curacy of St. Clement's, a parish lying over Magdalen Bridge, where a new church was needed, and a younger man than the rector to collect funds for building it. From this time he saw very little of Dr. Lloyd, who in 1827 was promoted to the See of Oxford, and died prematurely in 1829. At the former of these dates the Bishop knew of his intention to give himself up to the study of the Fathers, and expressed a warm approval of it.

Mr. Newman held the curacy of St. Clement's for two years, up to the time when he became one of the public tutors of his College. He held it long enough to succeed in collecting the 5,000*l.* or 6,000*l.* which were necessary for the new church. It was consecrated after he had relinquished his curacy, probably in the Long Vacation, when he was away from Oxford ; but so it happened by a singular accident that neither while it was building nor after it was built was he ever inside it. He had no part whatever in determining its architectural character, which was in the hands of a committee. The old church, which stood at the fork of the two London roads as they join at Magdalen Bridge, was soon afterwards removed ; and it thus was Mr. Newman's lot to outlive the church, St. Benet Fink, in which he was baptized, the school-house and playgrounds at Ealing, where he passed his boyhood, and the church in which he first did duty. At St. Clement's he did a great deal of hard parish work, having in the poor school, which he set on foot, the valuable assistance of the daughters of the rector, the Rev. John Gutch, Registrar of the University, at that time an octogenarian.

It was during these years of parochial duty that Mr. Newman underwent a great change in his religious opinions, a change brought about by very various influences. Of course the atmosphere of Oriel Common-Room was one of these ; its members, together with its distinguished head, being as remarkable for the complexion of their theology and their union among themselves in it, as for their literary eminence. This unanimity was the more observable inasmuch as, elected by competition, they came from various places of education, public and private, from various parts of the country, and from any whatever of the colleges of Oxford ; thus being without antecedents in common, except such as were implied in their being Oxford men and selected by Oriel examiners. Viewed as a body, we may pronounce them to be truly conscientious men, ever bearing in mind their religious responsibilities, hard or at least energetic workers, liberal in their charities, correct in their lives, proud of their college rather than of themselves, and, if betraying something of habitual superciliousness towards other societies, excusable for this at that date, considering the exceptional strictness of the then Oriel discipline, and the success of Oriel in the schools. In religion they were neither High Church nor Low Church, but had become a new school, or, as their enemies would say, a *clique*, which was characterised by its spirit of moderation and comprehension, and of which the principal ornaments were Copleston, Davison, Whately, Hawkins and Arnold. Enemies they certainly had. Among these, first, were the old unspiritual, high-and-dry—then in possession of the high places of Oxford—who were suspicious whither these men would go, pronounced them 'unsafe,' and were accused of keeping Copleston from a bishopric—a class of men who must not be confused with such excellent persons as the Watsons, Sykes, Crawleys, of the old London Church Societies and their surroundings, though they pulled with them; next and especially, the residents in the smaller and less distinguished colleges—the representatives, as they may be considered, of the country party, who regarded them as angular men, arrogant, pedantic, crotchety, and both felt envy at their reputation and took offence at the strictness of their lives. Their friends, on the other hand, as far as they had exactly friends, were of the Evangelical party, who, unused to kindness from their brethren, hailed with surprise the advances which Copleston seemed to be making towards them in his writings and by his acts, and were grateful for that liberality of mind which was in such striking contrast with the dominant High Church; and who, in Keble again—in spite of his maintenance of baptismal regeneration—recognised, to use their own language, a spiritual man. What a large number of the Evangelical party then felt, Mr. Newman as one of them felt also; and thus he was drawn in heart to his Oriel associates in proportion as he became intimate with them.

The Oriel Common-Room has been above spoken of as a whole; but the influence thence exercised on Mr. Newman came especially from two of its members, Mr. Hawkins and Mr. Pusey, of whom Pusey was external to what may be technically called the Oriel School. Though senior in age by just half a year, he was junior to Newman in both University and College standing, being elected at Oriel the year after Newman. He was a disciple of Lloyd's, not of Whately's, or perhaps it may be said not even of Lloyd's. The son of a man conspicuous for his religious earnestness and his charities, he left Eton and Christ Church for Oriel, not only an accurate scholar and a portentous student, but endowed with a deep seriousness and a large-minded open-handed zeal in the service of God and his neighbour, which he had inherited from his home. Newman first saw him on his dining, as a stranger, at Oriel high-table, when a guest of his Eton friend Jelf, and as a future candidate, as it was reported, for a fellowship. Newman used to speak in after life of this first introduction to one with whom eventually he was so closely united, and to 'the blessing of' whose 'long friendship and example,' as he said in the Dedication to him of his first volume of Sermons, he had owed so much. His light curly head of hair was damp with the cold water which his headaches made necessary for his comfort ; he walked fast, with a young manner of carrying himself, and stood rather bowed, looking up from under his eyebrows, his shoulders rounded, and his bachelor's gown not buttoned at the elbow, but hanging loose over his wrists. His countenance was very sweet, and he spoke little. This chronic headache nearly lost him his election in the following year. After commencing the paper work of the examination, he found himself from the state of his head utterly unable to complete it. He deliberately tore up the exercise on which he was engaged, and withdrew from the scene of action. But this abandonment of his expectations did not please his friends, and they would not allow it ; they forced him back, and one of the Fellows, then a stranger to him, Dr. Jenkyns, afterwards Canon of Durham, gathered up the fragments of his composition as they lay scattered on the floor, and succeeded so happily in fitting and uniting them together that they were used by his examiners as a portion of his trial. His headaches continued beyond his Oriel years, but he was always full of work. When Newman was offered the curacy of St. Clement's, it was at Pusey's suggestion, and Pusey was to have taken part in its duties, when Dr. Lloyd sent him off to Germany.

It is interesting to trace the course of Newman's remarks on Pusey in his private journal, commencing as they do in a high patronising tone, and gradually changing into the expression of simple admiration of his new friend. April 4, 1823, he writes, speaking of the election of Fellows : 'Two men have succeeded this morning' [E. B. Pusey and W. R. Churton] 'who, I trust, are favourably disposed to religion, or at least moral and thinking, not worldly and careless men'; and he goes on to pray that they may be brought 'into the true Church.' On the 13th he notes down : 'I have taken a short walk with Pusey after church and we have had some very pleasing conversation. He is a searching man, and seems to delight in talking on religious subjects.' By May 2 Newman has advanced further in his good opinion of him. He writes:

I have had several conversations with Pusey on religion since I last mentioned him. How can I doubt his seriousness? His very eagerness to talk of the Scriptures seems to prove it. May I lead him forward, at the same time gaining good from him ! He has told me the plan of his Essay for the Chancellor's prize, and I clearly see that it is much better than mine. I cannot think I shall get it; to this day I have thought I should.

And on May 17 he remarks :

That Pusey is Thine, O Lord, how can I doubt? His deep views of the Pastoral Office, his high ideas of the spiritual rest of the Sabbath, his devotional spirit, his love of the Scriptures, his firmness and zeal, all testify to the operation of the Holy Ghost; yet I fear he is prejudiced against Thy children. Let me never be eager to convert him to a *party* or to a form of *opinion*. Lead us both on in the way of Thy commandments. What am I that I should be so blest in my near associates !

Nothing more is said in these private notes about Pusey before the Long Vacation ; but hardly is it over when he notes down : 'Have just had a most delightful walk with Pusey : our subjects all religious, all devotional and practical. At last we fell to talking of Henry Martyn and missionaries. He spoke beautifully on the question, "Who are to go?"' On February 1 of the next year (1824) he notes down, 'Have just walked with Pusey; he seems growing in the best things— in humility and love of God and man. What an active devoted spirit ! God grant he may not, like Martyr, "burn as phosphorus !"' Lastly, on March 15, when the year from his first acquaintance with Pusey had not yet run out, he writes : 'Took a walk with Pusey : discoursed on missionary subjects. I must bear every circumstance in continual remembrance. We went along the lower London road, crossed to Cowley, and, coming back, just before we arrived at Magdalen Bridge turnpike, he expressed to me' .... There is a blank in the MS. The writer has not put into words what this special confidence was which so affected him. He continues : 'Oh, what words shall I use ? My heart is full. How should I be humbled to the dust ! <u>What importance I think myself of ! My deeds, my abilities, my writings !</u> Whereas he is humility itself, and gentleness, and love, and zeal, and self-devotion. Bless him with Thy fullest gifts, and grant me to imitate him.'

These extracts reached to within a few months of Mr. Newman's ordination, which took place on June 13, 1824, at the hands of Dr. Legge, Bishop of Oxford. It was by this important event in his life, and the parochial duties which were its immediate supplement, that he was thrown into a close intimacy with his other friend, Mr. Hawkins, then vicar of St. Mary's—an intimacy not less important in the mark it left upon him, though far other than 'his familiar intercourse with Pusey. Hawkins bore a very high character, and to know his various personal responsibilities, and his conduct under them, was to esteem and revere him ; he had an abiding sense of duty, and had far less than others of that secular spirit which is so rife at all times in places of intellectual eminence. He was clear-headed and independent in his opinions, candid in argument, tolerant of the views of others, honest as a religious inquirer, though not without something of self-confidence in his enunciations. He was a good parish priest, and preached with earnestness and force, collecting about him undergraduates from various colleges for his hearers. At this date—1824, 1825--on the ground of health he never drank wine, and was accustomed to say that he should not live beyond forty. He has already reached eighty-five years, and in the full use of all his faculties. On him, then, bound as he was by his parochial charge to residence through the year, Mr. Newman, then curate of St. Clement's, was thrown in a special way. In the Long Vacation, when the other Fellows were away, they two had Hall and Common-

Room to themselves. They dined and read the papers; they took their evening walk, and then their tea, in company; and, while Mr. Newman was full of the difficulties of a young curate, he found in Mr. Hawkins a kind and able adviser.

There was an interval of twelve years between their ages, but Mr. Hawkins was, in mind, older than his years, and Mr. Newman younger; and the intercourse between them was virtually that of tutor and pupil. Up to this time the latter took for granted, if not intelligently held, the opinions called Evangelical; and of an Evangelical cast were his early sermons, though mildly such. His first sermon, on 'Man goeth forth to his work and to his labour until the evening,' implied in its tone a denial of baptismal regeneration; and Mr. Hawkins, to whom he showed it, came down upon it at once on this score. The sermon divided the Christian world into two classes, the one all darkness, the other all light; whereas, said Mr. Hawkins, it is impossible for us, in fact, to draw such a line of demarcation across any body of men, large or small, because difference in religion and moral excellence is one of degree. Men are not either saints or sinners; but they are not as good as they should be, and better than they might be— more or less converted to God, as it may happen. Preachers should follow the example of St. Paul; *he* did not divide his brethren into two, the converted and unconverted, but he addressed them all, as 'in Christ,' 'sanctified in Him,' as having had 'the Holy Ghost in their hearts,' and this while he was rebuking them for the irregularities and scandals that had occurred among them. Criticism such as this, which of course he did not deliver once for all, but as occasions offered, and which, when Newman dissented, he maintained and enforced, had a great, though a gradual, effect upon the latter, when carefully studied in the work from which it was derived, and which Hawkins gave him; this was Sumner's 'Apostolical Preaching.' This book was successful in the event beyond anything else in rooting out Evangelical doctrines from Mr. Newman's creed.

He observes in his Private Journal, under date of August 24, 1824:

Lately I have been thinking much on the subject of grace, regeneration, &c., and reading Sumner's 'Apostolical Preaching,' which Hawkins has given me. Sumner's book threatens to drive me into either Calvinism or Baptismal Regeneration, and I wish to steer clear of both, at least in preaching. I am always slow in deciding a question; and last night I was so distressed and low about it that the thought even struck me I must leave the Church. I have been praying about it before I rose this morning, and I do not know what will be the end of it. <u>I think I really desire the truth, and would embrace it wherever I found it.</u>

On the following January 13 he writes:

It seems to me that the great stand is to be made, *not* against those who connect a spiritual change with baptism, but those who deny a spiritual change altogether. [Here he alludes to Dr. Lloyd, rightly or wrongly.] All who confess the natural corruption of the heart, and the necessity of a change (whether they connect regeneration with baptism or not), should unite against those who make regeneration a mere opening of new prospects, when the old score of offences is wiped away, and a person is for the second time put, as it were, on his good behaviour.

Here he had, in fact, got hold of the Catholic doctrine that forgiveness of sin is conveyed to us, not simply by imputation, but by the implanting of a habit of grace.

Mr. Newman, then, before many months of his clerical life were over, had taken the first step towards giving up the Evangelical form of Christianity; however, for a long while certain shreds and tatters[1] of that doctrine hung about his preaching, nor did he, for a whole ten years, altogether sever himself from those great religious societies and their meetings which then, as now, were the rallying ground and the strength

---

[1] This phrase, 'shreds and tatters,' had jarred on the reader (the Editor), who, encouraged to make comments, ventured to criticise what seemed its tone. A letter, treating on other matters connected with the task in hand, has this postscript:
'P.S.—I am surprised you should think that by shreds and tatters I meant to express contempt. Even a king's robe may be cut up into unintelligible bits. I have not looked out the passage; but I am sure I meant patches. Catholicism may be held in bits and pieces; but I will look out the phrase.'

of the Evangelical body. Besides Sumner, Butler's celebrated work, which he studied about the year 1825, had, as was natural, an important indirect effect upon him in the same direction, as placing his doctrinal views on a broad philosophical basis, with which an emotional religion could have little sympathy.

There was another great theological principle which he owed to Mr. Hawkins, in addition to that which Sumner's work had taught him. He has already mentioned it in his ' Apologia '—namely, the *quasi*-Catholic doctrine of Tradition, as a main element in ascertaining and teaching the truths of Christianity. This doctrine Hawkins had, on Whately's advice, made the subject of a sermon before the University. Whately once said of this sermon to Newman in conversation : ' Hawkins came to me and said, " What shall I preach about ? " putting into my hands at the same time some notes which he thought might supply a subject. After reading them I said to him, " Capital ! Make a sermon of them by all means. I did not know till now that you had so much originality in you."' Whately felt the doctrine to be as true as he considered it original.

Though the force of logic and the influence of others had so much to do with Mr. Newman's change of religious opinion, it must not be supposed that the teaching of facts had no part in it. On the contrary, he notes down in memoranda made at the time, his conviction, gained by personal experience, that the religion which he had received from John Newton and Thomas Scott would not work in a parish ; that it was unreal ; that this he had actually found as a fact, as Mr. Hawkins had told him beforehand ; that Calvinism was not a key to the phenomena of human nature, as they occur in the world. And, in truth, much as he owed to the Evangelical teaching, so it was he never had been a genuine Evangelical. That teaching had been a great blessing for England ; it had brought home to the hearts of thousands the cardinal and vital truths of Revelation, and to himself among others. The Divine truths about our Lord and His person and offices, His grace, the regeneration of our nature in Him ; the supreme duty of living, not only morally, but in his faith, fear, and love; together with the study of Scripture, in which these truths lay, had sheltered and protected him in his most dangerous years, had been his comfort and stay when he was forlorn, and had brought him on in habits of devotion, till the time came when he was to dedicate himself to the Christian ministry. And he ever felt grateful to the good clergyman who introduced them to him, and to the books, such as Scott's 'Force of Truth,' Beveridge's 'Private Thoughts,' and Doddridge's 'Rise and Progress,' which insist upon them; but, after all, the Evangelical teaching, considered as a system and in what was peculiar to itself, had from the first failed to find a response in his own religious experience, as afterwards in his parochial. He had, indeed, been converted by it to a spiritual life, and so far his experience bore witness to its truth; but he had not been converted in that special way which it laid down as imperative, but so plainly against rule, as to make it very doubtful in the eyes of normal Evangelicals whether he had really been converted at all. Indeed, at various times of his life, as, for instance, after the publication of his 'Apologia,' letters, kindly intended, were addressed to him by strangers or anonymous writers, assuring him that he did not yet know what conversion meant, and that the all-important change had still to be wrought in him if he was to be saved.

And he himself quite agreed in the facts which were the premisses of these writers, though, of course, he did not feel himself obliged to follow them on to their grave conclusion. He was sensible that he had ever been wanting in those special Evangelical experiences which, like the grip of the hand or other prescribed signs of a secret society, are the sure token of a member. There is, among his private papers, a memorandum on the subject much to the point, which he set down originally in 1821, and transcribed and commented on in 1826. In 1821—the date, be it observed, when he was more devoted to the Evangelical creed, and more strict in his religious duties than at any previous time—he had been drawing up at great length an account of the Evangelical process of conversion in a series of Scripture texts, going through its stages of conviction of sin, terror, despair, news of the free and full salvation, apprehension of Christ, sense of pardon, assurance of salvation, joy and peace, and so on to final perseverance ; and he there makes this N.B. upon his work :

I speak of conversion with great diffidence, being obliged to adopt the language of books. For my own feelings, as far as I remember, were so different from any account I have ever read that I dare not go by what may be an individual case.

This was in 1821 ; transcribing the memorandum in 1826, he adds :

That is, I wrote *juxta præscriptum*. In the matter in question, that is, conversion, my own feelings were *not* violent, but a returning to, a renewing of, principles, under the power of the Holy Spirit, which I had already felt, and in a measure acted on when young.

He used in later years to consider the posture of his mind, early and late, relatively to the Evangelical teaching of his youth, an illustration of what he had written in his essay on Assent, upon the compatibility of the indefectibility of genuine certitude with the failure of such mere belief as at one time of our lives we took for certitudes.[1]

We may assent [he there says] to a certain number of propositions altogether—that is, we may make a number of assents all at once ; but in doing so we run the risk of putting upon one level, and treating as if of the same value, acts of the mind which are very different from each other in character and circumstance.

Now a religion is not a proposition, but a system ; it is a rite, a creed, a philosophy, a rule of duty, all at once ; and to accept a religion is neither a simple assent to it nor a complex assent, neither a conviction nor a prejudice . . . not a mere act of profession, nor of credence, nor of opinion, nor of speculation, but it is a collection of all these various kinds of assent, *some* of one description, *some* of another ; but out of all these different assents how many are of that kind which I have called certitude ? For instance, the fundamental dogma of Protestantism is the exclusive authority of Scripture ; but in holding this a Protestant holds a host of propositions, explicitly or implicitly, and holds them with assents of various

[1] *Grammar of Assent*, p. 243.

character. . . . Yet if he were asked the question, he would probably answer that he was certain of the truth of Protestantism, though Protestantism means a hundred things at once, and he believes, with actual certitude, only one of them all.

Applying these remarks to his own case, he used to say that, whereas, upon that great change which took place in him as a boy there were four doctrines, all of which forthwith he held, as if certain truths—namely, those of the Holy Trinity, of the Incarnation, of Predestination, and of the Lutheran apprehension of Christ—the first three, which are doctrines of the Catholic religion, and, as being such, are true, and really subjects of certitude and capable of taking indefectible possession of the mind, and therefore ought not in his case to have faded away, remained indelible through all his changes of opinion, up to and over the date of his becoming a Catholic; whereas the fourth, which is not true, though he thought it was, and therefore not capable of being held with certitude, or with the promise of permanence, though he thought it was so held, did in the event, as is the nature of a mere opinion or untrue belief, take its departure from his mind in a very short time, or, rather, was not held by him from the first. However, in his early years, according to the passage quoted from his essay, he confused these four distinct doctrines together, as regards their hold upon him, and transferred that utter conviction which he had of what was revealed about the Three Persons of the Holy Trinity and the Divine Economy to his state of mind relatively to Luther's tenet of justification by faith only.

Having this confused idea of Christian doctrine, and of his own apprehension of it, and considering the Evangelical teaching true, because there were great truths in it, he had felt and often spoken very positively as to his certainty of its truth, and the impossibility of his changing his mind about it. On one occasion in particular he has recorded his feelings when he found himself affectionately cautioned by his Father, from his own experience of the world, against the Lutheran doctrine and a headstrong acceptance of it. This was shortly before he succeeded at Oriel, and he takes a note of it in his Private

Journal. In the course of conversation, availing himself of some opportunity, his Father is there reported to have said: 'Take care; you are encouraging a morbid sensibility and irritability of mind, which may be very serious. Religion, when carried too far, induces a mental softness. No one's principles can be established at twenty. Your opinion in two or three years will certainly change. I have seen many instances of the same kind. You are on dangerous ground. The temper you are encouraging may lead to something alarming. Weak minds are carried into superstition, and strong minds into infidelity; do not commit yourself, do nothing ultra.' On these prudent warnings his son observes, after prayer against delusion, pride, or uncharitableness, 'How good God is to give me "the assurance of hope"! If anyone had prophesied to me confidently that I should change my opinions, and I was not convinced of the impossibility, what anguish should I feel!' Yet, very few years passed before, against his confident expectations, his Father's words about him came true.

Fifty or sixty years ago the intellectual antagonist and alternative of the Evangelical creed was Arminianism. The Catholic faith, Anglo-Catholicism, Irvingism, Infidelity, were as yet unknown to the religious inquirer.

A cold Arminian doctrine, the first stage of Liberalism, was the characteristic aspect for the high-and-dry Anglicans of that day and of the Oriel divines. There was great reason then to expect that, on Newman leaving the crags and precipices of Luther and Calvin, he would take refuge in the flats of Tillotson and Barrow, Jortin and Paley. It cannot be said that this was altogether a miscalculation; but the ancient Fathers saved him from the danger that threatened him. An imaginative devotion to them and to their times had been the permanent effect upon him of reading at school an account of them and extracts from their works in Joseph Milner's 'Church History,' and even when he now and then allowed himself, as in 1825, in criticisms of them, the first centuries were his beau-ideal of Christianity. Even then what he composed was more or less directed towards that period, and, however his time might be occupied or his mood devotional, he never was unwilling to undertake any work of which they were to be the staple.

Thus in 1823 he drew up an argument for the strict observance of the Christian Sabbath from the writings of St. Chrysostom and other Fathers; in 1825-6, when he had not only Alban Hall and St. Clement's on his hands, but, in addition, the laborious task of raising sums for his new church, he wrote a Life of Apollonius and his Essay on Miracles. In 1826 he projected writing for the 'Encyclopædia Metropolitana' a history of the first three centuries of Christianity, and in 1827 he drew up a defence of infant baptism from the patristical testimonies furnished to him in Wall's well-known treatise. In the same year he gave a commission to his friend Pusey, who was then in Germany, to purchase for him as many volumes of the Fathers as came to his hand. And in 1828 he began systematically to read them.

LETTERS AND EXTRACTS CONNECTING CHAPTERS III. AND IV. OF THE MEMOIR

Surveying from a distance the excessive work of this period of his life, there stands in Mr. Newman's own hand the following admission :

This close application [to his Essay on Miracles] did not hinder my daily work in my parish and St. Alban Hall, visitings, &c., and two fresh sermons every Sunday. It was now first that I felt what, in the event, became a chronic indigestion from which I have never recovered. I overworked myself at this time.

The correspondence of this date illustrates what the Memoir has touched on, both of his literary labours and his early devotion to the Fathers. The following letter to his sister relates to his Essay on Miracles, which, months before, Mr. Hawkins had spoken of, as 'filling the window-seat' with books out of the college library.

J. H. N. to H. E. N.

January 26, 1826.

. . . Apollonius is a crafty old knave. After surveying the essay itself, I took hold of him, thinking to lift him up to the level of completion without much ado; but the old fellow clung so tight to me that I could hardly get rid of him. He asked me ever so many questions about my authorities for saying this or that of him, made me poke into dusty books in wild-goose chases, &c. &c. In fact, instead of despatching him in two days, I was ten. He detained me till St. Alban claimed me. You know I am going over to St. Mary's. [Qy. to be tutor at Oriel.]

Rev. J. H. Newman to Rev. E. Smedley.

January 27, 1826.

On thinking over your proposal concerning the article on the Fathers of the second century, I cannot but be apprehensive that it would be much too large an undertaking for the time that I could give to it in the course of a year. May I venture to inquire whether it would fall in with your arrangements were I to undertake the Fathers of the second and third centuries in one paper—that is, in fact, the ante-Nicene Fathers—engaging to send it to you this time two years. The period between the Apostolical Fathers and the Nicene Council would then be treated as a whole, embracing the opinions of the Church and so much of Platonism and Gnosticism as may be necessary to elucidate it.

P.S.—I fear I must decline the article on Music; my acquaintance with the subject is not at all sufficient to justify me in undertaking to write upon it.

Mr. Smedley declines the proposition of comprising the second and third centuries in one paper, in spite of its general advantages, as 'covering too large a space for the particular system of our work,' with suggestions how to meet the difficulty. 'Could you not find some convenient break—the reign of Pertinax, perhaps—which might enable you to terminate a first paper?' A proposal he does not seem to have acted upon.

Mrs. Newman to J. H. N.

February 17, 1826.

As you are to consider this a birthday letter, I must not omit begging you to accept the kindest wishes that a mother can offer to a son who has ever been her greatest consolation in affliction, and a comfort and delight at all times and in all situations. We are daily receiving great instruction and advantage, I trust, from the course of sermons you last sent us. We all agreed that a week was much too long to wait between each; and when we have read these repeatedly I hope you will let us have some more.

Again (March 6):

I assure you your sermons are a real comfort and delight to me. They are what I think sermons ought to be—to enlighten, to correct, to support, and to strengthen. It is, my dear, a great gift to see so clearly the truths of religion; still more to be able to impart the knowledge to others. You will, I am sure, duly appreciate the treasure, and make it valuable to many besides yourself.

These tender and happy mother's letters are given for a purpose which the reader will understand as time advances. Even now their tone is too confiding to be allowed to pass without some touch of warning.

To his Mother.

I feel pleased you like my sermons. I am sure I need not caution you against taking anything I say on trust. Do not be run away with by any opinion of mine. I have seen cause to change my mind in some respects, and I may change again. I see I know very little about anything, though I often think I know a great deal.

I have a great undertaking before me in the tutorship here. I trust God may give me grace to undertake it in a proper spirit, and to keep steadily in view that I have set my self apart for His service for ever. There is always the danger of the love of literary pursuits assuming too prominent a place in the thoughts of a college tutor, or his viewing his situation merely as a secular office—a means of a future provision when he leaves college.

The Oriel election and fellowship was this year a momentous one to Mr. Newman, as bringing him into intimacy with the friend whose influence he ever felt powerful beyond all others to which he had been subject. He writes of the election to his mother:

March 31, 1826.

... I go to Bath to-morrow morning, and while in the neighbourhood must employ myself in transcribing my essay, for I must have done it by a week hence. I return to Oxford on Thursday, and commence my labours at Oriel the following Monday. I gave up my church last Sunday, and my parish duty this day. I shall preach one or two sermons more. I did not send my letter to you before mid-day Saturday, and had then begun *neither* of my sermons for the following day. ...

By-the-bye, I have not told you the name of the other successful candidate—Froude of Oriel [Robert Wilberforce was the first]. We were in grave deliberation till near two this morning, and then went to bed. Froude is one of the acutest and clearest and deepest men in the memory of man. I hope our election will be *in honorem Dei et Sponsæ suæ Ecclesiæ salutem*, as Edward II. has it in our statutes.

To his Mother.

April 29, 1826.

I send Blanco White's book. We have just given a diploma degree to Blanco ... he is, however, too violent. I have received your letter, and have just despatched my famous essay by the night coach to town. ... I have felt much that my engagements of late drove me from you, hindered my conversing with you, making me an exile, I may say, from those I so much love.

But this life is no time for enjoyment, but for labour, and I have especially deferred ease and quiet for a future life in devoting myself to the immediate service of God.

A foregoing letter fixes the day when Mr. Newman was to enter upon his tutorial office. As it may interest some readers to know an undergraduate's first impressions of Mr. Newman, as tutor, some sentences may be given from old letters in the Editor's possession.

MR. THOMAS MOZLEY TO HIS MOTHER.

Oriel: April 28, 1826.

... I have at last had an interview with my new tutor, Mr. Newman, who gave me much good advice on the subject of themes, and gave me a manuscript treatise on composition written by Whately, who is a famous man here. This I have copied, and have all the week been furiously engaged in causes and effects and antecedent probabilities and plausibilities, which, as I have never read a line of logic, have been very abstruse.

Again, writing a month or two later:

June, 1826.

... Newman—my new tutor—has been very attentive and obliging, and has given me abundance of good advice. He has requested me to consider carefully what information and instruction I require for my course of reading, and also to determine what books to take up, and he will have a little conversation with me before the vacation.

The same pen, writing in December of the same year (1826):

... I have received very great attentions this term, both from my tutor (Newman) and the Dean. I go up to Collections next Thursday; after that I shall stay in Oxford a week to read Dr. Whately's 'Rhetoric' preparatory to making a careful study of Aristotle's 'Rhetoric' at home, which Newman, my tutor, strongly recommends.

Our college will make but a poor figure in the class list, which comes out, I believe, to-day. Our best is expected to be only a double second. Our men are getting so dreadfully dissipated; perhaps as bad as any in the University.

The following letter from Mr. Newman, in answer to his sister Harriett's petition that he will give her something to do, may suggest a task to some youthful, or indeed to some maturer, reader:

May 1, 1826.

You could not have proposed a more difficult question than in asking me to give you 'something to do.' I will write down a few suggestions as they occur to me; but whether they are rich or barren, difficult or easy, agreeable or disagreeable, I will not pretend to determine:

Compare St. Paul's speeches in the Acts with any of his Epistles, with a view of finding if they have any common features.

Make a summary of the doctrines conveyed in Christ's teaching, and then set down over against them what St. Paul added to them, what St. Peter, what St. John, and whether St. Paul differs from the other three in any points; whether of silence, or omission, or whether they all have peculiar doctrines, &c. &c.

. . . I am about to undertake a great work, perhaps. As I have not room to tell you about it, I must refer you to Jemima's letter.

Such a particular interest attaches to the name of Mr. Newman's youngest sister—Mary—whose early death was commemorated by him in many touching lines, and whose loss constituted that 'bereavement' which checked tendencies of thought at a critical time, as related in the 'Apologia'—that a letter of hers to her brother written at the age of fifteen or sixteen, characteristic in its nature and simplicity, as showing the mingled awe and familiarity which such an elder brother inspired, will not be out of place here :

May 5, 1826.

Dear John, how extremely kind you are. Oh, I wish I could write as fast as I think. I cannot tell why, but whatever I write to you I am always ashamed of. I think it must be vanity; and yet I do not feel so to most others. And *now* all I have written I should like to burn.

Thank you for your long letter, which I do not deserve. I wish I *could* see your rooms. Are they called generally by the titles you give them? I hope the 'brown room' is not quite so grave as the name would lead one to suppose. At least Harriett would not be in the number of its admirers. You know *brown* is not a great favourite of hers. I had no idea you lectured in your rooms. . . .

Oh, how delightful if you can do as you say! It really will be quite astonishing to have you for so long—but poor Frank! I wish, oh, that he might be with us too! . . . I did not imagine, John, that with all your tutoric gravity, and your brown room, you could be so absurd as your letter (I beg your pardon) seems to betray.

How very thoughtless I must be! I have proceeded so far without saying one word of your 'unwellness,' which ought to have come first; 1 hope it was worthy of no higher appellation. . . . In the Long Vacation, you know, we shall be able to nurse you. . . .

Well, I really think I have found out the secret of my difficulty in writing to you. It is because I never told you that difficulty. At least, I find I write much easier since my confession.

J. C. N. (HIS SISTER) TO J. H. N.

May 5, 1826.

I am very sorry to hear you have been so poorly. I feared you were not well when you were last here. The design you have formed of reading through the Fathers reminds me of Archbishop Usher; he was eighteen years in accomplishing the task, and he began at twenty. What is meant by 'the Fathers'? Surely not all the authors from the second century to Bernard?

June 6, 1826, Mrs. Newman writes on Mr. Francis Newman's double first, taken with especial distinction.

I think I must congratulate you equally with Frank on his success, as I suspect your anxiety on the occasion has been much greater than even his.

Again (June 13):

It is very delightful about Frank. I am more thankful on your account than on his. He is a piece of adamant. You are such a sensitive being.[1]

JOHN W. BOWDEN, ESQ., TO REV. J. H. NEWMAN.

August 4, 1826.

. . . Now *touchant les miracles*, do you recollect our remarking that all sceptical ways of accounting for the establishment of Christianity are much more marvellous and diffi-

---

[1] In November of this year Mr. F. W. Newman got a fellowship at Balliol.

cult of belief than the system which admits its miraculous nature ? I find in Dante exactly the same idea.[1] St. Peter asks him why he believes in the inspiration of the Scriptures : he refers to the miracles. But why believe those miracles themselves ? Then follows this passage : 'If the world turned itself to Christianity,' said I, 'without miracles, this one is such that the others are not the hundredth part of it.'

J. C. N. TO J. H. N.

August 5, 1826.

Mary desires her love, and begs that the next time you write you will be so kind as to enlighten her on the uses of reading the Fathers.

REV. SAMUEL RICKARDS TO REV. J. H. NEWMAN.

Ulcombe: June 28, 1826.

You must come and make acquaintance with Mrs. Rickards, that in future, when I write to you, as I hope I often may, I may send you her kind regards as well as my own.

Shortly after this date Mr. Rickards, himself a late Fellow of Oriel, planning that he and Mrs. Rickards should leave his parish in Kent for a few weeks, arranged with Mr. Newman to fill his place in the interval. As a Long Vacation rest, this suited Mr. Newman, and after Mr. and Mrs. Rickards' departure he and his sister Harriett arrived at Ulcombe, and occupied the deserted rectory.[2]

From the leisure of Ulcombe Mr. Newman writes to Mr. Keble : it is the first time the two names are seen in correspondence.

Ulcombe: September 1, 1826.

I have been commencing Hebrew in this retreat, an object I have long had in view and had begun to despair of accomplishing, and just finishing Genesis, though I had hoped to have made much further progress. The interest attending it has far surpassed all my anticipations, high as they were, and, though I clearly see I could never be a *scholar* without

---

[1] *Parad.* xxiv. 88-111.
[2] At this time the *Essay on Miracles* passed through the press.

understanding Chaldee, Syriac and Arabic, yet I think I may get insight enough into the language at least to judge of the soundness of the criticisms of scholars, and to detect the superficial learning of some who only pretend to be scholars. Is it not very difficult to draw a line in these studies? There seems no *natural* limit before the languages above mentioned are mastered. And is it not very tantalising to stop short of them? I should like to know whether those languages *are* so formidable as is sometimes said; in Greek we have a variety of dialects, and works in every diversity of style; can the Semitic tongues all together contain one hundredth part of the difficulty of Greek? Considering, too (as I suppose is the case with them all), their greater simplicity of structure? I wish we began learning Hebrew ten years sooner. Hoping we shall meet well and happily in October,

I remain, my dear Keble, most truly yours.

The following letter, opening with an amusing grievance, shows the writer in an unaccustomed vein :

TO HIS SISTER JEMIMA.

Ulcombe: September 5, 1826.

I know you will not consider me unmindful of you because I am silent. Three letters I have received from you, and yet you have not heard from me; but now I will try to make amends. You must not suppose that the letters you send to Harriett are in any measure addressed to me or read by me; if that were the case, I should be still more in your debt than I am. But Harriett is very stingy, and dribbles out her morsels of information from your letters occasionally and graciously, and I have told her I mean to complain to you of it. I, on the contrary, am most liberal to her of my letters. And in her acts of grace she generally tells me what you and Mary, &c. say in *her* words. Now it is not so much for the *matter* of letters that I like to read them as for their being written by those I love. It is nothing then to tell me that so and so 'tells no news,' 'says nothing,' &c.; for if he or she says *nothing*, still he or she *says*, and the *saying* is the thing. Am not I very sensible? You have received from H. such full information of our, I cannot say *movements*, but sittings, here, that it will be unnecessary for me to add anything.

I hope to finish Genesis the day after to-morrow (Thursday), having gained, as I hope, a considerable insight into the language. At first I found my analytical method hard work, but after a time it got much less laborious, and though as yet I have not any connected view of Hebrew grammar, yet the lines begin to converge and to show something of regularity and system. I think it a very interesting language, and would not (now I see what it is) have not learned it for any consideration. I shall make myself perfect in the Pentateuch before I proceed to any other part of Scripture, the style being, I conceive, somewhat different, and I wish to become sensible of the differences. I read it with the Septuagint.

On Mr. and Mrs. Rickards' return to Ulcombe an intimacy was at once formed; the ladies were friends from the first; Mr. Rickards's influence told at once on Harriett, and she ever retained for him the warmest admiration and respect for his judgment. To those who knew Mr. and Mrs. Rickards, it would seem natural that Harriett should write home an enthusiastic description of both, with a report, also, of her brother's 'ordeal,' as she termed it, Mr. Rickards doubtless bringing his penetration to bear on the man who, for several weeks, had had his parish in charge. A full sheet from Mrs. Newman and Mary remains in answer to this letter.

Mary—'Joy of sad hearts and light of downcast eyes'— in writing to her sisters, had habitually a style of her own, perfectly expressive, but embarrassed by requiring too much from her pen. Thus, at fourteen, wishing to impress on Harriett how clever she thinks her, 'what imagination you have,' she can only exclaim, ' How tiresome it is that in letters one cannot speak ! I wish I knew what inflections to put, and then you would see by the tone of my voice that I was in earnest,' and sensible of the restrictions of sober grammar, proposes a compact to Jemima. Jemima must supply the adjectives, &c. &c., and she the interjections.

MARY SOPHIA NEWMAN TO HER SISTER HARRIETT.

September 25, 1826.

I sit down, dear Harriett, in a frenzy of delight, sorrow, impatience, affection and admiration ; delight at your happiness, sorrow at your letter [Harriett had complained of headache], disappointment, impatience to see you, admiration at you all ! How much I should like to know Mr. and Mrs. Rickards ! And yet, I don't know, perhaps I should be afraid ; but no, I should not be afraid. O Harriett! I want to say such an immense number of things, and I cannot say one. I will try to be a little quiet ; but how is it possible while Mamma is reading to Aunt your charming description of John's 'ordeal'? Poor girl with a headache, poor girl— 'outrageous'; sweet girl! nice girl! dear girl! Oh, what shall I begin with ? Mamma's arrival on Friday quite revived me just as I was sinking in a torpid despondency. [Then follow home details, and apologies for writing in such a scramble.]

On the return of the pastor to his parish, Mr. Newman's task was done. He left Ulcombe, his sister remaining some time longer on a visit to her new friends.

H. E. N. TO J. H. N.

Ulcombe: September 25, 1826.

How strange it is to me that I cannot come and consult you as I have been so long happy and able to do ! Dear John, take care of yourself, and be sure you let me know from authority how you are. Mr. Rickards dreamed that you wrote saying you had been extremely happy here, and the only want you at all perceived in him was a hat.[1] You begged to present him with one. Is it not ridiculous? He must have discovered our thoughts by chiromancy.

J. H. N. TO HIS MOTHER.

October 13, 1826.

Mudiford is a very bracing place, and the air and bathing did me more good than the air and sea of Worthing or the Island. The sands are beautiful. The truth must be spoken : the air of Oxford does not suit me. I feel it directly I return to it. . . .

Of course the new arrangements in college will increase my business considerably. I don't know what the Fathers will say to it.

[1] A future letter will explain this.

The following letter is written in prospect of the Tutorship:

REV. J. H. NEWMAN TO REV. S. RICKARDS.

October 13, 1826.

. . . I am sorry to say the Provost [Copleston, about to be consecrated Bishop of Llandaff] has been very unwell at Chester ; he is better now. The news of Tyler's departure from Oriel nearly overset him. You, I suppose, recollect the circumstances which attended Tyler's election to the Dean's office. The Provost feels he is now losing one whom he selected from the Fellows as his confidant and minister ; and that, too, at the very moment when new duties take himself in part from the college. We who remain are likely to have a great deal of work and responsibility laid upon us ; *nescio quo pacto*, my spirits, most happily, rise at the prospect of danger, trial, or any call upon me for unusual exertion ; and as I came outside the Southampton coach to Oxford, I felt as if I could have rooted up St. Mary's spire, and kicked down the Radcliffe.

REV. S. RICKARDS TO REV. J. H. NEWMAN.

November 2, 1826.

I have no great village news to tell . . . . If I had not felt towards you as I do—that is, if you will allow me to say so—very warmly, I should have been much more punctilious in writing to you in the way of inquiries and thanks. This much, however, I may be bold to say, that my sense of the value of your late kind services is not lessened by finding, as I have found since you left, that the good folks of the village are quite determined never to forget you. They speak of you as if they were conscious you had done them good. Now this is comfort enough for any one man at a time, and I pray you to hoard it up, and take a glint of it only sometimes if you happen to be pestered and well-nigh tired out by a graceless booby congregation in the shape of a class. It is well for a man who is liable to such circumstances to have some bright parts of his life to look to, just to cheer him up and tell him that it does not all run to waste.

Much of the following letter has been given in the Memoir, and is therefore omitted here ; but one or two passages must be repeated, to give place to the strain of memory and reflection awakened by it. Transcribing this letter in 1860, Dr. Newman supplements it with the note in brackets.

REV. J. H. NEWMAN TO REV. R. WHATELY, D.D.

November 14, 1826.

My dear Principal,—I have just received, through Hinds, your kind and valuable present, for which accept my best thanks [Whately's 'Logic' on its first appearance]. On looking through it I find you have enriched your treatise with so much more matter that, compared with the article in the 'Encyclopædia,' it is in many respects a new work.

Much as I owe to Oriel in the way of mental improvement, to none, as I think, do I owe so much as to you. I know who it was that first gave me heart to look about me after my election, and taught me to think correctly, and—strange office for an instructor—to rely upon myself. Nor can I forget that it has been at your kind suggestion that I have been since led to employ myself in the consideration of several subjects [N.B.—In the articles in the 'Encyclopædia Metropolitana'] which, I cannot doubt, have been very beneficial to my mind.

[There is scarcely anyone whom in memory I love more than Whately, even now. How gladly would I have called upon him in Dublin, except that, again and again by his friends and my own, I have been warned off. He is now pursuing me in his new publications, without my having any part in the provocation. In 1836 he was most severe upon me in relation to the Hampden matter. In 1837 he let me call on him when he was in Oxford ; I have never seen him since. I ever must say he taught me to think. A remarkable phrase is to be found in the above letter—'strange office for an instructor, [you] taught me to *rely upon myself.*' The words have a meaning—namely, that I did not in many things agree with him. I used to propose to myself to dedicate a work to him if I ever wrote one, to this effect : 'To Richard Whately, D.D., &c. who, by teaching me to think, taught me to differ from himself.' Of course more respectfully wrapped up.—J. H. N., *November* 10, 1860.]

A passage like this needs in fairness some comment. Persons of strong views and convictions hold in memory their feelings and conflicts of feeling, but of course are unconscious of the expression of countenance that is apt to go along with strong disapprobation in temperaments of this class. They relapse into tenderness, and think nothing of the 'lofty and sour stage,' which has conveyed its meaning to the observer. A friend, looking back to a day when Whately, then Archbishop of Dublin, was in Oxford, 'remembers accusing Mr. Newman to his face of being able to cast aside his friends without a thought, when they fairly took part against what he considered the truth. And he said, "Ah, Rogers, you don't understand what anguish it was to me to pass Whately in the street coldly the other day." Possibly Whately's alienation from Newman might also have had its touch of anguish, never allowed to transpire.'

The following letter has an allusion to the cares of Mr. Newman's new office as college tutor :

TO HIS SISTER HARRIETT.

November, 1826.

. . . I have some trouble with my horses [college pupils], as you may imagine, for whenever they get a new coachman they make an effort to get the reins slack. But I shall be very obstinate, though their curvetting and shyings are very teasing.

November 9.

Pray wish Mary, from me, many happy returns of this day, and tell her I hope she will grow a better girl every year, and I think her a good one. I love her very much; but I will not say (as she once said to me) I love her better than she loves me.

REV. J. H. NEWMAN TO REV. S. RICKARDS.

Oriel College: November 26, 1826.

My dear Rickards,—In our last conversation I think you asked me whether any use had occurred to my mind to which your knowledge of our old divines might be applied. Now one has struck me—so I write. Yet very probably the idea is so obvious that it will not be new to you, and if so, you will not think it worth paying postage for. I begin by assuming that the old worthies of our Church are neither

Orthodox nor Evangelical, but intractable persons, suspicious characters, neither one thing nor the other. Now it would be a most useful thing to give a kind of summary of their opinions. Passages we see constantly quoted from them for this side and for that; but I do not desiderate the work of an advocate, but the result of an investigation—not to bring them to us, but to go to them. If, then, in a calm, candid, impartial manner, their views were sought out and developed, would not the effect be good in a variety of ways? I would advise taking them *as a whole*—a corpus theolog. and ecclesiast. —*the* English Church—stating, indeed, *how far* they differ among themselves, yet distinctly marking out the grand, bold, scriptural features of that doctrine in which they all agree. They would then be a band of witnesses for the truth, not opposed to each other (as they now are), but *one*—each tending to the edification of the body of Christ, according to the effectual working of His Spirit in everyone, according to the diversity of their gifts, and the variety of circumstances under which each spake his testimony. For an undertaking like this few have the advantages you have; few the requisite knowledge, few the candour, few the powers of discrimination —very few all three requisites together. The leading doctrine to be discussed would be (I think) that of regeneration; for it is at the very root of the whole system, and branches out in different ways (according to the different views taken of it) into Church of Englandism, or into *Calvinism, Antipædobaptism,* the *rejection of Church government and discipline,* and the *mere moral system.* It is connected with the doctrines of free-will, original sin, justification, holiness, good works, election, education, the visible Church, &c. Another leading doctrine would be that connected with the observance of the Lord's Day, connected with which the Sabbatarian controversy must be introduced. Again, on Church government, union, schism, order, &c.; here about Bible Society, Church Missionary (*sodes ?*), &c. Again, upon the mutual uses, bearings, objects, &c., of the Jewish and Christian covenants, on which points I shall be rejoiced to find them (what *I* think) correct. This is, indeed, a large head of inquiry, for it includes the questions of the *lawfulness of persecution, national blessings, judgments, union of Church and State,* and again of the profitableness, often, of the uses and relative value of facts at the present day, of the gradual development of doctrines, of election, &c. Again the opinions of these doctors concerning the Trinity and

Incarnation—how far they give in to Platonic doctrines, &c. &c. I have mixed subjects together unpardonably, and have made, as Whately would tell us, *cross divisions*. Never mind. The first subject, regeneration, is by far the most important and useful, I think. . . .

It is six years yesterday since I passed my examination; and if you knew all about me which I know, at and since that time, you would know I have very much to be serious about and grateful for. I trust I am placed where I may be an instrument for good to the Church of God. May you (as you are, and more than you are) be a blessing to all around you for miles and miles. And may we both and all the members of Christ work together in their respective stations for the edification of the whole body. This is Sunday, and I cannot better conclude my letter than by such a prayer.

Ever yours very sincerely,

JOHN H. NEWMAN.

The subject Mr. Newman proposes to Mr. Rickards was one for which he would seem naturally, as well as by his course of reading, well fitted; but he had an objection to 'big books.' The following characteristic answer gives his grounds for declining the proposed task:

REV. S. RICKARDS TO REV. J. H. NEWMAN.

January 9, 1827.

You entertained me by the magnificent work with which you design that I should ennoble myself; and by your so quietly taking for granted two such very debatable points as that I could write it and that other people would read it. Your plan pleased me much by its comprehensiveness and by its ingenuity too; but I do not quite agree with you in thinking that much can be done in these times of ours, through the weight of old authorities. I am not of opinion that any considerable regard would be paid to them except by a few thoughtful men, however well they might be collected; and even they would be hardly inclined to listen to a man offering to do this for them; and, in fact, I guess the materials will be found too stubborn and discrepant to work well in the form in which you are naturally so desirous to see them. My impression is that our old writers are excellent men to keep company with, if you wish to strengthen your powers by conversing with great and original thinkers; they will help you greatly to form a solid judgment for yourself, but they seldom give you a conclusion so wrought out as that you can use it for an argument in the shape in which they present it to you. Hooker and Bishop Sanderson are almost the only exceptions to this.

It seems to me, in these days, the way to draw attention and to make oneself useful, is rather by possessing oneself of the matter of those old venerable men than by leaning upon their names; by taking advantage of their fertility and fulness, and adding to these the clearness of conception and the strict yet luminous method of reasoning in which, I think, we have it in our power completely to outdo them. There is an old proverb, 'A man may say "on my conscience" *once a year,*' and I believe we must do much the same with the writers we are speaking of. We shall employ them to the most purpose by keeping them constantly in our own sight and out of other people's.

I am not dealing out this by way of admonition to you 'de legitimo usu Patrum'; but to tell you that I cannot write a big book.

REV. J. H. NEWMAN TO HIS SISTER HARRIETT.

November 25, 1826.

The term wears away. I have felt much the delight of having but one business [the college tutorship]. No one can tell the unpleasantness of having matters of different kinds to get through at once. We talk of its *distracting* the mind; and its effect upon me is, indeed, a *tearing* or *ripping open* of the coats of the brain and the vessels of the heart.

When I first wrote a thing—my first review—I expected to have opinions given me about it, to be corrected, &c. &c.; but now, old stager as I am, I have learned to take too 'large views' to look out for any immediate notice of a composition, such as 'Miracles,' in the 'Encyclopædia.' Whether it is the number of failures I have had in prize essays, &c. &c., have made me patient, or whether it is insensibility or fickleness, certain it is I rarely give a thought to the success of anything, though it has given me even as much trouble as this essay.

Mr. Blanco White plays the violin, and has an exquisite ear. I wish I could tempt him to Brighton.

The fourth and last chapter of the Memoir has now to be given.

AUTOBIOGRAPHICAL MEMOIR

CHAPTER IV

In 1826, as has been already said, Mr. Newman was appointed one of the Public Tutors of Oriel College, resigning the Vice-Principalship of Alban Hall and the curacy of St. Clement's. In 1827 he was appointed by Dr. Howley, the then Bishop of London, one of the preachers at Whitehall. In 1827–1828 he held the University office of Public Examiner in Classics for the B.A. degree, and for the Honour list attached to the examination. In 1828, on Mr. Hawkins becoming Provost of Oriel, he was presented by his College to the vicarage of St. Mary's, the University church. In 1830 he served as Pro-proctor; in 1831–1832 he was one of the University Select Preachers. This may be called his public career. He relinquished the college tutorship in 1832, and the vicarage, which was neither a University nor college office, in 1843. The other offices enumerated were of a temporary character.

As regards his tutorship at Oriel and his incumbency, both of which were permanent appointments, his separation from each of them in turn, though not abrupt, had something of violence in its circumstances. He had accepted each of them as if for an indefinite term of years, or rather for life. He did not look beyond them; he desired nothing better than such a lifelong residence at Oxford; nothing higher than such an influential position as these two offices gave him. How, by his own act, slowly brought into execution, he broke off his connexion with St. Mary's, he has described in his 'Apologia'; how he gradually, at the end of a few years, died out of his tutorship, shall be told in the pages that follow It is too important an event in his history to pass it over, together with the sentiments and motives which led to it; for, as the Oxford theological movement proper (so to call it) may be said to have ended in his resignation of St. Mary's, so it dates its origin from his and Hurrell Froude's premature separation from the office of college tutor.

The story, however, cannot be told without mention of the mournful differences which arose between Mr. Newman and his dear friend the new Provost of Oriel—Dr. Hawkins—who, on Dr. Copleston's promotion to the bishopric of Llandaff, at the end of 1827, succeeded to the Headship; but in a case in which each party in the quarrel held his own ground on reasons so intelligible and so defensible, and with so honest a sense of duty, the narrative which is now to follow will involve as little to the disparagement of Dr. Hawkins as of Mr. Newman.

There was a standing difference of opinion among religious men of that day, whether a college tutorship was or was not an engagement compatible with the ordination vow; and Mr. Newman's advisers of different schools had, with more or less of emphasis, answered for him the question in the negative. His friends of the Low Church party, though they might wish him to take orders early, had not thought of his doing so as the qualification, which it was then commonly considered, for holding the office of college tutor. He thus speaks on the point in his Private Journal of June 1823 :

Scott says, as a general rule, *not* soon. Hawkins says the same : Why bind yourself with a vow when there is no necessity, and which may mean something incompatible with staying at college and taking pupils? [He continues :] R. doubts the propriety of college tutors being clergymen ; Mr. Mayers (and he has been consulting Marsh of Colchester) advises immediate entrance into the Church by all means. 'Nothing,' he says, 'does the Church want so much as clergymen who, without the tie of regular duty, can make progresses among their brethren, and relieve them at certain seasons.'

So far his Private Journal; here we are principally concerned with Dr. Hawkins's view, as just given. It will be observed that, in his view of the principle laid down, he did not go so far as to pronounce college employments directly and formally unclerical, but it was a question with him whether they might not be so; they required an apology, and raised at first sight a reasonable scruple. The *onus probandi* that a college tutorship was in the instance of a clergyman allowable, lay upon its advocates, as (to take cases which some might think parallel) whether it was allowable for him to hunt, shoot, or go to the theatre. It was lawful for a time, or under circumstances, but anyhow, it was no fulfilment of the vow made at ordination, nor could be consistently exercised by one who was bound by such a vow as his lifelong occupation. Just this, neither more nor less, it is here believed was the decision of Dr. Hawkins.

But far other was Mr. Newman's view of the matter. He had as deep a sense of the solemnity of the ordination vow as another could have, but he thought there were various modes of fulfilling it, and that the tutorial office was simply one of them. As to that vow he has recorded in his Private Journal what he calls his terror at the obligation it involved. He writes the hour after he had received the Diaconate, 'It is over; at first, after the hands were laid on me, my heart shuddered within me; the words "For ever" are so terrible.' The next day he says, 'For ever! words never to be recalled. I have the responsibility of souls on me to the day of my death.' He felt he had left the secular line once for all, that he had entered upon a Divine ministry, and for the first two years of his clerical life he connected his sacred office with nothing short of the prospect of missionary work in heathen countries as the destined fulfilment of it. When then, as time went on, the direct duties of a college exerted a more urgent claim upon him, and he became Tutor, it must be understood that, in his view, the tutorial office was but another way, though not so heroic a way as a mission to idolaters, of carrying out his vow. To have considered that office to be merely secular, and yet to have engaged in it, would have been the greatest of inconsistencies. Nor is this a matter of mere inference from the sentiments and views recorded in his Journal. On occasion of his Father's death, three months after his ordination, he observes, 'My Mother said the other day she hoped to live to see me married, but I think I shall either die within college walls, or as a missionary in a foreign land,' thus coupling the two lives together, dissimilar as they were in their character. A few years later we find in his verses a like reference to college engagements, not as a clergyman's accident of life, but as his divinely appointed path of duty. He says that he is 'enrolled' in a sacred warfare, and that he would not exchange it for any other employment ; that he is a 'prisoner' in an Oxford 'cell,' according to the 'High dispose' of Him 'who binds on each his part'—that he is like the snapdragon on the college walls, and that such a *habitat* was so high a lot that well might he 'in college cloister live and die.' And, when it was decided that he was to be one of the Public Tutors, and he was about to enter upon the duties of his new office, he says in his Journal, ' May I engage in them, remembering that I am a minister of Christ, and have a commission to preach the Gospel, remembering the worth of souls, and that I shall have to answer for the opportunities given me of benefiting those who are under my care.' It will be seen presently why it is necessary thus distinctly to bring out Mr. Newman's view of the substantially religious nature of a college tutorship.

It was in Easter term, 1826, that Newman entered upon duties which he felt thus sacred, and he commenced them with an energy proverbial in the instance of 'new brooms.' He was one of four tutors, and the junior of them, and, though it would be very unjust to say of him that he intentionally departed from the received way of the College, it cannot be denied that there was something unusual and startling in his treatment of the undergraduate members of it who came under his jurisdiction. He began by setting himself fiercely against the gentlemen commoners, young men of birth, wealth, or prospects, whom he considered (of course, with real exceptions) to be the scandal and the ruin of the place. Oriel he considered was losing its high repute through them, and he behaved towards them with a haughtiness which incurred their bitter resentment. He was much annoyed at the favour shown them in high quarters, and did not scruple to manifest as much annoyance with those who favoured as with those who were favoured. He had hardly got through his first month of office when he writes in his Private Journal, 'There is much in the system which I think wrong; I think the tutors see too little of the men, and there is not enough of direct religious instruction. It is my wish to consider myself as the minister of Christ. Unless I find that opportunities occur of doing spiritual good to those over whom I am placed, it will become a grave question whether I ought to continue in the tuition.'

He was especially opposed to young men being compelled, or even suffered as a matter of course, to go terminally to communion, and shocked at the reception he met with from those to whom he complained of so gross a profanation of the sacred rite. When he asked one high authority whether there was any obligation upon the undergraduates to communicate, he was cut short with the answer, 'That question never, I believe, enters into their heads, and I beg you will not put it into them.' When he told another that a certain number of them, after communion, intoxicated themselves at a champagne breakfast, he was answered, 'I don't believe it, and, if it is true, I don't want to know it.' Even Hawkins was against him here; and when one of the well-conducted minority [1] of the gentlemen commoners—for, as has been said, it must not be supposed that there were none such—keenly feeling the evil of the existing rule from what he saw around him, published a pamphlet of remonstrance against it, Hawkins published an answer to him in defence of it.

In consequence, in much disgust with the state of the undergraduates at large, Newman turned for relief to his own special pupils, and primarily to the orderly and promising among them. He offered them his sympathy and help in college work, and in this way, as time went on, he gained first their attachment and then their affection. He set himself against the system of private tutors—that is, as a system, and except in extraordinary cases—viz. the system then prevailing

[1] ['In my letter of October 1884 in answer to Lord Malmesbury's report of my conduct at that time, I say that the well-conducted portion of the college was the majority. These separate statements need not be contradictory. The undergraduates were no stationary body, but continually changing in number. In the years between 1824-1828 what was the majority in one term, or half-year, might be the minority in another.']

of young graduates, bachelors or masters, undertaking the work of preparing candidates for the honours of the schools, and by their interposition between college tutor and pupil inflicting an expense on the latter, and a loss of legitimate influence on the former, which neither party was called upon to sustain. He laid it down as his rule, which in great measure he was able to carry out, that, on such of his pupils as wished to work for academical honours, he was bound to bestow time and trouble outside that formal lecture routine which was provided for undergraduates generally in the Table of Lectures put forth at the beginning of each term. With such youths he cultivated relations, not only of intimacy, but of friendship, and almost of equality, putting off as much as might be the martinet manner then in fashion with college tutors, and seeking their society in outdoor exercise on evenings and in Vacation. And, when he became vicar of St. Mary's in 1828, the hold he had acquired over them led to their following him on to sacred ground, and receiving directly religious instruction from his sermons; but from the first, independently of St. Mary's, he had set before himself in his tutorial work the aim of gaining souls to God.

About the time of his entering upon his vicarage, important changes took place in the Oriel staff of tutors, and that in a direction favourable to his view of a tutor's duties. The two seniors retired, their places being supplied by two young Fellows, Mr. Robert Isaac Wilberforce and Mr. R. Hurrell Froude, disciples of Mr. Keble, and both of them, as being such, in practical agreement with Mr. Newman, as to the nature of the office of college tutor. As Mr. Dornford, who was the senior of the new tutorial body, was far from indisposed to the view of his three colleagues, there ensued in consequence a sudden, though at first unobserved, antagonism in the college administration between Provost and tutor, the former keeping to that construction of a tutor's duties towards the young men which he had held hitherto, and which may be called the disciplinarian, and the four tutors adhering to the pastoral view of those duties. And thus, strangely enough, Mr. Newman, at the very moment of his friend Dr. Hawkins's entering upon the Provostship, became conscious for the first time of his own congeniality of mind with Keble, of which neither Mr. Keble nor he had had hitherto any suspicion, and he understood at length how it was that Keble's friends felt so singular an enthusiasm for their master.

It had been Froude's great argument in behalf of Keble, when the election of Provost was coming on, that Keble, if Provost, would bring in with him quite a new world, that donnishness and humbug would be no more in the college, nor the pride of talent, nor an ignoble secular ambition. But such vague language did not touch Newman, who loved and admired Hawkins, and who answered with a laugh that, if an angel's place was vacant, he should look toward Keble, but that they were only electing a Provost.[1] Little did Newman suspect that Froude's meaning when accurately brought out was that Keble had a theory of the duties of a college towards its alumni which substantially coincided with his own. Nor was it only deficiency in analysis of character which caused Froude's advocacy of his master to be thus ineffectual with Newman; by reason of that almost fastidious modesty and shrinking from the very shadow of pomposity, which was the characteristic of both Keble and Froude, they were, in a later year as well as now, indisposed to commit themselves in words to a theory of a tutor's office, which nevertheless they religiously acted on. Newman, on the contrary, when he had a clear view of a matter, was accustomed to formulate it, and was apt to be what Isaac Williams considered irreverent and rude in the nakedness of his analysis, and unmeasured and even impatient in enforcing it. He held almost fiercely that secular education could be so conducted as to become a pastoral cure. He recollected that Origen had so treated it, and had by means of the classics effected the conversion of Gregory the Apostle of Pontus, and of Athenodorus his brother. He recollected that in the Laudian statutes for Oxford, a tutor was not a mere academical policeman or constable, but a moral and religious guardian of the youths committed to him. If a tutor was this, he might, allowably, or rather fittingly, have received

[1] Pusey expresses the same feeling in his sermon on the opening of Keble College Chapel in 1876, where he says that 'We thought Hawkins the more practical man.'

Holy Orders; but if the view of Hawkins was the true one then he, Newman, felt he was taking part in a heartless system of law and form in which the good and promising were sacrificed to the worthless and uninteresting. On this he was peremptory, but in all this he received no sympathy from the new Provost, who, as far as he mastered Newman's views, maintained that Newman was sacrificing the many to the few, and governing not by intelligible rules and their impartial application, but by a system, if it was so to be called, of mere personal influence and favouritism.

This conflict of opinion, however, between Provost and tutor did not affect their united action all at once. For a time all went on well, with the prospect of a future tinted with that rose-colour which prevails at the opening of a new reign. The Provost loyally and energetically backed up his tutors in their measures for the enforcement of discipline and the purification of the College. He inflicted severe punishment on offenders; he showed no hesitation in ridding the place of those who were doing no good there either to themselves or to others. It began to be the fashion at Oriel to be regular in academical conduct, and admission into the tutors' set became an object of ambition to men hitherto not remarkable for a strict deportment. First classes were once more looming in the offing. With whatever occasional rubs and disputes between Provost and tutors, the former, as a man of straightforward religious principle and severe conscientiousness, could not but be much gratified at finding himself so well served by them, and they, eager and hopeful in their work, had no anticipation that they should not get on well with him. This was, on the whole, the state of things in 1828; but still there was at bottom that grave though latent difference in principle, as has been described above, which was too likely at one time or another to issue in a serious collision between the one party and the other.

At length the cause of quarrel came, and, when it came, it was so mixed up with both academical and ecclesiastical differences between the two parties, difficulties which it would involve much time and trouble, as well as pain, to bring out intelligibly now, that a compromise was hopeless. Its immediate occasion was a claim of the tutors to use their own discretion in their mode of arranging their ordinary terminal lecture-table—a claim which, on the Provost's denying it, they based upon the special relation existing, from the nature of the case and the University statutes, between each tutor and his own pupils, in contrast with his accidental relation to the rest of the undergraduates whom he from time to time saw in lecture.

The Provost practically made the relation very much one and the same in both cases; but at least three of the tutors— Newman, Wilberforce, and Froude—considered that their interest in their office was absolutely at an end, and they could not continue to hold it, unless they were allowed to make a broad distinction between their duties severally to their own pupils and those of other tutors.

A long discussion and correspondence followed, of which nothing came, reaching through 1829 to June 1830. Then the Provost closed it, by signifying to Newman, Wilberforce, and Froude his intention to stop their supply of pupils, as he had a right to do, thus gradually depriving them of their office, according as their existing pupils took their degrees and left the University. After expressing in a last letter on the subject the reluctance which he had all along felt to allude to any course of action which might have the air of a threat, he continues :

And I am most reluctant to do so still, but I yield to what you seem to desire, and feel bound, therefore, to say that, if you cannot comply with my earnest desire, I shall not feel justified in committing any other pupils to your care.

Among Mr. Newman's papers are letters written by Dornford and Froude at the very beginning and at the close of the controversy, and as they accurately express what Newman himself felt also on the points in debate, and afford him the sanction of their concurrence in his first step and in his last, they shall here be given.

Dornford's, written in December 1828, states distinctly his opinion that the arrangement of the college lectures, which was the point in dispute, lay with the tutors and not with the Provost. Froude's insists upon the practical effect upon himself, and upon his view of duty, of that particular arrangement of lectures which alone the Provost would hear of.

1. Dornford, under date of December 26, 1828 :

And now for your new plan of lecturing. There is much in it that I like, and at a first glance it seemed open to no objection ; but now it appears to me that it is much better adapted to 200 men than to 50, and . . . will add very much to the labour. . . . However, there can be no objection, I think, if you all feel strongly about it, to make the experiment and see how it works. And I perfectly agree with you here that we are not at all bound to consult anyone but ourselves on the adoption of it.

2. This was when the new system of lectures was just contemplated. When the Provost had finally disposed of it by depriving the tutors who advocated it of their office, Froude wrote to him as follows :

June 10, 1830.—I do not find that your explanation sets the system you recommend in a light in any respect different from that in which I have before considered it. I have, therefore, no need to deliberate long as to my answer.

In order to comply with such a system I should be obliged to abandon all hope of knowing my pupils in the way in which I know them at present, and, consequently, of retaining that influence over them which I believe I now possess.

Of this I can be certain from my knowledge of myself and from my present experience, slight as it may be.

But, in abandoning this hope, I should be giving up the only thing which makes my present situation satisfactory to myself, and should, therefore, have no inducement to retain it, except a wish to obviate the inconvenience which a sudden vacancy might occasion.

For this reason, in the event of its being proved to me that I cannot with propriety act contrary to your wish on this point, I shall be desirous of withdrawing from my situation at the earliest time which suits your convenience, and at any rate shall resign at Christmas.

He (Froude) wrote again on June 15 to the Provost thus :

I have never thought, as you suppose, that [your] view itself is necessarily at variance with the Statutes. When I appealed to them as a sanction of my conduct, it was not to show that they disallowed the *system* which you approve, but simply that they recognised *such a relation between tutor and pupil* as would justify me in acting on my own views, though they should not happen to be consistent with yours.

Unless I believed that they do recognise such a relation, I should feel bound either to acquiesce at once in the system which you approve, or to resign my situation in any manner that might best suit your convenience. But as it is I feel no less bound to consult to the best of my judgment for the good of those pupils that have been committed to me, and to act on this judgment, such as it is, till you think proper to revoke my authority over them.

When I speak of acting on my own judgment, I should mention in vindication of myself that, in *principle*, it coincides with that which Keble formed, when a tutor here, and which he still retains as strongly as possible ; and that almost in detail it has been suggested by the late Bishop of Oxford [Lloyd], who thought [however] that the Christ Church system was carried to an injurious length, and that some modification of it might be found that would combine the advantages of both.

And though I see the absurdity of assuming that whatever could suit Keble and Lloyd is suitable also to me, I would remind you that, while almost everyone who is put under me requires a *superintendence* which I find myself unable to give under your system, there are very few who require *instruction* beyond what any educated person is able to afford.

Mr. Newman had already written to the Provost to the same effect on June 8, and, according to his way, more abruptly.

My chief objection [he says] to the system you propose is, that in my own case, as I know from experience (whatever others may be able to effect), the mere lecturing required of me would be incompatible with due attention to that more useful private instruction, which has imparted to the office of tutor the importance of a clerical occupation.

To the same purpose he wrote afterwards to Mr. James, a late Fellow of the College, on December 8, 1831, a year and a half later, on occasion of a report that he had resumed his post as tutor :

Had the tutorship been originally offered me by the late Provost on the terms interpreted by the present, I never should have accepted it ; or, if so, only as a trial. I have ever considered the office pastoral, such that the tutor was entrusted with a discretionary power over his pupils. It was on this ground that, four years ago, I persuaded Robert Wilberforce to undertake it ; I have before now, while the Provost was a Fellow, expressed the same view to him. My decision, right or wrong, was made not in haste or passion, but from *long* principle ; and it is immutable, as far as any man dare use such a term of his resolves.

Mr. Newman's connexion with the college tutorship did not altogether terminate till the summer of 1832. As has been said, the Provost declined to give him more pupils ; but Newman was not disposed to surrender those whom he still had, both from the great interest he took in them, and their prospective success in the schools, and also as holding that the tutorship was a University office, of which the Vice-Chancellor only could directly deprive him. By the Long Vacation of 1832 his pupils had, all but a few, passed their B.A. examination ; and the two or three who remained he gave over into the hands of the Provost. At the end of the year he went abroad with Hurrell Froude and his father.

Perhaps it is worth noticing, though it does not seem to be set down in Mr. Newman's memoranda, that the main practical argument which the Provost urged upon him, on behalf of his continuing tutor on the old system of lecturing was, 'You may not be doing so much good as you may wish or think you would do, but the question is, whether you will not do some good, some real substantial good.' Mr. Newman used to laugh and say to his friends, 'You see the good Provost actually takes for granted that there is no possible way for me to do good in my generation, except by being one of his lecturers ; with him it is that or nothing.' In the year after his relinquishing the tutorship, on his return from abroad, the Tract movement began. Humanly speaking, that movement never would have been, had he not been deprived of his tutorship ; or had Keble, not Hawkins, been Provost.

Here closes Mr. Newman's Memoir ; henceforward he is to be represented by his letters.

END OF AUTOBIOGRAPHICAL MEMOIR

LETTERS
AND
CORRESPONDENCE

THE Autobiographical Memoir being now concluded, the letters are resumed from the commencement of 1827.

REV. J. H. NEWMAN TO HIS MOTHER.

Oriel College: February 1, 1827.

Doubtless you have expected to hear of or from me before this; but you know I am very busy. Shall I tell you my adventures in town if I had any? You know I was puzzled where I should lodge myself. Mr. E. recommended some hotel in Albemarle Street—he forgot the name. When I got there I found near a dozen hotels on each side of the way, and was obliged to choose one at a venture. They would not take me in without knowing my name, and I (though anticipating the absurdity which would follow) was obliged to give a card, and was then admitted. I stayed with the W.'s till past ten, and the ladies cajoled me into buying a trumpery piece of music, in the sale of which they were interested, and which they declared to be beautiful, heart-moving. I went to Cartwright, and underwent operations (for they were many) more severe than I ever experienced. I am sure many surgical operations would be less painful. . . . He told me they would pain me for some time in consequence, and, sure enough, I have been nearly in constant pain since, and my face is swollen up. But vinegar has made my *nerves* so much stronger that the toothache is not now the prostrating, overwhelming, down-throwing, flattening pain it was to me. The pain, however, of the operation was very considerable. . . . In the midst of my agony the wretch had the face to murmur out, 'A very ungrateful sensation this.'

I called on Bowden, as I passed Somerset House, and found him prepared for my arrival by a notice in the 'Morning

Post,' among the 'fashionable arrivals' (my card !). From what I have learnt since I fancy I figured among the fashionable departures. Fine subject for quizzing for my pupils !

The Bishop of Oxford died last night, and it is supposed that Lloyd will be his successor, though Copleston, Pearson, the Warden of Wadham, the Bishop of Sodor and Man, are respectively spoken of.

P.S.—I have not forgotten your wishes about some simple and plain commentary, yet I have not been able to satisfy them.

At this date—1827—the country was agitated by the question of Roman Catholic Emancipation, the Bill for which was passed in 1829. Mr. Newman's sister meets in society a clergyman who wishes to hear her brother's views on the question.

TO HIS SISTER HARRIETT.

March 19, 1827.

As to Mr. W.'s absurd question about my opinion on the Catholic question, tell him that I am old enough to see that I am not old enough to know anything about it. It seems to me a question of history. I am not skilled in the political and parliamentary history of Elizabeth, the Stuarts, and Hanoverians. How can I decide it by means of mere argument—theoretical argument, declamations about liberty, the antecedent speculative probability of their doing no harm ? In my mind he is no wise man who attempts, without a knowledge of history, to talk about it. If it were a religious question I might think it necessary to form a judgment; as it is not, it would be a waste of time. What would be thought of a man giving an opinion about the propriety of this or that agrarian law in Rome who was unacquainted with Roman history ? At the same time I must express my belief that NOTHING will satisfy the Roman Catholics. If this be granted, unquestionably they will ask more.

News came this morning of the Dean of Durham's death, late head of Ch. Ch. Pusey has lost a brother.

There is, as has been already shown, an easy tone in Mr. Newman's letters to his Mother which gives them a distinctiveness that may interest the reader, though the writer would have little thought of subjecting them to the eyes of strangers.

J. H. N. TO HIS MOTHER.[1]

March 30, 1827.

. . . Copleston has been very unwell. He is just returned from Tunbridge Wells, where he had been for about a fortnight, and thinks of returning again immediately. Whately is there and Dr. Mayo the physician, a late Fellow of Oriel, in whom the Provost has great confidence.

The new Bishop [Lloyd] presented himself in his wig in church last Sunday. He is much disfigured by it, and not known. People say he had it on hind part before. . . . Blanco preached a very beautiful sermon at St. Peter's last Sunday. What is the matter with Jemima, so mum is she? But she is industrious. Ah, I believe I owe her a letter, so the fault is mine. Young Oakley was elected Fellow of Balliol the other day.

Does the sea blossom? Are green leaves budding on its waters, and is the scent of spring in its waves? Do birds begin to sing under its shadow, and to build their nests on its branches? Ah! mighty sea! Thou art a tree whose spring never yet came, for thou art an evergreen.

There is a pastoral! With love to all, yours ever most dutifully,

JOHN H. NEWMAN.

Tell Mary I was quite delighted with her lines; they showed great elegance, poetical feeling, and good religious feeling, which is better still.

. . . I open my letter to answer your question from Mrs. O.

The *yearly* college expenses with us do not amount to 80*l*. This includes board, lodging, servants, dues, tuition, coals, washing, letters, and hair-cutting. I believe other colleges are about the same. The *great* EXPENSES *of a college residence are in the private extravagance of the young man.* If he will indulge in expensive wines and desserts, if he will hunt, if he will game, what can the college do? It forbids these excesses, indeed, and tries to prevent them; but where there is a will to do wrong there is a way. The college expenses of a careless man are indefinite.

[1] Lately settled at Eastern Terrace, Brighton.

J. H. N. TO HIS MOTHER.

May 7, 1827.

Tell Jemima Miss M. [Miss Mitford ?] is clever, but her naturalness degenerates into affectation and her simplicity into prettiness. She is rather the ape of nature—a mimic—*ars est celare artem.* But some of her pieces are very good, *e.g.* the old bachelor. Tell her she has no business to say *we* are getting old. Let her speak for herself. Tell her I am quite vigorous; particularly the last week, when I have hunted from the college two men. . . .

TO HIS MOTHER.

June 10.

. . . I find that sooner or later I must submit to enter the Schools, and I must prepare for it, so I intend this Vacation once for all to read up some works which, learned as I am, are yet strangers to me. At one time I thought I should have to go into the Schools after the Vacation, but now that seems improbable, and I certainly won't go without a six months' notice.

By the-bye, I have not told you the name of the individual who is to read with me [in the Long]. . . he will not occupy more than an hour a day. At least, I have consented to give no more, and *he* consents to be a *hermit* at Brighton and then at Hampstead [where Mr. Newman had undertaken duty for six weeks of the Vacation, occupying the vicarage during the incumbent's absence]. By-the-bye, talking of hermits puts me in mind of Keble's Hymns, which are just out. I have merely looked into them [the word 'hermit' occurs]. They seem quite exquisite. . . . To return to my pupil, I think you have heard his name before; it is Onslow. . . .

June 22.—Ah, the longest day is passed even before I *send* this, Mute Mary! Well, since writing the above, we have heard from Pusey; he passes through Oxford July 2, which tempts me to stay till that day here. . . . My friend G. [Golightly] comes on July 4. I like him much, as far as I know him, and doubt not, whether you see him little or much, you will like him too, though he is better to know than to see. We are having rows as thick as blackberries. What a thing it is to be vigorous, J. [Jemima], and to be dignified, H. [Harriett]. I am so dignified it is quite overpowering.

Yours ever most dutifully,

JOHN H. NEWMAN.

His Mother replies :

June 26, 1827.

It gives me great pleasure to see you appear so strong at the end of a troublesome term. I hope you will have effected a 'radical reform' by your vigorous measures, and that you are properly seconded.

The following letter is without date, but is written from Germany :

E. B. PUSEY, ESQ., TO REV. J. H. NEWMAN.

August 26, 1827.

I received the enclosed prospectus yesterday with an application, either personally or through friends, to contribute the accounts of the progress of God's kingdom which this country would supply. My acquaintance being both confined and, what I have, almost limited to one party of one religious denomination in this country, I should be utterly unable to give a general view either of the general progress or retrogradation in the whole or its parts. The great activity in almost every class, the variety of the phenomena, the approach, I think, of some crisis, infinitely increase the at any time great difficulty of judging of the religious state of a country, where the development proceeds from so many different points, of conjecturing the final issue, or of appreciating the importance of any particular set of facts as affecting the general result. A long study, &c., seems absolutely necessary either to conjecture what the result of the composition must be, which now seems, before many, nay perhaps before one, decennium is elapsed, unavoidable.

H. W. WILBERFORCE TO REV. J. H. NEWMAN.

July 5, 1827.

I cannot but feel most grateful to you for your kindness to me, which has indeed, I can say without affectation, been to me that of an elder brother.

Again, a month later :

I am quite jealous of Golightly, that he should be making

ground in your acquaintance, while I am deprived of the advantage which, however, I prize, I believe, as much as he can.

In September 1827 Mr. Newman visited Mr. Rickards at Ulcombe, Mr. Robert Isaac Wilberforce being there at the same time. Mrs. Rickards writes a report of her visitors to Miss Newman.

Ulcombe : September 12, 1827.

I trust we shall keep John till he must go to Oxford. We have great designs upon him, and I shall not rest till we have done our part towards accomplishing them—Samuel is even more vehement than I am, and will talk to more purpose—which are neither more nor less than to make him idle enough to rest himself; for we think his looks bespeak that he has been reading too hard. If he improves in looks at Ulcombe, how delightful it will be!

He was very tired all the evening, but we managed to talk a good deal, and R. Wilberforce was as merry as he generally is. This morning I was treated by all three gentlemen coming into the drawing-room after breakfast, when a long discussion began which lasted near two hours, after which they adjourned, R. W. to read, the other two to talk and walk about the garden, from whence they only just returned to be ready for dinner at two o'clock. And now here is John come to keep me company, or rather to be plagued by the children. I wish you only could see him with both on his lap in the great arm-chair, pulling off and then putting on his glasses. They are quite overjoyed to see him. . . .

Thursday.—This is a very rainy day. We have actually fires in each sitting-room. The gentlemen are all together in the larger room, employed upon the Epistle to the Romans, which is one of the things they are bent upon studying most diligently. I did not understand your warning respecting the designs afloat against Samuel. I have been asking him if he has discovered any. He says only that they seem determined to pump him well, and find out all he knows, enlightening him when he is deficient, &c. He says such examinations are worth more than three times as many hours of study alone. I hope the rest find the same to be the case. I cannot describe to you the enjoyment I have in listening. There is no intellectual pleasure so great or any from which one ought to profit so much as such conversation—but I shall talk of nothing else if I suffer my pen to go on on this subject. . . .

Last evening Mr. G.'s manuscript was read and commented on, but it was voted too prolix and dull to be continued. I do not know what we shall have to-night. We have read one of Keble's hymns all together and shall have more of them I hope.—Your affectionate friend,

L. M. R.

Later on, J. C. N., in a letter to her sister, says of this meeting of friends : 'They seem to have spent their whole time in their readings and discussions. Their lightest reading, John says, was Cudworth's sermons.'

J. H. N. TO HIS MOTHER.

Ulcombe : September 24, 1827.

The R.'s press most pressingly your coming here with Mary. . . . You must come before you return. I shall go from hence to the Wilberforce's ; when, I do not know. Rickards has given some most admirable characters of Froude, Blanco White, S. Wilberforce, and others.[1]

To explain a passage in the following letter from Ulcombe— Mrs. Rickards had an album in which she wished all her friends to write verses on flowers. The flower chosen by Mr. Newman was the Snapdragon. The verses begun when this letter was written were finished October 2. They may be found p. 17 of 'Verses on Various Occasions.'

TO HIS SISTER MARY.

Ulcombe : September 29, 1827.

Though I have a good deal to say, I doubt whether I shall say it, yet I hardly know why—perhaps I am lazy. Ulcombe is as pretty as it was last year ; the weather, however, has not been favourable, yet we have not neglected to take prodigious walks. We have seen Mr. Gambier twice, and the second time dined with him. He is a very interesting person. I applaud your determination to pass an independent judgment on what you read. It is very necessary to keep in mind the necessity of making up one's mind for oneself ; but I am rather stupid at this moment, or I would enter into a disquisition on the

---

[1] Mr. Rickards gave characters from handwritings. It was an especial favour reserved for intimate friends for him to do this in the presence of others.

subject. Tell Harriett that Mrs. Wilberforce has invited you (some or all) to Highgate with me. I think two might go, but who I leave to yourselves.

. . . What if I have begun some lines on a flower? I am not obliged to do it. What if I have not? Who can make me? . . . We have had discussions without end on all subjects, and have been reading various things most assiduously, but what the Schools will say I know not.

To HIS MOTHER.

Oriel College: October 18, 1827.

Our tutorial staff is very strong this term. Four tutors (Froude coming in additional), and Pusey as Censor Theologicus, that is, reviewer of the sermon notes. My Fathers are arrived all safe—huge fellows they are, but very cheap—one folio costs a shilling! and all in this extravagantly moderate way. . . .

St. Mary's is sadly out of order inside, as might be expected, but it will be all set right by Christmas, and on the whole the alterations will (I doubt not) be a vast improvement. Trinity Chapel is under a course of restoration. Merton Grove is at length finished, and Alban Hall is rising from its ruins. R. Wilberforce will reside (I fancy) this term.

I am much satisfied that you went to High Wood, though but for a day. I was much taken with Mr. Wilberforce. It is seldom indeed we may hope to see such simplicity and unaffected humility, in one who has been so long moving in the intrigues of public life and the circles of private flattery.

To HIS MOTHER.

October 22, 1827.

I have no lectures this term; my kind colleagues have set me at liberty for the Schools' sake. But I have to prepare, instead, the young candidates of distinction for their trial. This will at once accustom me to examining and be of service to them. I am, besides, reserved for general purposes. It is most useful to have a person reserved in this way. A *corps de réserve* for all contingencies, on the principle that the first Lord of the Treasury has so little to do. . . .

I have been admitted a Congregation Examiner to-day. I have taken the oaths.

Your ever most dutifully,
J. H. N

In allusion to anxieties which had lately been heavy upon her, Mrs. Newman writes to her eldest daughter:

November 5.

I have been a good deal plagued in various ways, but yet I hope the main things go on right. I have had various communications with dear John Henry; he is, as usual, my guardian angel.

E. B. PUSEY, ESQ., TO REV. J. H. NEWMAN.

Brighton: November 1827.

I have found a decided and gradual progress towards improvement since I have been here. I found even the fatigue of the journey a relief. Even the first day, when a deep fog hung heavy on land and sea, was reviving in some measure, and since it has been clear, the constant presence of the sea's deep roar, the sublimity of gazing on an interminable expanse of waters, with all the other feelings associated with this wondrous element . . . have removed for the most part depression of spirits. . . . When my nerves were laid to rest I at any time recovered them. I inhale sea air night and day. I bathe every morning at seven in the sea, and allow three hours in the day to the more immediate imbibing of sea air and exercise; and, what you will think more important, only get through the emending and writing notes on two chapters of Isaiah in the course of the day, my present object being to regain health. I do not grudge the time which it costs, and shall probably, even from this time, change the mode of life which my health could once stand.

Since writing the above I have seen Sir M. Tierney [the Brighton physician]; his views are not very encouraging. After a very short time he plainly said that my case was 'very nearly what they called a general breakdown of the system.' Such, I think, were his words. I did before much wish to return to Oxford, to resume the office, &c. . . . but after this statement, which is confirmed by the feeling of most painful weakness and liability to faintness, I fear it would be madness to attempt it.

At this time Mr. Newman's two younger sisters were visiting Mrs. Rickards at Ulcombe, from whence Mary writes to her brother; fragments of her letters are given, partly for the sake of the superscription on the packet in which they were found, and partly to show the charm of Mr. Rickards's personal influence on young people.

Ulcombe : November 27, 1827.

Is it not odd that Jemima and I should be here alone? Yet I feel quite at home. It is enough to make one feel glad only to look at Mr. Rickards, and Mrs. Rickards makes me laugh so. . . . O John! how absurd of me to tell you all this, which you know. How I long to see you! . . . I can fancy your face—there, it is looking at me. . . .

Again, writing on her return home :

Brighton : December 4, 1827.

I must tell you about Mr. Rickards. You know, as Harriett would say, he cannot let anyone alone ; so he has given me a great deal of good advice. He has recommended me several books to read—Ray's 'Wisdom of God in the Creation.' It is extremely interesting, but the style is so heavy that till I got used to it I found much difficulty. Two other books I am to read—' The Port Royal Art of Thinking,' and ' Watts on the Mind.' Mr. Rickards has also advised me to do what you used to make Harriett and Jemima do—turn ' Telemachus ' into verse.

What a nice creature Mrs. Rickards is! I always think of the word, I believe, you applied to her, 'fascinating,' for I think that is exactly what she is ; and it is so amusing to hear Mr. Rickards and her talk to each other.

I am so impatient to see you. How long is it before you come? Can it be three, nearly four weeks? I think it seems longer since I saw you than ever before. This letter is not to go till to-morrow—it will wait for our having seen Pusey.

Dearest John, your most affectionate sister,

M. S. N.

Upon the above letter is inscribed these words : 'Scarcely more than four weeks after, she suddenly died.'

J. H. N. TO HIS SISTER HARRIETT.

December 2, 1827.

Dear Pusey lodges at 5 Eastern Terrace. My Mother will send her card and he will call. He is very unwell ; his nerves very much tried. He is not well in mind or body. All of you be very dull when he calls, for he can bear nothing but dulness, such as looking out upon the sea monotonously.

I do not see how my Mother can be civil to him. He does not go out to dinner, and as to breakfast, it would be so strange to ask him.

Well, Copleston is a bishop and a dean. Shall we have a new Head or not? Which will be best, Keble or Hawkins?

E. B. PUSEY, ESQ., TO MRS. NEWMAN.

December 1827 [Saturday evening].

Mr. E. Pusey begs to present his best thanks to Mrs. Newman for her kindness in thinking of him, and for her obliging present. He has not yet been able to try it, but is sure that anything sent in so kind a manner must be palatable as well as beneficial.

It may, perhaps, be interesting to Mrs. Newman to know that there will be a vacancy in the Oriel Provostship. Mr. Pusey does not believe that it is any longer a secret, but it may be as well not mentioned beyond Mrs. Newman's immediate family. Should there be a difference of opinion as to the successor, it is a satisfaction to agree with J. N. on the subject.

The following entry in the 'Chronological Notes,' under date Nov. 26, 1827, marks the commencement of that illness which, in looking back, is, in the 'Apologia,' classed with bereavement :

Taken ill in the schools while examining, was leeched on the temples.

November 28.—R. Wilberforce took me off to Highwood. Consulted Mr. Babington.

December 14.—Went from London to Brighton.

This is the first mention of the valued medical adviser on whom Mr. Newman relied with unfailing trust till death removed his friend from him. Some letters remain of Dr. Babington's amongst Mr. Newman's papers.

The reader will remember that in the account of his failure, when he stood for honours in 1820, there is an allusion to this attack in 1827 as a repetition of the same symptoms, only in a severer form, from which he then suffered.

TO HIS MOTHER.

Highwood Hill: December 11, 1827.

I have been at Wilberforce's several days; finding myself tired with my Oxford work, he kindly proposed it and I accepted it. I find myself quite recruited, and return to Oxford to-morrow or Thursday. When you will see me I hardly know—the election of Provost may detain me; I had some idea of coming to you to-day, had I not sufficiently refreshed myself by coming here. See how dutiful I am to tell you all this, even at the risk of your thinking me unwell. It will be a great shame if my very candour and fairness in telling you I am tired make you think so.

Thank yourself, Mary and H. for your joint letter.

Golden Square: December 13.

It is my intention, God willing, to come down to you to-morrow for the vacation, though, doubtless (and I hope), I shall have to return to Oxford for the election. I am very much better, nay, almost well, but my kind medical adviser here (a friend of W.'s), with whom I dine and lodge till to-morrow, is against my returning to business.

The reader has not now to be told that at the election of Provost Mr. Newman voted for Mr. Hawkins. From the following letter it may be gathered that Mr. Keble had keen interests on the question, which, however, is a different thing from desiring for himself such a total change of life.

REV. J. H. NEWMAN TO REV. J. KEBLE.

Marine Square, Brighton: December 19, 1827.

Though I have not written to you on the important college arrangement which is under our consideration at present, and in which you are so nearly concerned, you must not suppose my silence has arisen from any awkward feeling (which it has not) or any unwillingness to state to you personally what you must have some time heard indirectly. I have been silent because I did not conceive you knew or understood me well enough to be interested in hearing more than the fact, any how conveyed, which way my opinion lay in the question of the Provostship, between you and Hawkins. This may have been a refinement of modesty, but it was not intended as such, but was spontaneous.

I write now because Pusey has told me that you would like to receive a line from any of the Fellows, even though you have already heard their feelings on the subject before us all; and I am led to mention my reason for not having written before (which I otherwise should not have done), lest you should think my conduct less kind to you than in intention it has really been. I have been so conscious to myself of the love and affectionate regard which I feel towards you, that the circumstance of my not thinking you the fittest person among us in a particular case and for a particular purpose seemed to me an exception to my general sentiments too trivial to need explanation or remark—to myself; but I have forgotten that to *you* things may appear different—that this is the first time I have had an opportunity of *expressing* any feeling towards you at all; and that, consequently, it would have been acting more kindly had I spoken to you rather than about you. Forgive me if I have in any way hurt you or appeared inconsiderate.

I have lived more with Hawkins than with any other Fellow, and have thus had opportunities for understanding him more than others. His general views so agree with my own, his practical notions, religious opinions and habits of thinking, that I feel vividly and powerfully the advantages the College would gain when governed by one who, pursuing ends which I cordially approve, would bring to the work powers of mind to which I have long looked up with great admiration. Whereas I have had but few opportunities of the pleasure and advantage of your society: and I rather suspect, though I may be mistaken, that, did I know you better, I should find you did not approve opinions, objects, and measures to which my own turn of mind has led me to assent. I allude, for instance, to the mode of governing a college, the desirableness of certain reforms in the University at large, their practicability, the measures to be adopted with reference to them, &c.

It is ungracious to go on, particularly in writing to you above others; for you could easily be made to believe anyone alive was more fit for the Provostship than yourself. I have said enough, perhaps, to relieve you of any uneasy feeling as regards myself: the deep feelings I bear towards you, these I shall keep to myself.—Yours ever affectionately.[1]

[1] The above letter from Mr. Newman to Mr. Keble will help to clear away the difficulties that have arisen as to Mr. Newman's part in the

REV. JOHN KEBLE TO REV. J. H. NEWMAN.

December 28, 1827.

I have made up my mind that it is on the whole unadvisable for me to allow my name to be mentioned on this occasion, and have written to Hawkins and Froude, and intend writing to Plumer to-night to say so. It was very kind in you to write to me, but surely your opinion required no explanation or apology. However partial one might be to oneself, your knowing so much more of Hawkins is enough to prevent anyone with a spark of common sense in his head from being hurt at your preference of him.

The first entry in the 'Chronological Diary' for the year 1828 is in these words :

January 5.—We lost my sister Mary.

In the 'Apologia' there is the following allusion to this event :

The truth is, I was beginning to prefer intellectual excellence to moral : I was drifting in the direction of liberalism. I was rudely awakened from my dream at the end of 1827 by two great blows—illness and bereavement.

It happened to the present writer to read—more than fifty years after this bereavement—a letter from Mary Newman to her Mother, so remarkable for sweet playfulness, and, if the term may be used, for the quality of simplicity, in its most bright picturesque form, that, on occasion of writing on some family concern to Cardinal Newman, it was natural to

election, which are noticed in Dean Burgon's *Twelve Good Men*. The following letter from Dr. Pusey is here given ; it was written on the same sheet of paper with that of Mr. Newman :—' My dear Keble,—N. having spared me a small space in his letter, which was written in consequence of seeing your kind answer to mine, I am very glad to be able to express my sincere gratitude for that kindness. I knew that whatever was done honestly would meet with your approbation ; but it is a satisfaction to have that expressed in such a manner. I suppressed much in my last letter that I would willingly have said, but dreaded its, at the moment, appealing insincere ; but I now find that it would probably give you less pain not to be the object of the choice of the Fellows than it will, I expect, be to me to vote otherwise than for you.—Affectionately yours, E. B. PUSEY.'

speak of the impression it had made. Shortly after came the following note from him, with an enclosure :

You spoke with so much interest lately of my dear sister Mary that I send you what I have just received from Maria Giberne.[1]

The letter brings the scene so vividly before the reader that its insertion will not be thought out of place here.

M. R. G. TO H. E. CARDINAL NEWMAN.

. . . But I do not want to talk of myself. I want to tell you of my entire sympathy with you in what you say and feel about the anniversary of our dear Mary's death. This season never comes round without my repassing in my heart of hearts all the circumstances of those few days—my first visit to your dear family. Who could ever behold that dear sweet face for any length of time and forget it again ? And again, who could ever have been acquainted with the soul and heart that lent their expression to that face and not love her ?

My sister Fanny and I arrived at your house on the 3rd [of January], and sweet Mary, who had drawn figures under my advice when she was staying with us at Wanstead, leant over me at a table in the drawing-room, and in that sweet voice said, 'I am so glad you are come ; I hope you will help me in my drawing.' I forget about the dinner and evening on that day, for I was doubtless under considerable awe of you in those first days ; but the next day Mr. Woodgate and Mr. Williams dined there, and dear Mary sat next you, and I was on the other side ; and while eating a bit of turkey she turned her face towards me, her hand on her heart, so pale, and a dark ring round her eyes, and she said she felt ill, and should she go away? I asked you, and she went : I longed to accompany her, but dared not for fear of making a stir. It was the last time I saw her alive. Soon after Jemima went after her ; and then your Mother, looking so distressed ; and she said, 'John, I never saw Mary so ill before ; I think we must send for a doctor.' You answered as if to cheer her, 'Ah, yes, Mother, and don't forget the fee.' How little I thought what the end would be ! Next morning Harriett came to walk with us about one o'clock—after the doctor had

[1] This lady, sister-in law of the Rev. Walter Mayer, has been described in *Reminiscences of Oriel*. She died at Autun, Dec. 2, 1885 in the Convent of the Order of Visitation.

been, I think—but though she said Mary had had a very bad night, she did not seem to apprehend danger. We went to dine with a friend, and only returned to your house about nine. I felt a shock in entering the house, seeing no one but you—so pale and so calm, and yet so inwardly moved; and how, when I asked you to pray with us for her, you made a great effort to quiet your voice, sitting against the table, your eyes on the fire, and you answered, 'I must tell you the truth: she is dead already.' Then you went to fetch vinegar, which I did not need, for I felt turned to stone. Fanny cried—I envied her her tears.

You told us a little about her, with gasping sobs in your voice, and then you left us. My tears come now in writing it, though they would not then. I never cry suddenly—I must think about it first. Now, dearest Father, I hope while I relieve my own heart by speaking of these sad scenes, I am not selfishly overtaxing your feelings; but I think you will not mind it, for you like to go over old times as well as I do, I think; and I cannot tell all this to anyone but you. Do you recollect that you and I are the only survivors of that event?

And then how can I ever forget all your kindnesses to me because of my toothache [she had undergone a painful, unsuccessful operation at the dentist's]? How your Mother sent out for soft cakes soaked with wine—the only thing I could manage to eat. You all seemed so unselfish in your grief, forgetting your own trouble to minister to my wants. I was deeply touched, and learnt a lesson which, though I have not practised as I ought, I have always striven to imitate : not to suffer myself to be so absorbed by my own feelings as that I could not feel for others.

This scene, recalled after fifty years, is given as fulfilling the promise or the prophecy made in the first freshness of sorrow, which forms the closing verse of the poem entitled 'Consolations in Bereavement.'

From these home scenes of trial Mr. Newman, in returning to Oxford, had to take share at once in a college election which had issues important to himself, and with which the fourth chapter of the Memoir is concerned.

J. H. N. TO HIS MOTHER.

January 31, 1828.

I was hastening to write a few lines to you before breakfast in time for our new Provost (as he will be in two hours) to take to town to save a day's post, when your letter came.

My journey fagged me much. I arrived here by half-past six. The Bishop [Copleston] was in the Common-Room, and I joined the party. He left yesterday morning. Yesterday I took a long and delightful ride, but the stench of the retiring waters in our quadrangle is odious, and the air in Oxford is thick and damp. The inside of St. Mary's is nearly complete.

The following letter from his Mother dwells on the subject foremost in her mind.

February 18, 1828.

My dear, dear Son,—It was very kind of you to write when you had such comforting news as your ' strikingly amended health.' I pray earnestly that it may continue to improve, and that you may be preserved from such accumulated and successive trials as it has pleased God you should experience in your entrance into life. The chastening Hand who brings these severe inflictions does mitigate them, and often, in greater mercy, renders them blessings ; such has it been to you, my dear, and through you to all of us. It is delightful to think that your dear departed sister owed so much of her religious and right feelings to you ; and her knowledge of her own insufficiency, and her submission and fitness to obey her awfully sudden call. These reflections, which call for our thankfulness, must soothe us for the bitter trials we have been repeatedly called on to endure.

Dr. Hawkins, as Provost, resigned St. Mary's. The following entries in the 'Chronological Record' give the dates:

March 9.—Did duty at St. Mary's in the afternoon, and preached.

March 12.—The Provost (Hawkins) resigned the living of St. Mary's.

March 14.—I was instituted by the Bishop of Oxford to St. Mary's.

March 16.—Did duty at St. Mary's, preaching.

March 20.—Inducted into St. Mary's by Buckley of Merton.
March 23.—I read in—*i.e.* read the Thirty-nine Articles.
March 27.—Disputed with Arnold for B.D. degree, Provost presiding.
March 28.—Dined with Provost to meet Arnold.

The following letter to his sister Jemima is taken from her collection of his letters. The reader of Mr. Newman's parochial sermons will recognise in that entitled 'The Lapse of Time,' passages which had their impulse in the thoughts here expressed.

Oriel College: March 9, 1828.

I hope you have not thought my silence unkind, dear Jemima. I have all along been going to write to you, but somehow or other, though I have not much to do, I find it difficult to make time. I am going out of the Schools, and Dornford (I fancy) will supply my place for the ensuing examination.

Dear Jemima, I know you love me much, though your disposition does not lead you to say much about it, and I love you too, and you (I trust) know it. Carefully take down, if you have not already, all you can recollect that dear Mary said on every subject, both during the time of her short illness and the days before; we shall else forget it. Would it not, too, be desirable to write down some memoranda generally concerning her?—her general character, and all the delightful things we now recollect concerning her. Alas! memory does not remain vivid; the more minute these circumstances the better. To talk of her thus in the third person, and in all the common business and conversation of life, to allude to her as now out of the way and insensible to what we are doing (as is indeed the case), is to me the most distressing circumstance, perhaps, attending our loss.[1] It draws tears into my eyes to think that all at once we can only converse *about* her, as about some inanimate object, wood or stone. But she 'shall flourish from the tomb.' And, in the meantime, it being but a little time, I would try to talk to her in imagination, and in hope of the future, by setting down all I can think of about her. But I must not selfishly distress you. God bless you, my dearest Jemima.

[1] See *Parochial Sermons*, vol. vii. p. 4, 'The Lapse of Time.'

J. C. N. TO HER BROTHER J. H. N.
March 17, 1828.

... I cannot bear to think that I should ever cease to feel as much towards dear Mary as I have all my life, but I think I am sure I shall not. I dare say strangers think us much at our ease, and in good spirits; but I always wish to say when I speak to anyone who did not know her, 'Ah, you little think what she was in herself and to us all.' Dear John, how you delighted me once when you said she was so singularly good! I never heard you speak so much about her, but I was sure you thought so; and indeed we, John, know more of her than you could know; I especially, who have been always with her.

TO HIS MOTHER.
April 1, 1828.

Last week I did my exercises for my B.D. degree, merely to keep Arnold company, since one man cannot dispute with himself [and he could get no one], and its being in Latin and in Collection week, I found it too hard work.

I take most vigorous exercise, which does me much good. I have learned to leap (to a certain point), which is a larking thing for a don. The exhilaration of going quickly through the air is for my spirits very good. I have a sermon to prepare for Warton to-morrow.[1]

TO HIS SISTER HARRIETT.
Oxford: April 21, 1828.

On my journey hither I comforted myself with writing the following lines. Do not show them to my Mother, if you think they would distress her.

CONSOLATIONS IN BEREAVEMENT.

Death was full urgent with thee, sister dear,
   And startling in his speed;
Brief pain, then languor till thy end came near:
   Such was the path decreed,
    The hurried road
To lead thy soul from earth to thine own God's abode.

---

[1] Rev. Walter Mayer's funeral sermon.

Death wrought with thee, sweet maid, impatiently;
    Yet merciful the haste
That baffles sickness ; dearest, thou didst die ;
    Thou wast not made to taste
        Death's bitterness,
Decline's slow-wasting charm, or fever's fierce distress.

Death came unheralded ;—but it was well ;
    For so thy Saviour bore
Kind witness thou wast meet at once to dwell
    On His eternal shore ;
        All warning spared,
For none He gives where hearts are for prompt change prepared.

Death wrought in mystery : both complaint and cure
    To human skill unknown :
God put aside all means, to make us sure
    It was His deed alone ;
        Lest we should lay
Reproach on our poor selves that thou wast caught away.

Death urged as scant of time: lest, sister dear,
    We many a lingering day
Had sickened with alternate hope and fear:
    The ague of delay ;
        Watching each spark
Of promise quenched in turn, till all our sky was dark.

Death came and went: that so thy image might
    Our yearning hearts possess,
Associate with all pleasant thoughts, and bright
    With youth and loveliness ;
        Sorrow can claim,
Mary, nor lot nor part in thy soft soothing name.

Joy of sad hearts and light of downcast eyes !
    Dearest, thou art enshrined
In all thy fragrance in our memories ;
    For we must ever find
        Bare thought of thee
Freshen our weary life, while weary life shall be.

I am conscious they need much correcting, which at times it will be a solace to me to give, but such as they are you will not dislike them. It goes to my heart to think that dear Mary herself, in her enthusiastic love of me, would so like them could she see them, because they are mine. May I be patient ! It is so difficult to realise what one believes, and to make these trials, as they are intended, real blessings.

To his Sister Jemima.

Oriel College: May 10, 1828.

... Poor Pusey came here last Monday. He is much thrown back, and his spirits very low. He proposes being ordained on Trinity Sunday. I suppose his marriage will take place shortly after. He, Pusey, is going to change his name to Bouverie; this, however, is quite a secret.

... In accordance with my steady wish to bring together members of different colleges, I have founded a dinner club of men about my own standing (my name does not appear, nor is known as the founder). We meet once a fortnight. One fundamental rule is to have very plain dinners.[1]

I am very regular in my riding [enjoined by his doctor], though the weather has not on the whole been favourable. On Thursday I rode over to Cuddesdon with W. and F. and dined with Saunders. It is so great a gain to throw off Oxford for a few hours, so completely as one does in dining out, that it is almost sure to do me good. The country, too, is beautiful; the fresh leaves, the scents, the varied landscape. Yet I never felt so intensely the transitory nature of this world as when most delighted with these country scenes. And in riding out to-day I have been impressed more powerfully than before I had an idea was possible with the two lines:

> Chanting with a *solemn* voice
> Minds us of our *better choice*.

I could hardly believe the lines were not my own and Keble had not taken them from me. I wish it were possible for words to put down those indefinite, vague, and withal subtle feelings which quite pierce the soul and make it sick. Dear Mary seems embodied in every tree and hid behind every hill. What a veil and curtain this world of sense is! beautiful, but still a veil.

Rev. E. Smedley to Rev. J. H. Newman.

May 17, 1828.

It is some time since, through your kindness, I opened a communication with Mr. Pusey, who gave me encouragement to hope that, as the historical portion of the 'Encyclopædia

[1] The members were: 1, R. H. Froude; 2, R. I. Wilberforce; 3, J. H. Newman; 4, J. Bramston; 5, Rickards; 6, Round.

Metropolitana' approached the birth of Mohammedanism, he might be inclined to assist us in Oriental history. As I very much wish to negotiate with him further, I take the liberty of requesting information from you, who, I think, may be able to furnish it.

REV. J. H. NEWMAN TO REV. E. SMEDLEY.

May 29, 1828.

Mr. Pusey is quite disposed to engage in the task you wish to impose upon him ; but, as was the case when he was applied to before, he feels considerable doubt whether his present studies will allow him to pledge himself to undertake it. He has for some time past been occupied in a translation of the Old Testament, to which he feels he must give an undivided attention for the whole of the next year.

For myself, my college engagements do not allow me to keep pace with the 'Encyclopædia.' I am now slowly turning my attention to Gnosticism.

Will you allow me to express the concern I felt at hearing there was some hesitation in the minds of the proprietors of the 'Encyclopædia,' concerning the right of the contributors to publish their papers in a separate shape ? For myself, I have no present intention of exerting the right, supposing it to be one, as I certainly understood it was, when I sent Mr. Mawman the article on 'Cicero and Apollonius.' . . . This feeling is entertained by every Oxford contributor whom I have heard mention the subject.

Dr. Whately requests me to inform you that his friend, Dr. Hampden, lately editor of the 'Christian Remembrancer,'[1] is not unwilling to have his name added to the list of contributors to the ' Encyclopædia,' if you have employment for him, and he considers you will find him a great acquisition.

REV. E. SMEDLEY TO REV. J. H. NEWMAN.

June 1828.

The history of Mohammedanism will not be approached yet awhile ; nevertheless, I much fear that, if Mr. Pusey's attention is engrossed by so important a subject as a translation of the Old Testament, we should have little chance of obtaining his assistance in time for our notice of the Koran.

[1] In its monthly form.

In June 1828 is entered into Mr. Newman's 'Chronological Notes' the following passage :

June 1.—Pusey ordained. [He read prayers for me in the evening at St. Mary's, and reminded me years afterwards that I said to him, 'If you read from your chest in that way it will kill you.' And, in fact, about 1832 he had read himself dumb.]

J. H. N. TO HIS SISTER HARRIETT.

June 4, 1828.

Pusey took orders Sunday last, and is to be married next week. His book has been out about ten days. It is sadly deformed with Germanisms : he is wantonly obscure and foreign—he invents words. It is a very valuable sketch, and will do good, but will be sadly misunderstood, both from his difficulty of expressing himself, the largeness, profundity and novelty of his views, and the independence of his radicalism. It is *very* difficult, even for his friends and the clearest heads, to enter into his originality, full-formed [*sic*] accuracy, and unsystematic impartiality. I cannot express what I mean : he is like some definitely marked curve, meandering through all sorts and collections of opinions boldly, yet as it seems irregularly.

Good-bye, my dear Harriett, both our minds are full of one subject, though we do not speak of it. Not one half-hour passes but dear Mary's face is before my eyes.

The following letter—the first that is found of his correspondence with Hurrell Froude—is notable also as showing an intimacy with Mr. Henry Wilberforce, and a recognition, veiled under a tone of disparagement, of the charm of his bright and playful wit.

REV. J. H. NEWMAN TO REV. R. H. FROUDE.

June 22, 1828.

I should have sent you more of a letter, but that plague, Henry Wilberforce, has been consuming the last half-hour before ten by his nonsensical chat. He bids me ask you whether you returned him a MS. on the Differential Calculus by Walker of Wadham. Did you read Pusey's book on the coach top as you intended ?

In July Mr. Newman joined his Mother and sisters at Brighton.

REV J. BLANCO WHITE TO REV. J. H. NEWMAN.

Brighton: July 16, 1828.

There is a spare bed in our [himself and pupil] lodgings, which we should be most happy if you would take. . . . The fact is, the noise of other lodgers in this house was most injurious to me, as it kept me awake for whole nights together. The only remedy was to take the spare bedroom. . . .

Whately was here two days ; unfortunately I was too ill to enjoy to the full the pleasure of his company. But it was really amusing to see him playing at ducks and drakes with D. [Blanco White's pupil], and beating him hollow. He ate and drank and joked like Hercules in the ' Alcestis.' There is no man with whom I have associated so many classical passages. What do you think of the following description of our friend going to an Oxford dinner ?—*Nunc in reluctantes* (*Magistros*) *Egit amor dapis atque pugnæ.* . . .

July 25, 1828, there is an entry in the 'Notes' :

Sent letter to the Bishop of London (Howley) accepting Whitehall preachership. [N.B. This is quite consistent with what is said in my 'Apologia.' At this time there were twelve preachers from each University. I agreed to be one of these, but when Blomfield soon after became Bishop of London he turned all twenty-four out, and began a plan of one (or two ?) from each University, and it was one of these (preacherships) which he sounded me about, and which I conditionally accepted.]

REV. R. I. WILBERFORCE TO REV. J. H. NEWMAN.

July 28, 1828.

I have a serious complaint to make against you, viz. that you have totally prevented me from preaching. According to my old notions, I could have got on tolerably well, and though I should have been dissatisfied with the execution, I should have believed myself on the right road. Now, you have convinced me I am altogether off the road, and every step I take I only get deeper in the mire. So you see you *must* preach both times if we take Elliott's Chapel (Q.E.D.)

REV. JOHN KEBLE TO REV. J. H. NEWMAN.

July 1828.

I have been thinking some time of claiming your promise of coming to see us, but we have been rather in a whirl of visitors, which as yet we have hardly got out of ; and my two companions [his father and sister] are neither of them used to seeing many friends together.

REV. J. H. NEWMAN TO REV. J. KEBLE.

11 *Marine Square, Brighton: July* 31, 1828.

I propose returning to Oxford by the end of next week, August 9. If then it meets your convenience, it would give me much pleasure to pay my Fairford visit in the course of the week beginning August 10. . . . Dornford has kindly offered me his Nuneham cottage, should I be able to prevail upon my Mother to take up her abode there for a part of the vacation, in which case I should probably post myself there too.

I have just heard of the appointment of John Sumner to Chester, which has given me sincere pleasure. I suppose it will be generally popular. . . . I am employed in reading with great interest Heber's Journal. . . . I think it may do a great deal of good. Most pious men who have gone out, have hardly had that flexibility and elasticity of religious principle which can accommodate itself to the world, and have worked stiffly. Henry Martyn, in spite of the romantic interest attending him, is (is he not ?) an instance.

Yours ever affectionately.

The name of Dr. Pusey and his work for the Church have become such world-wide facts, that it may interest the reader to see some criticisms (one notice has already been given) of his first work before his name was widely known.

REV. S. RICKARDS TO REV. J. H. NEWMAN.

August 7, 1828.

You know R. Wilberforce is kind enough to come here next month ; as you could not come again I feel that in him I have the man upon whom, next after yourself, I should be most delighted to leave over my flock. I have read your favourite Pusey's book [about Germany], and I am so nearly disappointed in it that I can hardly permit myself to speak to you about it; and yet I can still less bring myself to be silent on the subject. It appears to me the hasty work of a man not formed or conditioned to move in haste; struggling partly under a vast accumulation of matter, partly under press of time, and mainly under a more than common difficulty of combating successfully with such untoward circumstances. The style, surely, is often odious; his spirit, more surely, very delightful; and I cannot think he has made out his case with sufficient fulness and clearness, nor drawn the result towards which he tends nearly enough to a point. If it succeeds in gaining much attention I am clearly wrong. I am aware that the reverse will be no proof that I am right.

REV. R. H. FROUDE TO REV. J. H. NEWMAN.

August 12, 1828.

I hear from Robert Wilberforce that you are returned from Brighton, and mean to stay in Dornford's cottage at Nuneham. He tells me that you are at present much better, but fears that you will go again into the Schools. If you really intend this, I envy, without approving, your resolution; but I sincerely hope you will not be called to exert it. . . .
. I have a brother now at home [William Froude] who is coming to Oriel next term, and will make a very good hand at mathematics unless he is very idle.

After plans for his Mother's and sisters' stay at Nuneham, Mr. Newman tells his sister Jemima of his first visit to Keble, then living with his father. He writes after a rainy season :

Oriel College: August 19, 1828.

The glass was rising the whole of the last week, and now stands almost at fair; besides, there was a change of the moon yesterday, and yesterday and to-day are certainly more auspicious. . . . As we unfortunately dined out on the Friday, I, after all, saw little of the Fairford party, so much so that I was discontented with myself. They have ·a very nice garden – not large, but nice—and a tree-surrounded paddock, most retired and quiet, with a walk round it. Mr. Keble said it was all the world to Elizabeth (his daughter), who travelled round it in a chair many miles in the course of the year. It is quite an affecting and most happy world. He was born and has lived in Fairford all his life. . . . Keble's verses are written (as it were) on all their faces. My head ran so upon them that I was every minute in danger of quoting them. Mr. Keble as well as John shows much playfulness and even humour in his conversation. But it was such dull weather when I was there, it made us all stupid.

The letter then diverges to other persons and things, ending with :

. . . What a gossiping letter this last half has been ! It is quite a girl's letter. Ah ! I feel ashamed.

REV. J. KEBLE TO REV. J. H. NEWMAN.

August 20, 1828.

The higher powers here were sorry to let you go without their benediction ; so the sooner you come to receive it, all quite properly, the better.

On the question of the tutorship Mr. Robert Wilberforce writes to Mr. Newman :

September 3, 1828.

I wish to embody the ideas in which we agreed when at Brighton, in relation to the appointment of some one period when the freshmen of each year should come up. The advantages of it appeared, I think, to be :

1. The increased facility of dividing the men into proper classes. At present perhaps one set of freshmen have entered upon a course of historical reading, and made some way in it—when a single one comes up, who is put in temporary lectures with men of quite different standing, that he may wait till enough are come to form a second historical class.

2. A further advantage would be that the men would not so soon become indifferent to exposing themselves before one another as they do at present. *Now*, when a freshman is put into a lecture with senior men, and sees them neglect all preparation, he learns to do the same. A lecture composed entirely of freshmen is always most easy to manage.

3. Another advantage would be that the tutor would be able to judge more accurately of the progress of his pupil by comparing his advance with that of his contemporaries.

4. Another difficulty at present existing, is that felt in giving advice to a pupil as to the quantity of subjects he should undertake, the preparation he should make for the Schools, &c. It is only, of course, by observing a number of persons, seeing how long they went on attending [or not attending—J. H. N.] to fresh subjects, and when they began to concentrate their attention, that we can form any rule for our guidance in giving such advice.

5. As regards the men themselves. It is a great advantage to them to know whereabouts they are in their academical life. Many respectable men spend a great deal of time in study during the early part of their residence ; but, postponing perhaps an accurate attention to scholarship, or the reconsideration of what they have done, suddenly find themselves without time for so doing. Were there a larger number who went on together, they would be in a certain degree a check upon one another.

6. Were more men brought together, a greater degree of stimulus would be given to them. If a man finds himself inferior to one who came up before him, he does not think of referring it to any deficiency in exertion.

The thing cannot be effected immediately, though I don't see why it should not be done next year. The temporary inconvenience of the men cannot weigh against their own permanent good, which is the object proposed.

If anything of this kind is to be done, it would be advisable, perhaps, to suggest it to the Provost [Hawkins], that, if approved by him, it might be submitted to the absent Fellows, who, as owners of rooms, are interested in it.

REV. J. BLANCO WHITE TO REV. J. H. NEWMAN.

September 11, 1828.

I desired the Provost to acquaint you with the mental squall which has for the twentieth time driven me out of my intended course. I was quietly paddling across a little pool of Greek and Latin, just to land my pupil in the Schools on the lee side of the infamous scopuli,[1] at the mouth of that longed-for haven, when in an unguarded moment I was blown off into the broad and tempestuous sea of Reviews, exposed to the attacks of the 'genus irritabile,' both large monsters and small fry, which take their pastime therein. Was it

[1] 'Infames scopulos Acroceraunia,' Hor. *Od.* I. iii. 20.

rashness, was it ignorance, that exposed me to this unexpected trial? It was neither, my dear friend. Dr. Mayo came on purpose from Tunbridge Wells to make me the proposal of the editorship. He found me sick of Livy and Thucydides, promised me an addition of health from a more enterprising occupation, spoke of comforts for approaching old age, and made me in a moment start up from my drowsiness as young and as bold as if I had been five-and-twenty, and had just left Oxford with a double first.

Reflection soon came to tell her sad tale; but it was too late: and here I am with an engagement upon me which I dare say alarmed at one time the formidable Gifford [Editor of the 'Quarterly.' Murray tried to get Blanco White over to him, giving up the prospect of the 'London Review.'—J. H. N.], who had the sting of a wasp at the tip of each of his fingers. There is but one way for such an ἄοπλος creature as myself to be saved from being crushed—my friends must stand round me, especially my Oriel friends. Well, then, sharpen your pen and give me an article on any subject you like, Divinity excepted for the present, for of that I expect a flood. You must not decline, my dear Newman. You must also do me the kindness to engage Pusey to write something for me. Will you inquire the direction of Mills of Magdalen for me? Do you think your brother would write for me? I want materials for two numbers before I publish the first.

I intend to spend a month in Oxford during the next full term. I will keep lodgings there till the fate of the Review is ascertained.

Mr. Newman seems to have answered Blanco White in a friendly and encouraging tone, for within a fortnight he writes in reply:

REV. J. BLANCO WHITE TO REV. J. H. NEWMAN.

September 23, 1828.

It gives me great pleasure to find that you consider the intended Review almost as an Oriel cause. But you must contribute to its success with your pen. I know how difficult it is to persuade a mind like yours to write without preparation; but I should strongly advise you to venture upon the strength of your *household stuff*—on the reading and reflection of many years. Write without much concern; you are sure to write well. Take up any book you like; imagine yourself in our Common-Room, myself in the corner, Dornford passing the wine, &c., and tell us your mind on paper. Should you prefer a subject connected with your daily occupations, tell us how the leading classical writers should be read. You must have marked a number of passages which come home to the bosoms and business of men. Have you a taste for Memoirs? Would you like to write those of Dr. Parr ? I write this day to Dornford for a military article. Neate has proposed two very good subjects. . . .

A day or two later he acknowledges another letter from Mr. Newman, in which it appears he had suggested two subjects: one on poetry, which was written at once, and has been reprinted among the author's works under the title 'Poetry with reference to Aristotle's "Poetics,"' and a second on music, which seems to have remained an idea only. The Review, for reasons given in a note to the republished article, ended with its second number.[1] Blanco White writes to a friend, May 20, 1829, 'My compact with the evil spirit, the demon of the book-market, is almost at an end. . . . I hope very soon to be entirely free from the nightmare of the "London Review."'

J. H. N. TO HIS SISTER HARRIETT.

August 20, 1828.

To-day I have brought together the letters I have received since August 1826, just two years (348 letters). It is a pleasant yet painful employment. As I was sorting them into years, my eye caught a hand [Mary's] which so discomposed my

[1] The following is extracted from 'Note on Essay 1,' in *Essays Critical and Historical*, vol. i. p. 27 :—

' The time was favourable for a new *Quarterly*, so far as this, that the long-established *Quarterly* was in the crisis of a change of editors. In fact, its publisher entered into correspondence with Mr. White with a view to an arrangement which would supersede the projected Review . . . the new publication required an editor of more vigorous health and enterprising mind, of more cheerful spirits and greater powers of working, and with larger knowledge of the English public than Mr. White possessed; and writers less bookish and academical than those, able as they were, on whom its fate depended. Southey, by anticipation, hit the blot. As a whole, the Review was dull.'

head that I have been obliged to lock them all up again, and turn my thoughts another way. I ought not to be talking of it now, but who can refrain ?

REV. J. KEBLE TO REV. J. H. NEWMAN.

October 9, 1828.

I hear Pusey's name mentioned as likely to succeed Nichol [N.B. as Regius Professor of Hebrew]; tell me how the matter goes. The only fear I have is that he may not be quite old enough ; and also I am a little apprehensive of his reading himself to death. For I suppose, by the Rule of Three, Fellowship : Canonry : : Headache : Apoplexy. I hope you are all well and comfortable at the Nuneham cottage.

THE BISHOP OF LLANDAFF TO REV. J. H. NEWMAN.

[*Note* by J. H. N.—This letter is a good specimen, from the 'My dear sir' at the beginning to the 'My dear sir' at the end, of his real kindness, yet ingrained donnishness.]

October 28, 1828.

My dear sir, . . . What you say about the commencement of Michaelmas term at Oriel quite startled me. The 18th was the second Saturday in term, the established day of meeting. It used to be a mistake that some of our junior Fellows made, supposing St. Luke's day to be a day of audit business. *Our* audit (I still cannot help calling it so) is to finish *before* St. Luke's day. Everything therefore is concluded on the morning of the 17th, and why the young men should not come in on the following day I do not know, except that the fifth of Dr. Hill's reasons for drinking is also applicable to the case of prolonging vacations.

I hope your health is quite restored, and I am inclined to conclude that it is by your silence on the subject. Dornford also is not the worse, I trust, for his Highland rambles. I was glad to hear of him from a lady who met him *en route*.

It is well that Oriel has so good a treasurer as yourself. Without meaning any reflection on former treasurers, I think you will improve the system ; at least you will not be content with copying precedent blindly, but will accommodate your method to the changes which time is for ever bringing on,

and study continual improvement, which is the way in all things to prevent both degeneracy and revolution.
I beg to be kindly remembered to the Provost, and to all your colleagues, and am, my dear sir,

LL.

REV. BLANCO WHITE TO REV. J. H. NEWMAN.

November 8, 1828.

I have read your MS. in all the hurry of pleasure. I will read it again with all the composure of a critic, if I can, for you are a treacherous writer, you slip so softly through the critic's fingers. Well, then, my dear friend, you must write for me constantly ; you want an outlet for your mind and heart, which are running over where there is no call for their riches. Tell the world at large what you feel and think. Talk with the people of England through my journal, and let me have the benefit of their delight. I write in a great hurry, and yet I cannot help inclining to poetry in my style, such is the effect of your article. Adieu, my Oxford Plato.

J. H. N. TO HIS SISTER HARRIETT.

After describing a busy day :

November 11, 1828.

. . . My ride of a morning is generally solitary; but I almost prefer being alone. When the spirits are good, everything is delightful in the view of still nature which the country gives. I have learned to like dying trees and black meadows —swamps have their grace, and frogs their sweetness. A solemn voice seems to chant from everything. I know whose voice it is—her dear voice. Her form is almost nightly before me, when I have put out the light and lain down. Is not this a blessing ?

Dear Pusey is gazetted. I hope he will not overwork himself. How desirable it seems to be to get out of the stir and bustle of the world, and not to have the responsibility and weariness of success ! Now, if I choose to wish a scheme, and in my solitary rides I sometimes do, I should say, ' Oh, for some small cure of a few hundreds a year, and no preferment, as the world calls it.' But you know this is wishing for idleness, and I do not think I shall have this obscurity, because I wish for it. Yet, see, I talk of the comfort of retirement—how long should I endure it were I given it. I do not know myself.

REV. DR. PUSEY TO REV. J. H. NEWMAN.

January 10, 1829.[1]

Your opinion on my [Hebrew] Lectures [*i.e.* as relates to beginners] is precisely what I had myself felt. It was always my own theory that as little grammar as possible should be taught at first, *i.e.* until the student is sufficiently familiar with the language to take interest in the instances, &c., and the general structure of a language so different from our own; until, in fact, he be in some degree acquainted from his own experience with the problems which are to be solved. I am very much obliged to you for all your hints, and hope to profit by them, especially as they confirm my own practical views, though these had begun to give way before the interest which I myself felt in the theories of grammar. I hope for more criticisms from you soon.

REV. J. H. NEWMAN TO REV. S. RICKARDS.

Oriel College: February 6, 1829.

My dear Rickards,—I have been out of humour with you for your abuse of Pusey[2]—and that's the truth. However, I shall say nothing about it, only hoping you may gain wisdom as you grow up, and it's no harm wishing this for any of us. You have heard of our proceedings at Oriel, I presume, from X., but I do not account him a very fair judge. Not, indeed, that I know what he said, or even that he said anything; but it is natural he should say something, and it's almost certain he would say wrong. He annoys me by his way of railing against the Provost, and I shall tell him so some day. If he has railed to you, don't believe him. We have gone through the year famously; packed off our lumber, parted with spoilt goods, washed and darned where we could, and imported several new articles of approved quality. Indeed, the College is so altered that you would hardly know it again. The tangible improvements of system have been, first, the diminishing the Gentlemen Commoners from twenty to eight or nine;

---

[1] This date given, but with a doubt expressed as to *exact* correctness.
[2] *See* Letter on p. 165.

then the dismissal of the Incurables; then the rejecting unprepared candidates for admission—the number is awful, some twice; then the giving chance vacancies to well-recommended and picked men; then the introduction of paper work into the Collection examinations; then the refusing testimonials to unworthy applicants; then the revival of a Chapel sermon at the Sacrament; then the announcement of a prize for Greek composition. The most important and far-reaching improvement has been commenced this term—a radical alteration (not apparent on the published list) of the lecture system. The bad men are thrown into large classes, and thus time saved for the better sort, who are put into very small lectures, and principally with their own tutors, quite familiarly and chattingly. And, besides, a regular system for *the year* has been devised. But we do not wish this to be talked about. We hope soon to give some Exhibitions or Scholarships. All these alterations are, you observe, additional to that grand act at the election, of throwing open two Fellowships. Pretty well, we hope, for a year. Hawkins's spirits are not what they used to be, and persons who have known him long say he is ageing. I have sometimes been made quite sad at the sight of him. But this, of course, *entre nous*. He has not (nor should a Head) taken the initiative in these innovations, but has always approved—sometimes kept abreast with us—and at Collections has slain the bad men manfully. It is said in College by the undergraduates that, 'Now, alas! the Provost was as bad as a Tutor.' Whereas, at Collections they used to hope the Provost would retaliate on the Tutors the blows they received from the latter.

J. H. N. TO HIS SISTER JEMIMA.

February 8, 1829.

I began my Littlemore Evening Catechetical Lecture last Sunday. I am now returned about an hour from it, and am not fatigued. I hope no one will interrupt while I write to you, for everything is hushed around me. Why is a feeling of calm melancholy pleasing? Is it that the languor after exertion gives rise to a pleasing bodily temperature, or is it mental? I was much struck with this evening's first lesson.[1] It seemed to apply to the Church. You know I have no

[1] That Sunday was the Fifth Sunday after Epiphany. Therefore by the Old Lectionary the evening first lesson was the 64th of Isaiah.

opinion about the Catholic Question, and now it is settled I shall perhaps never have one; but still, its passing is one of the signs of the times, of the encroachment of Philosophism and Indifferentism in the Church.

From this state of pensive calm melancholy there follows the rebound, which is a characteristic of Mr. Newman's nature, and which may be observed throughout his course.

To HIS SISTER HARRIETT.

February 17, 1829.

Peel resigned; Ch. Ch. *gave him up.* This was a great thing, and among others I exerted myself to gain it. Unluckily our meddling Provost just then returned from London, where Oxford men, being chiefly Liberal lawyers, were for Peel. He joined the Merton men—Whately, Shuttleworth, Macbride, &c.—in nominating Peel. He suddenly formed a committee in London, and—vigorously employing the Ch. Ch. interest, which Ch. Ch. had precluded itself from using—began an active canvass. The party opposed to Peel's re-election consisted of all the College Tutors and *known* resident Fellows in Oxford; but they agreed in one point, only differing in their view on the Catholic Question, but all thinking Mr. Peel unworthy to represent a religious, straightforward, unpolitical body, whose interest he had in some form or other more or less betrayed. Besides, they thought it an infamous thing if Oxford was to be blown round by the breath of a Minister, signing a petition one day and approving of the contrary next. At the first meeting they could agree only *not* to have Mr. Peel, and so the protest stands in the papers. On Saturday they proceeded to nominate their candidate, and the difficulty of doing this was the strength of their opponent. They at length selected Sir R. Inglis. So urgent was the case, and so strong our dislike of Mr. Peel, that it was done *unanimously* in an hour's meeting. But the Peelites, having Ch. Ch., having London, and an early day of election (our voters being mostly clericals from the country), above all having the Government interest, will, I doubt not, get their way. Let them. I would have signed a protest had there been no opposition. The great Captain, wise as he is, has thought the Church and Oxford his tool—and that we should turn round at the word of command. When Oxford is spoken of, the *residents* are always meant. Oxford, by seventy residents, has rejected Mr. Peel, and, if it elects him, elects him by non-resident lawyers. It is said we shall all be in great disgrace, and that certain persons have ruined their chance of promotion. Well done. I rejoice to say the Oriel resident Fellows have been unanimous anti-Peelites [Denison and Neate were Probationers, not M.A.'s], and I have just heard that the modest Keble has come forward with a paper of questions against Mr. Peel, signed with his own fair name. I have no fault whatever to find with the other side, except that they have presumed to bring in the non-residents against the residents, which, I dare say, they think quite fair. Pusey is against us, thinking Peel an injured man, and us hot-headed fellows. The Bishop of Oxford [Lloyd]—whom I wish to love and do love—will, I fear, be much hurt with what I and others are doing; he has already in his time promoted, or helped in the promotion of, four Oriel Fellows [Pusey, Jelf, Churton, Plumer].

To HIS MOTHER.

February 26, 1829.

At three o'clock to-day Sir R. Inglis was head of the poll by 70—190 Peel, to 260 Inglis. He ended [to-day] by being 40 ahead.

I will tell you why the Provost is 'meddling'—because when Ch. Ch. had *resigned* Peel, he chose to turn the opposition to him, without inquiring, into a *cabal*; and suddenly got up an opposite party without speaking to any of us [*i.e.* the Oriel Common-Room] on the subject, and brought clamour and faction in, when Ch. Ch. was quietly seeking for a member, and would most probably have chosen a man moderately favourable to Catholic Emancipation. This I call awkward 'meddling'; and if he fails he will have burned his fingers. If he succeeds he will bring in by a poor majority a man who has hitherto come in unanimously—this is a sorry triumph.

I am deeply grieved at something else. Blanco White (I know his way so well) wrote a letter to some Oxford friend stating his change of views about Catholic Emancipation. Why not let him change with the mass of the nation? No, it served the purpose of the Peelites to bring his name forward. He is asked to publish—generously and devotedly he does it;

and thus he is made the victim of an electioneering purpose. He has brought upon himself all sorts of attacks, odious personal attacks.

It is too bad to inflict upon individuals favourable to Catholic Emancipation the most difficult task of striking a balance between their disgust of Mr. Peel and their friendly disposition towards the Catholic question. Hence some Emancipatists have taken one side, some another; some have remained neuter; some have taken a side and half repented—all have felt a difficulty. This, I say, all arose from the indelicacy of those who thrust Mr. Peel on the University.

To his Mother.

March 1, 1829.

We have achieved a glorious victory. It is the first public event I have been concerned in, and I thank God from my heart both for my cause and its success. We have proved the independence of the Church and of Oxford. So rarely is either of the two in opposition to Government, that not once in fifty years can independent principle be shown. Yet, in these times, when its existence has been generally doubted, the moral power we shall gain by it cannot be overestimated. We had the influence of Government in unrelenting activity against us—the 'talent' so called of the University, the town lawyers, who care little for our credit, the distance off and the slender means of our voters—yet we have beaten them by a majority of 146 votes, 755 to 609. The 'rank and talent' of London came down superciliously to remove any impediment to the quiet passing of the great Duke's bill; confessing at the same time that of *course* the University would lose credit by turning about, whatever the Government might gain by it. They would make use of their suffrage, as members of the University, to degrade the University. No wonder that such as I, who have not, and others who have, definite opinions in favour of Catholic Emancipation, should feel we have a much nearer and holier interest than the pacification of Ireland, and should, with all our might, resist the attempt to put us under the feet of the Duke and Mr. Brougham.

Their insolence has been intolerable; not that we have done more than laugh at it. They have everywhere styled themselves the 'talent' of the University. That they have rank and station on their side I know; and that we have the inferior colleges and the humbler style of men. But as to talent, Whately, with perhaps Hawkins, is the only man of talent among them; as to the rest, any one of us in the Oriel Common-Room will fight a dozen of them apiece—and Keble is a host; Balliol too gives us a tough set, and we have all the practical talent, for they have shown they are mere sucking pigs in their canvass and their calculations. Several days since, their London chairman wrote to Mr. Peel assuring him of complete and certain success. They strutted about (peacocks!) telling our men who passed through London that they should beat by eight to one, and they wondered we should bring the matter to a poll. We endured all this, scarcely hoping for success, but determining, as good Churchmen and true, to fight for the *principle*, not consenting to our own degradation. I am sure I would have opposed Mr. Peel had there been only just enough with me to take off the appearance of egotism and ostentation; and we seriously contemplated about ten days since, when we seemed to have too slight hopes of victory to put men to the expense of coming up, we the resident seventy, simply and solemnly to vote against Mr. Peel, though the majority against us might be many hundreds. How much of the Church's credit depended on us residents! and how inexcusable we should have been, if by drawing back we had deprived our country friends of the opportunity of voting, and had thus in some sort betrayed them.

Well, the poor defenceless Church has borne the brunt of it, and I see in it the strength and unity of Churchmen. An hostile account in one of the papers says, 'High and Low Church have joined, being set on rejecting Mr. Peel.'

I am glad to say I have seen no ill-humour anywhere. We have been merry all through it.

TO HIS MOTHER.

March 13, 1829.

What a scribbler I am become! But the fact is my mind is so full of ideas in consequence of this important event, and my views have so much enlarged and expanded, that in justice to myself I ought to write a volume.

We live in a novel era—one in which there is an advance towards universal education. Men have hitherto depended on others, and especially on the clergy, for religious truth;

now each man attempts to judge for himself. Now, without meaning of course that Christianity is in itself opposed to free inquiry, still I think it *in fact* at the present time opposed to the particular form which that liberty of thought has now assumed. Christianity is of faith, modesty, lowliness, subordination; but the spirit at work against it is one of latitudinarianism, indifferentism, and schism, a spirit which tends to overthrow doctrine, as if the fruit of bigotry and discipline—as if the instrument of priestcraft. All parties seem to acknowledge that the stream of opinion is setting against the Church. I do believe it will ultimately be separated from the State, and at this prospect I look with apprehension—(1) because all revolutions are awful things, and the effect of this revolution is unknown; (2) because the upper classes will be left almost religionless; (3) because there will not be that security for sound doctrine without change which is given by Act of Parliament; (4) because the clergy will be thrown on their congregations for voluntary contributions.

It is no reply to say that the majesty of truth will triumph, for man's nature is corrupt; also, even should it triumph, still this will only be ultimately, and the meanwhile may last for centuries. Yet I do still think there is a promise of preservation to the Church; and in its Sacraments, preceding and attending religious education, there are such means of Heavenly grace, that I do not doubt it will live on in the most irreligious and atheistical times.

Its enemies at present are: (1) The uneducated or partially educated mass in towns, whose organs are Wooler's, Carlisle's publications, &c. They are almost professedly deistical or worse. (2) The Utilitarians, political economists, useful knowledge people—their organs the 'Westminster Review,' the 'London University,' &c. (3) The Schismatics in and out of the Church, whose organs are the 'Eclectic Review,' the 'Christian Guardian,' &c. (4) The Baptists, whose system is consistent Calvinism—for, as far as I can see, Thomas Scott, &c., are inconsistent, and such inconsistent men would in times of commotion split and go over to this side or that. (5) The high circles in London. (6) I might add the political indifferentists, but I do not know enough to speak, like men who join Roman Catholics on one hand and Socinians on the other. Now you must not understand me as speaking harshly of individuals; I am speaking of bodies and principles.

And now I come to another phenomenon : the talent of the day is against the Church. The Church party (visibly at least, for there may be latent talent, and great times give birth to great men) is poor in mental endowments. It has not activity, shrewdness, dexterity, eloquence, practical power. On what, then, does it depend ? On prejudice and bigotry.

This is hardly an exaggeration ; yet I have good meaning and one honourable to the Church. Listen to my theory. As each individual has certain instincts of right and wrong antecedently to reasoning, on which he acts—and rightly so —which perverse reasoning may supplant, which then can hardly be regained, but, if regained, will be regained from a different source—from reasoning, not from nature—so, I think, has the world of men collectively. God gave them truths in His miraculous revelations, and other truths in the unsophisticated infancy of nations, scarcely less necessary and divine. These are transmitted as 'the wisdom of our ancestors,' through men—many of whom cannot enter into them, or receive them themselves—still on, on, from age to age, not the less truths because many of the generations through which they are transmitted are unable to prove them, but hold them, either from pious and honest feeling (it may be), or from bigotry or from prejudice. That they are truths it is most difficult to prove, for great men alone can prove great ideas or grasp them. Such a mind was Hooker's, such Butler's ; and, as moral evil triumphs over good on a small field of action, so in the argument of an hour or the compass of a volume would men like Brougham, or, again, Wesley, show to far greater advantage than Hooker or Butler. Moral truth is gained by patient study, by calm reflection, silently as the dew falls—unless miraculously given—and when gained it is transmitted by faith and by 'prejudice.' Keble's book is full of such truths, which any Cambridge man might refute with the greatest ease.

To his Sister Harriett.

March 16, 1829.

I am continuing in fact my letter to my Mother. Well, then, taking the state of parties in the country as it is, I look upon the granting of the Catholic claims not so much in itself as in the principle and sentiments of which it is an indication. It is carried by indifference, and by hostility to the Church.

I do not see how this can be denied. Not that it is not a momentous measure in itself; it is certainly an alteration in our Constitution, and, though I am used to think the country has not much to dread from Romanistic opinions (the danger seeming to be on the side of infidelity), yet there is a general impression, which Blanco White's book confirms, that infidelity and Romanism are compatible, or rather connected with each other. Moreover, it is agreed on all hands that the Emancipation will endanger the Irish Protestant Church; some even say it must ultimately fall.

All these things being considered, I am clearly in *principle* an anti-Catholic; and, if I do not oppose the Emancipation, it is only because I do not think it expedient, perhaps possible, so to do. I do not look for the settlement of difficulties by the measure; they are rather begun by it, and will be settled with the downfall of the Established Church. If, then, I am for Emancipation, it is only that I may take my stand against the foes of the Church on better ground, instead of fighting at a disadvantage.

That Emancipation is necessary now I think pretty clear, because the intelligence of the country will have it. Almost all who have weight by their talent or station prefer, of the alternatives left to us, concession, to an Irish war. But that the anti-Catholic party, who have by far the majority of number, should have been betrayed by its friends suddenly, craftily, and that the Government should have been bullied by Mr. O'Connell into concessions, is most deplorable. Perhaps there are circumstances in the background of which we know nothing. I have thought, perhaps, the Duke wants to have the energies of the country free and ready for a Russian war.

I do not reckon Pusey or Denison among our opponents, because they were strong for concession beforehand; and Pusey, I know, thought most highly of Mr. Peel's integrity and generosity.

REV. JOHN KEBLE TO REV. J. H. NEWMAN.

March 28, 1829.

In good earnest I do not repent, nor can I imagine anything, humanly speaking, at all capable of making me repent, of the line I took in the late election; except, indeed, that Sir Robert [Inglis] were to fight a duel, which, however, I *can* hardly imagine.

I do repent of some unkind thoughts and words which I fear I was guilty of at first towards Mr. Peel, and it is my expression of this feeling to one or two correspondents which, I presume, has won for me the most undeserved honour of being enrolled among the new converts. . . .

On moral grounds, therefore, I am disposed to respect and admire him; but on political grounds I am more and more pleased that he was not elected. To say the truth, I never wish to see a Minister of State or leader of a party representing the University again. I had rather have a straight-forward country gentleman.

J. H. N. TO HIS MOTHER.

March 29, 1829.

They wish me to go into the Schools again. I have refused it point-blank and unconditionally.

I must have tired you about the Catholic question. The Duke, even though right in his policy itself, seems to be acting quite unjustifiably in passing the measure against the loud and decided voice of the nation. However admirable it may be in a great captain, it is unworthy of an honest statesman. The people have been betrayed by those in whom they confided. The forced submission, too, of the Lords to the Commons is an alarming precedent.

Mr. Newman has spoken in his Memoir of his relations with Dr. Lloyd. The reader will recall the description given of him in his lecture-room. The following letter shows how warm his feelings were towards him personally.

TO HIS SISTER HARRIETT.

June 4, 1829.

We were much alarmed about the Bishop of Oxford (Lloyd) about ten days before his death. You may suppose Pusey is in a good deal of distress. I do not doubt that vexation and anxiety had much to do with his (Lloyd's) illness. He had all the odium of Mr. Peel upon him. His speech in the House got him into trouble, though as far as the *argument* is concerned he seemed to me to be quite right. He has been assaulted in the papers continually, and in a brutal way, beside the coldness of private friends, and, as I know, the anonymous attacks in the shape of letters addressed to him. Pusey's appointment, moreover, was made matter for abusing him, and perhaps Pusey's book.

His death shocked me much ; it must most men. Apparently in sound and robust health, with the certainty of the noblest preferment before him, probably the Archbishopric of York. No one could tell what his complaint was—he had a violent cough, which they thought the whooping-cough, and his lungs were found inflamed after death ; but he also had a bilious fever for certain, and others speak of other complaints. He took so little care of his health by exercise, that I do not wonder at his constitution giving way when attacked suddenly and violently.

I had the greatest esteem, respect, and love for him as a most warm-hearted, frank, vigorous-minded and generous man. His kindness for me I cannot soon forget. He brought me forward, made me known, spoke well of me, and gave me confidence in myself. I have before my mind various pictures of what passed in his lecture-room ; how he used to fix his eyes on me when he was pleased, and never put his Ch. Ch. friends unduly forward. I wish he ever had been aware how much I felt his kindness.

Oriel Fellows of mark of the third and fourth decade of this century have been made known to the reader through the portraiture of one of their number. It has startled the Editor to find the following sketch of the artist himself in the first promise and blossom of his youth. The reader will remember that Mr. Newman, in writing this letter, was addressing a late Fellow of Oriel.

REV. J. H. NEWMAN TO REV. S. RICKARDS.

April 28, 1829.

I do not expect to finish this by post-time ; but here goes. You are a cunning fellow to write me a letter just before our election. Well, I understand your meaning, so I tell you we have elected two Oriel men, *nomine* Mozley and Christie. The particulars of the election I will tell you when we meet, should I recollect them at that time. In the meantime know, in brief, that I never was at so perplexing and anxious an election, though all in which I have been concerned have been important ones.

I am persuaded we have done what we ought to do. Mozley, if he turns out according to his present promise, will be one of the most surprising men we shall have numbered in our lists (*ut apud Orielensem Orielensis de Orielensi aliquid jactem*); it will be some time doubtless before he comes to maturity. He is not quick or brilliant, but deep, meditative, clear in thought, and imaginative. His $\eta\theta os$ is admirable, and during his residence with us he has conducted himself unblamably; he is amiable and, withal, entertaining in parlance, and, to sum up all, somewhat eccentric at present in some of his notions. And now you will confess that I have given you a full description. His standing was quite a chance, and connected with some interesting circumstances too minute for a letter.

The excitement of the election over, Mr. Newman returned with freshened appetite to the course of reading to which he had devoted himself.

TO HIS SISTER HARRIETT.

June 25, 1829.

I am so hungry for Irenæus and Cyprian I long for the vacation.

On leaving Brighton, July 21, the family party settled for the Long Vacation at Horspath, Mr. Newman riding in to Oxford in the morning and returning to dinner. Both at Horspath and Oxford there was music. 'Woodgate's piano' was sent to Horspath. Quintets, in which Blanco White took a part, are often mentioned. 'Henry Wilberforce' had lodgings near, and read with Mr. Newman. 'S. Wilberforce' came over from Checkendon. It was an harmonious period, that might well live in the memory of all concerned in it, and perhaps raise gloomy contrasts as time went on.

The first letter preserved from Newman to Hurrell Froude shows the interest of the two friends in the Tutorship, and the harmony of their opinions in the conduct of their office:

REV. J. H. NEWMAN TO REV. R. H. FROUDE.

August 15, 1829.

... He [N.B. a youth examined for entrance] is at present a youth somewhat unformed in manner, *rusticior paulo*; but I am somehow not displeased with such men. For, though they come up quizzes somewhat, they form sound men in these bad days, and I liked the ἦθος of the youth, though there was something odd in his exterior. I have also entered for you one of two brothers, by name ———. They are frank youths. They are to be gentlemen commoners, which I could not help, and, to tell the truth, if we can get gentlemen commoners to *our taste*, I do not know why they should be sent elsewhere, where they will want the sound instruction and pastoral care of Adam de Brome. They will not, I am sure, do us discredit. They come with a very high character from Eton. I wish I could speak of another youth as favourably, who, I fear, will give us much trouble. I *could* not pluck him; but he is only just so much prepared as to neglect his lectures if he has a mind.

Mozley[1] just now made his appearance in my rooms, having arrived for a few weeks' hermitage here. ... Dornford was, on the whole, I think, pleased with what he saw in Ireland, but did not see much, and was disappointed in the Irish character (its wit, I believe). I like what he says as far as it goes. He met some very clever Irish lads (Roman Catholics) who knew a great deal about their own tenets, and argued well. He seems to think a reformation to Protestantism quite chimerical, and likes the idea of a gradual improvement in the Roman Catholic system itself. This is Arnold's system too, bigot! And why it is not a good one I do not know.

You prophesied ill of the weather, yet for enjoyment it has been excellently well adapted; except the last day or two: I sleep at Horspath, ride in here to breakfast, and ride back to dinner, and get wet through (yesterday, for instance) now and then. I am doing nothing, *i.e.* recovering arrears. I have been from four to six hours at it daily, and have not done. While I am about it I shall go through all my papers and letters, burn and arrange, and by the end of the vacation be quite comfortable; but as to the Fathers *ne hilum quidem*.

[1] Thomas Mozley, elected Fellow of Oriel April 1829.

I *must*, in the course of time, give up the tuition and be a gentleman, or, rather, a Fellow. [N.B.—I meant (as I was wont to hold) that a Fellow ought not to be a mere tutor, but take a substantial place as a student, writer, &c.]

REV. E. B. PUSEY, D.D., TO REV. J. H. NEWMAN.

1829.

I have sent the first five chapters of my book, including Inspiration of the Fathers, to the press. There are some parts which I want you much to see, especially one in which, *à propos* of Irenæus, I have made some observations (I believe, in your spirit) on the Inspiration of the Church ; and, as if justifying Irenæus, have said that there was nothing harsh in supposing that those who wilfully, &c., separated from the Church, excluded themselves from some of the benefits intended by God for us, since some can only, it appears, be thus conveyed ; and I have said proof might be brought from the partial manner in which Christianity has generally been embraced by separatist bodies. What think you of this ? I shall send them in hopes that you will criticise freely that others may not severely.

The 'Morning Star' [his little child Lucy] longs to shine upon you, although her rays are sometimes, and not unfrequently, watery.

REV. J. H. NEWMAN TO REV. R. H. FROUDE.

September 11, 1829.

Much as you boast of your situation on the water, and justly, yet I doubt after all whether it is finer than the inland Shotover. The weather indeed has been sad, but the lights most exquisite. I never saw tints half so enchanting. Certainly rain brings with it this compensation.

I wrote first to Robert Wilberforce, and since he on the whole declines, I write to you to know whether you feel at liberty to join me [in the care of my parish] ; at least can you propose any one ? . . .

I mean ultimately to divide the duty of St. Mary's from Littlemore, and wish the person I gain to take Littlemore at once, having nothing to do with St. Mary's. This ensuing audit I shall begin my stir about a chapel, which, when (if) built, will be his. Till then I fear I must confess he will be without public duty. As to the vacations, I do not suppose there will be much difficulty in arranging them. I would divide the residences with him. At least you can give your counsel.

[N.B.—The Provost was to the last opposed to dividing off Littlemore as a separate cure from St. Mary's. Crawley alone, who settled at Littlemore, was able at length, about 1843, to persuade him. He went and had a talk with him, I prophesying that he would not succeed. As the building a chapel tended to the separation of the cure, as an almost necessary ultimate result, I think I am right in saying that the Provost always steadily threw cold water on the building. It was not begun till 1835.]

I have been reading a good deal lately of the times of the first James and Charles, the Parliamentary debates of the day, &c., and am struck by the resemblance of those times and these—all times may be like all times for what I know.

My home party at Horspath has been delighted with the place in spite of the weather, and my Mother is much better. I am dismayed at the decreasing limits of the vacation, though this is most ungracious, considering it is at least an accident of full term to bring the Tutors together. It is a shame to rail at Oxford as so many of us do. We have all sorts of comforts and advantages there, yet it is fashionable to abuse it in the abstract.

I suppose Pusey's book will be out in the autumn [N.B. Answer to Rose]. His view of inspiration I think you will be much pleased with. It is one which has by fits and starts occurred to me. He has put it into system, and I do believe it is the old Orthodox doctrine. He holds the inspiration of the Church and of all good men, for example Socrates; and, indeed, I never could find out why Hooker is not to be called inspired.

REV. R. H. FROUDE TO REV. J. H. NEWMAN.

Keswick: September 27, 1829.

. . . I am very much gratified to find that you and Pusey take a view of inspiration which exactly (as far as I understand you) agrees with mine. I have got it written in a crude form, as it occurred to me when I first heard the subject canvassed; and shall have great satisfaction in talking it over with you. I hope Pusey may turn out High Church after all.

A propos of these last words, the following letter is given, written within the year 1829, but with no fuller date :

REV. E. B. PUSEY TO REV. J. H. NEWMAN.

I do not know how to thank you for all the trouble which you have taken. I wish I could do justice to the subject. . . . The notices, however, will be useful to me. In Beveridge I have found something to my purpose, though he is higher Church than I. . . .

H. W. WILBERFORCE, ESQ., TO REV. J. H. NEWMAN.

[Writing from his brother's.]

Checkendon: September 28, 1829.

I have given Sam your kind invitation to visit you at Horspath, and, as I expected, he values it most truly. To-morrow we intend to ride over. I hope we shall be there in time for your dinner. I hope when we have got Sam safe we may prevail on him to stay, instead of returning to the solitary home he has here. In the meantime there is no danger of my being idle, Sam being fully employed; so that Aristotle and Horace will profit rather than suffer by my day's delay.

On October 23, Mrs. Newman and her daughters moved to Mr. Dornford's cottage at Nuneham. It was a dreary wintry time. Before Christmas, snow lay thick on the ground and frost made slippery paths. The change was great from Horspath. The added chill of solitude told on the elder sister, whose letters also indicate that she could not go along with her brother in his growth of view, and possibly had some mistrust of the new influence which was telling upon him.

FROM HIS SISTER HARRIETT.

November 14.

We go on very quietly in these parts. . . . I hope you can give us a decent lengthened call. I should like a quarter of an hour's quiet talk with you.

. . . We have long since read your two sermons; they are

very High Church. I do not think I am near so High, and do not quite understand them yet.

As secretary of the Church Missionary Society, to which office he had been elected March 9 of this year 1829, Mr. Newman's mind was much occupied with the system on which it was conducted. Early in the following year there are private entries on the subject, thus: 'Sketched letters about Church Missionary Society,' &c. The following letter, to the Rev. John Hill, Head of St. Edmund Hall, gives the first note of this dissatisfaction.

REV. J. H. NEWMAN TO REV. JOHN HILL.

December 1829.

I have just found that the sermons [1] preached at St. Ebbe's Church last Sunday, in aid of the funds of the Church Missionary Society, have been supposed to be authorised by the Oxford Association; and, considering that the doctrine reported to be contained in them is not at all in necessary connexion with that professed by the Church Missionary Society, I am anxious to consult with you [N.B.—He and I were the secretaries] about the propriety of adopting, if possible, some measure calculated to remove so erroneous an impression, and of introducing the subject to the meeting on Monday.

I have written at once, since I am not certain it will be in my power to call on you to-morrow, and I am unwilling that you should not be informed of my feeling on the subject as soon as possible.

REV. JOHN HILL, VICE-PRINCIPAL OF ST. EDMUND HALL, TO REV. J. H. NEWMAN.

December 12, 1829.

The collection on behalf of the Church Missionary Society at St. Ebbe's last Sunday, and the appointment of the preachers, originated in the minister of that parish; nor has the Society, I conceive, anything to do with either, except to view thankfully the contributions thus freely offered to its funds.

[1] By Bulteel and Sibthorp.

It is true that one of the preachers employed some expressions in his sermon which the other considered to be not altogether correct, who therefore felt it right to allude to the subject in the afternoon. But while it is open to the friends of each to converse with them on the subject according to their own judgment, surely the committee or secretaries of the Society are not authorised to interfere, as those opinions had no reference to the Society, nor were adduced as the sentiments of the Society. As to myself, I would not, on any account, allow myself to become a party to any measure which might appear like a disclaimer against either of the individuals in question. I should, on the contrary, deem such a proceeding totally inconsistent with Christian candour and love. Both the men are devoted servants of Christ, and actuated in an eminent degree by love of God and man—as their whole conduct and spirit testify. Both are, as to the general character of their preaching, faithfully announcing the Gospel of Jesus Christ. With regard to the point of difference between them, I conceive (so far as I can judge from the reports I have received of their sermons, and from my previous knowledge of their sentiments) that Mr. Bulteel is most correct, because more clearly adhering to the spirit and language of Scripture; yet I entertain at the same time a very high regard for the piety and usefulness of Mr. Sibthorp; nor can I believe that the difference between them on the particular subject in question is so great as some casual expressions may have led some to suppose.

Mr. Newman's further action towards the Missionary Society belongs to the following year, 1830, but it was one of the questions occupying his mind at this time, along with all the business his bursarship brought upon him at the close of the year.

In all pecuniary matters involving responsibility Mr. Newman was rigidly exact—enforcing punctilious promptitude and accuracy on juniors working under him. That in his College office (as treasurer) he gave satisfaction may be gathered from the following playful recognition of his services.

Rev. W. James to Rev. J. H. Newman.

December 3, 1829.

'Two hundred pounds and possibilities is good gifts,' to use the phrase of a revered and learned Welshman of old—Sir Hugh Evans. The opening of your letter led me to expect something very different—more in accordance with the state of the times; so that when I came to 200*l.* actually put to my account at Hoare's, I felt as if my most sanguine expectations had been far outdone. And then came the 'possibilities.' If you were to treat us so every year I shall vote that you be made perpetual treasurer. Far from thinking you late in writing—knowing something of your engagements—I did not expect to hear before the end of term, and now you have so amply satisfied whatever cravings I had as to possibilities, I shall wait with the utmost patience.

With all these cares and duties on his hands, the last words of the year show a sense of pressure.

J. H. N. to H. E. N.

Oriel College: *December* 31, 1829.

I have nothing to say except that, if I had but one-tenth part to do of what I really ought in various ways, I should have quite enough.

The Christmas vacation was mainly spent at Nuneham with his Mother and sisters, Mr. Newman walking from and to Oxford day after day.

The passages in brackets occurring in the following letter are, as the reader has already been told, comments or explanations introduced by the writer of the letter in the course of copying at an after date. The transcripts were made in 1860, and the passages in brackets would be added in the course of transcription.

Rev. J. H. Newman to Rev. R. H. Froude.

Oriel College: *January* 9, 1830.

I have taken it into my head to write you a letter, which, if it be merely a well-wisher for a new decennium, will have its object; but I shall attempt to impart to you my thoughts and remarks on various subjects; and, first, I am glad to see that the Bishop of London [Blomfield], in sermons just published, maintains the propriety and expedience of the Athanasian Creed—this is important—and so does Bishop Mant, in a twaddling (so to say) publication. Now, though there are parts of the Creed I would willingly see omitted, if it could be done silently, and could not defend if attacked, yet, as to cut it out would be to lose the damnatory clauses, and to curtail it even would be to flatter the vain conceit of the age, I am heartily pleased at this firmness of the Bishop's, and notice to you that you may conceive worthier thoughts of him.

[I can explicitly state what I meant in this passage. One of my first declared departures from Whately's teaching, who, among other views, leant to Sabellianism, was in a sermon I preached in College Chapel on Easter Day, 1827. Hawkins, Whately, and Blanco White all asked to read it afterwards, and none liked it. I have it still, with their pencil comments upon it. It took the view of the doctrine of the Holy Trinity which I afterwards (in 1831-1832) found to be the Ante-Nicene view, especially on the point of the 'subordination of the Son,' as Bull (whom at that time I had not read) brings it out in one of his chapters. This view, I considered, was taken in the Nicene Creed, and I thought there was a marked contrast between it and the statements of the Athanasian Creed on the sacred doctrine. Of course, to this day I hold, and must ever hold, there *is* a difference of statement, though it is a difference of statement only, not of sense or substance. What I meant when I wrote the above was that the Athanasian Creed was written in a less scriptural style than the Nicene. For instance, one of my objections was this : that the Athanasian Creed says that 'the Son is equal to the Father.' Now this either means 'equal' in His *Personality* or 'equal' in His Divinity to the Father; but in neither alternative is the expression correct; for in His Divinity He is not equal to the Father, but the *same* as the Father; and in His Personality He is not *equal*, but *subordinate* to the Father.]

I am pleased, moreover, to see that the 'British Critic,' which is under his influence, not only contained an article on the Union of Church and State (as you know, supposed to be written by him) and defending it on the *right*, not the

Warburtonian, grounds, but he has had besides *two* articles lauding Laud, which is very different from the 'Spirit of the Age,' and not at all in the spirit of the poor 'Remembrancer,'[1] which, in its last number, has offered to give up the Cross in Baptism.

I have doubt whether we *can* consider our King as a proprietor of land on the old Tory theory. The rightful heir was lost in the Revolution; then the nation took [usurped] the property [proprietorship] of the island [time has sanctioned their violence] and gave it to William, and then to George, on *certain conditions* . . . that of being chief *magistrate*. Has not the Constitution since that time been essentially a republic? Is it not our duty to submit to being accounted such? though we ought to make a stand against farther innovation?

Ogilvie wished me to lend him Arnold's Sermons. I am glad to tell you he returned the book with an expression of much satisfaction and agreeable surprise. Some sermons, of course, he objected to; but 'the impression was decidedly favourable.' [N.B.—This is an allusion, I think, to a donnish phrase, used by and to the Provost, in the Collections Tower, of the undergraduates, in their presence.] I have read some more of them; one cannot but agree with Ogilvie in opinion.

If I possibly can I shall vote for the new Examination Statute. I cannot but fear, if it be rejected, men will be appointed [*i.e.* as examiners] who are likely to make great innovations, losing sight completely of those old principles which, in drawing up this, the Provost has kept in view. Cardwell, Mills, Burton, Short, Hampden, &c.—would they not exclude Aristotle, and bring in modern subjects? I should like to make Modern History, or Hebrew, &c. &c., necessary for the M.A. degree; and, strange to say, any Master of the Schools might *require* something of the sort (so I am told) without new statute, merely by [the University's] omitting to suspend the Dispensation for Determination. [N.B.—Among my papers are the answers in 1830-31, which I gave to a Committee, appointed by Heads of Houses, which had proposed questions to the Tutors.]

I have thought vows [*e.g.* of Celibacy] are evidences of

---

[1] The reader of to-day must be reminded that, of the periodicals here mentioned, the *British Critic* did not come into the hands of the party connected with the Movement till 1838, and the *Christian Remembrancer*—at the date of this letter a Monthly—not till 1844.

want of faith [N.B. trust]. Why should we look to the morrow ? It will be given us to do what is our duty as the day comes ; to bind duty by forestalment is to lay up manna for seven days ; it will corrupt us. In a very different way, still quite a parallel, as exhibiting a *want of faith* [*i.e.* trust] *vid.* Origen's conduct instead of a vow.

With my sister's help I have been adjusting Keble's poems to Bennett's chants, and find some of them suit admirably. It is the only kind of music which brings out their sweetness without overpowering it.

Qy. What is meant by the right of private judgment ? The *duty* I understand : but no one can *help* another's thinking in private : *vid.* dialogue between Rex Pentheus and Bacchus in Horace.[1] [N.B.—I suppose 'the right of private judgment' means 'the right of *holding*, expressing, maintaining, *advocating*, proselytising to our private judgment and decisions.']

The following letter illustrates what is said in the 'Apologia' (p. 45)—'Also I used irony in conversation when matter-of-fact men would not see what I meant.'

REV. R. I. WILBERFORCE TO REV. J. H. NEWMAN.

January 13, 1830.

Cunningham [of Harrow] is to be at Oxford to-night, and I wanted to inform you that he has got a strange notion of your dialogue with him, and has been propagating the same. He says you asserted there was no use, or next to none, in preaching under any circumstances ; that you took a lower view of it than any person he had met with, &c. In case you meet him I think you should be careful not to let drop anything that can be taken hold of.

REV. J. H. NEWMAN TO J. W. BOWDEN, ESQ.

Oriel College: January 16, 1830.

I regret to say I am kept here till Term begins—my principal Vacation engagements being a most odious Bursarship, which, besides teasing me by an inconceivable number of little businesses in Term-time, has hitherto tied me especially to this place in Vacation as the only leisure time for its greater

[1] *Epist.* i. 16. 73.

duties. It is very well to have such business, when it is one's main business ; but as a business by the way it is insupportable. It has, I believe, been more than anything else the cause of my continued indisposition ; and now deprives me of a pleasure which I would put second to no other that could be mentioned.

We are to have a three months' winter, I suppose. It has been my practice to walk of a day to Nuneham to dinner, and then back in the morning to breakfast. I have been more at home since July than I ever have since I came to Oxford. Shotover is, in our minds, quite a classical place ; especially as Milton once lived near it, before he was contaminated by evil times and the waywardness of a proud heart ; and King Charles and his Bishops seemed to rise before us along the old road which leads from Oxford to Cuddesdon. We have been paying a good deal of attention to the history of those times, and I am confirmed as a dull staid Tory unfit for these smart times.

Which way is the world marching ? and how *we* shall be left behind when the movement is ordered by the word of command ! The *Times* now begins to vote the King's office an abuse and a job. But this is a wise talk about nothing at all, if the future is but a shadow to us, as it is.

The Mr. Wilson to whom the following relates was subsequently President of Trinity.

To his Mother.

January 26, 1830.

Mr. Wilson's [of Trinity] accident was of a frightful description. On Monday he was cleaning his gun, when it went off and shot him through the left wrist. He was obliged to have it immediately amputated. Indeed, they told him unless the operation took place he could not live five hours, so shattered were the bones. What made it still more distressing was that, after it was over, a second amputation was found necessary higher up.

Again :

I called on Wilson on Saturday. He was very composed and cheerful, up and moving about as usual. He bears his misfortune with a serenity of mind which to me is perfectly incomprehensible. I feel quite ashamed of myself; for I seemed much more distressed at it than he was.

Mr. Newman was now passing a pamphlet on the Church Missionary Society, of which he was secretary, through the press.

TO HIS SISTER J. C. N.

Oriel College: January 29.

The printers are so tedious I shall not have the letter *out* till Monday. I am printing 500 copies, and if it takes (which I do not expect, but take the chance of), I shall send it campaigning all over the country. I shall make Woodgate, perhaps our friend Mr. Rickards, distribute it in Kent, and a Mr. Bramston[1] (you may have heard me mention) will, I hope, distribute it in Essex. I shall send it to Davison at Worcester, and Benson in town, and to the Bishops of London, Lincoln and Llandaff—perhaps Exeter. Perhaps the Bishop of Ferns! Ha ha!—are you not laughing? I am. There is a fine fricassee of fowl before the eggs are laid. By-the-bye, Mr. B. told me that the Bishop of London has informed him that *his only* objection to joining the Society is the existence of public meetings. Well, but what am I doing in Oxford? Why, I have sent it (*i.e.* shall) to Bishop, Archdeacon, Dean, two canons, and all parochial ministers in Oxford; to Vice-Chancellor, Proctors, ten Heads of Houses, and about thirty-five M.A.'s—in all sixty-three persons. Now, if it be a silly thing, why, I am exposing myself and doing what is unsafe; but one must run risks to do good, and fortune favours the bold; so I must hug myself if no one else will hug me.

In the 'Chronological Notes' is the entry: '*February* 1.— Sent round my printed letter about the Church Missionary Society.' Mr. Newman's friends wrote their thoughts on it. Mr. Bramston (once described by Mr. Newman as 'a mild Evangelical') says:

[1] Afterwards Dean of Winchester.

REV. JOHN BRAMSTON TO REV. J. H. NEWMAN.

February 18, 1830

Worthless as my testimony may be, I cannot help being convinced that you are right. It is important to put on record (even if it goes no further) a Churchman's apology for a Society which is considered by all unthinking and careless persons as decidedly sectarian. Tell me whether you have any favourable results to communicate at Oxford . . . and whether you are likely to have any public meetings this year.

In this part of the country it is joined by those clergymen only who keep aloof from mixed society, and who, from that circumstance, are viewed with a degree of ill-will by worldly people. I should like, however, to put your suggestions before some friends of mine if you have any to spare.

A friend of a different school, mindful of the late defeat of Mr. Peel, for the reason embodied in the letter, affects a cynical turn in his sympathy.

REV. H. A. WOODGATE (FELLOW OF ST. JOHN'S) TO REV. J. H. NEWMAN.

February 22, 1830.

. . . I have sent one of your letters [on the Church Missionary Society] to the Bishop of Rochester, to Archdeacon Pott, and have put another in the way of reaching Mr. Norris of Hackney, who, I find, is a Churchman in a better sense of the word, and not like Lord Eldon, whom he disapproves of entirely, considered as a friend of the Church. I have withheld the author's name as you requested me, but told them there was no cause for alarm, as he was one who, however he might once have betrayed symptoms of sectarianism, or be called Evangelical, was now as staunch a Churchman as Addison's landlord, who, when he could not find time to go to church, headed mobs to pull down meeting-houses ; that you drank Church and King every day in a bumper after dinner [N.B.—All this is a cut at my joining the opposition against Sir R. Peel in 1829, the writer being in Sir R. Peel's committee], voted for Sir R. Inglis, stood neutral on petitions, and sang 'God save the King,' and 'A health to Old England, the King and the Church,' every night after supper.

I perfectly agree with you on theory [*i.e.* the Letter], but when I remember how many societies of this nature owe their origin or increase to sectarian bodies, who are only called into existence by the indifference or neglect of Churchmen, I should almost fear a decline of their prosperity if taken entirely out of the former and placed in the hands of the latter exclusively. Although visibly improving, still the Church, or at least that portion of it—those on whom the care of these things would then devolve, seems often to paralyse by the frigidity of its touch any institution that comes in its way. However, if it is a positive duty, we must not hesitate, &c.

In the 'Chronological Notes' is this entry:

March 8.—Turned out of the Secretaryship of the Church Missionary Society because of my pamphlet.[1]

Circumstances gave this incident a marked place in Mr. Newman's memory. A letter on the subject, written at this date, by a friend of Mr. Newman's, may interest the reader.

THOMAS MOZLEY TO HIS ELDEST SISTER.

March 14, 1830.

. . . Newman, as I forgot to tell you in my last, has been completely discomfited in the matter of the Missionary Society. His proposal to put an end to public meetings was carried in the committee, which consists, I believe, only of clergymen in offices, and such laymen as they, the subscribers at large, choose to appoint. But last Monday, when there was a general Meeting to elect officers, when they generally re-elect the old ones and just fill up vacancies, he was ousted by an immense majority, Bulteel and his satellites and half Edmund Hall being in attendance. He has, to be sure, given the Low Church party great provocation, beyond his proceedings in the committee, by writing and sending to all the resident clergy of Oxford (University) a pamphlet setting forth on what principles a good Churchman might join a Society which admitted Dissenters, and by what management the Society might be exclusively attached to the Church, working under episcopal jurisdiction : thus, on the one hand, subjecting to

[1] A statement of the facts of the case, written by Mr. Newman, will be found in vol. ii. of *The Via Media of the Anglican Church*.

proper discipline and rule a good deal of misguided power and zeal ; and, on the other, presenting to the Church of England, which has all along been very deficient on this very point, an engine made ready to her hands. And this to be effected merely by taking advantage of the opening offered to them by the Society itself, making all clergymen who choose to subscribe members of the committee, although, of course, a great secession of the Low Church party was to be expected. Very few indeed approve of this plan, or think it practicable ; but Newman is not a man to be deterred by temporary failures. He is, indeed, better calculated than any man I know, by his talents, his learning, by his patience and perseverance, his conciliatory *manners*, and the friends he can employ in the cause—of whom I hope to be one—to release the Church of England from her present oppressed and curtailed condition.

The following letter from Mr. Rickards may be given as containing a scheme of reform in Church temporalities put forward at this date. The Preachership of the Temple had been proposed to Mr. Rickards.

REV. S. RICKARDS TO REV. J. H. NEWMAN.

Ulcombe : May 26, 1830.

Your letter relating to the Temple I considered well. Upon close and particular inquiry I ascertained that we could not live in or near London without income ; and that if I did take it, it must be with the earnest hope of speedy preferment —such a hope you will not wonder I did not choose to entertain ; I thought it neither a safe nor a worthy guest in a preacher's house ; so I told Benson [Master of the Temple] the reason, and passed the matter by. I did this with sorrow, and after deliberation ; because I found the congregation was remarkably well disposed towards me, and many even expressed a strong wish that I should be settled among them.

Yesterday, at our visitation, the Archdeacon told us mournfully that measures are about to be taken to provide for the better maintenance of the clergy who have only one *small* living, by making them the only persons eligible to Prebends in the different cathedrals. If the information is correct, you and I may stand a chance of a *great* living ; and the marvellous sight will be seen of greedy men running after little ones.

It will be a pleasant scene enough to watch a man actually manœuvred into a good benefice, and very angry about it without daring to say so.

I think Benson knows something about Mr. Rose, and feels an interest in looking to see whether he will get out of his scrape [with Pusey ? – J. H. N.] or flounder about in it. I guess that he has a higher value for Rose's talents than I have ; but I know hardly anything about the matter, except that I wish somebody would be so good as to convince me that he is a very first-rate man, because I find it mighty inconvenient to stir among Cambridge men and not to think him so. But let him be what he may in this respect, from all that is said it seems he will be a bishop before long, and so, I hope, he is all I am told he is.

To this letter is appended the following note :

Here Rickards wrote hastily. I am a bad hand at criticising men, but the admiration and love I had for Rose were inspired, I think, by his elevation of mind, his unflagging zeal, his keen appreciation of what was noble and saintly, his insight into character, and his vigorous eloquence.—J. H. N.

J. H. N. TO H. E. N.

June 9, 1830.

Yesterday I withdrew my name from the Bible Society in a note to Macbride, who took it very kindly. I said that the objections that caused me to retire from it were felt by me as such when I first subscribed to it, but that then I viewed them as indirect, not necessary, consequences, and that the more men who felt them subscribed, the greater prospect there was of their being obviated ; but now, on the contrary, I viewed them as practically direct, and there being no *principle* recognised by the Society on which Churchmen could fall back and take their stand, no accession of members of the Church could tend to remove them.

REV. E. B. PUSEY, D.D., TO REV. J. H. NEWMAN.

June 14, 1830.

I have just seen Burton, who wishes to explain himself that he did not intend to ask you whether *he* should appoint you, but whether you would undertake the office [I suppose of

Select Preacher] should the Board appoint you. Burton
wishes to see you also about another office—the second class
of Select Preacher. [N.B.—I think this was a plan, never
carried out, of University sermons through the year (the plan
was rejected by Convocation, June 25, 1830), in which the
Vicar of St. Mary's naturally would take part.—J. H. N.]
You will be glad to hear that since I saw you we have had a
little son born.

J. H. N. TO HIS MOTHER.

June 18, 1830.

It is at length settled that the Provost gives us no more
pupils—us three (R. Wilberforce, Froude, and me)—and we
die gradually with our existing pupils. This to me personally
is a delightful arrangement; it will naturally lessen my
labours, and at length reduce them within bearable limits,
without at once depriving me of resources which I could not
but reckon upon while they lasted. But for the College I
think it a miserable determination. [Adding, a day or two
after :] Now that I shall have more time I am full of projects what I shall do. The Fathers arise again full before me.
This vacation I should not wonder if I took up the study of
the Modern French Mathematics.

Riding from Oxford to Brighton, on a visit to his Mother,
he writes on his way thither :

Guildford: June 30, 1830.

I arrived here at nine this morning. I am philosophising,
but I have not yet brought out my speculations enough to say
on what subject. Is not that the meaning of *musing*—namely,
thinking about something or other, we cannot tell what?
Hence the word *music*, which suggests feelings without ideas,
and to *amuse*, which means to please without addressing the
reasoning powers. Now should this, as being unsealed, fall
into the hands, or rather eyes, of cab or coach man, what will
he think about it? Well, that is the very thing—I *told* you
I am musing.

If I do not come punctually to-morrow morning, consider
my horse is tired.

On his return journey he again writes to his Mother from
Guildford :

Guildford: July 15, 1830.

I am just returned from Horsham Church. I wish churches were open in every place that a traveller stopped at. I conjecture they were some centuries ago. Though we have gained more, we certainly have lost something by old Luther.

To his sister Harriett he gives his final experience of travel :

July 19, 1830.

My journey was prosperous. On the whole I lost five miles by error of the ways. There are no direction posts, the milestones are defaced, the labourers in the fields are deaf, and the few intelligent persons one meets have a strange way of correcting their senses by their reasoning faculty. By going 'straight on,' they mean going the 'right way.' I had two instances of this. In one case the left-hand road was the right one, but the man said ' go straight on.' I believe they habitually consider the road they know best the ' right road.'

In the following letter Mr. Newman talks of himself in a vein of melancholy not usual with him :

Oriel College: July 20, 1830.

My dear Rickards,— . . . I was amused by your speculations about myself, while I could not but be grateful for the interest you take in my proceedings. Sometimes I am in a humour to talk about myself easily, and if that were the case now, you should have the benefit or mischance of it ; but I am not in a communicable mood. I will but say it is now many years that a conviction has been growing upon me (say since I was elected here) that men did not stay at Oxford as they ought, and that it was my duty to have no plans ulterior to a college residence. To be sure, as I passed through a hundred miles of country just now in my way to and from Brighton, the fascination of a country life nearly overset me, and always does. It will indeed be a grievous temptation should a living ever be offered me, when now even a curacy has inexpressible charms. And I will not so far commit myself as to say it must be wrong to take one under all circumstances. Is it not vastly absurd my talking in this way, when I have no more chance of such preferment than of a living in the moon ? Well, but this is the only great temptation I fear, for as to other fascinations which might be more dangerous still,

I am pretty well out of the way of them; and at present I feel as if I would rather tear out my heart than lose it, though when once fairly caught, my views doubtless would change. Now you must not complain of this egotistical letter, for I have nothing else to fill my paper with. One thing I have earnestly desired for years, and I trust in sincerity—that I may never be rich; and I will add (though here I am more sincere at some times than at others) that I never may rise in the Church. The most useful men have not been the most highly exalted. Hooker and Hammond were simple presbyters. Nor have the most favoured been highest. St. Peter was neither the beloved disciple, nor did he labour more abundantly than they all, yet he was the President (at least for a time) of the Apostolic College. Men live after their death —they live not only in their writings or their chronicled history, but still more in that ἄγραφος μνήμη exhibited in a school of pupils who trace their moral parentage to them. As moral truth is discovered, not by reasoning, but by habituation, so it is recommended not by books, but by oral instruction. Socrates wrote nothing. Authorship is the second best way. How grand all this is, and how conducive to indolence and self-indulgence! I shall turn philosopher, rail at the world at large, and be content with a few friends who know me. Perhaps you went up with the University address to the King.

REV. J. H. NEWMAN TO REV. R. H. FROUDE.

July 28, 1830.

I was not at all unwilling for the College's sake that your brother should take his honours with us, and then be transplanted elsewhere.

We are speculating here on the issue of your undertaking to convey your horse down into Devonshire. We hope you are safe arrived, but no tidings have reached Oxford. The fine weather at length come is a time for speculation, you know. I have had many bright thoughts, and intended to communicate some, but they are departed—that is the worst of speculations. We hold them like Hæmon, ἐν ὑγραῖς ἀγκάλαις.[1] Perhaps I had better begin with facts.

[1] The words, though found in a fragment of Euripides (Fr. 836), do not occur in the *Antigone*. They may be a reminiscence of

ἐς δ' ὑγρὸν
ἀγκῶν' ἔτ' ἔμφρων παρθένον προσπτύσσεται.—Soph. *Antig.* 1236.

I knocked my horse up by over-despatch on my way down to Brighton—*i.e.* I took too long stages at first. The consequence was she came down the last morning, her knees quite uninjured, but my nose cut pretty deep with the silver of my glass. It seemed to promise a scar, but will be nothing. I shall leave off glasses in riding. So I finished by walking twenty-one miles in a broiling sun on a dusty road. By-the-bye, how neatly I have implied my tumble above as a matter of course! In my journey back I was more wary, and brought her home quite fresh.

When I was at home, I wrote out all that correspondence which I mean to be a document to my heirs; and I made a bold inroad into Trigonometry, and have this morning got through about a quarter of Hamilton's Conics. [N.B.—I was beginning a new course of mathematics by analytics and differentials; I had been more accustomed to geometrical proof, fluxions, Newton, &c.] I suspect I shall have little time for it now, what with Wood, Christie, parish, and other matters.

The Senior Proctor [Dornford] got great credit for his display at the presentation of the address. The King gave him an opportunity for an off-hand speech which is thought happy. 'Mr. Proctor,' he said, 'I hope you keep up discipline in your University'; to which Dornford replied, 'Yes, sir, *for* we inculcate the most loyal principles.' [This is the answer that Whately is so savage with.]

Robert Wilberforce comes in a fortnight's time. Mozley [T.] evanuit altogether. I am sure we *must not* say a word to make him believe we wish him to stay. It will spoil him; we must be αὐτάρκεις, and above such weakness. I think of setting up for a great man; it is the only way to be thought so. I have ever been too candid, and have in my time got into all sorts of scrapes. [N.B. (added at a later date)—How strange I should say so then, when the very words about my officious candour and my scrapes of afte years are continually in my thoughts now!] I shall learn wisdom rapidly now. Besides, men must have *their run*, if they are worth anything. M. is now roaming: if he is ever to come round, it is not by telling him to do so.

The French are an awful people How the world is set upon calling evil good, good evil! This Revolution [ending in abdication of Charles X.] seems to me the triumph of irreligion. What an absurdity it is in men saying, 'The times will not admit of an establishment,' as if the 'times' were anything else than the people. It is the people who will not admit of it. Yet coxcombs wag their heads and think they have got at the root of the matter when they assure one that the times, the spirit of the times, makes it chimerical to attempt continuing the Catholic Church in France. The effect of this miserable French affair will be great in England.

On the prospect of an election to the Poetry Professorship, R. H. Froude writes:

August 1, 1830.

. . . From several conversations with Keble, I am sure he would, on the whole, like to be Poetry Professor, if he could become so without canvassing, and if the College would send out his cards. He retains a great affection for the classics, and wishes that he had some business to spend time on them. He also thinks that a connexion of high $\mathring{\eta}\theta o\varsigma$ with poetical feeling might be useful, and has a great fancy for illustrating the theory out of Virgil, Lucretius, &c.

The following letter tells its own tale of one member of the home circle of a nature and a temper so difficult as to be a life-long trial to all concerned.

To his Mother.

August 27, 1830.

My head, hands, and heart are all knocked up with the long composition I have sent Charles. I have sent him twenty-four closely-written foolscap pages all about nothing. He revived the controversy we had five years ago. I have sent him what is equal to nine sermons.

F.'s departure has had its sufficient share in knocking me up, and much more will it, I fear, discompose you and my sisters. Still, it is our great relief that God is not extreme to mark what is done amiss, that He looks at the motives, and accepts and blesses in spite of incidental errors. What, indeed, else would become of any of us? Frank so completely put himself into His hands that we can have no fear for him, whatever becomes of his projects.

My hand is so tired and my head so dull, you may excuse my leaving off.

The following letter to his sister gives an insight into Mr. Newman's manner of literary work; with certain rules, to which probably he always adhered. It was a natural wish on her part to help him in the mechanical part of his literary labours, but he shows that no such work was with him mechanical in the sense of the mind not sharing in it, and taking an active part.

To HIS SISTER J. C. N.

September 1830.

. . . First, with many thanks, it is impossible for you to assist me in the transcription of the folio pages. The rough copy is a riddle, besides that things strike me as I go on, so that I like to have the opportunity of reviewing myself. C.'s letter to me you might have written out, but here I found it an advantage to do so myself; it put me in so much clearer possession of his position and mine in contrast, than any reading could do: and I only regretted that I had not done so before answering him. My letter would have been, not in substance different, but more scientific. Be guided by me, if ever you get into controversy, whether in private or in (faugh!) the public prints, *write out* first the letter you are to answer. I shall always do it in future. Experience brings wisdom.

A letter to Froude at this date concludes:

. . . As for poor —— I am going to write him a letter, but I am desponding. All my plans fail. When did I ever succeed in any exertion for others? I do not say this in complaint, but really doubting whether I ought to meddle.

Added later:

[N.B.—It is remarkable to me to find myself making the very complaints then, thirty years ago, which are ever rising in my mind *now*. My sermon on Jeremiah, in Plain Sermons,[1] was written in 1829, 1830, or 1831.]

The following letter, in answer to an application for help in a projected Ecclesiastical History, again shows Mr. Newman's advocacy of thoroughness in all literary work.

[1] See *Parochial and Plain Sermons*, vol. viii.: 'Jeremiah a Lesson for the Disappointed.'

REV. J. H. NEWMAN TO REV. DR. JENKYNS.

I hardly know what answer to make to your inquiry without knowing more of particulars. For instance, what I feel most clear about is this: I never would undertake to write lightly on any subject which admits of being treated thoroughly. I think it is the fault of the day. Now this probably will be a great objection to my engaging in a professedly popular work. Not that it is necessary to compose a long treatise, but more time (I feel) ought to be given to the subject than is consistent with the dispatch of booksellers, who must sacrifice everything to regularity of publication and trimness of appearance. An Ecclesiastical History, for example, whether long or short, ought to be derived from the original sources, and not be compiled from the standard authorities. [My 'Arians' was the result of this application.—J. H. N.]

At the end of the Long Vacation of 1830 Mrs. Newman and her daughters left Brighton and settled at Rose Hill, Iffley. This house—'Eaton's Cottage,' two cottages turned into one picturesque dwelling—was before long exchanged for Rose Bank, Iffley, where Mrs. Newman remained till her death in 1836. Some entries in the 'Chronological Notes' show the interest Mr. Newman felt in preparing Rose Hill, his Mother's cottage home. Other notices of the time have also their interest; sometimes telling much in little.

August 6.—Walked with Pusey and his wife to see the cottage at Rose Hill.

August 26.—Frank went for good [to Persia]. God guide us in His way!

September 13.—News came of poor Bennett's death by coach overturn. [The University's and my organist. A man of genius.] Walked with H. Wilberforce to Rose Hill to go over Eaton's Cottage.

September 30.—Walk with Froude to Rose Hill to inspect the furniture.

October 22.—My Mother and sisters came to Rose Hill, arriving about 4 P.M.

November 7.—Preached for Church Missionary Society St. Mary's collection, 16*l*. 11*s*. 6*d*.

November 9.—Introduced my sisters to the people at Littlemore.

November 12.—Dined with Provost to meet Mr. Wilberforce.
November 30.—St. Andrews; boys chanting for first time.
December 10.—Class paper came out. H. Wilberforce first and second.

The opening of 1831 found Mr. Newman 'weak and deaf' from overwork, also subject to want of sleep, with now and then sleepless nights; but ready for his pupils when Term began; for it will be remembered he did not give up those already his when the change in the tutorship came. The one absorbing public interest of 1831 was the Reform Bill. The following letter gives Mr. Newman's thoughts on the Church aspect of the question.

REV. J. H. NEWMAN TO J. W. BOWDEN, ESQ.

March 13, 1831.

I fully agree with you about the seriousness of the prospect we have before us, yet do not see what is to be done. The nation (*i.e.* numerically the πλῆθος) is for revolution. . . . They certainly have the physical power, and it is the sophism of the day to put religious considerations out of sight, and, forgetting there is any power above man's, to think that what man can do he may do with impunity.

I fear that petitions against Reform would but show the weakness of the Conservative party by the small number which could be got together. At all events, I believe the University has never come forward on questions purely political, or at least before others. Besides, the Church has for a long time lost its influence as a body—*Exoriatur!* Nor do I think it is in a humour to exert it on this occasion, if it had any. It is partly cowed and partly offended. Two years back the State deserted it. I do not see when, in consequence of that treachery, the State has got itself into difficulties, that the Church is bound to expose itself in its service.

Not that the Church should be unforgiving; but, if others think with me, *what* great interest has it that things should remain as they are? I much fear society is rotten, to say a strong thing. Doubtless there are many specimens of excellence in the higher walks of life, but I am tempted to put it to you whether the persons you meet generally are—I do not say consistently religious; we never can expect that in this world —but believers in Christianity in any true sense of the word. No, they are Liberals, and in saying this I conceive I am saying almost as bad of them as can be said of anyone. What will be the case if things remain as they are? Shall we not have men placed in the higher stations of the Church who are anything but real Churchmen? The Whigs have before now designed Parr for a Bishop; we shall have such as him. I would rather have the Church severed from its temporalities, and scattered to the four winds, than such a desecration of holy things. I dread above all things the pollution of such men as Lord Brougham, affecting to lay a friendly hand upon it. . . .

You may not thank me for this long meditation; and to tell the truth I cannot, even in this long account of my thoughts, express them fully.

Do you know that my brother Frank has gone out of the country as a missionary? He left Oxford last August, and was to arrive at Bagdad by the middle of January.

You ask me what I am doing. Why, I am going to be an author, but anonymously? I am thinking of writing two works on theological subjects, for a library which is coming out under the Bishop of London's sanction. And I am retiring from the tuition.

REV. E. B. PUSEY, D.D., TO REV. J. H. NEWMAN.

Hastings: March 17, 1831.

I am truly glad that you have undertaken the work on the Articles, as I think it is very much wanted, and there seems scarcely a commencement of what you will do satisfactorily, an illustration of the historical sense and the language employed in them. With regard to the Councils, though, as generally treated, they are the driest portion of Ecclesiastical History, I should think an account of them might be made both interesting and improving, by exhibiting them in reference to, and as characteristic of, the ages in which they occurred. You may also be of much service, I hope, in stemming heterodoxy, one of whose strongest holds is, perhaps, the so-called history of doctrines. I do not think there will be much to be gained for your object from German writers. Some of the Fathers, or rather parts of the Fathers, you must, of course, read; but this will all aid towards your great object. I should think this little essay would be of great use to yourself, towards nerving you for that design. Oh, for a conclusion of the Catalogue and the time when my hands will be free! But all in God's good time.

I may regard myself now as quite well, although my chest is still not strong.

The following letter to Mr. Rose, written some months before their personal acquaintance began, relates to the Ecclesiastical History on which Mr. Newman had lately written to Dr. Jenkyns.

REV. J. H. NEWMAN TO REV. HUGH JAMES ROSE.

March 28, 1831.

I have allowed myself to delay my answer to your obliging letter from a sense of the importance of the undertaking to which you invite me. I am apprehensive that a work on the Councils will require a more extensive research into Ecclesiastical History than I can hope to complete in the time to be assigned me for writing it. Otherwise I am well disposed towards it.

You do not mention the number of Councils you intend should be included in the History. May I trouble you to give me a description of the kind of work you desire, and what books you especially refer to in your letter as the sources of information, and what time you can grant me?

I fear I should not be able to give my mind fully to the subject till the autumn, though I wish to commence operations sooner. If I undertook it, it would be on the understanding that it was to be but introductory to the subject which Mr. Jenkyns mentioned to you—the Articles.

I had considered a work on the Articles might be useful on the following plan : First, a defence of Articles ; then the history of our own. Then an explanation of them founded on the historical view. Then a dissertation on the sources of proof—for example, revelation or nature, the Bible or the Church, the Old or New Testament, &c. Then some account of the terms used in Theology as a science—*i.e.* Trinity, Person, merits of Christ, Grace, Regeneration, &c. And, lastly, some general view of Christian doctrines to be proved from Scripture, and referred to their proper places in the Articles. It seems to me much better thus to collect the subjects of the Articles under heads than to explain and prove each separately, with a view both to clearness of statement and fulness in the proof from Scripture.

Will you consider it out of place in one so little known as myself to add, that, though I am most desirous you should be put into full possession of my views, and at all times wish to profit by the suggestions of others, and am not aware I differ in any material point from our standard writers, yet, intending to take on myself the entire responsibility of everything I write, I should be unwilling to allow any alteration without the concurrence of my own judgment? And if the changes required were great, I should cheerfully acquiesce in my MS. being declined, rather than consent to suppress or modify any part of it which I deemed of importance.

In saying this, perhaps, I am raising actual difficulties in my wish to avoid possible prospective ones; yet, in a matter of this kind, I deem it best to use as much openness as possible, begging your indulgence of it, and being entirely disposed to welcome in turn any frank statement of your own sentiments which you may find it necessary to communicate to me.

After the academical success of his brilliant pupil—H. W. Wilberforce—the father and Mr. Newman exchange letters.

WILLIAM WILBERFORCE, ESQ., TO REV. J. H. NEWMAN.

Kensington Gore: April 21, 1831.

... I scarcely need assure you that your testimony in my dear Henry's favour is not a little gratifying to me. And I can truly assure you that the pleasure it gives me is much enhanced by the high respect for the principles, the judgment, and the means of information of the individual by whom that favourable opinion was expressed. I believe I had been led to underrate the probabilities of Henry's succeeding in his competition for the fellowship, and therefore I was less disappointed. I know not your opinion as to the profession to which he should devote himself. You probably have heard that he has entered into one of the Inns of Court, though declaring that it is contrary to his inclination. I leave the decision entirely to himself. Allow me, before I conclude, to express my hopes, that, whenever we may have the opportunity of cultivating each other's personal acquaintance and friendship, you will allow us to embrace it. That it may please God to grant you a course of usefulness and comfort is the cordial wish of yours very sincerely,

WILLIAM WILBERFORCE.

The 'Chronological Notes' show that there were still pupils to occupy time and heart. Entries occur up to the end of the year. Thus:

April 30.—H. Wilberforce went for good.
May 6.—Introduced Rogers to my Mother.
May 18.—Classical list out, Wood and Wilson (his pupils) firsts.
June 4.—Mathematical class list out, Perkins first class [a pupil of mine, now dead. I don't recollect that I knew him intimately], Wilson second.
June 11.—Second day of Collections; finished my men— and so ends my Tutor's work.

In the Long Vacation Mr. Newman paid a long-remembered visit to Dartington, the home of Hurrell Froude.

TO HIS MOTHER.

Dartington: July 7, 1831.

I despatched a hasty letter yesterday from Torquay which must have disappointed you from its emptiness, but I wished you to know my progress. As we lost sight of the Needles twilight came on and we saw nothing of the coast. The night was beautiful, and on my expressing an aversion to the cabin, Froude and I agreed to sleep on deck. [Froude in consequence caught a cold which turned to the epidemic influenza, and was the beginning of his long fatal illness.— J. H. N.] I have for a long while almost vowed never to sleep in those gregarious cabins. I robbed my berth of a blanket, in which I enveloped my blessed person, and putting over it my cloak, stretched myself on a bench. At one o'clock, passing Portland Lights, the swell was considerable, as it always is there.

When I awoke, a little before four, we were passing the Devonshire coast, about fifteen miles off it. By six we were entering Torbay, and by seven we landed at Torquay. We had debated whether to go to Plymouth, or to land at Dartmouth, or at Torquay—our decision would have been furthered on our finding the steamer's flag was a tricolour; but was ultimately made by a desire for breakfast, &c.

Limestone and sandstone rocks of Torbay are very brilliant in their colours, and sharp in their forms; strange to say, I believe I never saw real rocks before in my life. This consciousness keeps me very silent, for I feel I am admiring what everyone knows, and it is foolish to observe upon.

You see a house said to have belonged to Sir Walter Raleigh; what possessed him to prefer the court at Greenwich to a spot like this? Really the abstract vague desire of distinction does seem to me the most morbid unnatural feeling going. I can understand a man tempted by a definite tangible prize, or a dependent man setting out to seek his fortune; but not that gluttonous indefinite craving for honours and reputation.

Now I know I am writing great nonsense! but since I should say it in words if I were with you, I will write it down.

I know I am writing in a very dull way, but can only say that the extreme deliciousness of the air and the fragrance of everything makes me languid, indisposed to speak or write, and pensive. My journey did not fatigue me to speak of, and I have no headache, deafness, or whizzing in my ears; but really I think I should dissolve into essence of roses, or be attenuated into an echo, if I lived here. Certainly I am not more original in my remarks and disposed to start a conversation than an echo, as the people here as yet find, though they may not yet have discovered my relationship to an essence.

What strikes me most is the strange richness of everything. The rocks blush into every variety of colour, the trees and fields are emeralds, and the cottages are rubies. A beetle I picked up at Torquay was as green and gold as the stone it lay upon, and a squirrel which ran up a tree here just now was not the pale reddish-brown to which I am accustomed, but a bright brown-red. Nay, my very hands and fingers look rosy, like Homer's Aurora, and I have been gazing on them with astonishment. All this wonder I know is simple, and therefore, of course, do not you repeat it. The exuberance of the grass and the foliage is oppressive, as if one had not room to breathe, though this is a fancy—the depth of the valleys and the steepness of the slopes increase the illusion—

and the Duke of Wellington would be in a fidget to get some commanding point to see the country from. The scents are extremely fine, so very delicate yet so powerful, and the colours of the flowers as if they were all shot with white. The sweet peas especially have the complexion of a beautiful face. They trail up the wall mixed with myrtles as creepers. As to the sunset, the Dartmoor heights look purple, and the sky close upon them a clear orange. When I turn back and think of Southampton Water and the Isle of Wight, they seem by contrast to be drawn in Indian ink or pencil. Now I cannot make out that this is fancy; for why should I fancy? I am not especially in a poetic mood. I have heard of the brilliancy of Cintra, and still more of the East, and I suppose that this region would pale beside them; yet I am content to marvel at what I see, and think of Virgil's description of the purple meads of Elysium. Let me enjoy what I feel, even though I may unconsciously exaggerate.

To HIS SISTER HARRIETT.

Dartington: July 15, 1831.

The other day the following lines came into my head. They are not worth much, but I transcribe them.

> There stray'd awhile amid the woods of Dart
> One who could love them, but who durst not love;
> A vow had bound him, ne'er to give his heart
> To streamlet bright, or soft secluded grove.
>
> 'Twas a hard, humbling task, onwards to move
> His easy captured eye from each fair spot,
> With unattached and lonely step to rove
> O'er happy meads, which soon its print forgot:
> Yet kept he safe his pledge, prizing his pilgrim lot.

The weather has been beautiful here. The whole house has had the influenza, and been unable to go out of doors, and in consequence I have as yet seen nothing, and been nowhere. I was not sure I should not catch it myself. I have had a sermon [namely, in my first volume of 'Parochial Sermons' on the Pool of Bethesda: 'Scripture, a Record of Human Sorrow'] to write for to-morrow, which I do believe to be as bad a one as I have ever written, for I was not in the humour, but I do not tell people so; it may do good in spite of me.

To his Mother.

Dartington: July 20, 1831.

In twelve days I have written you five letters. I am amused, then, there should be a complaint of my silence.

I mean to leave this place on Friday by an afternoon coach, and you may expect me at Rose Hill about five or six on Saturday. I send you a philosophical poem [1] on the origin of poetry, tendered by me the other day for a lady's album.

Possibly for a like distinction the following lines may have been penned, composed, as they must have been, amid a gathering of young people, to whom fair weather would be all important for showing off their beautiful country. The reader will remember that St. Swithin's Day falls on July 15, the date of this letter.

Dartington: July 15, 1831.

> Gently, wet saint, descend, nor sluice
> Our summer's broad sunshine;
> Or hasten autumn's riper juice,
> And let thy rain be wine.

Rev. R. H. Froude to Rev. J. H. Newman.

Dartington: July 29, 1831.

People down here regret your departure; so I hope that the benefit you have derived from your excursion may some time or other bring you down again.

Rev. J. H. Newman to Rev. R. H. Froude.

Oriel College: August 10, 1831.

I am just come in to Oxford for a while, and find a letter from Mozley, in which he sends you the following message: 'I have heard of Bulteel's proceedings through the newspapers. If Froude remembers his proposal, and you think St. Ebbe's a fit sphere for me, I should be much obliged to you if you would take any steps that may not be inconvenient to you to procure the curacy for us, making what use you like of my name.'

I don't know whether you have heard Bulteel is about to leave Oxford; he has communicated it to his parishioners from the pulpit.

---

[1] *Verses*, p. 55, 'Seeds in the Air.'

Keble, who was here yesterday, wishes you to have a country parish; he did not give his reasons. I have nothing to say except that my work [N.B. 'The Arians'] opens a grand and most interesting field to me; but how I shall ever be able to make one assertion, much less to write one page, I cannot tell. Any one, pure categorical, would need an age of reading and research. I shall confine myself to hypotheticals; your 'if' is a great philosopher, as well as peacemaker.

The preceding letter seems to imply that the idea had been for R. H. Froude and T. Mozley to take a parish in conjunction.

REV. R. H. FROUDE TO REV. J. H. NEWMAN.

August 16, 1831.

Since you may wish to have a definite categorical answer to Mozley's question, I will say No. . . . Whatever you may think, I have a serious wish, and, if I could presume to say so, intention of working at the Ecclesiastical History of the Middle Ages. Willie [his brother] continues very steady, getting up at half-past five, and working without wasting time till two or three. . . . I think I am myself improved in composition, and attribute it to imitation of Plato.

REV. JOHN KEBLE TO REV. J. H. NEWMAN.

August 24, 1831.

I wish you would come and stay a day or two with us. You would find us all *uninfluenced* now, and the master of the house [his father] so gay as to read prayers at Fairford Church on Sunday. Moreover, I want some of your criticism, for somehow I can't get it out of my head that you are a real honest man.

We don't hear a very good account of Pusey, and are much inclined to suppose that he does not take care of himself. Do you know of anybody who would be fit and likely to take the place of second Master at Rugby, with emolument of 500*l.* or 600*l.* a year, in case Arnold should not succeed in an arrangement which I believe he has in view?

BONAMY PRICE, ESQ. (Master at Rugby), TO
REV. J. H. NEWMAN.

August 1831.

The resignation of Mr. Moore having created a vacancy among our Masters, it has been suggested to us that Mr. Blencowe—a Fellow of your college—would be a very fit person to become his successor, and might not be unwilling to accept the situation. I have, therefore, taken the liberty of begging your opinion of him in reference to an engagement of this sort; judging that, from your personal acquaintance with him, there was no person to whom I could more properly apply than to yourself. His well-known character in the University leaves no room for doubt on the score of attainment, but your own experience in tuition must have convinced you, that there are many other requisites for the successful carrying on of the work of education. I do not know that anything in particular is needed for Rugby more than for any other school, except that Dr. Arnold has a sort of idiosyncrasy for a man who is $\dot{\alpha}\gamma\alpha\theta\grave{o}\varsigma\ \pi\alpha\iota\zeta\epsilon\iota\nu$. At least we all feel from experience that cheerfulness of temper and a ready turn for amusing oneself are amongst the most valuable qualifications for a schoolmaster. I hope you will excuse the liberty I thus take of asking for what I know you may feel much reluctance to give; but I trust I may plead my apology on the ground of the importance of the matter, and the necessity imposed on Dr. Arnold of procuring as certain information as he can. I hope you continue to receive favourable accounts of your brother. I have had a letter from him, written in very good spirits, and, I am glad to add, showing evidence that general and classical literature has lost no interest with him.

J. H. N. TO HIS MOTHER.

September 18, 1831.

Dr. Whately is made Archbishop of Dublin.

REV. JOHN KEBLE TO REV. J. H. NEWMAN.

September 1831.

I am quite astonished at what you tell me about Whately, and can only say I hope he and the Irish Church may be the better for it this day six months. It will be a step in that direction if they have made no truckling bargain with him to sacrifice the temporalities to a reformed Parliament, if such be their good pleasure. If you see him, pray assure him of my very sincere and constant good wishes on so trying an occasion.

The following letter shows how fixed Mr. Newman's mind was on Oxford as his lifelong home.

,TO MISS M. R. GIBERNE.

Oriel College: September 22, 1831.

I was very much vexed that I should have been away when you paid my sisters a visit here last July. I will not allow you have seen Oxford yet. It was a most informal proceeding to be lionised, as you were, by one who was under no monastic vow to love it and be true to it for life.

REV. JOHN KEBLE TO REV. J. H. NEWMAN.

September 22, 1831.

We shall be happy to see you next week, and perhaps I may have the pleasure of introducing you to a friend of mine —an Oriel incumbent—Penrose, of Coleby, worth your knowing if you never met him.

REV. JOHN KEBLE TO REV. J. H. NEWMAN.

September 30, 1831.

Mr. Lily [Scout], or rather, my dear Newman, for when I am about it I may as well speak to a friend as not, the purport of this note is to inquire about two pair of shoes which Hill says have never made their appearance in our house since I last came from Oxford ; so we suppose they are pursuing their studies in the room I then occupied, viz. ground floor on the right, Jenkyns's staircase. If so, please to have them sent me &c. . . . otherwise I shall be very unfit to accept the many invitations which, no doubt, I shall receive from high personages in London next week.

I must now thank you very heartily for your patient

endurance of all the prose and *verse* which was inflicted on you last Monday and Tuesday, and what is more, I don't care how soon I have an opportunity of the same kind again. Penrose went off this morning to rub off a little of the Tory dust which he might have contracted during his stay here, by a visit to William Short, of Chippenham. Then he goes to my brother's, then to Rugby, so that he will stand a fair chance of getting home in a tolerably neutral state.

During the summer and autumn of 1831 are entrances in the 'Chronological Notes' which tell, in short, events of private or public interest.

1831. *August 2.*—Rogers [Lord Blachford] came and read with me, stationing himself at Iffley.

August 20.—Took tea with Rogers to meet Gladstone.

September 1.—Made Rural Dean.

September 18.—Heard that Whately was appointed Archbishop of Dublin, as Rogers and I were walking over Magdalen Bridge into Oxford.

October 4.—Whately and Hind left for Ireland.

October 10.—Went over by coach to Cotton, at Denchworth, walking from the Lamb.

October 12.—Walked back to Oxford, through clay fields, streams, and miry roads, about fifteen miles. [It was in this walk that I devised the mode of writing sermons which is my published mode. One, however, of that mode, is the one which I wrote at Dartington in the foregoing July—some of my old style are among the published ones.] [1]

October 14.—My rule was to lecture at Littlemore every Friday.

October 21.—Resumed my task at the Councils ['The Arians'], though with many interruptions, for a while.

October 24.—On my return from my walk found present from my pupils, consisting of the Fathers.

The following letter is certainly remarkable as showing how unconscious Mr. Newman was of the gulf that was separating him from Dr. Whately and his school.

---

[1] Being asked what was his former style, he spoke of Simeon's style, divisions 1, 2, 3, into different heads.

To his Sister H. E. N. (at Stowlangloft).

October 16, 1831.

For some time Whately's promotion teased me much, and in a selfish way. As far as he himself is concerned, one must always feel sorrow about it, for I think he will not now have a day of peace till his life's end, any more than the Abbot Boniface after quitting the Abbey of Dumdrennon; and he thinks all this too. But my first annoyance was as to my own prospects, for I foresaw he would ask me some time or other to join him at Dublin, and not only did I feel it would seem selfish and ungrateful and cowardly not to do so, but I feared it might turn out to be my duty on direct grounds, and had even thought (that is, for some time) that a post in Ireland was the one thing which seemed to have claims enough to draw me from Oxford:—perhaps you have heard me say so.

However, by this time I think my mind is quite made up that it is my duty to remain where I am, so remain I shall. (Is it not good to answer before I am asked?) My reasons for remaining are these: first, I am actually engaged to Mr. Rose for a succession of works [historical, of the Councils, J. H. N.] the composition of which is quite incompatible with the duties of a post about an Archbishop; next, this engagement will be in itself a channel of exclusive usefulness, which I should be abandoning just as I had begun it; thirdly, the study of theology is very much neglected at Oxford, and I may be doing peculiar service to the place (by 'peculiar' I mean what others will *not* do) by cultivating it; fourthly, if times are troublous, Oxford will want hot-headed men, and such I mean to be, and I am in my place; fifthly, I have some doubts whether my health would stand an Irish engagement. Many minor reasons might be added to the above. I dread Whately proposing something [He never did; he knew me better than I knew myself - J. H. N.], but expect nothing immediate, though at first I did.

You may assure Rickards from me, that I am a reformer as much as he can be. I should like (as far as I can understand the matter) to substitute the First Prayer Book of King Edward for the present one; but such reforms are not popular, that is the worst of it; so that practically I do become an anti-reformer in the modern sense of the word. I am thankful the Bishops have lately played so bold a part, but I fear they will still give way, a large number of them being frightened 'at the sound themselves have made.'

The Provost has again negatived my proposition of doing something for Littlemore. . . .

To his Mother.

October 24, 1831.

I have to-day received a very valuable present of books from many of my new friends and pupils, consisting of thirty-six volumes of the Fathers; among these are the works of Austin, Athanasius, Cyril Alexandrinus, Epiphanius, Gregory Nyssen, Origen, Basil, Ambrose, and Irenæus. They are so fine in their outsides as to put my former ones to shame, and the editions are the best. Altogether, I am now set up in the patristical line, should I be blessed with health and ability to make use of them.

Rev. S. Rickards to Rev. J. H. Newman.

Stowlangloft: October 25, 1831

Harriett tells me a little about your employments, and when I can get rid of the regret I feel that the College has lost you,[1] I am well pleased to know they are what they are. I very earnestly hope they will put you into Whately's place [Headship of Alban Hall]; that ought to be vacant by this time; I am glad you are so sanguine about Oxford, it helps me to keep up my spirits about it, when else they would be apt to fail. Most people there fall so short of one's expectations, just when they have got to the point when they might begin to realise them.

This is an odd neighbourhood into which we are got here, and thronged with a set of rather rich, moderately learned, and immoderately liberal clergy. The spirit of the Bishop of Norwich has got into them so thoroughly, that if they had not shown themselves so earnest for the late Bill, one might have thought that they reckoned a decisive opinion the chief crime. Of course, here and there we have a hot man on one extreme side pitched against a still hotter on the other side. But the effect of these seems to be only to make the mass more certain than ever, that they are the wise happy men. There was a stir

[1] By Mr. Newman retiring from the tutorship.

made a few weeks ago, which I helped to make, to bring the
clergy to meet together once a month within a given district.
It may still come to something, but it is at present at a standstill;
and two of the oldest and more influential clergy, who professed
to like the thing in most respects, still gave it as their opinion
that it was unnecessary, *because* all things that could be discussed had been discussed already in books, and the books
might be bought as they were wanted. As far as I have been
able to observe, hitherto, the people are either of the lowest
order of Dissenters, and this to a vast extent, or else they are
Churchmen without a jot of Christian knowledge. I wish you
could come and see us, that I might talk to you of many things
whereof I cannot write. I can say but little to you until you
do, for I feel scarcely to know anything about you. Accept
our love, and let it fetch you speedily.

MRS. NEWMAN TO J. H. N.

[On the first alarm of the cholera in England.]

Rose Hill: November 12, 1831.

. . . Should it [the cholera] increase, I wish you could
have that cottage at Littlemore for head-quarters for nurses
to be on the spot, without mixing with uncontaminated families,
and for a depôt of medicines, &c. And I should think it a
privilege, while health permits, for you to consider me *head
nurse.* I have the whole in my head, should it be ordained
that our vicinity is to suffer under the visitation. Pray take
care of your own health. *Your* usefulness is before you, I
trust for the comfort of many, for many years.

Towards the close of 1831 the Notes have frequent mention
of the cholera.

November 5.—News of the cholera in Sunderland.

November 6.—Prayers against the cholera in College
Chapel.

November 15.—Had papers about the cholera for my
parishioners.

November 17.—We sent out Keble's cards. Candidate for
Poetry Professorship.

December 8.—Keble elected Poetry Professor.

December 9.—No sleep at night. Preached University
sermon in the afternoon. My first as Select Preacher.

December 17.—Went round the parish with cholera committee.

December 19.—Resumed opusculum after many weeks' interruption. [I was working too hard at 'The Arians.' It was due the next summer, and I had only begun to read for it, or scarcely so, the summer past.]

December 26.—T. Mozley disappointing me, wrote and preached lecture for morning service.[1]

The correspondence of the year 1832 opens with what Mr. Newman calls a sad letter from Mr. Hurrell Froude, as giving an unfavourable report of his own health. In the course of it he enters a protest on his friend's method of working on the opusculum then in progress, and then continues :

REV. R. H. FROUDE TO REV. J. H. NEWMAN.

. . If you go on fiddling with your introduction you will most certainly get into a scrape at last.

I have for the last five days been reading Marsh's Michaelis, which I took up by accident, and have been much interested by it. I see that old Wilberforce [Robert] owes to it much of the profundity which I have before now been floored and overawed by. It has put many things into my head that I never thought of before.

REV. J. H. NEWMAN TO REV. R. H. FROUDE.

January 13, 1832.

Your letter was most welcome, sad as it was; I call it certainly from beginning to end a sad letter, and yet somehow sad letters, in their place and in God's order, are as acceptable as merry ones.

What I write for now is to know why you will not trust your brother [N.B. William Froude] to come up by himself. Let him go into your rooms, and do stop in Devonshire a good

[1] 'It is justice to the delinquent to give his recollections on the occasion. "He [Newman] never complained of an unexpected addition to his work, or any interruption. I had undertaken a saint's day sermon. An hour before the time I presented myself a defaulter. I could not do it. Newman threw aside the work he was busily and eagerly engaged in and wrote a sermon, which, when delivered, might indicate days of careful preparation."—*Reminiscences chiefly of Oriel and the Oxford Movement*, vol. i. p. 207.

while; in which time you not only may get well, but may convince all about you that you *are* well—an object not to be neglected.

... Your advice about my work ['The Arians'] is not only sage, but good; yet not quite applicable, though I shall bear it in mind. Recollect, my good sir, that every thought I think is thought, and every word I write is writing, and that thought tells, and that words take room, and that, though I make the introduction the *whole* book, yet a book it is; and, though this will not steer clear of the egg blunder, to have an introduction leading to nothing, yet it is not losing time. Already I have made forty-one pages out of eighteen.

Rickards has had in his parish a true instance of Asiatic cholera, as large as life. I believe he is but a few miles from the place where the Sunderland coal barges unload. The poor man died in three or four hours. No other case has occurred, but there is much English cholera about. He was dirty, out of health, in bad circumstances, a suspected man, and in a very dejected state of mind.

REV. JOHN KEBLE TO REV. J. H. NEWMAN.

January 16, 1832.

I am very sorry we are not to see you, but don't much wonder at it, considering the twenty-six tomes of the Concilia [alluding to 'The Arians'].

As it happens, I could have come up now, for I have written and transcribed enough of something meant for Latin [N.B.—I suppose his first Poetry Lecture], but I think I am more in the spirit of the law by waiting till the 31st.

I am very sorry to hear of Froude [N.B.—This was the first symptom of his illness]. I don't think he takes care of himself.

REV. WILLIAM PALMER OF WORCESTER[1] TO REV. J. H. NEWMAN.

January 22, 1832.

I would not willingly run the risk of displeasing you, yet I cannot refrain from attempting to express, however faintly,

---

[1] [Author of *Origines Liturgicæ*.—J. H. N.]

the pleasure which your discourse this day afforded me. [N.B.—This is Sermon IV. of my University sermons.¹]

How entirely and completely did I go along with all you said so wisely and so truly! How thankful did I feel to Divine Mercy for raising up preachers of righteousness! In times of sorrow and depression, when evil seems to prevail over all the earth, there is an inexpressible consolation to the broken spirit to see and know that there are still some faithful found.

February 20 there is mention of a distressing letter from Froude, and the following letter from Archdeacon Froude shows how serious he felt his son's case to be.

VEN. ARCHDEACON FROUDE TO REV. J. H. NEWMAN.

February 22.

If the doctor advises it, I have offered to be Hurrell's companion to the Mediterranean or any other part of the world that may be supposed most favourable in such a case as his. I own my faith in the advantages to be gained by going abroad is not very great, unless they can be procured under the most favourable circumstances. At any rate, I think your suggestion for his giving up the office of treasurer shall be followed.

We hear of severe weather in town and the northern part of the kingdom; here we have had a fortnight of the most delightful time I ever remember at this season.

REV. J. H. NEWMAN TO REV. R. H. FROUDE.

April (Lent) 1832.

As I grew idle and did not know what to say, I gave up my subject (for the University pulpit), and determined to preach a practical discourse fit for Lent. Therefore I have written a sermon[2] against Sir James Macintosh, Knight. I still have some need of your imprimatur, and send you 'Sermon Notes,' to which I shall expect an answer by return of post should you discern anything heretical, &c.

[1] The title of Sermon IV. is 'The Usurpation of Reason.' The text, Matt. xi. 19: 'Wisdom is justified of her children.'
[2] See Sermon VI., *University Sermons.* Title: 'On Justice, as a Principle of Divine Governance.' Text, Jer. viii. 11: 'They have healed the hurt of the daughter of my people slightly, saying Peace, peace, when there is no peace.'

VOL. I.   Q

Sir J. M. asserts that imperative *per se* as is the voice of conscience, yet the *test* of its correctness is its tending to the general good. In other words, he supposes benevolence unlimited and absolute to be the attribute of the Divine governance, and the end the general good; and that it is impossible ('a contradiction in terms') for anyone who holds (as all must hold as soon as it is stated) the general good to be the most desirable conceivable end of the world's course, to love and revere, *i.e.* to have religious feelings towards a Deity of mixed and imperfect benevolence. Accordingly that the feeling of justice in the mind is but a divinely appointed *expedient* for promoting the general good; and so again of purity.

I first speak of the cheerful hopeful view of human nature which prevails at all times (especially since the glorious 1688!). Such was Paley's, Addison's, Blair's, and now Maltby's, and the Liberals'. It is nominally like the Christian's cheerfulness, but superficial, &c. . . .

Before quoting Sir James, I come to the *arguments* which I wish your critical judgment on. Justice is amiable as well as Benevolence (here I go somewhat beyond Butler; part 1, ch. 3, is it? Therefore be sharp). That we do not commonly love and revere Justice arises from our being sinners and fearing it. The saints in heaven glorify God, *because* 'just and true are his ways,' &c.—*vide* Revelation.

REV. R. H. FROUDE TO REV. J. H. NEWMAN.

Fairford: April 6, 1832.

On the whole I like both the subject and the τόποι, especially that on which you tell me to be sharp. Perhaps the love of order is too minute; but I will make two or three remarks on the arrangement, &c.?

Might not something be said on the silliness of attempting to reduce all our moral instincts to one generally, &c.?

REV. J. H. NEWMAN TO REV. R. H. FROUDE.

April 12, 1832.

. . . As to your ' Annotationes in Neandri Homiliam,' to be sure I have treated them with what is now called 'true respect,' for I have spoken highly of them and done everything but use them. I did not have them till Saturday morning; so, having your authority for what I wanted—*i.e.* the soundness of the main position and the τόποι—I became indolent.

The following letter to a former pupil is of so private a character that it certainly could not have been inserted here but that the receiver has already put it into print in the Addenda to his 'Reminiscences of Oriel College.' It is therefore given as a specimen of Mr. Newman's letters of counsel to young men under his influence. The sentences which introduce the letter may be given from the 'Reminiscences.'

The new idea of Cardinal Newman as a mere dialectician and orator is so utterly repugnant to all my thoughts and feelings about him, that I am tempted to add a letter which I have early referred to. When . . . I returned all Newman's letters, I lamented that I had not seen this for many years, and concluded I must have lost it. I was deceived by the most important matter of the letter not appearing on the first page. Newman had a better recollection of its contents, and, finding it among the rest, returned it. The letter was written just fifty years ago [at the date 1882], while Hampden was delivering his Bampton lectures, and Newman himself was deep in his 'Arians.'

REV. J. H. NEWMAN TO REV. THOS. MOZLEY.

Oriel College: May 13, 1832.

My dear Mozley,—J. Marriott has taken Buckland in this neighbourhood, on his going into orders in the autumn, but the curacy being vacant in June, the place will be several months without pastor. Stevens has told me this, and on my hinting to him the possibility of its suiting you for this interval, wished me to write to you; so I do. The place you know from our Wadley excursions. You distinguished yourself by racing up the lime groves with Wilberforce, and rested under the fragrant firs. The population about 600 (?). The distance twelve miles from Oxford. There is a cottage which is used as a parsonage for the curate. I hear you are thinking of duty, else I should not have mentioned it, considering your late illness. It has been very unfortunate that you were obliged to give up your engagement with Round, but all is for the best. I am truly rejoiced to find your desire for parochial employment has not diminished, and your opinion of your own health not such as to deter you. For myself, since I heard your symptoms, I have not been alarmed, but some persons have been very anxious about you. I trust you are to be preserved for many good services in the best of causes. I am sure you have that in you which will come to good, if you cherish and improve it. You may think I am saying a strange thing, perhaps an impertinent and misplaced, and perhaps founded on a misconception, yet let me say it, and blame me if it be harsh—namely, that had it pleased God to have visited you with an illness as serious as the Colchester people thought it, it would almost have seemed a rebuke for past waste of time. I believe that God often cuts off those He loves, and who really are His, as a judgment, not interfering with their ultimate safety, but as passing them by as if unworthy of being made instruments of His purposes. It is an idea which was strong upon the mind of my brother, during his illnesses of the last year, while he did not doubt that his future interests were essentially secure. I doubt not at all that you have all along your illness had thoughts about it, far better than I can suggest; and I reflect with thankfulness that the very cause of it was an endeavour on your part to be actively employed; to the notion of which you still cling; yet I cannot but sorrowfully confess to myself (how much so ever I wish to hide the past from my own mind) that you have lost much time in the last four or five years. I say I wish to hide it from myself, because, in simple truth, in it I perceive a humiliation to myself. I have expected a good deal from you, and have said I expected it. Hitherto I have been disappointed, and it is a mortification to me. I do expect it still, but in the meanwhile time is lost, as well as hope delayed. Now you must not think it unkind in me noticing this now, of all times of the year. I notice it, not as if you needed the remark most now, rather less, but because you have more time to think about it now. It is one especial use of times of illness to reflect about ourselves. Should you, however, really acquit yourself in your own mind, thinking that the course you have pursued, of letting your mind take its own way, was the best for yourself, I am quite satisfied, and will believe you, yet shall not blame myself for leading you to the question, since no one can be too suspicious about himself. Doubtless you have a charge on you for which you must give account. You have various gifts, and you have good principles. For the credit of those principles, for the sake of the Church, and for the sake of your friends, who expect it of you, see that they bring forth fruit. I have often had—nay have—continually anxious thoughts about you, but it is unpleasant to obtrude them, and now I have hesitated much before I got myself to say what I have said, lest I should only be making a fuss; yet believe me to speak with very much affection towards you. Two men who know you best, G. and C., appear to me to consider you not at all improved in your particular weak points. I differ from them. Perhaps I am exaggerating their opinion, and men speak generally and largely when they would readily, on consideration, make exceptions, &c. But if this be in any measure true, think what it implies? What are we placed here for, except to overcome the εὐπερίστατος ἁμαρτία,[1] whatever it be in our own case?

I have no great news for you from this place. Poor Dornford is laid up with a low fever. Wood has left us, and in a week or two commences the law in London. The few days he was in Oxford, after the decision of our election, were sad indeed: they made Froude and me quite uncomfortable, not as not fully participating in the act of the College (of which doubtless he has given you an account), but from the notion of W.'s going. Under any circumstances it is a painful thing on both sides when a man leaves residence and parts from his friends; but I am not to lose him, as we are to be very regular correspondents. Wilson is in residence this term, good fellow as he is. What a pleasant thing it would be to have more fellowships than eighteen—that is, if we could always have such good men to put into them!

Ever yours very affectionately,
J. H. NEWMAN.

In the June of 1832 Mr. Newman became personally acquainted with the Rev. Hugh James Rose, rector of Hadleigh, whose name is connected with the start of the Movement. Mr. Rose was then on a visit to Mr. Palmer, of Worcester. The entries in the 'Chronological Notes' imply that he was at once welcomed into the band of friends invited to meet him.

June 2.—Mr. Rose in Oxford. Met him at Palmer's at dinner.
June 3.—Called, with Pusey, on Mr. Rose. This was the termination of their quarrel about German writers.

---

[1] Heb. xii. 1.

June 4.—Froude and I dined at Palmer's to meet Mr. Rose.
June 6.—Dined with Ogilvie to meet Rose.

The impression made on Mr. Rose by his reception at Oxford is shown in the following passage in a letter to his late host.

REV. W. PALMER TO REV. J. H. NEWMAN.

. . . He (Rose) says : I assure you that I have not spent so delightful a week for many years ; and that I derived the very highest gratification which such times as these admit, from seeing such a body of learned, powerful and high-minded men as I had the good fortune, through your kindness, to meet at Oxford. Convey my best thanks to Mr. Ogilvie for his attention to me ; and my kind regards to Mr. Newman, assuring him that his MS. [I suppose the 'Arians'] has just come into my hands safe, and that I am taking it into the country.

All through June Mr. Newman had been engaged upon his 'Arians,' or, to give its original title, 'First Volume of Councils.'

Mr. Froude had warned his friend not to go 'fiddling on' with his preface. Mr. Newman's solicitude over this first work showed itself throughout. He grudged no pains ; wrote and re-wrote ; read passages to his home circle ; sought the criticism of his friends. Mr. Henry Wilberforce made free to tell him that the style was not, to his judgment, equal to that of his sermons ; finally, he notes in his diary, 'the last days of my working upon the "Arians" I was tired wonderfully, continually on the point of fainting away, quite worn out.'

Absorbed as these passages show Mr. Newman to have been in his literary work, the correspondence of this time proves his mind to have been very much occupied with the questions involved in his accepting the office of Dean of his College.

REV. J. H. NEWMAN TO REV. H. JENKYNS.
June 28, 1832.

My dear Jenkyns,—The more I think about it, the more it seems to me to be the business of the College to consider whether they will make me Dean, rather than mine whether I will accept their offer. So I have come to the conclusion to take the office, if it comes to me ; and leave the responsibility of first moving in the matter to them. At the same time, as a member of the College, and bound moreover in duty to it, I am desirous of clearing and expediting the business by any explanations it may be in my power to give.

Ever yours,
J. H. NEWMAN.

REV. J. H. NEWMAN TO REV. H. JENKYNS.
June 30, 1832.

My dear Jenkyns,—I write, instead of coming to you, in order to be explicit. It certainly strikes one that the College, being electors, have the direct responsibility of electing.

Had I anything to communicate either about myself or the Provost, I ought to do so ; but I have nothing. For the Provost, I maintain I can know no more than yourself what will happen on his part ; and for myself, I am not conscious of cherishing any specific plan or novel principle about College discipline, &c., which I am desirous of bringing into operation, or I would say so frankly. Did I know of any *unsurmountable* obstacle to my discharging the duties of the office efficiently, for my own sake, I would decline it. But an experiment it certainly is—an experiment, which I do not say I will do my utmost (if it is made) to bring to a successful issue, for of course I am already bound to that, but which would lead me, on taking the office, to anticipate the *chance*, whether from your wish or my own, of my not holding it another year. I can say no more than this ; and all this, only in *evidence*, so to say ; for you all are the judges, not I.

Why should I, being satisfied with what I am, go out of my way to bring responsibility on myself ? At the same time I can say with sincerity that to be elected Dean is a mark of confidence which I have done nothing to deserve.

Excuse this long talk, which is more than I thought it would be. Now to your questions.

1. I do not recollect the words of the Statute, but without waiting for precise terms, I fully think that the Dean is bound to assist and act under the Provost in maintaining the discipline and good order of the College.

2. I fully allow that the discretion of the Dean is limited, *i.e.* its particular acts stopped by the veto of the Provost.

But here I will make some remarks; though, since they do not interfere with the above, they may seem irrelevant.

(1) I conceive the Dean at liberty to maintain things as he finds them, when he wishes : *i.e.* without dreaming of interfering with the Provost's discretion, I hold the Dean to have the right of acting himself by existing rules; *e.g.* supposing (to take an absurd case) it were proposed that the gentlemen commoners should sleep out of College, the Dean need not be a party to such arrangement.

(2) I think the Dean has the right of determining whether or not he is acting up to his duty as prescribed by statute and custom; *e.g.* supposing my feelings go strongly against administering the Sacrament to an individual, and the Provost wishes me, and I refuse—here his veto cannot come in; he can only say 'you are not acting up to your office'; a point to be decided by my judgment, not his.

(3) Is not the Dean *the* chaplain of the College, *i.e.* the sole officiator in the *ordinary* service of the Church ? *i.e.* I exclude the Communion Service.

I throw out these observations as they occur to me—but at present they seem correct.

Ever yours,
J. H. NEWMAN.

REV. J. H. NEWMAN TO REV. H. JENKYNS.

July 4, 1832.

My dear Jenkyns,—I agree entirely in your view, abstractedly considered, that the Dean has no independent authority, and is but a Vice-Provost. But abstract views are little to the purpose, as you observe—you have yourself given it as your opinion that the Dean, as any other officer, must have a discretionary power in *fact*; and whether this arises from the Provost's granting it or not, and therefore is or is not subject to his limiting, is not a practical question. I grant it is so originated, so limited ; but the difficulty is, how shall we know that all parties to the proposed arrangement agree to the previous question and allow the Dean's actual discretionary power ? Now, of course, it would be the height of disrespect and indelicacy to ask the Provost whether he has altered his (practical) views on this subject, and I for my part hardly think it necessary, were it ever so proper ; for men change their line of conduct without knowing it themselves, and I think it probable the Provost would. But if other persons have a suspicion, which I have not, that the Provost will not practically allow the principle which you allow ; let them not think of making me Dean, for no good could come of the arrangement. On my part I avow without reserve, if it be necessary to speak strongly, that it would be, in my opinion, underhand in me to attempt any change which I believed the Provost to consider important, without giving him the opportunity of interposing, *i.e.* without acquainting him with it. Even as Tutor, an office which, though in his gift, may appear to some to be held not strictly of him, but of the University—I never made changes *in fact* (though the above were my abstract views) without full written explanation to those who were senior to me in the tuition, and their sanction upon it. Much less should I do so in a place which, though not in the Provost's gift, is in the abstract that of a mere assistant to him in certain specified functions.

At the same time, I never will *pledge* myself to mention to the Provost all I do on my own discretion ; there being a multitude of little things which one who has the superintendence of others does at the moment and forgets at once—and the discriminating between great matters and little must, I conceive, rest with his own judgment. However, let me come to the practical point of the Sacrament ; for if the question is to turn on this, we are both of us losing time.

I have at present no formed opinion about administering it to the mass of undergraduates ; but if I have to make up my mind (which I cannot do all at once on an important subject), I think it very likely I shall make it a point of conscience to act upon it. Then the question will be whether the Provost will make it a point of conscience, on the other hand, to bid me administer it when I object. If so, dropping abstract views, it is frank to say, I should not consider myself bound to obey him in a matter so solemn. I will further say, that, at this very time (I may change my opinion next week) I am disinclined towards the present rule of (practically) obliging the undergraduates to communicate.

I will say no more in answer to your letter, before I can see whether this brings things to an issue ; merely adding that to *ask* the Provost whether he would allow me this discretion about the Sacrament, seems to me wrong ; it is like imposing conditions on him, and I think he should be supreme ; his discretionary power being limited solely by the practicability of governing well by means of it.

Yours,
J. H. NEWMAN.

In July of this year Mr. Newman visited Cambridge, going from thence to Mr. Rickards. To his Mother he gives his first impressions of Cambridge.

Cambridge: July 16, 1832.

Having come to this place with no anticipations, I am quite taken by surprise and overcome with delight. This, doubtless, you will think premature in me, inasmuch as I have seen yet scarcely anything, and have been writing letters of business to Mr. Rose, and Rivingtons. But really, when I saw at the distance of four miles, on an extended plain, wider than the Oxford, amid thicker and greener groves, the Alma Mater Cantabrigiensis lying before me, I thought I should not be able to contain myself, and, in spite of my regret at her present defects and past history, and all that is wrong about her, I seemed about to cry '*Floreat æternum.*' Surely there is a *genius loci* here, as in my own dear home ; and the nearer I came to it the more I felt its power. I do really think the place finer than Oxford, though I suppose it isn't, for everyone says so. I like the narrow streets ; they have a character, and they make the University buildings look larger by contrast. I cannot believe that King's College is not far grander than anything with us ; the stone, too, is richer, and the foliage more thick and encompassing. I found my way from the town to Trinity College like old Œdipus, without guide, by instinct ; how, I know not. I never studied the plan of Cambridge.

Mr. Rose is away ; he is very ill, which accounts for his silence. Should you see Froude, tell him he *is* married.

P.S.—Let me know about the cholera. I trust we shall have no cases, but it would distress me deeply should a case occur while I am away.

REV. WM. PALMER OF WORCESTER TO REV. J. H. NEWMAN.
July 18, 1832.

I was anxious to see you before I left Oxford, but called at your rooms more than once in vain. I often think of you, and not without some anxiety, when I reflect that the cholera is now in Oxford ; and though it is true that few persons in the better classes of society have taken it yet, it is impossible to avoid feeling some uneasiness when it is likely to come into the vicinity, perhaps the presence, of a valued friend. Let me hear, my dear friend, of your health, and may God have you under His protection.

I congratulate you very sincerely on getting rid of MS. Few sensations in life are more agreeable. It is like taking a load off the conscience. I cannot tell with what interest and satisfaction I look forward to a perusal of the results. [N.B.—My work on the Arians.]

Mr. Newman returned to Oxford on the 24th of July, and reports 'Cholera in St. Clement's.' That it was not confined to the poorer classes is well known. The following letters show the general impression of alarm.

H. W. WILBERFORCE, ESQ., TO REV. J. H. NEWMAN.
July 27, 1832.

. . . I did not know whether I might not say that I should be coming to see you at Oxford. I had hoped that my Mother would consent, but the deaths in the upper classes this week in London have too much alarmed her. Mrs. R. Smith was a cousin of my Father's. She was well on Sunday morning, seized at noon while on her way to church, and, in spite of the most prompt attendance of the most eminent practitioners, dead by midnight.

Lord Carrington writes to my Father that the London gentry are flying in every direction.

In the 'Chronological Notes' is written:

There had been no case of cholera in St. Mary's and Littlemore. The cases, I think, were all in the parishes which were upon the clay.

FREDERIC ROGERS, ESQ., TO REV. J. H. NEWMAN.
Blackheath: July 23, 1832.
. . . I have to thank you again for your present at parting. I have not yet discovered (though I think I have gone through most of it two or three times) where the liberty lies which you asserted yourself to have taken with me : but I do see enough of the private nature to feel *extremely* complimented at being allowed to see them, and being trusted with a copy.

[Rogers, having passed his examination, seemed now to have done with Oxford ; so I gave him the little book as if in parting.]

I have seen Wood and Wilson lately. Wood rather knocked up by conveyancing. But he is by this time in Yorkshire, where he will remain till November. He wants a little lecturing from you ; he goes to bed *late*. . . .

REV. J. H. NEWMAN TO F. ROGERS, ESQ.
Oriel College: July 25, 1832.
I soon heard the speed of your operations at Rivington's, but from Mr. Rose I have only just heard. Through a variety of circumstances I have been in suspense till yesterday about the fate of my MS. Turrill, indeed, delivered it at once, but a note to Mr. Rose, which I had not in time for you, was sent wrong by Rivington. Thus over-care is often defeated by itself. Directly you went, I felt unwell, and the next night had to send for Mr. W. Nothing ought to have alarmed me, but I had been near fainting more than once, and altogether (fear being more imaginative at night-time— did you never find this ? it partly accounts for the fear of ghosts), I must confess I played the fool. Continuing, however, indisposed, I was obliged to leave my work, and went to Cambridge in hopes of finding Mr. Rose, but he had left from illness, and I went on to Rickards, and fetched back my sister, finding your letter on my return yesterday. I am glad you have commenced your wanderings, and the violoncello, though they do not proceed contemporaneously. You have no chance of seeing me : I am so uncertain. After you went, we had a fatal case of cholera at Littlemore. It was not in my parish, but it made us very busy, being so very near. Between a fort-

night and three weeks having past without a second case, we consider we are as safe as any other part of the neighbourhood : though I have heard, on my return, that the obstinate blockheads have actually first, not burnt, but buried, and now again actually dug up, the bed furniture of the poor patient which they were ordered to destroy. Is not this the very spirit of Whiggery : opposition for its own sake, striving against the truth, because it happens to be commanded us ; as if wisdom were less wise because it is powerful ? and can we wonder at the brutishness of the Israelites in the desert, with such specimens before our eyes ? As to the cholera, it is not yet formidable here, I am thankful to say, or I should not have gone away. (I have wandered—I meant to say, that perhaps it might come on and keep me here, and prevent my ramblings.) We have had altogether about forty cases—confined, I believe, to St. Ebbe's, St. Aldate's, the Jail, &c., though we cannot, of course, boast, were it but for the bad luck of it. For myself, in these things it is well to be a fatalist ; I am practically so. Whether imagination would get the better, did I actually *see* a case, I cannot tell, but at present I am unable to realise the danger. Surely one's time is come, or it is not ; the event is out of our power. David's meaning is evident to me in a way I never understood it before. When he speaks of falling into hands higher than human, he means to say that the pestilence is beyond the physicians ; but famine is not beyond the chief butlers and bakers of Israel. The difficulty is to unite resignation *with* activity. Here we are only called to be resigned, which is comparatively easy. Then, again, when one argues about oneself, there is on one's own mind the strong impression (I know it is not a good argument, but fear is but an impression, and this works by a counter-imagination) that one is destined for some work, which is yet undone in my case. Surely my time is not yet come. So much for the cholera.

I can hardly tell you what I would say about the verses I put into your hands. It was their private nature which constituted the liberty, for why should I tell you of things which do not pertain to you ? It is, literally, being impertinent. Nor am I satisfied with your reference to the Buckland occurrence,[1] for there is every difference between a stranger and

[1] The 'verses' were an early collection of poems kept, though printed, so strictly private, and for so limited a number of readers, that it was an effort to give it to intimate friends beyond this inner circle. Several of the poems, however, now find a place in the book of *Verses*. The

a friend. However, I see by your letter that you suffer me, and that is enough. Do not think this absurd. We may feel things to be done in kindness, which yet our judgment condemns as out of propriety; and what I feared was, you might have an instinctive feeling that I had done what I ought not, though my own judgment, having become puzzled, might not have seen it. And even as it is, I sometimes feel quite ashamed of myself for having given you the book, and have all manner of absurd spectres dancing before me, the nephews of *mauvaise honte* (I cannot make out who their father is), which is more painful than guilt.

I propose going away next week to Brighton and Tunbridge Wells. I *had* a plan of going through part of Wales with Palmer of Worcester, in the autumn. It would be curious if we met. Davies is dead, and there will be two vacancies next year. They say Marriott of Balliol is to be a formidable competitor to you and W. How I should rejoice if you and W. succeed! It is far from impossible. I suppose Wood stands at Merton! It would complete one's happiness did he get in there. Wilson tells me that wretch H. W., instead of settling to some serious work, has been falling in and out of love in Yorkshire. *Cura ut valeant oculi tui.*

P.S. Calcott's is the best introductory book on thorough bass that I know. Shield is a goose.

REV. BLANCO WHITE TO REV. J. H. NEWMAN.

Redesdale: August 24, 1832.

. . . I hope when we go to Dublin in November I shall be able to finish a first volume containing the history of perse-

' Buckland occurrence ' may possibly apply to the following extempore stanzas, written for a lady who was to him a stranger, who had committed her Album to a mutual acquaintance (the present Editor) with an urgent petition that Mr. Newman should be persuaded to contribute some lines to her book. This petition was preferred as a joke, but a certain pair of kittens which had great prominence given to them by his host (the Rev. Thomas Mozley), who lavished on them much wit and humour, suggested these lines, written in pencil:

Two kittens gain our pleased caress	No airs deform the modest Fair,
And share our rival praise;	No gibe the silent Wit.
One has the rarer cleverness,	
One Beauty's winning ways.	So is it minds of noblest mould
	Still choose a peaceful life;
Thoughtless of self, a friendly pair,	Their friends the flag of war unfold
In musing mood they sit;	And trim the party strife.

cution till the end of the ninth century. The second volume, if I live to write it, will be the history of the Inquisition properly so called. I long to see your book [the 'Arians'].

In spite of violent prejudice, the Archbishop [Whately] cannot but gain ground in the esteem of all good men that come near him. But oh, my dear Newman, what furious bigots are to be found here in the Protestant party! I have heard a sermon, beautifully written and delivered, that shocked me more than any speech of Mr. Hume, considering where it was delivered. Satire, sarcasm, everything objectionable, from the pulpit, and the congregation in an open titter. I expected 'hear hear' at every moment; and yet the preacher is high Evangelical.

. . . What will the Morton Pinckney people say when they see the new Rector [Thomas Mozley]? Will they not suspect that he has run away from Lecture and gone there for fun to personate his tutor? He is, however, an excellent young man, and I trust the parishioners will soon find out his growing good qualities.

REV. ISAAC WILLIAMS TO REV. J. H. NEWMAN.

August 25, 1832.

. . . I will let you know about my coming back another time; but, my dear Newman, you have yet to learn how to be a vicar, or you would see the impropriety of saying to a curate 'I am obliged to you for staying'; for it is my business to be here always. I am reading a little Chrysostom, which I find a great comfort and delight.

REV. E. B. PUSEY, D.D., TO REV. J. H. NEWMAN.

1832.

The sermon which I preached for *you* at Grove met with the fate which it would have been more entitled to had you preached it; it extracted 70*l.*, and was 'ordered to be printed.'

Now to myself the sermon appears infinitely less calculated to be printed than even the former one; because it is more in the form of a sermon than the other; and there is no one subject discussed in it, as I was obliged to make it very popular.

How far might this incidental protest against the sad neglect of our heathen countrymen in our great towns or our villages, or the greater publicity given to the success with which the exertions here have, in this case, been blessed, be likely to produce other similar ?

To solve this I send you my sermon ; but I must *insist* that you will not even look at it if you are hurried still with your work, or need repose.

Should you advise this to be printed (which I think you will not), what should you do with regard to the other ?

Be sure you will be acting most kindly to me by consulting your own comfort. I was truly glad to hear from Mrs. Newman that you were much better.

REV. R. L. COTTON TO REV. J. H. NEWMAN.

September 8, 1832.

The consecration day was, indeed, a day much to be remembered. Pusey's sermon was very beautiful, and is in the press. . . . I did not hear that he was injured by preaching, and have seen both his brothers since, and inquired after him. What progress has there been in the cholera ?

REV. R. H. FROUDE TO REV. J. H. NEWMAN.

September 9, 1832.

I have had my ups and downs since I saw you. [N.B. viz. July 31, when he left Oxford for home. It was when the cholera was imminent, and we parted as if, perhaps, we might not see each other again. With reference to the memory of that parting, when I shook hands with him, and looked into his face with great affection, I afterwards wrote the stanza

> And when thine eye surveys
> With fond adoring gaze,
> And yearning heart, thy friend,
> Love to its grave doth tend.

and the latter in close proximity to the former : ταῦτα δὲ πάντα θεῶν ἐν γούνασι κεῖται.] I will not go into details, for all is at last as well as possible ; but you were right in saying it would be a slow job [N.B. this refers to his sister, I think] ; perhaps much pain is yet to come, but all must go right.

You will be glad to hear that I have made up my mind to spend the winter in the Mediterranean, and my father is going with me the end of November ; and we shall see Sicily and the south of Italy. We are both very anxious that you should come with us. I think it would set you up.

REV. DR. HAWKINS TO REV. J. H. NEWMAN.

Rochester: September 12.

I was grieved to hear some time ago from Pope that you had not been well. I hope you do not allow Messrs. Rose and Lyell to work you hard. Writing is a most deceitful employment; hurting you the more, the more you are interested by it; and you are always disposed to exert yourself too much. We have had good accounts of the Whatelys and B. White. We have excellent accounts of Pusey, who is going to print his sermon at the consecration of a church.

REV. J. H. NEWMAN TO REV. R. H. FROUDE.

September 13, 1832.

As to your proposal for me to accompany you, it is very tempting. It quite unsettled me, and I have had a disturbed night with the thought of it. Indeed, it makes me quite sad to think what an evidence it has given me of the little real stability of mind I have yet attained. I cannot make out why I was so little, or rather not at all, excited by the coming of the cholera, and so much by this silly prospect which you have put before me. It is very inconsistent, except, perhaps, that the present novelty has come upon me suddenly. But enough of philosophising.

I am much tempted by your proposal, for several reasons, yet there is so much of impediment in the way of my accepting it. I cannot divest myself of the feeling that I may be intruding upon your father; but, supposing this away, I see much in favour of the scheme. Probably I never shall have such an opportunity again. I mean that of going with a man I know so well as yourself. And going with a person older than myself, as your father, is to me a great temptation. <u>I am indolently distrustful of my own judgment in little matters, and like to be under orders.</u> [N.B.—My leaving them, in the event, at Rome, and going through Sicily by myself is a curious comment upon this.]

Then what a name the Mediterranean is! And the time of the year, for I think summer would be too hot for me; and the opportunity of getting there without touching Gallic earth (for I suppose you go by water), which is an abomination. And if I ever am to travel, is not this the time when I am most at liberty for it? My engagements being slighter now than they have been these many years, and than they are likely to be hereafter. And I feel the need of it ; I am suspicious of becoming narrow-minded, and at least I wish to experience the feeling and the trial of expansiveness of views, if it were but to be able to *say* I had, and to know how to meet it in the case of others. And then I think I may fairly say my health requires it. Not that I ever expect to be regularly well as long as I live. It is a thing I do not think of ; but still I may be set up enough for years of work, for which, at present, I may be unequal.

But you must tell me (1) as to time. I could not allow myself to be absent from England beyond Easter (say the beginning of April). Would it not be possible for me to part company with you ? (2) As to expense, which, I apprehend, will be a serious subject. . . . (3) As to my health. It is quite enough that *you* should be an invalid ; but it would be an ungracious πάρεργον for me to fall sick also. Now I cannot answer for my health. If all of a sudden I fell ill ?

My book [the 'Arians'] has long been out of hand. I suspect that Rose thinks it scarcely safe, and Rivington thinks it dull. However, I am quite satisfied with Rose ; he is in ecstasies with parts of it, and, I sincerely believe, delays it under the wish to make it as good as possible. He seems to like the first chapter least, which is now in Lyell's hands. Rose is a very energetic, well-principled fellow. I have seen a good deal of him ; whether he is firm remains to be seen. I will believe no one till he has committed himself.

Do send Mr. Rose one or two more architectural articles before you go.

REV. J. H. NEWMAN TO REV. R. H. FROUDE.

October 4, 1832.

Perhaps I had better write instead of waiting till we meet, for you may have made up your mind by that time. [N.B.—In his letter of September 27 Froude gave me private reasons for desiring after all to remain in England.] Now, then, let me entreat you that nothing but the force of plain duty keep you from going abroad. You require it. The complaint with which you are threatened is extremely slow in its advances (and therefore insidious) when persons get to your age. I have now a case at Oxford which has been coming on for four full years ; and it began in a slight imperceptible cold.

As to myself, *I* had rather postpone going, without liking to give up the prospect you have opened ; so do not let me come in any way into your deliberations, as I suppose you will not. Did I consult my wishes I should stop at home. I grudge the time, the expense, the trouble, the being put out of one's way, &c. But it may be a duty to consult for one's health, to enlarge one's ideas, to break one's studies, and to have the name of a travelled man ; this last being a pleasure also—ὑπεροχῆς γάρ.¹

I have been entirely idle the last month. The violin has been my only care, and, though I have not practised or progressed much, yet I see that I could easily play better than I ever did, and with *regular* attention might do what I pleased. But of all trades under the sun the worst is that of music in a blow-up ; for Euripides's complaint still holds good, and the lyre is only heard in feasts. Yet 'music hath charms,' and it were better to ask the *Date obolum* after a tune than to beg without pretence.

As the reader knows, the original plan for spending the winter in the Mediterranean was adhered to, and the party sailed from Falmouth early in December.

REV. J. H. NEWMAN TO REV. R. H. FROUDE.

October 1832.

I am more and more convinced one ought to do everything one can to avert a *civil* commotion ; and now incline to the hope that the Whig spirit will keep in and the Church be set adrift. If this were the case we should be so very independent of things temporal ; for we only, as individuals, should suffer. But a revolution involves the sufferings of others, and, consequently, our obligation to defend them, which is a tie. I should do all I can to support the Whigs so far forth as they are Conservative.

I am afraid of making too much of little things and resting in them. Let us make broad comprehensions. I hope you like this doctrine ; certainly it does not do to split on trifles. One must use the οἰκονομία. I agree with you about preaching [*i.e.* extempore preaching]. I have had from time to time divers thoughts about turning evangelical *so far*, only I am afraid. If Oxford was any place *but* Oxford, I certainly would have a weekly lecture—ἐπιδείξεως χάριν.

¹ Arist. *Rhet.* ii. 12.

REV. JOHN KEBLE TO REV. J. H. NEWMAN.
November 1832.

I send this lecture [his fourth] with a request that either you or Froude or Ogilvie will run your eye over it, and say what is wrong. I meant to have delivered it last week, but I thought Mr. Vice-Chancellor would rather not, as he was expecting their Royal Highnesses. There are three matters in the lecture to be discussed :—(a) The song of Ragnar Lodbrog, where it is to be found most authentical? (b) What book gives the best specimens of the 'Welsh Triads'? (c) That little Lapland song of which I have tried to translate a stanza ('I saw the moon rise clear'); is it in any sense genuine? I had it from Rickards ages ago, and shall write to him.

By the time these matters are settled another ten days will be over; and, settled or not, I propose coming up on Monday the 12th, and predicating the 13th. I send the third lecture in case you should think it worth looking over too.

I long to know how Froude is. The sooner he comes now [to Fairford] the better, or you either. My dear N., I am sadly afraid you will be giving us the slip as the time of your voyage draws near, and my brother wants to see you, and I want you to see him.

You will see that I have reserved much of what we talked of for another lecture. I was sure the yawns else would have been direful.

REV. C. P. GOLIGHTLY TO REV. J. H. NEWMAN.
November 7, 1832.

I sit down to inform you, though very reluctantly, that I have given up Deddington. Blencowe's rejection of my offer is fatal to the whole scheme. I can think of no other person. Consider how difficult it is in these days to meet with any young man, of *real zeal*, who is not Calvinistic, or has not some objections to some of the services of the Church. In short, how few young men are there of real zeal who care a rush for authority.

REV. E. B. PUSEY, D.D., TO REV. J. H. NEWMAN.
November 8, 1832.

Our dear little one, who by your ministry was made a member of Christ's Church, has been removed from all struggle and sin before it knew them. Her departure was sudden; but we have great room to thank God for His mercies in everything relating to it. She promised fair to be a meek and quiet spirit here, but she is gone (which, since it is so, must be far better) 'her Father's household to adorn.' We would see *you* gladly any day after this week, but cannot meet mixed society on Tuesday.

REV. J. H. NEWMAN TO REV. E. B. PUSEY, D.D.

November 10, 1832.

I trust the change of place and the retirement of the country have been a blessing to you and Mrs. Pusey, as I am sure they have. It only requires to be alone for receiving the comfort which almost necessarily attends any dispensation from Above. Of course, only parents can tell the sorrow of the loss of a child. But all persons can see the nature of the comfort contained in it—the comfort of knowing that you have given an immortal spirit to Heaven, and of being released from all responsibility of teaching her right from wrong, and from the uncertainties of her final destiny. You have done what her age allowed. She has been dedicated to God, and He has received the offering. For me, I have had a great privilege in being the means of her dedication. It is the only service which we are given to perform with a rejoicing conscience and a secure mind. [N.B.—I mean that the belief in the *opus operatum* saves one from the feeling that one's own sin has weighed on it.] And, on recollection, it becomes doubly precious, and a festival work, when, as in the case of your dear little one, we see the certainty of its having been accepted.

FREDERIC ROGERS, ESQ., TO REV. J. H. NEWMAN.

November 12, 1832.

I am delighted to find that at last I stand a chance of seeing you. I shall most certainly be at Hatchett's at one o'clock. Can you then come down here with me and spend a day or two with us ? I am sure you must be an idle man now.

The following note and poem are appended by Mr. Newman to the foregoing letter :

I went down with Rogers to Blackheath, Nov. 14, for the first time. I dined there and returned to London. It was my first time of seeing his (F. R.'s) family. Father, mother, sisters, and I think some brothers. In consequence I wrote the lines which stand first in the 'Lyra Apostolica,' 'Where'er I roam.' One of the sisters died on September 22, 1837.

HOME.

Where'er I roam in this fair English land,
The vision of a temple meets my eyes:
Modest without: within all-glorious rise
Its love-enclustered columns and expand
Their slender arms. Like olive plants they stand,
Each answering each in home's soft sympathies.
Sisters and brothers. At the altar sighs
Parental fondness, and with anxious hand
Tenders its offering of young vows and prayers,
The same and not the same. Go where I will
The vision beams! ten thousand shrines all one.
Dear fertile soil! what foreign culture bears
Such fruit? And I through distant climes may run
My weary round, yet miss thy likeness still.

Oxford, Nov. 16, 1832.

The author of 'Reminiscences of Oriel' says: 'It never was possible to be even a quarter of an hour in his [Newman's] company without a man feeling himself incited to take an onward step, sufficient to tax his energies or his faith.' The following letters on taking leave of his friend and pupil, who had just taken a high degree, perhaps illustrate this demand upon the energies of men in proportion as he valued and estimated them.

November 19, 1832.

I have been thinking you may be at present exposed to danger from the state of your eyes; thus—Are you not naturally idle? and are you not now *reduced* to a state of idleness? Beware of getting into a way of muddling away your time; shuffling through the day doing nothing, &c. I know that when you get to the Bar you must work; yet there are degrees of exertion, and it is possible to be absent with your books before you. I throw out this merely because it strikes me, as a raw material which you may convert as far as possible into something real and practicable.

To the same friend he had written previously:

You have an active mind and are not lonely without books, and I almost think that idleness, or rather vacancy, is the best time for thought.

Again to the same, who seems to have replied on the question of muddling:
November 22, 1832.

When I spoke of muddling, it was merely that I thought your eyes at present kept you from doing *anything*, and that you were literally idling. I did not mean that you must be reading or thinking. You may hunt in Hampshire three days in the week, and I shall never call it muddling; that is, *it will not incapacitate you from working in its season.* But to be doing absolutely nothing *is* injurious.

VEN. ARCHDEACON FROUDE TO REV. J. H. NEWMAN.
November 24, 1832.

I heard yesterday from Falmouth that a steamer now fitting up at Woolwich is *likely* to take out the Mediterranean mails on December 7, and that we are to go out in her.

. . . If my correspondent is correctly informed, the ship is the same that took the Bishop of Exeter and myself to Scilly last year. She is, I think, the largest packet in the service, and was at that time fitted up in the most comfortable way imaginable, and her captain was a worthy obliging person. She is 800 tons and is called the 'Hermes.'

F. ROGERS, ESQ., TO REV. J. H. NEWMAN.
November 26, 1832.

. . . The letters which we can get for you for Italy, I fear, we cannot manage till after you have left England. Do you think them worth forwarding?

Among the tasks which Mr. Newman proposed to Mr. Rogers, as an idle man, was the writing of verses. His last letter despatched just before sailing touches upon this.

REV. J. H. NEWMAN TO F. ROGERS, ESQ.
Oriel College: December 1, 1832.

As to my notion about verses, do not be so surprised—I had a reason. If you do not already write them, I can only say the sooner you do the better, for while your eyes are bad, it would be an amusement. But the truth is that we have in contemplation to set up a verse department in Rose's Magazine for all right purposes; and I am (not beating up, but) looking for recruits. Do not mention this, but we have hopes of making an effective quasi-political engine, without every contribution being of that character. Do not stirring times bring out poets? Do they not give opportunity for the rhetoric of poetry, and the persuasion? And may we not at least produce shadows of high things if not the high things themselves?

On Sunday, December 2, 1832, as Select Preacher, Mr. Newman preached the sermon on Saul.[1] On Monday, December 3, he set out by the Southampton coach for Whitchurch, writing on the same day.

TO HIS MOTHER.
Whitchurch: December 3, 1832.

It is soon to make you pay postage. . . . Here I am at Whitchurch from one till eleven! I had hoped to be alone, and I should have despatched several copies of verses; but a person claiming to be H.'s brother has made his appearance, and, as going to Exeter as well as myself, claims to share my room and society. So I am practising for the first time the duty of a traveller, which is sorely against the grain, and have been talkative and agreeable without end; . . . now that I have set up for a man of the world it is my vocation. I have been so hurried I have had no time to think, but at times it seems to be miserable going away for so long. Yet I doubt not, in after life, I shall look back on this day as a bright day and full of interest, as the commencement of one of the few recreations which I can hope, nay, or desire to have in this world, for the only cessation from labour to which I may look without blame. I really do *not* wish (I think) that it [this present cessation] should be anything else than a preparation and strengthening time for future toil; rather I should rejoice to think that I was in this way steeling myself in soul and body for it.

In the afternoon service yesterday, the second Psalm [for singing] was Ps. 121, Merrick's version. Now I cannot think

---

[1] 'Wilfulness the sin of Saul,' *University Sermons*.

the organist chose it on purpose, yet chosen on purpose it must have been by some one or other. So it seems like an omen or a promise.—Yours ever dutifully.

P.S.—Some time since Mrs. Copley sent me her History of the Bible. . . . Get Williams to see or write to her, with a message from me, and the gift of a book in turn. . . . Some book *on the Church* or like 'Thomas à Kempis,' or Taylor's 'Holy Living,' or against schism, so that it is not offensive. And I have wished some time to give James [the man-servant] Beveridge's 'Private Thoughts,' or some such book. Williams will help you here; and I have promised my laundress a book of the same kind. And I wish to give a gown to Bobbin's mother, but have not told him. H. W. [Henry Wilberforce], perhaps, will try to worm some of my sermons out of you, to *carry out of Oxford*—do not let him.

To his Mother.

Falmouth, December 5, 1832.

I arrived here between seven and eight o'clock this morning as expeditiously as I could hope. My companions are not yet arrived, as far as I can make out; but I have not long done breakfast, and did not get up till one o'clock. I got to Exeter at 1 P.M. yesterday, and set off by the Falmouth mail at seven in the evening.

A night journey through Devonshire and Cornwall is very striking for its mysteriousness; and it was a beautiful night, clear, frosty, and bright with a full moon. Mere richness of vegetation is lost by night, but bold features remain. As I came along, I had the whole train of pictures so vividly upon my mind, that I could have written a most interesting account of it in the most approved picturesque style of modern composition, but it is all gone from me by this time, like a dream.

The night was enlivened by what Herodotus calls a night engagement with a man, called by courtesy a gentleman, on the box. The first act ended by his calling me a d—— fool. The second by his insisting on two most hearty shakes of the hand, with the protest that he certainly did think me very injudicious and ill-timed. I had opened by telling him he was talking great nonsense to a silly goose of a maid-servant stuck atop of the coach; so I had no reason to complain of his choosing to give me the retort uncourteous. . . He assured me he reverenced my cloth. . . . It is so odd, he thought I had attacked him under personal feeling. I am quite ashamed of this scrawl, yet since I have a few minutes to spare I do not like to be otherwise employed than in writing.

I have already experienced several of those lesser inconveniences which become great as soon as they are dwelt upon, but shrink to their proper size when the mind is occupied by any more important object, whether of this world or the next. First, Fisk had *not* repaired the rent in the side of my cloak. Next, the buckle of my new carpet-bag broke before I set out, and the key broke in opening it at Exeter. I was obliged to improvisate a padlock, which again has got wrong in my journey here, and now a man is at it again. Thirdly, my portmanteau has been cut, but not badly. Fourthly, Harriett's purse has torn itself. Such is the present state of my expedition.

Our vessel is the 'Hermes'; it is the largest vessel in the Malta service. It has been seen miserably perplexed with the gales off the Downs, and is now expected hourly. Do not tell anyone any part of the nonsense I have been scrawling. P.S. The Froudes are just come.

Before entering upon the series of letters from abroad, extending from December 11, 1832, to July 1833, the Editor thinks it well to transcribe the following caution from the writer of them, without any further interference with the letters as they stand. Writing July 26, 1885, he says: 'Further—so widely has the world been thrown open since fifty years ago, that I may be very wrong in my *descriptions* and *statements of facts* of all kinds.—J. H. N.'

To his Mother.

On board the 'Hermes': December 11, 1832.

I wish you to receive the first letter I write home from foreign parts.

To-day has been the most pleasurable day—as far as externals go—I have ever had that I can recollect; and now, in the evening, I am sleepy and tired with the excitement. We are now off Cape Finisterre. Lights were just now visible from farmhouses on shore, which is, maybe, fifteen miles off. This morning early we saw the high mountains of Spain—

the first foreign land I ever saw, having finished most prosperously our passage across the formidable Bay of Biscay. The land first discovered was Cape Ortegal and its neighbourhood, magnificent in its outline; and, as we neared it, marked out with three lines of mountains; in some places very precipitous. At first we were about fifty miles off them, then twenty-five perhaps. At the same time the day cleared, and the sea, which even hitherto had been very fine, now became of a rich indigo colour; and, the wind freshening, was tipped with white edges, which, breaking into foam, turned into momentary rainbows. The sea-gulls, quite at home, were sailing about; and the vessel rocked to and fro with a motion which, unpleasant as it might have been, had the wind been from the south-west, was delightful as being from shore.

<u>I cannot describe the exquisite colour of the sea,</u> which, though not striking as being strange or novel, is unlike anything I have ever seen; so subdued, so destitute of all display, <u>so sober</u>—I should call it, so gentlemanlike in colour; and then so deep and solemn, and, if a colour can be so called, so strong; and then the contrast between the white and the indigo, and the change in the wake of the vessel into all colours — transparent green, white, white-green, &c. As evening came on, we had every appearance of being in a warmer latitude. The sea brightened to a glowing purple, inclined to lilac; the sun set in a car of gold, and was succeeded by a sky, first pale orange, then gradually heightening to a dusky red; while Venus came out as the evening star with its peculiar intense brightness. Now it is bright starlight.

We passed Corunna in the afternoon, but too far off to see more than the mountains above it. We shall not make Malta by Christmas Day. I think it very probable I shall not be home by Easter. . . . As to my work [the 'Arians.'—J. H. N.] I ought to give several months of correction to it, which I might give in the Long Vacation.

I have not been idle in the matter of verse-making. I have written a copy a day since I have been on board, besides others at Falmouth and Whitchurch.

The Captain is a very pleasant man. There are three midshipmen, and one above them, who may or may not be called lieutenant; for steam vessels are anomalies (they are all of the navy, as is the case with all packets now) There are, besides, a purser and a doctor. They are, all of them, young men from twenty to twenty-five; have seen a great deal of all parts of the world, have much interesting information, and are very gentlemanlike. It amuses one to scrutinise them. One so clever, the others hardly so. They have (most of them) made very few inductions, and are not in the habit of investigating causes—the very reverse of philosophers. They have good spirits and are very good-humoured. . . . Do not I write well, considering the sea is rocking up and down, up and down ? I am surprised at the ease with which I walk the deck—that is, at my having got my sea legs; and altogether how easily I do many things which seem difficult; and am disposed to think that hitherto [in past years] I have been working under a great pressure, and, should it please God ever to reverse it, I shall be like steam expanding itself. I shall end with one or two matters of business if I can recollect them. Should a letter come to me from the Bishop of London, offering me a Whitehall preachership, get Christie [J. F.], to whom I have spoken, to write him word (I use the expressions I wish him to use) that, since I was honoured with an interview, 'circumstances have arisen which have decided me in *declining* that flattering mark of his notice, should it be offered me, which, he said, was possible.' . . .

Excuse me if I have made blunders in this letter; it is too long to read over.

To his Sister Harriett.
On board the ' Hermes': December 12, 1832.

We are again out of sight of land, having been out in order to double Cape Finisterre. We lost the Lizard about five o'clock on Saturday, and after that did not see land till yesterday (Tuesday) morning, about ten. The interval was occupied in passing round 'the Bay,' which we did almost by a straight line from Falmouth to Cape Ortegal. Seldom at this time of year is a voyage so prosperous.

In giving his experience of sea-sickness Mr. Newman certainly did not look for a wide class of readers, but thought was busy; the impulse to analyse was strong in him; and he could reckon on amused sympathy; and perhaps may have it still.

My sea-sickness, if it may be so called, left me in twenty-four hours. It is an uncomfortable feeling certainly; but in saying that, I have said the worst of it. Never certainly had I ailment more easy to bear; and, so far from having my spirits depressed, I could do nothing but laugh at the oddity of my plight. It began on going down to dinner on Saturday. The motion is felt much more below, and the cabin is close. A strange feeling came over me; the heaving to and fro of everything seemed to puzzle me from head to foot, but in such a vague, mysterious way, that I could not get hold of it, or say what was the matter with me, or where. On I ate: I was determined, for it is one of the best alleviations. On I drank, but in so absurdly solemn a way, with such a perplexity of mind, not to say of body, that, as I have said, I laughed at myself. How I wished dinner over! Yet, on I sat, heaving up and down, to and fro, in an endless, meaningless motion; <u>a trouble without a crisis</u>: the discomfort of an uneasy dream. I went upstairs and got better. Then I lay down and was well. Got up at eleven at night, walked about, and was better again—went to bed and slept soundly. Sunday morning I was languid and qualmish; lay down on the deck and got well, but was afraid to stir. We had great difficulty to read the service. Archdeacon Froude was very bad and in bed. R. H. F. was getting well, but I did not like to let him try by himself. However, he read, and I was able to respond. I was better and worse all day, and after bed-time had no more trouble up to this time, when I eat and drink, loll about, read and write as usual. Sea-sickness is to me a very light evil; lying down is an instant specific for it, and eating a certain alleviation and fortifying against it.

I am only just now getting reconciled to my berth, which yet is very far superior to most, if not all, accommodations of the kind. I will not speak of its smallness, more like a coffin than a bed, nor of its darkness; but, first, think of the roll of the vessel to and fro. The first night my side was sore with the rub, rub of the motion. Then fancy the swinging, the never-ended swinging—you knock your head, you bruise your arms, all the while being shelved in a cupboard five feet from the floor. Then the creaking of the vessel; it is like half a hundred watchmen's rattles mixed with the squeaking of Brobdingnag pigs, while the water dashes, dash, dash against the side. Then overhead the loud foot of the watch, who goes on tramping up and down for more or less the whole night. Then in the morning the washing of the deck; rush comes an engine-pipe on the floor—ceases, is renewed, flourishes about, rushes again : then suddenly half a dozen brooms, wish-wash, wish-wash, scrib-scrub, scratching and roaring alternately. Then the heavy flump, flump of the huge cloth which is meant to dry the deck as a towel or duster. Last, and not least, the smell. In spite of airing it, the berth will smell damp and musty ; at best it is close ; there is no window in it ; it opens into the cabin, which at night is lighted with oil. Added to this, the want of room for your baggage, and your higgledy-piggledy state ; and you will allow I have given you enough of discomfort. Yet one day like yesterday outweighs them all ; and, in fact, they are vanishing fast To be sure, a valetudinarian could not bear it. I think that it would quite have knocked me up a year or two since : and as for those who, in advanced stages of consumption, are sent abroad, it must be a martyrdom : yet, I repeat, our vessel is a peculiarly convenient one.

But I am glad to say I am getting over all these things. First we have decided on going on with the vessel to Zante, Patras, Corfu, and to take Malta as the vessel comes back ; thus we are sure of remaining on board for a month and more to come ; so I shall unpack, which will be a comfort. . . . You must know that each berth has two sleeping-shelves, one above the other, which are both occupied when the vessel is full (fancy the misery). But we have no cabin passengers on board beside ourselves ; so we have our berth each to himself. Now the under shelf I shall empty of bedding and arrange my baggage there. There are several little shelves, too, on which I shall place various little articles and books. . . . Next I am getting to understand my berth, and the way of lying in it comfortably ; and certainly I cannot deny that it is snug, though odd. I get not to mind the noises, and I have effected a better ventilation.

This is all I have to say at present. Meanwhile, I transcribe one of my follies, having done it before breakfast this morning.

> Ere yet I left home's youthful shrine
> My heart and hope were stored
> Where first I caught the rays divine,
> And drank the Eternal Word.
>
> I went afar, the world unrolled
> Her many-pictured page ;
> I stored the marvels which she told,
> And trusted to her gage.

> Her pleasures quaffed, I sought awhile
>   The scenes I prized before ;
> But parent's praise, and sister's smile,
>   Stirred my cold heart no more.
>
> So ever sear, so ever cloy,
>   Earth's favours as they fade,
> Since Adam lost for one fierce joy
>   His Eden's sacred shade.'

I have written one on Athanasius, and a sort of song ; and one on the Church of Rome, and I wish to take Old Testament subjects, but cannot yet seize them.

I wonder what news you have at home all this while. How strange it is to have given up all thoughts about the French and Antwerp ! But, hearing nothing, we are forced, in self-defence, to forget what otherwise is so interesting. Rose has answered our proposal about the 'Lyra Apostolica' in the most flattering manner. I hope he will let us do as we will.

To his Sister Jemima.

The 'Hermes': December 12, 1832.

Having nothing at present to tell you, I have invented something, which I now send you.

> They do but grope in learning's pedant round
>   Who on the fantasies of sense bestow
>   An idle substance, bidding us bow low
> Before those shades of being which are found
> Stirring or still on man's scant trial ground ;
>   As if such shapes and moods, which come and go,
>   Had aught of Truth or Life in their poor show
> To sway or judge, and skill to sain or wound.
> Son of immortal Seed, high-destined Man !
> Know thy dread gift, a creature, yet a cause,
> Each mind is its own centre, and it draws
> Home to itself, and moulds in its thoughts' span,
> All outward things, the vassals of its will,
> Aided by Heaven, by earth unthwarted still.

> O Aged Saint ! far off I heard
>   The praises of thy name ;
> Thy deed of power, thy skilful word,
>   Thy zeal's triumphant flame.

Off the Lizard, December 8.

I came and saw; and, having seen,
Weak heart, I drew offence
From thy prompt smile, thy simple mien,
Thy lowly diligence.

The Saint's is not the Hero's praise;
This have I found, and learn,
Nor to profane Heaven's humblest ways,
Nor its least boon to spurn.

To-night the fire-flies are most beautiful, and the water phosphoric. We are in latitude 41° about. It is curious to see the Great Bear close to the water's edge. I was familiar enough with the Celestial Bear [this is an allusion to Whately] to make it feel odd to see him near the horizon; yet he quite squints, like a word ill spelt. I wish I could draw in your style a picture of men taking the log—that is, finding the rate the vessel is going. A rope is thrown into the sea with certain knots to mark the rate. It is briskly unwound from a roller as the vessel moves, while another man holds a minute glass. About four or five men are employed in it, and the grouping is very good.

December 13.—I have had before my eyes the last two hours visions such as I can hardly believe to be real : the Portuguese coast, in all that indescribable peculiarity of foreign scenery which paintings attempt. Whether it is in the clearness of the air or other causes, it is as different from England as possible, and I can hardly say how. The cliffs are high, composed of sandstone. They form a natural architecture—pyramids, and these in groups. The water, which is beautifully calm, breaks in high foam; the sun is bright and casts large shadows on the rocks and downs. Above, all is exposed, barren, or poorly cultivated; an immense plain, irregularly surfaced, slopes down to the brink of the cliffs, a beautiful pale reddish-brown. Through the glass we see houses, flocks of sheep, windmills with sails like a spider's web, martello towers with men lounging about the walls, woods of cork-trees with very long stems, all as clear and as unnaturally bright as you can fancy. To the south the town Mafra, which we are passing; above the magnificent heights of Torres Vedras. Cintra is to the south, and we are expecting it. It is so very tantalising that we cannot land and really determine that it *is* a country. It is like a vision. It is the first foreign soil I have come near. The line of Torres Vedras is now most distinct. We are passing a point beyond which we see nothing. But I suppose Cintra and Lisbon are on the other side.

Since I wrote the above the lines of Torres Vedras and the rocks underneath have passed before us like a pageant. The cliffs are high and bold, all sorts of colours, a greenish-reddish-brown, very sober. Above the cliffs are the country houses of the nobility, scattered along rising plains which terminate in a sharp bold outline, receiving and screening the lines of Torres Vedras. At the base of the cliffs the waves are dashed, the foam rising like Venus from the sea. I never saw more graceful forms, and so sedate and deliberate in their rising and falling. The colour of the heights a strange bluish-greyish something or other, very subdued.

Eight o'clock P.M.—In the afternoon we had two more sights: the rock of Lisbon, and the other side of the Torres Vedras, with the mouth of the Tagus. The latter is the most strange sight of this day. Am I only five days from England? Am I in Europe? I expect America to be different; but is it possible that what seems so unlike home should be so near home? How is the North cut off from the South! What colouring! A pale greenish-red which no words can describe, but such as I have seen in pictures of Indian landscape—an extremely clean and clear colour. We shall make Cadiz by to-morrow evening, while Williams is lecturing at Littlemore. The sunset has been fine—the sky bright saffron, the sea purple. The night is strangely warm. Latitude 39° or 38°. The Great Bear almost in the water. The glass 66° in my berth, which is cooler than the cabin, which opens upon the external air.

December 14.—The weather gets warmer and warmer, though I believe we are in astonishing fortune for the time of year. This morning porpoises are about us, and we nearly ran over two large turtles. The first object at sunrise was Cape St. Vincent. We had just spoken with a fisher-boat with four men. Whether it is the atmosphere or sky, the colours were very picturesque; the clearness of the air I cannot describe. I end, having room, with a verse:

> Poor wanderers, ye are sore distrest
> To find that path which Christ has blest,
> Tracked by His saintly throng;
> Each claims to trust his own weak will;
> Blind idol! so ye languish still,
> All wranglers, and all wrong.

> He saw of old, and met your need,
>   Granting you prophets of His creed,
>   The throes of fear to suage;
>   They fenced the rich bequest He made,
>   And sacred hands have safe conveyed
>   Their charge from age to age.
>
> Wanderers! come home! when erring most,
>   Christ's Church aye kept the faith, nor lost
>   One grain of Holy Truth;
>   She ne'er has erred as those ye trust,
>   And now shall lift her from the dust,
>   And reign as in her youth!

TO HIS MOTHER.

Gibraltar: on board the 'Hermes': December 16, 1832.

I went on deck this morning at sunrise, and took a survey of this place which one has heard of so much. We are in the harbour close by the Mole, lying under the inside of the Rock. Everything is foreign. To the N.E. by compass is the range of mountains which I spoke of to Aunt when I saw them at the other side at Cadiz. Under them, and close at hand, we see the town of St. Roque, and the hill called the Queen of Spain's Chair, because it is said she was placed at the top of it to see the siege of Gibraltar. To the east, in perspective, the Rock begins; and on the side of it lies the old Moorish town, which is still the seat of the mixed Gibraltar population. The old Moorish fort is visible, but I see nothing more. The great batteries, I am told, lie under.

The population is limited by rule to 18,000, in order to provide against the risk of an excess during a siege; but this rule is evaded, and the town held three times that number at the time of the yellow fever, two or three years since. The population is said to be very dense and dirty, with a great many Jews. The town is cut off from the garrison by walls of defence, and an open space, which is planted and called the Almeidah. Still closer to us are the barracks (still on the Rock), with the Government houses, officers' lodgings, &c. Under, and close opposite to our starboard stem, lie several Dutch coalers detained by the embargo. Right opposite on the other side of the vessel, and on the N.W., runs the Mole close to us, covered with coal, which the foreign jabbering heavers are conveying into the vessel.

The whole scene is something quite different from anything I have seen during this wonderful week, and unlike any picture or panorama I have met with.

The Rock has a magnificent outline, very sharp in the ridge ; the other and outer side (which we do not see) being perpendicular down to the Mediterranean. It is coloured with all sorts of hues—grey, red, white and green—all, of course, subdued. The space between the town and garrison is traversed by a road lying on the side of the cliff, with gardens on both sides. It is fringed with orange-trees as high as a mountain-ash (to judge from a distance), with long stems. The grass is tinted in places with a bright yellow, which, in England, we should judge to be buttercups. The garrison buildings are very picturesque. The barrack itself is a long, whitish, handsome building ; but about it are houses in groups—high, and turning all ways- painted of all colours. Close to us is a large, dull red shed or storehouse, low and long, with gables ; above them are buildings faced with blue, cream colour, brown, white and red.

The water is so clear we can see, plainly as if they were out of it, innumerable fish of considerable size playing about in all directions. Galleys and boats are moving about, one pulled by more oars than I could count. The morning is very bright—indeed, as the day gets on (now it is 10 A.M.), too bright for the beauty of the scene. Early the surgeon of the garrison came alongside of us, and we were each asked particularly about the cholera, whether we had been in cholera districts, &c. From his manner we are sure we shall be allowed to land ; but the Board of Health does not meet till after church ; so, instead of going to church on shore, we shall enjoy the black dust of the coal. The yellow quarantine flag dangles from our mast-head. Having at this moment nothing to write, I add a sonnet which I meant to have sent to Aunt :

> Are these the tracks of some unearthly Friend ?
> His footprints, and his vesture skirts of light,
> Who, as I talk with men, conforms aright
> Their sympathetic words, or deeds that blend
> With my hid thought ;—or stoops him to attend
>   My doubtful—pleading grief ;—or blunts the might
>   Of ill I see not ;—or in dreams of night
> Figures the scope in which what is will end ?
> Were 1 Christ's own, then fitly might I call
> That vision real ; for to the thoughtful mind
> That walks with Him, He half unveils His face ;
> But when on common men such shadows fall,
> They dare not make their own the gifts they find,
> Yet, not all hopeless, eye His boundless grace.

Last night the stillness, after a week's rattling and roaring, had a most singular effect ; it was so unnatural. I never felt anything like it, and cannot describe it. I had, in consequence, a very good night—the first for a week—it was very soothing.

Eight P.M.—Our fate is decided, we are not to be released till 2 P.M. to-morrow. The St. Roque Spaniards, who are members of the Board of Health, are the cause of our quarantine. This has been a most uncomfortable day ; a Sunday without the signs of a Sunday I can hardly understand. The vessel not being allowed to stop over to-morrow, the men have been all day engaged in bringing on coal. It has been one scene of confusion, dust flying about—the cabin, in consequence, closed—the native coalmen jabbering about nothing at all ; the sun blazing on deck ; service impossible ; the crew very busy or very idle and listless. The warmth of the weather is quite strange, but not relaxing at all. Yesterday we left off all our fire, which even before was nominal, and dined with open skylights. The nights are brilliantly starlight, yet without anything like frost. Mars, to all appearance, almost in the zenith.

I shall be heartily sick of not hearing from you till I get to Naples, which is the first place to which letters may be safely directed. . . . I add a sonnet,[1] and some verses :

> Whence is this awe, by stillness spread
>   O'er the world-fretted soul ?
> Wave reared on wave its boastful head,
> While my keen bark, by breezes sped,
> Dashed fiercely through the ocean bed,
>   And chafed towards its goal.
>
> But now there reigns so deep a rest,
>   That I could almost weep.
> Sinner ! thou hast in this rare guest
> Of Adam's peace, a figure blest ;
> 'Tis Eden seen, but not possessed,
>   Which cherub-flames still keep.

> O Lord ! when sin's close marshalled line
>   Urges Thy witness on his way,
> How should he raise Thy glorious Sign,
>   And how Thy Will display ?
> Thy holy Paul, with soul of flame,
>   Rose on Mars'-hill, a soldier lone ;
> Shall I thus speak the Atoning Name,
>   Though with a heart of stone ?

---

[1] Never published.

'Not so,' He said :—' hush thee, and seek,
With thoughts in prayer and watchful eyes,
My seasons sent for thee to speak,
And use them as they rise.'

To his Sister Harriett.

On board the 'Hermes': December 18, 1832.

I have sent you from Gibraltar, by the 'Flamer' steam-packet, a parcel containing two letters to my Mother, and one inside parcel, with six letters besides, to you and Jemima, to Aunt, to the Archdeacon (Oxford), to the Provost, to Pope.

We left Gibraltar at 9 P.M. yesterday, and are now on the open Mediterranean—the sea without a billow, and a strange contrast to the Atlantic; and in the distance the dim shadows of snowy mountains, ranging up the Spanish coast to the N.E. Africa out of sight.

But I must go back to give you an account of our brief visit to Gibraltar. I no longer wonder at younger persons being carried away with travelling, and corrupted; for certainly the illusions of the world's magic can hardly be fancied while one remains at home. I never felt any pleasure or danger from the common routine of pleasures, which most persons desire and suffer from—balls, or pleasure parties, or sights—but I think it does require strength of mind to keep the thoughts where they should be while the variety of strange sights—political, moral, and physical—are passed before the eyes, as in a tour like this. (I have just been called up to see the mountains of Grenada, which we have neared; they are enveloped in a sheet of snow.)

With this remark I proceed to give you some poor account of our visit to Gibraltar, the first foreign land I ever put foot on.

We were to have obtained pratique, as it is called (I cannot learn the right meaning of the word), at 2 P.M. yesterday (Monday), but by the good offices of one of Archdeacon Froude's friends, who was afterwards our guide and host, a meeting of the Board of Health was effected in the morning, and we were allowed to land about half-past twelve. Col. Rogers, of the Artillery (the officer in question), took Archdeacon Froude in his gig, and gave Hurrell and me horses, and off we set to the southern point of the Rock—Point Europa. Here the Rock is thrown about into a vast variety of forms with deep fissures or valleys, and most picturesque groups in consequence. It is

of a grey colour, varied here and there with a reddish sand.
What the solid Rock is composed of I am ashamed to say I
do not know ; but it may be the same as the rock which is
always forming around it—namely, a sandstone cemented
and indurated by water passing through limestone. In consequence, it has an oolitic appearance, and sometimes a granitic.
There are various caves abounding in stalactites in consequence.
The lime is so adhesive that they mix no glutinous substance
in the whitewash made of it, as they do in England ; and
when used for walks, instead of gravel, we observed it looked
as solid as a granite pavement. The old Moorish fortifications
are entirely made of it—that is, of *the earth* of the place.
They are entirely made of earth rammed tight together in a
framework, which is afterwards removed after the manner of
the Pisans, which the Duke of Bedford introduced to England
some time since at Woburn Abbey.

So much on the nature of the rock. As we rode up the
carriage-way the Rock seemed to heighten marvellously. It
had so hung over us, and at the same time receded from us,
when we were in the vessel, that it seems but a few hundred
feet high, being really 1,500 feet. But now our up-hill ride
convinced us, though our eyes were unconvinced ; still, I can
give you no account of the guns and batteries, which I do not
understand ; of course, they are very imposing. Before us lay
the range of African mountains, which differ in shape from
the Spanish. The African seems to be of volcanic origin—
conical and independent like waves. Ape's hill rises 3,000
feet from the sea, being the termination of the Atlas chain.
Behind we saw this part of the Atlas distinctly, covered with
snow, I think ; the range is very high, the highest mountain
being 10,000 feet. Further towards the east, about Fez, the
range is highest, being in one place 14,000 or 15,000 ; I forget
which.

The Rock of Gibraltar, where we now were, presented a
very broken surface, being more like haycocks or a ploughed
field than anything else. In the intervals grow large aloes,
the flowers still remaining ; geraniums clothe them as ground-
ivy may a bank in England. As we went along the road,
huge cactuses sprawled over the walls. I did not know they
grew so large ; they were as thick as the trunk of a good-
sized tree. The oranges were in full fruit, and various other
hot-house plants. We went round the side as far as the
Monkey Cave, where we were fortunate enough to see some of

the monkeys skipping like birds all over the surface. The Colonel considered we were in high luck. He was in Gibraltar two years before he saw one; yet we also saw some afterwards on the north. At the furthest extremity we reached, the cliff descends right down to the sea from the top, 1,500 feet! with hardly a break, certainly none of consequence. There are caverns at the bottom.

After entering the town we went first to the convent, which is now the Government House. Archdeacon Froude had introductions with him to a number of superior officers, and he took this opportunity of staying half an hour with Col. Mair, the Governor's Secretary, with whom we lunched. He is a very young-looking man for a Colonel, remarkably handsome and agreeable, and of a literary turn. On looking over his table I was surprised and amused to see the 'British Magazine' there among the books.[1] We had a delightful lounge in the convent garden, which even at this season is luxuriant and fragrant. Immense cactuses, the date, the orange, the lemon, the custard-apple, the turpentine-tree, the dragon-tree; last, and not least, the palm, about eighteen feet high, and a most singular tree—a perfect garden of Alcinous. Col. Mair told us that in a month's time the garden would be one mass of odours and splendours. Col. Mair gave us some superb Cyprus wine, and then we set off to join Col. Rogers again.

. . . I will transcribe for you a sort of ecclesiastical carol which I wrote as an experiment, but which I am by no means confident is a successful one.

> Faint not, and fret not, for threatened woe,
> Watchman on Truth's grey height!
> Few though the faithful and fierce though the foe,
> Weakness is aye Heaven's might.
>
> Infidel Ammon and niggard Tyre,
> Ill-attuned pair, unite;
> Some work for love, and some work for hire,
> But weakness shall be Heaven's might.
>
> Eli's feebleness, Saul's black wrath,
> May aid Ahitophel's spite;
> And prayers from Gerizim, and curses from Gath,
> Our weakness shall be Heaven's might.

---

[1] This was afterwards explained to Mr. Newman when, on his return to England, he found Col. Mair was brother-in-law to Mr. Rose—the editor—at whose table he afterwards met him.

Quail not and quake not, thou Warder bold,
    Be there no friend in sight;
Turn thee to question the days of old,
    When weakness was aye Heaven's might.

Moses was one, yet he stayed the sin
    Of the host in the Presence bright;
And Elias scorned the Carmel-din
    When Baal would scan Heaven's might.

Time's years are many, Eternity one,
    And one is the Infinite;
The chosen are few, few the deeds well done,
    So scantness is still Heaven's might.

P.S. *December* 26.—I purpose sending you this letter from Corfu overland, and I shall send a packet of letters and a chest of oranges by the 'Hermes' on its return. I send you some verses.

How can I keep my Christmas feast
    In its due festive show,
Reft of the sight of the High Priest
    From whom its glories flow?

I hear the tuneful bells around,
    The blessed towers I see;
A stranger on a foreign ground,
    They peal a fast for me.

O Britons! now in scoffings brave,
    How will you meet the day
When Christ reclaims the gift He gave
    And calls the Bride away?

Your Christmas then will lose its mirth,
    Your Easter lose its bloom;—
Abroad a scene of strife and dearth;
    Within, a cheerless home!

TO HIS SISTER JEMIMA.

On board the 'Hermes': December 18, 1832.

I finished Harriett's letter abruptly; the paper ending like the night in the narratives of Scheherazade. This day has been just fitted for writing these letters: first, as being the very next day after my visit to Gibraltar; next, we have been nearly all day out of sight of land; thirdly, I am indisposed to any exertion of body—such as walking the deck—from the labours of yesterday. The sun has been so hot to-day we have had an awning on deck. Porpoises and sword-fish have been sporting about us; the sea being as calm and the motion of the vessel as slight as that of a steamer going to Richmond on the Thames. . . . We expect to make Algiers by Thursday morning. Col. Rogers walked down with us to the water's edge. He is a hospitable, warm-hearted, and considerate man. We are much indebted to him. It does not diminish our debt to him, that it broke the monotony of his military life to entertain strangers. He spoke in high terms of the Mess, but lamented that so few officers were single men, so that he had but a small society. As our boat went off to the vessel, I saw again the electric phenomenon which I mentioned in a former letter; and its beauty cannot be exaggerated. The edge of the water, where it broke against the pier, was all on fire. Wherever the oar went it was a sheet of soft liquid flame, sparkling besides, wherever the splashes fell. It was as if the under surface of the water was fire, and the oar turned it up. We got back to the vessel very tired. It set off about nine. I slept soundly, and found myself this morning in the open sea.

When Marshal Bourmont was here two years ago, his criticism on Gibraltar was that its fortifications were overdone. This may be true, but such a judgment will vary with possession and non-possession.

By a curious coincidence an assistant chaplain of my name is expected here. Accordingly the report got about that he had come, and Arch-*bishop* Froude had come to consecrate the chapel. . . .

Having nothing more to say, I conclude with some verses:

> Tyre of the West, and glorying in the name
>   More than in Faith's pure fame,
> O trust not crafty fort nor rock renowned,
>   Earned upon hostile ground;
> Wielding Trade's master-keys, at thy proud will,
> To lock or loose its waters, England! trust not still.
>
> Dread thine own power! since haughty Babel's prime
>   High towers have been man's crime;
> Since her hoar age, when the huge moat lay bare,
>   Strongholds have been man's snare.
> Thy nest is in the crags; ah! refuge frail!
> Mad counsel in its hour, or traitors, will prevail.
>
> He who scanned Sodom for his righteous men,
>   Still spares thee for thy ten;
> But should vain hands pollute the temple wall,
>   More than His church will fall;
> For as Earth's kings welcome their spotless guest
> So gives He them by turn to suffer or be blest.

To his Mother.

On board the 'Hermes': December 19, 1832.

One great convenience of a voyage is that time is given one to record one's thoughts as they occur, and to see things without the bustle of moving and an over-rapid succession. And I am glad that this has been my fortune at the earlier part of my tour, when my impressions from new objects are more vivid than they will be in a short time. Yet, however interested I have been in what I have seen, I do not think I have ever for a moment so felt as not to have preferred, had the option been given me, to find myself suddenly back again in the midst of those employments and pleasures, that come to me at home in the course of ordinary duty (perhaps the moment when I first saw Cadiz, with the hope of landing, is an exception), so that I have good hope I shall not be unsettled by my present wanderings. For what are all these strange sights but vanities, attended too, as they ever must be, with anxious watchfulness lest the heart be corrupted by them, and by the unpalatable necessity of working up oneself to little acts of testifying and teaching, which mere indolence, not to say more, leads one to shrink from! So that I really do think that the hope of benefiting my health and increasing my usefulness and influence, are the main considerations which [cause me to] absent myself from you and Oxford. Yet even [such] thoughts do not reconcile me to the length of time I shall be away, which is so vast as quite to make me despond; and under these forlorn feelings I cannot but limit my view to the present day, and enjoy the novelties and wonders before me, dismissing all thoughts of the places which are yet to be undergone before I get back. You must not suppose me melancholy because I say all this; it is, of course, an habitual feeling with me which I now express, partly because I have leisure for it, partly because I happen still to be somewhat fatigued with the exertions of the day before yesterday. We are now still making for Algiers, being out of sight of land. The weather most delightful, with a breeze aft.

What has inspired me with all sorts of strange reflections these two days is the thought that I am in the Mediterranean. Consider how the coasts of the Mediterranean have been the seat and scene of the most celebrated empires and events which are in history. Think of the variety of men, famous in every way, who have had to do with it. Here the Romans and Carthaginians fought; here the Phœnicians traded; here Jonah was in the storm; here St. Paul was shipwrecked; here the great Athanasius voyaged to Rome. Talking of Athanasius, I will give you some verses about him:

> When shall our Northern Church her champion see,
>   Raised by Divine decree,
> To shield the ancient Truth at his own harm?
>   Like him who stayed the arm
> Of tyrannous power, and learning's sophist-tone,
>   Keen-visioned Seer, alone.
>
> The many crouched before an idol-priest,
>   Lord of the world's rank feast.
> In the dark night, 'mid the Saints' trial sore
>   He stood, then bowed before
> The Holy Mysteries,—he, their meetest sign,
>   Weak vessel, yet divine.
>
> Cyprian is ours, since the high-souled primate laid
>   Under the traitorous blade
> His silvered head. And Chrysostom we claim
>   In that clear eloquent flame
> And deep-taught zeal in the same woe, which shone
>   Bright round a Martyr's throne.
>
> And Ambrose reared his crosier from the tomb,
>   Though with unequal doom,
> When in dark times our champion crossed a king—
>   But good in everything
> Comes as ill's cure. Dim Future! shall we need
>   A prophet for Truth's Creed?

December 23.

I write this before we get to Malta, which is to be to-morrow morning, lest new sights should confuse old ones. A severe gale, from which I am just recovering, has prevented my writing what I have to tell while I saw it. I began this letter on Wednesday, the 19th. On Thursday morning, which was very fine, we neared Cape Tenez, a fine headland—but I shall weary you with my descriptions. The sun was behind it, and as it ascended and shot its rays downwards, the surface, which had before been purple, became varied into hills and ravines, beautifully coloured of a rich sienna. Mount Atlas soon showed itself again, and went with us the greater part of the day. A sublime range, indeed, with its head every now and then in the clouds, and three or four tiers of heights under it, till the eye came down to the cliffs overhanging the sea—*vide* the first fifty lines of the 'Odyssey.' Only in a steam vessel can one approach so near the land. About dinner time—three o'clock—we neared Algiers, which, in its way, is as interesting a sight as we have had. I wish I could do justice to it.

On going on deck there lay before the eye a huge hill covered with heath, with folds and recesses and a roundish form. On this hill—I suppose a mile or two from the town—were perched about a number of very white houses, apparently of Frank merchants, looking very desolate, as if they wondered how they got there. They seemed to have no gardens, lodges, farmyards, or outhouses, such as make an English country house look like a small village. At length the town opened upon us. It lies on the side of a slant, not very steep, apparently, and is of a triangular form, not reaching to the top of the hill, with the fortifications in front of its base. The French tricolour floated from them. The houses are closely jammed together, and are of a discoloured yellow. They have very small windows, some high narrow arches at bottom. The western side of the steep (I did not observe the other) is flanked by a high wall. A mosque stands without it, and there are several within. A considerable space walled in is still further west, and at the foot of the heathy hills. The fortifications run along the water's edge with one high tower; here Lord Exmouth took his station. The French, on the contrary, landed in the bay to the east, and attacked the city behind.

A boat was put off to us to receive the despatches, rowed by four natives - strange-looking fellows—two with somewhat Saracenic features ; the other two puzzled me, being very like the old Egyptians : yellow, with skin like leather—you could hardly believe it to be skin—and fine regular features. One of them, with a remarkable vacancy of countenance, took no notice of us, though we were staring at him, or of our vessel : a vacancy like a statue, most strange. This nest of insects, with 4,000 sick in the city—which is small and has such a reputation for the plague that, had we touched anything belonging to them, even their boat, we should, I suppose, have incurred three weeks' quarantine at Malta—affected to put us in quarantine on account of the cholera, and were prompt in assuring us we must not land ; and would not receive our letters till they were cut through (to let out the cholera, I suppose), and then only at the end of a pair of tongs. How odd it is I should have lived to see Algiers !

After Algiers we saw nothing worth speaking of. We made the small island of Galita yesterday (the 22nd). This morning (the 23rd) we neared Cape Bon, and saw the track to Carthage. An island lies to the west, and the course is between the two. Nothing I had seen so touched me as this. I thought of the Phœnicians, Tyre, of the Punic Wars, of Cyprian, and the glorious Churches now annihilated; the two headlands looked the same then as now; and I recollected I was now looking at Africa for the last time in my life. It disappeared towards noon, and as it diminished, Pantellaria came in sight, a fine volcanic island, thirty miles in circumference. We passed close by its small town. It has an unfathomable lake in the centre, once the crater of a volcano. Its inhabitants are mixed Italian and Arabic. It is a dependency of Sicily. And now we are making quickly for Malta.

I am greatly wearied by the gale we encountered after Algiers, which was severe enough to make half the sailors sick. . . .

Malta: December 24.

I am quite recruited now, and proceed: I care little for sea-sickness itself, but the attendances on it are miserable. . . . The worst of sea-sickness is the sympathy which all things on board have with it, as if they were all sick too. First, all the chairs, tables, and the things on them much more, are moving, moving up and down, up and down, swing, swing. A tumbler turns over, knife and fork go, wine is spilt, as if encouraging like tendencies within you. In this condition you go on talking and eating as fast as you can, concealing your misery, which you are reminded of by every motion of the furniture around you. At last the moment comes; you are seized; up you get, swing, swing, you cannot move a step forward; you knock your hips against the table, run smack at the side of the cabin, try to make for the door in vain, which is your only aim. [There being no ladies on board, the three voyagers were allowed berths in the ladies' cabin; but dinner was in the men's cabin.] You get into your berth at last, but the door keeps banging; you lie down, and now a new misery begins—the noise of the bulkheads: they are sick too. You are in a mill; all sorts of noises, heightened by the gale, creaking, clattering, shivering and dashing. Your bed is sea-sick, swinging up and down, to your imagination, as high and as low as a swing in a fair, incessantly. This requires strong nerves to bear; and the motion is not that of a simple swing, but epicyclical, thus ⊙ a ⊙, a being the point where the motion begins, and then back again. And, last of all, the bilge water in the hold ; a gale puts it all in motion. Our vessel was hastily sent off from Woolwich, before it was properly cleaned ; and the smell was like nothing I ever smelt, suffocating. What would I have given to have been able to sleep on deck on Thursday night last ! But the hail and sleet made it impossible. Of course I had no rest.

Another trouble : you know a lee shore is always formidable to sailors. Now we were off a coast without a harbour in it, the wind shifting about from the N.W. to N.E. This, indeed, is little to a steamer, which moves against the wind. But on Wednesday our engines had got damaged, and taken a long time to mend, and we fancied they might not be strong enough to make way against the gale, which was severe. About two in the morning the engines stopped ; we did not know why. So I got up and went on deck, and was relieved by being told all was right, but it had been an anxious matter.

The next day, Friday, the usual swell followed, which is sadly fatiguing. I have not had a night's sleep since I left England, except when we were quiet at Gibraltar, and it is wonderful how little I suffer from it. I am sore all over with the tossing, and very stiff, and so weak that at times I can hardly put out a hand. But my spirits have never given way for an instant, and I laughed when I was most indisposed. And now we are safe at Malta, and hope, please God, to have a quiet night before Christmas Day. We start for Corfu on Wednesday, but it is the passage of only a day or two ; we remain there six days, and then back to the Lazaret ; then I shall try to write verses. Not a day has passed since I embarked without my doing a copy. When I was most qualmish I solaced myself with verse-making. I send 'Bide thou thy time,'[1] ' Moses,' ' Woe's me.'[2]

> Bide thou thy time !
> Watch with meek eyes the race of pride and crime
> Sit in the gate, and be the heathen's jest,
>   Smiling and self-possest.
> O thou to whom is pledged a victor's sway,
>   Bide thou the victor's day !

---

[1] 'The Afflicted Church.'   [2] 'Jeremiah.'

Think on the sin
That reaped the unripe seed ; and toiled to win
Foul history-marks at Bethel and at Dan—
No blessing, but a ban ;
Whilst the wise shepherd hid his heaven-told fate,
Nor recked a tyrant's hate.

Such need is gain ;
Wait the bright advent that shall loose thy chain !
E'en now the shadows break, and gleams divine
Edge the dim distant line.
When thrones are trembling, and earth's fat ones quail,
True Seed ! thou shalt prevail !

Moses, the patriot fierce, became
  The meekest man on earth,
To show us how Love's quickening flame
  Can give our souls new birth.

Moses, the man of meekest heart,
  Lost Canaan by self-will,
To show where Grace hath done its part,
  How sin defiles us still.

Thou Who hast taught me in Thy fear,
  Yet seest me frail at best,
O grant me loss with Moses here,
  To gain his future rest !

'Woe's me !' the peaceful prophet cried,
  ' Spare me this troubled life ;
To stem man's wrath, to school his pride,
  To head the sacred strife !

' O place me in some silent vale
  Where groves and flowers abound ;
Nor eyes that grudge, nor tongues that rail,
  Vex the truth-haunted ground !'

If his meek spirit erred, opprest
  That God denied repose,
What sin is ours, to whom Heaven's **rest**
  Is pledged, to heal earth's woes ?

To his Sister Harriett.

On board the ' Hermes ': December 25, 1832.

We are keeping the most wretched Christmas Day, and it seems a sad return to that good Providence who has conducted us here so safely and so pleasantly. By bad fortune we are again taking in coals on a holy day, and as the captain's orders are precise about his stay, there seems no alternative. But what provokes me is that the coal will be got in by the afternoon, and they are making preparation for a Christmas dinner, which seems incongruous. This morning we saw a poor fellow in the Lazaret close to us, cut off from the ordinances of his Church, saying his prayers with his face to the house of God in his sight over the water; and it is a confusion of face to me that the humblest Romanist testifies to his Saviour as I, a minister, do not. Yet I do what I can, and shall try to do more, for I am very spiteful.

Yesterday morning, Monday the 24th, we saw Gozo on first coming on deck (by-the-bye, Graham Island, which went down, was about fifteen miles from Pantellaria, which I spoke of to my Mother). Next we passed Camino, and then came Malta. These three are called the Maltese Islands. We passed along the north side; on our left, in the distance, being the height above Girgenti in Sicily. One of the first sights we came to in Malta was St. Paul's Bay, where tradition goes that the Apostle was wrecked. Above St. Paul's Bay is Città Vecchia, where probably was the Roman garrison spoken of, Acts xxviii. They say there are many antiquities there.

Malta is a strange place, a literal rock of a yellowish brown; the coast presents an easy slope towards the sea, and the plain is intersected by a number of parallel walls to keep up the soil. They say here they have had a month of rain, and that the weather changed yesterday. In what good fortune are we! It was certainly a beautiful day, like July, no sign of winter; but it is only what we have had nearly the whole of our passage. This is the rainy season here, I believe. The night turned cold, and there was much rain and heavy in the early morning, and it has been raining now.

Immediately on our mooring (opposite to the Lazaretto) we were put under the care of a guardian who watches over our quarantine, both to keep us from others and others from us. A queer set of fellows they are, with yellow collars. We are in the smaller port off the Manual Battery. There is a bright sun upon the light-brown rock and fortresses. The sea a deep green; a number of little boats, some strangely rigged, others strangely rowed, pushing to and fro, painted bright colours; not a few Greek trading-vessels of a respectable size. Their flag is blue and white striped. I never saw a finer group than the coalheavers on the wharf. There are about a dozen of them of all ages, slight and elegantly formed men, many of them—they stood for perhaps half an hour, waiting for our being ready, each in his own attitude, and grouped.

In the afternoon we got into one of our boats, and rowed round the quarantine harbour, for which leave is granted. First we went to the parlatorio, which is the place of intercourse between men in and out of quarantine. It is a long naked building or barn divided into several rooms, and cut lengthway from end to end by two barriers parallel, breast high. Between these two, guardians are stationed to hinder contact, the men in quarantine on one side, the townsmen on the other, the latter being either friends of the imprisoned party, or pedlars, traffickers, &c. A crowd of persons are on the prison side, each party under the conduct of its own guardian; for if these parties were to touch each other the longer quarantine would be given to the party which had the smaller number. If I were to touch a Greek, I should have fifteen days of quarantine. The strange dresses, the strange languages, the jabbering and grimaces, the queer faces driving a bargain across the barrier, without a common language, the solemn absurd guardians with their staves in the space between, the opposite speaker fearing nothing so much as touching you, and crying out and receding at the same time, made it as curious a sight as the free communication of breath, and the gratuitous and inconsistent rules of this intercourse made it ridiculous. But the British Government is forced to be strict in its rules by the jealousy of other Powers. By being so, Malta becomes a gate for the whole Continent, and the Lazaret here is much more comfortable than elsewhere, so that it is lucky for us that it is so. Yet, absurd as the system is, I believe the plague is strictly contagious. They say that before now its circle has been gradually narrowed till it actually has been shut up in a box.

The most interesting sight in the parlatorio was a number of Greeks. Their most graceful and becoming dresses, their fine countenances and shapes and attitudes, and the thought of their ancestors, not only heathen but Christian, contrasted with the fact, which no one can doubt, that they are now as a people heartless and despicable, sunk below the Turks their masters, made me feel very melancholy. But the power which out of the wild olive-tree formed an Origen or an Athanasius, can transform them too. Fancy being rowed in an open boat without a greatcoat on a December evening, and not feeling cold. The sun went down gloriously and the sky was of an indescribable gold colour. The only object of interest which struck me on our return, was a vessel towed by about a dozen of small boats, like a number of ants bringing in some large insect into their nest.

The bells are beautiful here, as at Gibraltar and Cadiz, deep and sonorous, and they have been going all the morning, to me very painfully [for reasons above given]. We went after breakfast across the plank to the Lazaretto to choose our rooms for our return to Malta. It is as like a prison as one pea to another, yet it is a fine one too. The loss of fifteen days quite casts us down. After several courts we came to a quadrangle of curious but simple architecture. A flight of steps leads to a gallery which runs round it outside, almost half-way up, and is supported by a strange kind of prop

It is imposing. In this gallery are openings into our apart ments. We may have as many of them as we please, and all for nothing. They are fine rooms, fifty by thirty at least (we measured them); the roof is arched, the walls whitewashed, the floors stone pavement. No furniture (they say we can buy furniture almost for nothing, for a few dollars); there *are* bed-*steads*. We find everything. We have taken two rooms; we shall sleep in one and live in the other. I should not have been unwilling to have been there for a few days for the fun of the thing, nor do I care for the *length*, but for the *waste* of time. But we *must* have had a quarantine somewhere; in the north of Italy I suppose, if we went overland, and for our fifteen days we have gained a sight of Gibraltar, and shall see the Ionian Isles besides Malta itself. No one knows whether, in the course of events, it may not be our turn to be put into a worse prison than this. We shall make ourselves as comfortable as we can, eat and drink. I shall write, and perhaps hire a violin. After all, it is a great waste of time when life is so short, and one has so much to do. I thought of learning Italian. I know enough to read a good deal, but as to speaking you must be among the people.

I hear there is an overland post from Corfu, which I shall avail myself of, to send a letter to you. Ah! those sad bells; there they go again. I have not time to read this over, and this applies to all my letters. The Malta windmills have six

sails, and are strengthened against the wind by a rod at right
angles to the sails from their centre, with strings from it to
their ends.

To his Sister Jemima.

Between Zante and Patras: December 29, 1832.

At this moment our prospects are clouded, though it is
nothing to you to know this some six weeks hence. We are
threatened with twenty-one or fifty days' quarantine on our
return to Malta. Don't go and tell anyone. Of course, we
get into difficulties, *and* we get out; but if only the getting in
is known, it is a good joke to hearers. At Malta we were
assured by the quarantine people we should have but fifteen
days for visiting the Ionian Isles, and we were sure of having
nearly as much for touching at Gibraltar. Now we find that
Lord Nugent has, out of his own head, put the Isles in
pratique with the Morea, which is in twenty-one or forty or
fifty days' quarantine with Malta. This we learned on touching at Zante (pronounced Zant). Besides, we have taken on
board passengers from the Morea.

Our new passengers are the military Governor of Cerigo,
old Cytherea [Col. Longley], and the Consul of Pátrās [Mr.
Crowe], and their account of the state of the Morea is deplorable. It is literally overrun with banditti; and a traveller
cannot touch on the coast without being robbed. We have
had numerous instances of this in the case of military men or
messengers with despatches. The coast, too, swarms with
little pirates who have look-outs on the hills, who signal, and
the pirate vessels run into places where our men-of-war cannot
follow them. In such a state is the country that the factions,
tired of mutual inflictions, have in some instances had recourse
to the Turkish authorities on the other side the Gulf, for
arbitration or redress, as the Belgians may be doing to
Holland. Russia is at the bottom of these troubles, in order
to gain the post of arbitration and then of sovereignty, when
the Porte falls, which seems soon expected. She has encouraged a portion of the National Senate to withdraw from the
seat of Government, and set up for themselves against the
new Regency, which is now in progress from Germany with
King Otho. The English Consul, now on board, was forced
to fly from Patras, sending his wife and family on board an
English man-of-war—Sir John Franklin's. Meanwhile, the
Turkish dominions are orderly, and, while the coast from

Patras to Corinth is impossible, Athens may safely be visited. Indeed, one of the schemes that has dawned on us, if we are driven hard, is to make for Janina, and so for Athens. I am called on deck. Ithaca is in sight.

It is so strange in a vessel: you go on at your employment downstairs; you are called on deck, and find everything new. A scene is spread before you as if by magic, and you cannot believe it is real. I am now in the Greek sea, the scene of old Homer's song and of the histories of Thucydides. Yesterday was the most delightful day I have had. The morning was wet — being the first rain — except a shower perhaps at Malta (I forget), since leaving England. I am sorry to find we are in the rainy season. Last night it rained incessantly; a pouring rain you have no idea of at home. We could see Zante, at the distance of sixty miles, with Cephalonia on the left. The latter is different from anything I have seen; the outline, formed by what is called the Black Mountain, of a bluish black; which, being more or less covered with snow at top, looked like polished marble. We sailed between them and then we saw the Peloponnesus in the distance — kindling what different thoughts from the Morea! — the coast, blue from the distance, with two purplish rocks, isles or promontories, in front, and behind a long and high range of snow mountains; to the left, far in the distance, the Acarnanian coast, somewhere about the mouths of the Achelous.

Night fell before we reached Zante (the town), but we got into a boat and made for shore. We wandered about the town, and curious it is—(I have just been called to see a magnificent snow mountain towards the north-west point of the Peloponnesus; the outline is wonderful; a sheer descent; the day very unfavourable, thick and cloudy)—a triangular space or *Place* surrounded by good-looking houses — a guardroom, &c., with towers, a great many streets beyond it, narrow and flagged, or like flagging. What appeared the chief street had arcades running along on each side, giving it a handsome appearance. The shops all open, without fronts, like booths in England; the halls of private houses open, with stairs and a gallery; a good many churches. Most people were abed, we were told: those who were about were singing, walking fast perhaps the while: some singing in parts, particularly in shops, as at a shoemaker's. We went into the principal inn — such a strange place — into a billiard-room, into several coffee- and smoking-rooms, a barber's, a wine-merchant's, a currant-merchant's, a pipe-seller's. We were surprised at the wealth of this shop. The pipes were from 100 dollars (20*l.*) downwards. At a nondescript shop, a young urchin was buying his obol worth of oil and bread for supper. We saw a barrel of Cornish pilchards, which have long been in use here. We drank some of the *vin ordinaire*—which we thought very good of the kind—red and white. The men were miserably filthy, and the countenances of many, who were drinking or playing backgammon, &c., slovenly and sottish. We were told they were the principal men of the place.

By-the-bye, I think I have made up my mind about going to operas, &c. I think it allowable—as far as merely going to *see the place*, &c.—in the same sense in which it is allowable to visit the country at all—*e.g.* I see no objection to going into a heathen country for the sake of seeing it, and going into a playhouse is nothing more than this. If I may not go into a place because bad men are in it, where *can* I go ? If, indeed, I go for the sake of the amusement—which would be the case if I *frequented* it—then it would be a different matter; but I go and see, as I go and see a coffee-house, a billiard-room, or a mosque. Nor am I supporting persons in a bad way of life —that is, the actors - for if no one went but strangers, as a matter of curiosity, they would have a poor living. Theatres are set up, not as objects of curiosity, but of amusement. I am only seeing what is established and supported ; not establishing and supporting it myself.

To return. When we rose this morning—raining as it was —the view, which the night had hidden, was so lovely, that we deplored our fate, which hindered our seeing the place at more advantage. Virgil calls the island 'nemorosa'[1]—it still deserves the title. The whole face of a beautiful and varied rock was covered with olive-trees in an exquisite way. They say that the view over the heights, which takes in Cephalonia, is one of the finest in these parts. We have lately passed Ithaca ; the outline is very broken and abrupt, but it was in mist, and we could not make much of it.

Since I wrote the above, the day has just so much brightened as to give the effect of light and shadow ; and I am lost in enjoyment. The mountains are multiplied without end, one piled on the other, and of such fine shapes and colours; some very high and steep like giants, and black at top, or bleached with snow ; and to think that here were Brasidas, Phormio, Demosthenes, Cimon, and the rest !

[1] *Æn.* iii. 270.

7 P.M.—We are at Patras. I have seen Rhium and Antirrhium. The chain of Parnassus rises before us, shrouded with clouds, which the eye cannot pierce, yet the imagination can. I have landed on the Peloponnese. High snowy mountains, black rocks, brownish cliffs—all capped with mist, shroud us. The sunset, most wild, harmonises with the scene.

TO HIS MOTHER.

On board the 'Hermes': December 29, 1832, 9 P.M.

As every day brings its own matters, I begin at once this letter, though I have only just now finished writing to Jemima, to tell you about our landing at Patras, which is, in one sense, the most considerable place in the Morea, as being the place of export for the trade, chiefly the currant trade, of the west of Europe. We called here to deliver despatches for the new Greek Government at Napoli, in Argos, about ninety miles off. From this place it is most accessible, though the banditti make the road very dangerous.

The fortress of Patras is strong, and was bombarded by the English several years since, when the allied Powers were driving the Turks out of the Morea. I believe they did not succeed with it; anyhow, it is at present occupied by a self-constituted authority, in the shape of a brigand, who would not give up to the French, and now professes he will, or will not submit to King Otho, according as he likes him or no. The town was destroyed during the disturbances, and is now slowly rebuilding, the work being interrupted this year by the continued disorder of the country. We were told we ought to use caution in paying a visit to the place at night, as plunderers were about; and it unluckily happens here, as at Zante, that we scarcely arrived before nightfall. The first news which greeted us at the Russian Consul's was that King Otho was actually on his way, and that we had a chance of seeing him at Corfu. Considering the state of the country, we were amused to learn he was coming (besides a suite of high officers), with thirty ladies, a hundred horses, and a throne finer than anything in Europe. He sent to the man-of-war which is to convey him, to inquire how many German stoves they had on board in provision against cold weather. I suppose that this was an act of gallantry towards the ladies. We are assured by the Resident of Cerigo, who is sitting by me, that there is not at Napoli, whither they are going, any possible accommodation for ladies at all ; so that they will be literally houseless.

We walked about the new-built town, or rather its foundations. It will be very handsome. We went through the market or bazaar, crowded with people ; stopped some time in a billiard-room, where some Russians were playing, and sat and took coffee in a room full of small Greek merchants. The dresses of the men are most picturesque ; the 'snowy camese,' spoken of by Byron, then an embroidered waistcoat, a plaited and frilled white petticoat to the shins, and a large greatcoat with the arms hanging down behind, the 'shaggy capote'; their faces and figures very fine ; evidently a mixture of races. The coffee was almost the best I ever tasted, and so refreshing I could fancy I had been drinking wine. We returned after a ramble of about an hour.

December 30.

I do not forget it is dear Harriett's birthday, and it is signalised by our passing Ithaca. I could not have believed that the view of these parts would have so enchanted me. When I was for hours within half a mile of Ithaca, as I was this morning, what did I not feel ! Not from classical associations, but the thought that what I saw before me was the reality of what had been the earliest vision of my childhood. Ulysses and Argus, which I had known by heart, occupied the very isle I saw. It is a barren huge rock of limestone, apparently, a dull grey, poorly covered with brushwood, broken into roundish masses with deep ravines, on which, principally, cultivation had dared to experimentalise ; though the sides of the hill were also turned up. Olive-trees have made their appearance; the vines, being cut down in the winter, are invisible from the water. On a hill in the centre and narrowest part of the island is a height called the Tower of Ulysses. We could see through the glass parts of the Cyclopean ruins which surmount it. Their make is far anterior to the historical period. Homer calls the island 'dear and little.'[1] I gazed on it by the quarter of an hour together, being quite satisfied with the sight of the rock. I thought of Ham,[2] and of all the various glimpses which memory barely retains, and which fly from me when I pursue them, of that earliest time of life when one seems almost to realise the remnants of a pre-existing

---

[1] See *Od.* ix. 27-37. Cf. vi. 208, xiv. 58.

[2] Ham, near Richmond, where some of his earliest years were passed.

state. Oh, how I longed to touch the land, and to satisfy myself that it was not a mere vision that I saw before me !

We were on the western side of it, running between it and Cephalonia. The channel is from two to four miles broad, as still as a pond, except that it flows ; it is, indeed, a majestic river, the depth, I believe, being out of soundings. Behind us lay the entrance to the Gulf of Corinth, the Morea, and, in the distance, Zante. As we emerged from the strait, we saw on our right the fine ranges of the Acarnanian Mountains, which are certainly the finest in shape and grouping I have seen. The whole scene was wonderfully grand. The masses of Ithaca and Cephalonia behind us ; small islands of rock, breaking the view of Acarnania ; its mountains rising as a number of ridges, blue in front, with bright snowy heights, with the sun upon them, behind ; Sta Maura (Leucadia) before us ; the famous promontory of Leucas close by ; lastly, we come to Sappho's Leap—still so called—which is certainly a high cliff to fall from. By this time, it being about eleven, we went down for the prayers. We are told we can have no notion of the Greek climate by this specimen of it.

Corfu is close at hand. I shall go on deck. Meanwhile take some verses. Thus I complete my fortieth set :[1]

> My father's hope ! my childhood's dream!
> The promise from on high !
> Long waited for ! its glories beam
> Now when my death is nigh.
>
> My death is come, but not decay;
> Nor eye nor mind is dim ;
> The keenness of youth's vigorous day
> Thrills in each nerve and limb.
>
> Blest scene ! thrice welcome after toil
> If no deceit I view ;
> O might my lips but press the soil,
> And prove the vision true !
>
> Its glorious heights, its wealthy plains,
> Its many tinted groves,
> They call ! but He my steps restrains
> Who chastens whom He loves.
>
> Ah ! now they melt . . . they are but shades ;
> I die !—yet is no rest,
> O Lord ! in store, since Canaan fades
> But seen, and not possest?

---

[1] The title ' Moses seeing the Land.'

On board the 'Hermes,' Corfu: January 1, 1833.

A happy New Year to you all at home. Ever since we got here it has been pouring furiously, and almost incessantly, and the accommodations are so suspicious on shore that as yet we remain here on board. . . .

There are passages in the following letter to his sister which show a reaction from the tension under which Mr. Newman's mind had been held by the scenes around him.

To his Sister Harriett.

On board the 'Hermes,' Corfu: January 2, 1833.

This morning is the first tolerably clear day we have had. Monday and Tuesday have been days of incessant violent rain. On going on deck I was really astonished at the view. Even to-day is not a bright day, so I have a poor idea what the view really is; but I see quite enough: high mountains of a brilliant white or slate colour, folded in long plaits like a table-cloth artificially disposed along a rising and falling outline, without crease or rumple; rocks of a rich brown, looking so near that you think you could touch them, and others of a pale sad colour, like Malta. We are to have a good ride to-day; the roads are said to be excellent, and soon dry. It is an overpowering thought to recollect that the place looked precisely the same in the times of Homer and Thucydides, as being stamped with the indelible features of the 'everlasting hills.'

Here that famous faction fight began which eventually ran through Greece; and what a strange contrast was the scene last night at the Palace—the ball on the anniversary of Constitution Day—at the magnificent palace of a nation in the time of Thucydides not merely barbarous, but unknown. Dresses, novel to them, and unbecoming, but rendered fashionable as being the garb of their masters, soldiers in a like costume, and Greek names and faces in the midst of them all; all mixed up and dancing together, as if it were the most natural thing in the world. Let me set it down in my books, a proposition settled and indisputable, that no change is so great as to be improbable. (*Himself*)

January 4.

I have a great deal to say, but fear I shall forget it. No description can give you any idea of what I have seen, but I will not weary you with my delight; yet does it not seem a strange paradox to say that, though I am so much pleased, I am not interested ? That is, I don't think I should care—rather I should be very glad—to find myself suddenly transported to my rooms at Oriel, with my oak sported, and I lying at full length on my sofa. After all, every kind of exertion is to me an effort : whether or not my mind has been strained and wearied with the necessity of constant activity, I kno v not ; or whether, having had many disappointments, and suffered much from the rudeness and slights of persons I have been cast with, I shrink involuntarily from the contact of the world, and, whether or not natural disposition assists this feeling, and a perception almost morbid of my deficiencies and absurdities—anyhow, neither the kindest attentions nor the most sublime sights have over me influence enough to draw me out of the way, and, deliberately as I have set about my present wanderings, yet I heartily wish they were over, and I only endure the sights, and had much rather *have* seen them than *see* them, though the while I am extremely astonished and almost enchanted at them.

The bad weather has almost left us. On Tuesday the rain was so violent and the sea so rough, we thought we should not be able to land for dinner. We managed it—not without a drenching—and went in the evening to the Palace, where almost the whole island was assembled. We were told we should see a great variety of costumes ; but the rain kept the country people away, and there were not above ten Greek dresses in the room. There is an affectation among the people of the English costume. The most remarkable sight was Madame M. (the late Mrs. Heber) and her husband in Greek dresses. He is certainly a striking-looking man, with a fine profile, and an expression of benignity and dignity. The rooms are magnificent. We had dined at the Artillery mess, and found the officers the same intelligent gentleman-like men as they were at Gibraltar. The Artillery, I believe, is superior to the rest of the army. The mess is the best appointed, they having the advantage of waggons, &c., to carry their things about with. Certainly they live in sumptuous style. Major Longley (brother of Longley of Harrow), who is resident at Cerigo, was our host, and Archdeacon Froude had letters to Colonel Armstrong. Our reception was an amusing contrast to our entertainment at the Commander of the Forces, Sir Alexander Woodford's, with whom we dined the two last days. He has been extraordinarily civil, and even asked us a third time—Saturday. This company was entirely military ; a number of dandy officers, aides-de-camp, &c., brimful of the indifference which is now the fashion. At dinner, a formidable round table neither top nor bottom, Greeks to wait, a service of plate, dishes handed round, no conversation. However, I made a slight acquaintance with one of these, who seems to have good about him. He interests me, because in a measure I enter into his state of mind. He has a good deal of talent and taste—a German scholar, passionately fond of Weber's music—feeling his superiority to the generality, who follow base pleasures, yet (seemingly) substituting refinement for religion. He has kindly undertaken to get me some Greek airs transcribed, which I mean to send you.

On Wednesday and Thursday we took rides about the country, the first of twenty miles, the next of thirty; and how am I to speak of their strangeness? There was nothing to remind you of England but the high roads, which are capital, on Macadam's plan. Olive is nearly the only tree; there are forests and parks of them, through which the road winds. The leaf must be monotonous in summer, but it is beautiful now. The tree is very like a willow, such as in Christ Church Walk; the trunk and branches being more graceful and white. It does not grow to a great size commonly. The trunk separates into parts when it is old. Often it presents a network appearance, as honeycombed. The tree, I think, never dies; as one portion goes another shoots out. However—(Monday, January 5, having left Corfu; Ithaca in sight)—the olive in Corfu is of no great age. They were planted in Venetian times, a great many of an inferior kind. There is great uncertainty in the right of property in them. A tree is sometimes divided among two or three persons—the divisions of land are vague. The olive requires scarcely any cultivation, except care that the roots are not left bare, which happens in a rocky soil with occasional heavy rain and steep banks. There is very little corn grown, Indian corn instead; the land is too swampy for the former. Sir F. Maitland attempted drainage, but failed.

But I have digressed from my ride. The beautiful cypress was another strange sight. It stands when grown in groups of two or three, shooting up in black graceful spires amid the olives. The shaft is used for the masts and yards of the lateen-rigged vessels. It is beautifully straight. The orange-tree, again, is in full fruit, with its bright-polished leaf; I did not observe many wild, and none that were wild with fruit. The fig is not in leaf. We had a loss, too, as regards the colours of the ground, which in spring, we were told, is covered with a profusion of wild flowers (I have got the seeds for my Mother,[1] but not of the most striking flowers). Even at this season the brushwood and hedgerows are beautiful. The myrtle, which is profusely spread over the country, is of a rich brown-green. The vines are cut down at this season, and look like stumps. There is a dwarf holly, too, and the arbutus, all evergreen; here and there the cactus and the aloe.

The moving portion of this strange scene was as strange as the trees themselves. Peasants on horseback (mules are scarce and fetch a high price), two persons on one, with their legs on one side and their load before them; they have few carts—I didn't see one market-cart - flocks of goats, sheep, not woolly like ours, but with soft fleeces like hair, flowing, and with queer graceful little bodies; cows, like wild cows, with strange necks and backs, and of a dun or iron-grey colour.

The landscape itself is beautifully varied; finely-formed heights, intersected with plains, deep ravines, villages, or rather towers, perched up upon the hills. Both days we digressed from the road, cutting across country. In that way we had a specimen of what travelling is in Greece; you may cut across almost anywhere, but for the most part at a walk. You descend by beds of rivers, you cross rocks. How horses go I can't conceive; fancy riding over the ruins of a brick wall, and you will have an idea of it, except that the stones are not sharp. The rock here is chiefly limestone, and the weather polishes it. The steps up to the houses are all marble—strange at first sight. The villages in a deplorable condition, and seem once to have been more important than they are now. The people are marvellously idle. In Corfu the streets swarm with men doing nothing; and the roads are full of them. In a village where we stopped, a horse having lost a shoe, a collection of idlers of all ages came round us; all dirty and uncombed. The children are fine-looking, and some of the men; the women keep indoors. Their bread is very fair (the corn comes from Poland and the Black Sea through Odessa); though in these parts, from Spain to Corfu, they leaven it. This gives it a sour taste when it is old. The population of Corfu by itself is said to be 40,000, which is almost incredible, though the statement comes from one who ought to know. Our rides across country have given me some definite notion of the state of travelling in Greece in the

---

[1] Mrs. Newman was fond of flowers and devoted to gardening.

times of Thucydides, &c. (also I have some drawings). It is astonishing I should have so long read about a country without realising it, and I am amazed how it ever *became* one country ; how its inhabitants ever had intercourse with each other, how they ever could go to war, &c. &c. ; for it is one heap of mountains thrown together in the wildest way conceivable.

The town of Corfu is very picturesque in the Venetian style. The churches are very numerous—as in Oxford (they say) there is a pot-house every ten houses, so of the churches here. Dissenters are unknown in the Greek Church. There seems much superstition here. On Saturday we saw the church and body of St. Spiridion, who was one of the Nicene Fathers, though doubtless it is not his body. He is the patron saint of the island ; each of the seven has its own. The churches are Venetian ; but why it was that the Venetians extended the Greek communion I have not made out. St. Spiridion's is small, but handsomely fitted up, though not so much more so than a country church which I by chance went into. I was surprised ; the two were so much alike in arrangement and decoration. A number of paintings in gilt frames, not badly executed, the subject the history of Genesis and the Last Judgment ; large silver lamps ; stalls, like in cathedrals, for the chief persons and the infirm—for the Greeks stand in prayer for the most part. At the east end a number of pictures in parallel niches—apostles, prophets, &c. Lower down, our Saviour, the Virgin, St. Gregory, &c., Moses. A door opens into what in England is called the chancel—where seems to be the high altar—the Consecration, I suppose, being private ; in St. Spiridion the saint's silver tomb and body.

The Greek clergy of these islands, as of the Morea, are of a lower rank, as our Methodists. They are said to be very ignorant, but moral in their lives. They interfere little, or not at all, with their flocks, who pay them their offerings and receive the rites of religion as a *quid pro quo*. There seems to be no endowments, but the clergy are dependent on their people. There is a bishop to each island, paid by the Government 250*l*. per annum each. There seems to be no excommunication. The Greeks are very rigid in their fasts ; besides the forty days in Lent, they have forty before Christmas, and some others. At these times they eat no meat ; the pirates are as rigid in keeping them as others. I turned over the leaves of one or two books in the country church ; one was a collection of prayers by John of Damascus. There was little objectionable that I saw in either of the books ; much that was very good. There was a prayer to the Virgin, a prayer to the Guardian Angel ; but the doctrine of the Trinity was the prominent subject of all of them. The pictures I spoke of abounded in representations of the Deity ; in one I saw the Trinity. St. Michael seems a principal saint here ; his figure is prominent in the pictures of the Last Judgment. At St. Spiridion's people were ever coming in, weeping and bowing and kissing the pictures.

There are two Latin churches at Corfu, and one English —the garrison church. The Chaplain is Mr. Leeves, of the Bible Society. I had not been to church for five weeks till yesterday, and it was quite a comfort to get there. I had hoped there might have been the Sacrament. Yesterday, the 6th, was the Greek Christmas Day. Mr. Leeves has been very kind ; we dined with him yesterday. We first met him at Col. Baker's, where I dined twice ; and the second time, Friday, the Froudes also. They are friendly and kind people. I called on Mrs. Baker on Saturday, and sat with her an hour and a half. She gave me all the seeds she had (they are tender and require a greenhouse), and directed me to the Lord High Commissioner's Gardens, about two miles out of the town. I went there, but unluckily he was out.

In one of the villages we rode through on Wednesday there is a church built by Jovian. Unluckily, we did not know it at the time. On Saturday we dined again at the Artillery mess, and very well-informed men they are. We were all extremely pleased with a Mr. Askwith, who went about with us every day. He has been a great traveller in Greece this year, and was full of information. On Friday we went to see the ruins of the old town. The fortifications on Vido, a small island opposite to the town of Corfu, are in progress. When they are completed the defence of the place will be committed to them—the Citadel and Fort Neuf ; the others, viz. Fort Abraham, St. Salvador, &c., being abandoned. They are very strong, of Venetian construction, but would require a vast number of men to man them. Sir A. Woodford has a fine pepper-tree in his garden ; his geraniums are superb. I told you that at Zante a man's shop was full of expensive cherry-sticks for pipes, and argued thence that at least some of the people were well off. Now, I find, he has been in the practice of showing off this one stick, which he bought years ago. This shows how cautious one should be in receiving the facts and inferences of travellers. The weather has been dry and fine since Tuesday.

January 7.—*Very* cold. There is a great deal of snow on the Albanian mountains. We set off last night, passing the eastern side of Ithaca, and now are making for Patras, where I hope to present my letter from Bowden to Sir John Franklin. The Albanian mountains are said, one portion of them, to be a hundred miles off from Corfu—yet they seem quite close. We had wild boar from Albania at Corfu. Turkeys are the principal fowl, and they are brought from Albania; those which are ready fattened for the table cost 3*s*. apiece. Ithaca wine has a good deal of flavour, and not at all heavy. It has grown upon me. I have been much surprised at the cheapness of living at Corfu. We have been making many inquiries to guide us in our Sicilian expedition. The high road is furnished with excellent inns, but we mean to diverge, and to live like gipsies.

In the meantime here are some verses for you.[1]

<blockquote>
The better portion didst thou choose, Great Heart,
  Thy God's first choice, and pledge of Gentile grace!
  Faith's truest type, he with unruffled face
Bore the world's smile, and bade her slaves depart;
Whether, a trader, with no trader's art,
  He buys in Canaan his first resting-place,
  Or freely yields rich Siddim's ample space,
Or braves the rescue and the battle's smart,
  Yet scorns the heathen gifts of those he saved.
  O happy in their souls' high solitude
Who commune thus with God, and not with earth,
  Amid the scoffings of the wealth-enslaved!
  A ready prey, as though in absent mood
They calmly move, nor hear the unmannered mirth.[2]
</blockquote>

At sea: December 27, 1832.

---

[1] Those poems that were transcribed in the letters home are inserted in the letters; but they present an insufficient idea of the impulse given to Mr. Newman's mind by new scenes, witnessed in freedom from his accustomed studies and cares. In illustration, the names and dates of poems written in December, but not inserted in the letters, are given below:—

The Isles of the Sirens . Dec. 13	The Course of Truth . Dec. 24
Absolution . . . Dec. 14	Sleeplessness . . . Dec. 26
Memory . . . . Dec. 15	The Greek Fathers . Dec. 29
Fair Words . . . Dec. 17	The Witness . . . Dec. 30
Penance . . . . Dec. 23	

[2] Title, 'Abraham.'

Thrice blest are they who feel their loneliness ;
To whom nor voice of friend nor pleasant scene
Brings that on which the sadden'd heart can lean.
Yea, the rich earth, garb'd in her daintiest dress
Of light and joy, doth but the more oppress,
   Claiming responsive smiles and rapture high,
   Till, sick at heart, beyond the veil they fly,
Seeking His Presence Who alone can bless.
   Such, in strange days, the weapons of Heaven's grace;
When, passing by the high-born Hebrew line,
He forms the vessel of His vast design.
   Fatherless, homeless, reft of age and place,
Severed from earth, and careless of its wreck,
Born through long woe His rare Melchizedek.[1]

Corfu: January 5, 1833.

January 10, 1833.

We are now off Malta, and have had a swell which again caused sea-sickness. We came off Patras at night, so I lost Sir J. Franklin. Next morning—the 8th—we saw the range of Arcadian mountains, and in the distance Parnassus. We landed at Zante. From the hill above the town there is a fine view of the plain, where almost all our pudding currants are grown—a flat of about ten miles, surrounded with hills, studded all over with houses, before each a square drying plot for the currants. So many are grown that the duty this last year on the exports was 95,000*l*. Sir J. Franklin has been off Patras in his sloop for eighteen months, and neither he nor his crew have touched land once. What an imprisonment! King Otho was expected at Corfu to-day.

I do so long to hear from you ; there is just a chance of my hearing at Malta by the packet that left London about the 19th. I dream about you all, and that letters are brought me ; but, when I begin to read, they are illegible, or I wake up, as if there were men trying to tell me and others preventing it. And the ship bells are so provokingly like the Oriel clock, that I fancy myself there. Whether my health is improved I cannot tell. I long for the fifteen days of peace in the Lazaret. This is my last day on the 'Hermes.' How much have I seen in the course of five weeks! Tell Williams he may see my little poems to stimulate him.

    I saw thee once, and nought discerned
      For stranger to admire —
    A serious aspect, but it burned
      With no unearthly fire.

---

[1] 'Melchizedek.'

Again I saw, and I confe-sed
    Thy speech was rare and high;
And yet it vexed my burdened breast,
    And scared, I knew not why.

I saw once more, and awe-struck gazed
    On face, and form, and air;
God's living glory round thee blazed—
    A Saint—a Saint was there!

Off Zante: January 8, 1833.

Banished the House of sacred rest,
    Amid a thoughtless throng
At length I heard its creed confessed,
    And knelt the Saints among.

Artless his strain and unadorned,
    Who spoke CHRIST'S message there;
But what at home I might have scorned,
    Now charmed my famished ear.

Lord, grant me this abiding grace,
    Thy Word and Sons to know;
To pierce the veil on Moses' face,
    Although his speech be slow!

At sea: January 9, 1833.

---

[1] If e'er I fall beneath Thy rod,
    As through life's snares I go,
Save me from David's lot, O God!
    And choose Thyself the woe.

How should I face Thy plagues? which scare,
    And haunt, and stun, until
The heart or sinks in mute despair
    Or names a random ill.

If else—then guide in David's path,
    Who chose the holier pain;
Satan and man are tools of wrath—
    An angel's scourge is gain.

Off Malta: January 10, 1833.

[1] 'David Numbering the People.'

REV. J. H. NEWMAN TO J. W. BOWDEN, ESQ.

Lazaretto, Malta: January 20, 1833.

. . . Only imagine my pleasure at being in these places! I was in silent wonder; and everything so grand and beautiful, and the mode of conveyance such that I could look on without stop and without fatigue. I had Homer's 'Odyssey,' Virgil, and Thucydides with me, and seemed transported back to their times, for everything looks now just as it did then. Mountains cannot change. . . .

I have only told you part, though the most interesting, of our hitherto tour. We have seen Gibraltar, Cadiz, and Algiers. The African mountains are most imposing. There are several tiers of them, the most distant being Mount Atlas, which ran alongside of us from Tangiers to Algiers. Over against Gibraltar it rises 10,000 feet. Well did Homer in the beginning of the 'Odyssey' speak of it as supporting the heaven (as having μακρὰς κίονας οὐρανοῦ[1]). It has just that effect if you take the Mediterranean as the great centre of the earth, and the sky stretched over it as a curtain.

TO HIS SISTER JEMIMA.

Lazaretto, Malta: January 15, 1833.

You will now receive my letters only at intervals. However, I shall put two into the post here which you will receive about March. I begin at once from this house of my imprisonment, though I am tempted to delay, for my hand is quite tired with writing. My dear Mother will say I am doing too much; but to one who has been employing his mind actively for years, nothing is so wearisome as idleness, nothing so irksome as dissipation. I assure you, I feel much more comfortable now than when I was on that restless element which is the type of human life, and much less wearied in prison than in seeing sights.

We seem to have narrowly missed getting to Napoli, and so on, perhaps, to Athens; for Archdeacon Froude had letters to Sir H. Hotham, &c., and I to Captain Swinburne, who set

[1] *Odyss.* i. 53, 54.

off to meet King Otho the day after we came here—and might possibly have taken us, had we been a little sooner; but I cannot bring myself to regret what, nevertheless, I should have rejoiced in.

The 'Hermes' left this place on Saturday last—the 12th—and I saw it go off with strange feelings. I had been securely conveyed in it for five weeks, during which time I had never once slept ashore. It was a kind of home; it had taken me up from England, and it was going back there. I shall never take a voyage again. As it went off, I seemed more cast upon the world than I ever had been, and to be alone—no tie remaining between England and myself; nor any assignable path by which I can get back.

We are very comfortable here. The weather has turned fine, having been unusually wet for three months. We found the same complaints off the Morea. At Cerigo the glass had been as low as 40°. At Corfu our first two days were uninterrupted rain; the last five beautifully clear; the last two very cold, almost bitter. When we returned to Patras there had been ice. At Zante, on the contrary, nothing but rain. Patras is a finer climate than Zante—that is, for agriculture. They are sure of two months' fine weather just when the fruits are ripening. People frighten us with forebodings about the weather during our Sicilian expedition. They say February is the rainy month. The climate must be perfectly delightful, though hot, of course, in summer there. I am writing in a large room twenty feet high, without furniture, opening into others far larger, and all the windows, which are casements, entirely open—that is, in fact, I am sitting in the open air. The floors are stone. We use a fireplace at breakfast and dinner, for boiling eggs and heating our milk. I believe in the whole Lazaret there is but one fireplace beside our own. We burn olive wood. I assure you we make ourselves very comfortable. We feed well from an hotel across the water. The Froudes draw and paint. I have hired a violin, and, bad as it is, it sounds grand in such spacious halls. I write verses, and get up some Italian, and walk up and down the rooms about an hour and a half daily; and we have a boat, and are allowed to go about the harbour.

This Lazaret was built by the Knights for the Turks, and many a savage fellow, I dare say, has been here, but they leave no trace behind them. We have four rooms besides a kitchen; two facing the water; the farther of them we do not use at all; the other is our sitting and eating room; it looks out upon the Greek and other vessels, the fortifications of Valetta, some few houses of the town, two windmills, and the great church of St. John. No. 3 is a very large room 48 by 30, I suppose, and 20 to 22 high, arched. There are deep recesses through the wall for the windows, which form dressing-rooms for Hurrell and me. Our beds, at right angles to the depth of the wall, blocking them up. Our bedsteads are iron, with light musquito curtains. There we lie, with one or two thin blankets, and a very hard mattress. No. 4 is a kind of hall which we do not use. No. 5 is the kitchen. We have ired a man-of-all-work to wait on us. No. 6 is the balcony running round the inside of the quadrangle; a staircase descending from it at 7 into a court which opens by large gates upon a terrace over the water, where we have a small confined walk upon the flags. On this common ground all persons on quarantine may show themselves; they may sit on the same seat successively, but they must not touch. One soon gets accustomed to this; nobody touches nobody. I have only to add that my dressing-room window opens upon the chimney of the baking-room for letters; and the sharp, sour smell often reminds me of Frank's letters which have been baked and doctored there.

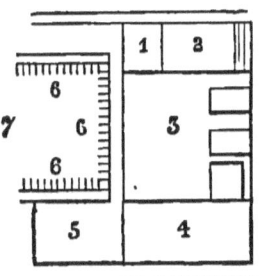

Yesterday we met at the parlatorio Sir John Stodart, Chief Justice, to whom both Froude sand I had letters. He gave us a good deal of curious information about the state of the Catholic Church in Malta. It seems Malta was not taken, but capitulated to us; and one of the provisions was that the laws and the religion should be inviolate. Now, the clergy here were independent altogether of the State in such a way as hardly in any other Catholic country at present. Till 1813 nothing was done, for the Government thought the island might be ceded at the peace; but, after Bonaparte's defeat in Russia, they resolved on keeping it. A Commissioner was sent out to adjust the legal and ecclesiastical system. Sir J. Richardson went on with it—when here in 1826—and Sir John Stodart is going on with it now. He is introducing trial by jury, which at first sight is a problematical improvement. As to the clergy, they were tried in courts of their own (as in Becket's time), and irresponsible to the civil power. How was this to be altered? For a Catholic to violate the rights of the Church is a mortal sin, from which not even the Bishop—no one but the Pope—can release him. Supposing, then, the King to make it law that the clergy should be subjected to the State courts, the execution of such a measure would, of course, rest with native magistrates; let them then enforce it against a priest, and then go to their confessor. The priest cannot absolve them; he has not the power: he can do nothing without the Pope's assent. This exemplifies the admirable system of the Papacy as an instrument of power. Accordingly, representations were made to the Pope—at that time Leo XII.—and, though he was considered strict in his adherence to the privileges of the Church, the Government managed to gain a continual dispensation for the Catholic magistrates here: and that thus the clergy are virtually subject to the State courts. This system of dispensations is in force in Austria.

There is another difficulty about the Bishop, who is under the Archbishop of Palermo; for which reason, and also as claiming the suzeraineté of Malta, the King of Naples claims to appoint him. I believe this is not adjusted yet, though there is no dispute just now. The Maltese are a very industrious race—a contrast to the Ionians. The most industrious servants at Corfu are Maltese. There was a plan some time since to relieve the place of its abundant population by sending them there; but, whether from the difference of religion or other cause, it did not answer. Malta increases by a thousand souls a year. It has the largest population on the smallest territory of any place in the world—above 100,000. Sir John Stodart said he had a plan for colonising them to Negropont. I suppose it would not do.

January 23.

We are just out of quarantine. We shall be in Malta ten days. Do not tell people, of course; but we had mysterious night visitants in the Lazaret, which have broken my night's rest, even worse than the sea, and have given me a cold. We can account for them to a certain point, but no further, a characteristic of most such stories. My companions both distinctly heard steps in room 4 about two o'clock of the night of the 17th and 18th. They are perfectly convinced on the point; we are locked in. About the same time I dreamed that a man came to me (our servant I thought) and told me it was only an hour from rising time, and as we were going on a boat expedition next morning, I wished to be punctual. I was so fully impressed with the reality of it, that I lay awake for some time on my back, not thinking it a dream, and have almost ever since woke at that hour and fancied it morning [I certainly heard steps about my bed]. On talking it over in the morning, we recollected we had heard noises before.

On Sunday night last, the 20th, I was awakened by a noise in room 2 as I thought, so loud that I smiled to myself, and said : ' Clearly this is too earthly to be anything out of the way.' When it had been repeated twice at intervals, it struck me that someone might be taking away Mr. Froude's effects (who sleeps in a window of that room), and who was audibly fast asleep. So the fourth time it occurred, I hallooed out ' Who's there ? ' and sat up in my bed ready to spring out. A deep silence followed, and I sat waiting a considerable time, and thus I caught my cold. From that time to the time we left I heard nothing. Now I must tell you that on the night of the 17th our next-door neighbour left the Lazaret about two o'clock and walked along the external gallery ; but the wall between our room and the gallery is ten feet thick. You may say the noises came from some strange transmission of sound ; or you may say that the quarantine island is hardly Christian ground. Anyhow, we cannot doubt that evil spirits in some way or other are always about us ; and I had comfort in the feeling that, whatever was the need, ordinary or extraordinary, I should have protection equal to it.[1]

[1] Those who have heard Dr. Newman converse on the spiritual world will recall the impressiveness and sincerity of conviction in his manner. After his visit to Barrow-on-Trent, October 6, 1874, Elizabeth Mozley, writing to her brother, Dr. Mozley, touches on this :—
 ' One sees that Dr. Newman's great power (and it came out on the question of modern miracles, spiritual manifestations, &c.) is a certain vivid realisation of the unseen, or rather that there is an unseen that you cannot see. " How can people say what is, or is not, natural to evil spirits ? What is a grotesque manifestation to us may not be so to them. What do we know about an evil spirit ? " The words were nothing, but there was an intensity of realisation in his face as he said them, of a reality and of his ignorance about it, that was a key to me as to the source of his influence over others. The *sight* of belief in others is next to seeing yourself ; **and men cling to it.**'

To his Mother.

Malta: January 26, 1833

The weather has been unusually severe here. My cold caught in the Lazaret ripened the day I came out of it into the most wretched cough I ever recollect having, as hard as the stone walls, and far more tight than the windows. This is Saturday, and we came out on Wednesday morning, and all that while, with the exception of one imprudence, I have been a close prisoner, nay, in my bedroom. Yesterday morning I was not up till twelve o'clock, an event unprecedented in my history, as far as memory goes. To-day I am much better, but not well. I have engaged an Italian master.

I have seen St. John's Church, and most magnificent it is. It is in the same style as St. Peter's; in richness and exactness, minuteness and completeness of decoration, far exceeding anything I have ever seen. I shall go to it once or twice more to get some more accurate notion of it. It is built with a nave with side aisles leading to separate chapels or altars, *e.g.* the French chapel, the Italian, the Spanish. It is covered throughout with the most costly marbles and with gilding; a multitude of pictures—some very fine—some statuary, splendid tapestries, and silver lamps and candlesticks of course. In the Chapel of the Communion are the famous silver rails which were saved from the clutches of Bonaparte by being painted to look like wood; he took away the gold rails. By this and similar acts the French have made themselves hated here. The Knights of St. John (the Baptist, not the Evangelist) were not allowed to leave away their property, accordingly immense sums were available for religious works. It is said they brought from Rhodes property to the amount of 300,000*l.* a year.

I have hitherto seen little of the Greek and Latin churches, but what I have seen fires me 'with great admiration.' I do not perceive that my opinion has in any respect changed about them; but it is fearful to have before one's eyes the perversion of all the best, the holiest, the most exalted feelings of human nature. Everything in St. John's Church is admirable, if it did not go too far; it is a beautiful flower run to seed. I am impressed with a sad presentiment, as if the gift of truth when once lost was lost for ever. And so the Christian world is gradually becoming barren and effete, as land which has been worked out and has become sand. We have lasted longer than the South, but we too are going, as it would seem.

As to the number of sects which have split off from the Church, many of them have already ended in Socinianism and heresy worse than any in Rome or Constantinople. All this does not interfere with good men being in any Church, nor is there any proof that we have more than they, though if you cut away from us those who are in no sense Churchmen, though called so, I think there are more in us, as far as appearances go. By-the-bye, what answer do Protestants make to the *fact* of the Greek Church invoking saints, over-honouring the Virgin, and substituting ceremonies for a 'reasonable service,' which they say are the prophetic marks of Anti-Christ? I do not see that the Romanists are more than advanced Greeks, the errors being the same, though less in degree in the latter.

I was speaking just now of the Maltese disliking the French. They are said to like the Russians, as the Greeks do; but there is so much contradictory testimony. All agree that they are a very industrious race, being an exception to the general Mediterranean character; I suppose they are Arabs or Moors in great measure. Paul was Grand Master of the Order, and I suppose the Russians narrowly missing getting the island, instead of us, their troops, which were to have co-operated with the English, being suddenly called off to act together with the French against us, they appointed wealthy men as commanders of their vessels in these parts, with orders to spend a good deal of money among the Maltese population. About five years ago they quite enriched the place. At present there is extreme poverty. We are told that, if any other people were so distressed, there would be a mob of 4,000 or 5,000 starving men every morning at the Governor's palace.

I cannot help thinking how we have been favoured in the weather. The two packets which came out the two months before successively had uninterrupted bad weather. A steamer, which set out four days before us, damaged its engine, and put into Lisbon for three weeks, arriving here as we returned from Corfu. The brig that took out Lord Nugent also suffered. This is a most curious town: the people are very kind, and we overflow with invitations; but somehow I do not like the place, though I have seen little of it. I shall be glad to be quiet at Rome or Naples for a while. Rome is the city of the Apostles, and a place to rest one's foot in, whatever be the after-corruption. We shall go almost by the track of St. Paul from Malta to Rome.

January 27.

Yesterday, in my solitude, I finished my Patriarchal Sonnets. I now have completed fifty-four sets for Rose, and am not anxious to do any more; but, when thoughts come into my head, it is impossible to resist the temptation of fixing them. It is Sunday morning. I think of St. Mary's and Littlemore. We do not know how great our privileges are. All the quiet and calm connected with our services is so beautiful in memory, and so soothing, after the sight of that most exciting religion which is around me—statues of the Madonna and the Saints in the streets, &c. &c.—a more poetical but not less jading stimulus than a pouring forth in a Baptist chapel. How awful seems (to me here) the crime of demolition in England! All one can say of Whigs, Radicals, and the rest is, that they know not what they do. Archdeacon Froude has just forbidden my going to church on account of my cold. I have been to church only once since I left England.

> Many the guileless years the Patriarch spent
>   Blest in the wife a father's foresight chose;
>   Many the prayers and gracious deeds which rose,
> Daily thank-offerings, from his pilgrim tent.
> Yet these, though written in the heavens, are rent
>   From out truth's lower roll, which sternly shows
>   But one sad trespass at his history's close—
> Father's, son's, mother's, and its punishment.
>   Not in their brightness, but their earthly stains
> Are the true Seed vouchsafed to earthly eyes.
>   Sin can read sin, but dimly scans high grace;
> So we move heavenward with averted face,
>   Scared into faith by warning of sin's pains;
> And saints are lowered that the world may rise.[1]

Valletta: January 23, 1833.

> O specious sin and Satan's subtle snare,
>   That urges sore each gentlest, meekest heart
>   When its kind thoughts are crushed and its wounds smart,
>   World-sick to turn within, and image there

[1] 'Isaac.'

Some idol dream to lull the throbbing care!
So felt reft Israel when he fain would part
With living friends; and called on memory's art
To raise the dead and soothe him by despair.
Nor err they not, although that image be
God's own; nor to the dead their thoughts be given,
Earth-hating sure, but yet of earth enthralled;
For who dare sit at home and wait to see
High Heaven descend, when man from self is called
Up through this thwarting outward world to Heaven?'[1]

O purest semblance of the Eternal Son!
Who dwelt in thee, as in some blessed shrine,
To draw hearts after thee, and make them thine;
Not parent only by that light was won,
And brethren crouch'd who had in wrath begun,
But heathen pomp abased her at the sign
Of a hid God, and drank the sound divine
Till a king heard, and all thou bad'st was done.
Then was fulfill'd Nature's dim augury,
That ' Wisdom, clad in visible form, would be
So fair that all must love and bow the knee';
Lest it might seem, what time the Substance came,
Truth lack'd a sceptre, when it but laid by
Its beaming front, and bore a willing shame.[2]

Lazaret, Malta: January 20, 1833.

Latest born of Jesse's race,
Wonder lights thy bashful face,
While the Prophet's gifted oil
Seals thee for a path of toil.
We, thy angels, circling round thee,
Ne'er shall find thee as we found thee
When thy faith first brought us near
In thy lion-fight severe.
Go! and mid thy flocks awhile
At thy doom of greatness smile;
Bold to bear God's heaviest load,
Dimly guessing of the road—
Rocky road, and scarce ascended,
Though thy foot be angel tended.

Two-fold praise thou shalt attain,
In royal court and battle plain;
Then comes heart-ache, care, distress,
Blighted home, and loneliness;
Wounds from friend and gifts from foe,
Dizzied faith, and guilt, and woe;

---

[1] 'Israel.'   [2] 'Joseph.'

Loftiest aims by earth defiled,
Gleams of wisdom sin-beguiled.
Sated power's tyrannic mood,
Counsels shared with men of blood,
Sad success, parental tears,
And a dreary gift of years.
Strange, that guiltless face and form
To lavish on the scarring storm !
Yet we take thee in thy blindness,
And we buffet thee in kindness :
Little chary of thy fame,
Dust unborn may bless or blame;
But we mould thee for the root
Of man's promised healing Fruit;
And we mould thee hence to rise,
As our brother, to the skies.[1]

Lazaret, Malta: January 18, 1833.

January 28.

I am properly taken at my word. I have been sighing for rest and quiet. This is the sixth day since I left the ' Lazaret '; and I have hardly seen or spoken to anyone. The Froudes dine out every day, and are out all the morning of course. The two last days they have been on a visit to a friend [I wished and insisted on their doing all this]. Last night I put a blister on my chest, and, never having had one on before, you may fancy my awkwardness in taking it off and dressing the place of it this morning. I ought to have had four hands. Our servant was with the Froudes, and the people of the house are so dirty, cheating, and ignorant of English, that they make a mistake whatever is told them. Never was such a take-in as this place : we were recommended to go elsewhere. Well, I am set upon a solitary life, and therefore ought to have experience what it is ; nor do I repent. But even St. Paul had his ministers. I have sent to the library and got ' Marriage ' to read ! Don't smile – this juxtaposition is quite accidental. You are continually in my thoughts, of course. I know what kindness I should have at home ; and it is no new feeling with me, only now for the first time brought out, that I do not feel this so much as I ought. Thank God, my spirits have not failed me once. They used, when I was solitary, but I am callous now. Last night, as I put on my blister, I reflected it was just a week since I caught my cold at the Lazaret by speaking to a ghost. I wonder how long I shall last without any friend

[1] 'The Call of David.'

about me. Scripture so clearly seems to mark out that we should not be literally solitary. The Apostles were sent two and two, and had their attendants, so I suppose I should soon fail. I am glad Frank [in Persia] has the comfort of friends about him.

February 2.

Since I wrote, Dr. Davy (to whom we had letters through Mr. Hawkins among others) has recommended me a simple remedy, which has almost, if not entirely, cured my cough—fifty drops of antimonial wine three times a day. My morning dose has made me feel not qualmish but languid till breakfast-time, but otherwise I have had no inconvenience from the remedy at all, and it is wonderfully efficacious.

February 14.

Just arrived at Naples. I am *quite* well, as if I had never had a cough. We have seen Egesta, Palermo, and Messina.

To his Sister Harriett.

Naples: February 16, 1833.

Our two days' impression of Naples is very unfavourable. We find a climate variable, capricious, bleak, stormy, and miserable; moreover, the streets overrun with mud and water, not dripping, but pouring from the houses. We find everyone we come in contact with—custom-house officers, shopmen, and populace—thieves and cheats, having been subjected, every step we have taken, to all sorts of provoking impositions. We find such despicable frivolity, so connected with religious observances, as to give the city a pagan character. I am in vain trying to find out whether there are any letters from you to me at the post-office. They are so careless that some persons have been kept from their letters before now for five weeks, and yet I do not know what other direction to give you than Naples. We shall stay here about a fortnight. I got my Mother's letter yesterday from the Neales. My present notion is to get Edward Neale to go through Sicily with me in April. The Froudes have decided on giving up Sicily and going home by the Rhine.

Well, we left Malta on the 7th. Its climate is uncertain and stormy in winter, though more than usually so this season. Some days, after we left the 'Lazaret,' were piercingly cold. Dr. Davy told me there was an endless passage of wind from Africa to Europe during the winter, and that the barometer was always very unsettled. I was confined to my room nearly the whole fortnight we were out of quarantine. The Neapolitan steamer came (on Monday the 4th) just as I was getting quite well of my cough. On Tuesday I went to St. Paul's Bay by water; and this expedition, with walking a little about the streets, is all I have seen of Malta. The houses are superb. They are great palaces. The Knights spent their money in houses and fortifications. The houses in Messina, Palermo and here are very splendid, but they are inhabited in floors; whereas in Malta one man—say Dr. Davy —has the whole house, with its square court within, galleries, &c. The rooms are magnificently lofty, and every part of stone. The streets are straight, and at right angles to each other; the fortifications prodigious in point of size and extent, but not worth much in a military point of view, each Grand Master adding to his predecessor's work without unity of plan or use for modern purposes. St. John's Church properly belonged to the Government, and might have been made the Protestant Church, as it was built by the Knights, and not part of the island's Church property; but, by mismanagement, it was given to the Romanists, or perhaps it was impossible for us to do otherwise. The present Protestant chapel is insufficient to contain more than the chief English families; the multitude of English being left to either total neglect of religious observance, or to the Roman Catholic priests, or the Wesleyans, as the case may be.

I forget what opinion I gave about the attachment of the Maltese to the English; our final and confirmed opinion was that they do not like us. England has laid a heavy corn tax on them, which galls them much; 120,000$l.$ is thus raised, which is profusely laid out in quasi-sinecures, and, after all, a balance is transmitted to England. Few Maltese are put into any posts of importance. It is urged, on the other hand, that responsible men, Englishmen of wealth, must be put into places which yet it is confessed none but Maltese deputies can execute. So much about Malta.

We left Malta on board the 'Francisco,' a Glasgow-built steamer beautifully appointed, with passengers to the number of seventy or eighty, who had come from Naples to see the island. There was Prince Galitzin, and the wife of the Governor of Wallachia and Moldavia, and counts and princes numberless, who spat about deck and cabin without any concern, Poles, Russians, Germans, French. The only gentlemen-like men were the princes of Rohan,[1] Carlists, who prosecuted Madame de Feucheres last year. The elder one was a sedate and pleasingly-mannered man, with a countenance like Henri IV. Our voyage was singularly prosperous—a calm sea and a warm atmosphere. We got to Messina in twenty-four hours, and landing at one in the morning, encountered the misery of custom-house officers for the first time, and a strange language (it was our first foreign ground), and unluckily as we landed it began to rain copiously. We were two days at Messina, and starting thence on Saturday evening (last) arrived at Palermo early Sunday morning. There the steamer stayed two days; on Wednesday morning we left Palermo and arrived here with a swift passage in twenty hours on Thursday. Thus I give our itinerary before speaking of Sicily.

Little as I have seen of Sicily, it has filled me with inexpressible delight and (in spite of dirt and other inconveniences) I am drawn to it as by a loadstone. The chief sight has been Egesta (Segesta), its ruins with its temple. O wonderful sight! full of the most strange pleasure—strange from the position of the town, its awful desolateness, the beauty of the scenery, rich even in winter, its historical recollections by contrast with the misery of the population, the depth of squalidness and brutality by which it is surrounded. It has been a day in my life to have seen Egesta. From the moment I saw Sicily I kept saying to myself, ' This is that Sicily '; but I must stop if I am to find room in this letter for Messina and Palermo, though really my mind goes back to the recollections of last Monday and Tuesday, as one smells again and again at a sweet flower.

[1] The following passage is from a letter of Miss Frere's, pp. 241-242 in Sir Bartle Frere's Memoir of the Right Hon. John Hookham Frere. It is written from Malta, Feb. 11, 1833:—
' These two Frenchmen (great people, they had been in the steamer with us, Rohans, I think), of finished manners, like the very best style of English breeding, made a pleasant contrast with our three English strangers, Archdeacon Froude, his son, and another clergyman, their friend, who have a becoming simplicity and placidity of deportment, very agreeable also. We were sorry at their going, just as we found out that we liked them. The son, on whose account they are travelling, is quite well; but the friend, Mr. Newman of Oriel, was confined with some ailment of his chest. My brother had some good talk with him one morning, and would have liked to introduce his Aristophanes to him, had there been fair opportunity. The brother of this Mr. Newman is a young man of great promise who has left the fairest prospect of advancement in England to go a missionary to Persia.'

February 17.

Another day of pouring rain, and a miserable scirocco, howling as at Corfu. The wretches at the post-office, to whom I have been five times, and most of the times by their own appointment, have not yet examined whether there are any letters due to me from you, though I cannot doubt there are. Well, for my narrative :—When we rose on the Friday morning, the 8th, Sicily laid alongside us in mist, Etna invisible, at least its top. As we approached the coast, we saw a vast number of ridges running up the country, steep, sharp, and covered with olives and vines, every now and then a sand-course into the sea, the bed of a *fiumara* or torrent. We were off Taormini : Italy on the other side in mist. We landed by about ten o'clock, and having so many on board, had a difficulty in getting lodged. In spite of the threatening weather, we walked up a high hill, 2,000 feet (the next day was beautiful), and I saw at my feet the Straits of Messina, with Scylla and Charybdis and the fine coast of Calabria, with Reggio. Charybdis is now the site of the Mole, and consists of little whirlpools, which in consequence have spent themselves. But both it and Scylla are still dangerous for small sailing vessels, which, getting into the current from the one, are sent forward upon the other.

We went into many of the churches both here and at Palermo, and saw somewhat of the Roman service, which is less reverent than the Greek, being far more public. There is no screen, the high altar is in sight. Palermo is a far richer and finer place than Messina ; some of the churches are magnificent. It is a beautiful city, and contains 160,000 inhabitants. It lies in a splendid bay of bold mountains, snow-capped in part. On the extreme right as you enter is Monte Pellegrino, which in ancient times, I think, Amilcar held for three years against the Romans. The whole scenery is wild and fearful, with a very rich valley lying at the foot of it, in which the city is placed. Far on the left you see Etna, a mass of white with a small cloud above its summit. The city mainly consists of two streets intersecting each other at right angles, and one of them perhaps a mile long. The houses are very fine ; numerous convents, which run along the upper floors—shops, &c., being below. There is a splendid promenade running along the water's edge. It was the carnival time, and the main streets were thronged with people as full as London. Fancy this at the length of a mile. The beggars were incredibly importunate, thrusting their hands into one's face and keeping them there for several hundred yards, till they came to the end of their beat, when others succeeded them. They have a miserable whine, in all parts of the island that we have seen, so as to make one quite nervous. The streets are filthy beyond expression, and the mixture of greatness with littleness is strange to an Englishman. They are paved side to side with flags; there is no footway. At Naples they are not so filthy as in Sicily, and the beggars less troublesome, but the boys at Naples are thieves. Froude has already lost a handkerchief, and I have had one half pulled out of my pocket, and have caught one or two boys peeping into it.

We dined last Tuesday at Palermo with Mr. Ingham, one of the principal British merchants, and yesterday (at Naples) with Moberly's brother-in-law, Mr. Bennett, the chaplain here. I ought to give you an account of an Italian dinner as we first became acquainted with it on board the steamer, after waiting till we were very hungry. First a course of cheese, pickles, anchovies, raw sausages of mule's flesh—then soup, then some boiled meat, then fish, then cauliflower, then a fowl; lastly, pastry with dessert. You are never helped twice. I see now the meaning of the English phrase, 'cut and come again.' Yet sometimes, as at Mr. Ingham's, this dinner becomes quite superb. All over the South, according to our experience, after two or three glasses of wine, the cloth not being removed, coffee (one small cup) is brought in, which is followed by some liqueur, and so the entertainment ends.

To his Sister Jemima.

Naples: February 19, 1833.

We have fallen on bad weather at Naples. The books tell us that a perpetual spring is here; but more piercing winds, and more raw, wretched rains, I have scarcely ever felt. For invalids the place is emphatically bad; especially when they don't see the harm of linen wet from the wash. But yesterday, when we went to Baiæ, was a magnificent day. On Thursday evening we went to the Opera. In spite of my reasonings, which I continue to think sound, I felt so great a repugnance to going, that, had I been alone, I should not have gone. There was nothing there to offend me, however, more than that the whole city offends me. It is a frivolous, dissipated place. This is carnival time, and all sorts of silly saturnalia between King and people are going on. Religion is turned into a mere occasion of worldly gaiety—as in the history of the Israelites—and the sooner we are out of so bad a place the better. And now I shall leave mention of Naples, which even in its scenery much disappoints me, after the glorious Sicily and the majestical bay of Palermo.

That bay is, in my eyes, far finer than that of Naples. It is not to the purpose that we have had bad weather here, for I am speaking of outlines. The bay of Naples is partly surrounded by lumpish cliffs. In Palermo you have a theatre of the most graceful mountains. Here is the difference between Sicily and Greece. As far as the drawings I have seen, and my experience, such as it is, confirms them, in Greece the view is choked up with mountains; you cannot move for them. But in Sicily you have ample plains,[1] and the high ground rises out of them at its ease, calmly, and with elbow-room. This is the beauty of the bay of Palermo; but other influences come in to move me. I saw the most interesting (profane) country after Egypt; and its history—beginning with the highest antiquity—unites in due time both with the Greek history and the Roman. It was the theme of almost every poet and every historian, and the remains in it of the past are of an earlier antiquity and more perfect than those of other countries. And now it lies in desolation under a bad Government. Not tricked out in the vanities of modern times, but as if in mourning, yet beautiful as ever. These thoughts suggested the following sonnet:

> Why, wedded to the Lord, still yearns my heart
> Upon these scenes of ancient heathen fame?
> Yet legend hoar, and voice of bard that came
> Fixing my restless youth with its sweet art,
> And shades of power, and those who bare their part
> In the mad deeds that set the world in flame,
> So fret my memory here.—Ah! is it blame
> That from my eyes the tear is fain to start?

---

[1] The following comparison illustrates the ground of that harmony with Mr. Newman's nature which so attracted him to Sicilian scenery. Writing to his sister, J. C. M., in 1847, he says:
'In myself I like an extensive view with tracts bold and barren in it. Such as Beethoven's music seems to represent.'

Nay, from no fount impure these drops arise;
'Tis but the sympathy with Adam's race
Which in each brother's history reads its own.
So let the cliffs and seas of this fair place
Be named man's tomb and splendid record stone.
High hope pride-stained, the course without the prize.¹

Messina: February 9, 1833.

At Palermo the wife of the Governor of Moldavia and Wallachia took the whole town. After being boxed about from place to place, we contrived to secure two rooms, which we pronounced to be unbearably filthy. But it is astonishing how our standard falls in these parts. On our return from Egesta we pronounced them to be, 'after all, very fair apartments.' We got into them by ten or eleven on Sunday.

That night we went to bed early, and were called at three next morning to commence our journey to Egesta, for we were resolved to make the most of our time, the vessel starting on Wednesday morning for Naples. By four we were off. A travelling carriage, drawn by three mules with bells, a driver and his boy behind, and a servant hired as a guide for three days, formed our set-out. We stop in the town at a café for something warm in the shape of coffee, for we have a journey of forty-three miles before us over a cold mountain country; and then eight or nine miles to and fro on mules before we were to eat or drink again. A morsel of bread was our sole breakfast. The revellers were returning home from the grand masquerade as we recommenced our journey, the mule-bells ringing and clinking in the dark, till we came to the suburbs, and began our long ascent of twelve miles. What a wonderful prospect broke on us with the day—wild, grey, barren eminences tossed about, many with their heads cut off by clouds, others lighted up by the sun! Then we descended into a stupendous valley, a sheer descent of rock on each side of us, of perhaps a thousand feet, meeting at an acute angle, and the road then cut on one of them. Then followed a richly fertile plain, large every way, full of olives, corn, vines, with towns interspersed, the bay of Castel-a-mare bounding it, around which bold and beautiful mountains rear themselves. After passing through one town we came to Scala di Partenico, where we changed horses, and soon came to Alcamo, thence to Calatafimi, which ended our drive, by half-past one. I now begin to understand how Sicily was a corn country, not merely in vales and plains, but up slopes of long hills which are cultivated up to the top, and in the midst of rocks and precipitous descents.

¹ 'Messina.'

I recommended a slight 'refection,' as Lady Margaret would say, before starting on our mules; so, after an egg or two, we set off for the Temple, which is four miles off, and which came in sight suddenly, after we had advanced about a mile. Oh that I could tell you one quarter what I have to say about it! First, the surrounding scene on approaching it is a rich valley—now, don't fancy valleys and hills as in England; <u>it is all depth and height, nothing lumpish</u>—and even at this season the colouring is rich. We went through groves of olive and prickly pear, and by orange orchards till we came to a steep hill covered with ruins. We wound up the ascent—once doubtless a regular road to the city gate—and, on surmounting the brow, we saw what we had seen at a distance (and what we saw also afterwards at the end of a long valley on leaving the plain of Castel-a-mare for Palermo), the Temple. Here the desolation was a striking contrast to the richness of the valley we had been passing. The hill on which we stood was covered with ruins, especially of a theatre. Opposite to it, a precipitous rock started out of the ravine below. On the hill beyond it there were, as on our hill, ruins; and we conjectured they might mark the site of the Greek town, but on the circular hill there was nothing but a single Temple. Such was the genius of ancient Greek worship—grand in the midst of error, simple and unadorned in its architecture: it chose some elevated spot, and fixed there its solitary witness, where it could not be hid. I believe it is the most perfect building remaining anywhere—Doric—six gigantic pillars before and behind, twelve in length, no roof. Its history is unknown. The temples of later and classical times have vanished—the whole place is one ruin, except this in the waste of solitude. A shepherd's hut is near, and a sort of farmyard—a number of eager dogs—a few rude intrusive men, who would have robbed us, I fancy, had they dared. On the hill on which the theatre stood was a savage-looking bull, prowling amid the ruins. Mountains around and Eryx in the distance. The past and the present! Once these hills were full of life! I began to understand what Scripture means when speaking of lofty cities vaunting in the security of their strongholds. What a great but ungodly sight was this place in its glory! and then its history; to say nothing of Virgil's fictions. Here it was that Nicias came; this was the ally of Athens; what a strange place! How did people take it into their heads to plant themselves here? At length we turned about, and got back to Calatafimi by six o'clock. And now I ought to tell you about Calatafimi and the towns we passed through to get there, in order to complete the picture, but I have not done it and cannot.

I send two songs *à la mode de* Walter Scott.

> When mirth is full and free,
> Some sudden gloom shall be;
> When haughty power mounts high,
> The Watcher's axe is nigh.
> All growth has bound; when greatest found
> It hastes to die.
>
> When the rich town, that long
> Has lain its huts among,
> Rears its new structures vast,
> And vaunts,—it shall not last!
> Bright tints that shine are but a sign
> Of summer past.
>
> And when thine eye surveys,
> With fond adoring gaze
> And yearning heart, thy friend,—
> Love to its grave doth tend.
> All gifts below, save Truth, but grow
> Towards an end.[1]

Valletta: January 30, 1833.

> When Heaven sends sorrow,
>   Warnings go first,
>   Lest it should burst
>   With stunning might
>   On souls too bright
> To fear the morrow.
>
> Can science bear us
>   To the hid springs
>   Of human things?
>   Why may not dream
>   Or thought's day gleam
> Startle, yet cheer us?
>
> Are such thoughts fetters,
>   While Faith disowns
>   Dread of earth's tones,
>   Recks but Heaven's call,
>   And on the wall
> Reads but Heaven's letters?[2]

Between Calatafimi and Palermo: February 12, 1833.

[1] 'Prosperity.'   [2] 'Warnings.'

To his Mother.

February 28, 1833.

We leave Naples for Rome to-morrow morning. You may send me letters directed either to Naples, to Mr. Oates, 70 Vicolo Freddo, or to Rome, till just after the Oriel election, which is April 12 ; a letter will get to me by May 2 at Rome or Naples on my return (please God) from Sicily homeward. I suppose I shall get to England by the beginning of June.

We returned yesterday from Pæstum. We have not achieved Vesuvius. To return to Sicily.

I left Jemima without an account of the condition of the lower classes in Sicily. I will now give you a traveller's description, which is proverbially superficial. The mixture of grandeur and dirt in the towns is indescribable, and to an Englishman incomprehensible. There, at Naples and at Palermo and Messina, the beggars are fearful, both in their appearance and their importunity. One fellow at Messina stuck by us for two hours. At Palermo they have beats ; here at Naples their horribleness has most struck me : at Palermo their dirt and squalidness. Oh, the miserable creatures we saw in Sicily ! I never knew what human suffering was before. Children and youths who look as if they did not know what fresh air was, though they must have had it in plenty—well, what water was—with features sunk, contracted with perpetual dirt, as if dirt was their food. The towns of Partenico and Alcamo are masses of filth ; the street is a pool ; but Calatafimi, where we slept !—I dare not mention facts. Suffice it to say, we found the poor children of the house slept in holes dug into the wall, which smelt not like a dog-kennel, but like a wild beast's cage, almost overpowering us in the room upstairs. I have no sleep all night from insects of prey ; but this was a slight evil. The misery is increased from the custom of having the stable on the ground floor and the kitchen on the first. The dwelling is on the second floor. Yet it is pleasing to discern a better seeming class amid the misery ; even at Alcamo there were tidy clean-looking women, and outside the towns much washing was going on. A great number of the Sicilians and Calabrians we have seen are a striking and bright-looking race—regular features and very intelligent. Sparkling eyes, brownish skins, and red healthy-looking cheeks. At Amalfi yesterday we were quite delighted with them.

The state of the Church is deplorable. It seems as if Satan was let out of prison to range the whole earth again. As far as our little experience goes, everything seems to confirm the notion received among ourselves of the priesthood, while on the other hand the Church is stripped of its temporalities and reduced to distress. The churches at Messina and Palmero are superb, and there is a fine church at Monreale, which is the see of the Primate (there are, perhaps, ten sees in the island). It is worth 10,000*l*. a year, but the present bishop compounds with Government for 2,000*l*. I think I heard that originally the Sicilian Church was expected to support the poor, but that the bishops compounded for this by giving a certain sum to Government, which is now spent in paying Government pensions. We have just heard of the Irish Church Reform Bill. Well done ! my blind Premier, confiscate and rob, till, like Samson, you pull down the Political Structure on your own head ! At Naples the poverty of the Church is deplorable. All its property we are told is lost. The grandfather of the present King, the Lazzaroni king, began the confiscation ; the French completed it. Thus these countries have the evils of Protestantism without its advantages – that is, Anglican Protestantism ; for there are no advantages whether in schism like Dissent, or Socinianism such as Geneva's. But here, too, they have infidelity and profaneness, as if the whole world (Western) were tending towards some dreadful crisis. I begin to hope that England after all is to be the 'Land of Saints' in this dark hour, and her Church the salt of the earth. We met in the steamer an American who was a pompous man, and yet we contracted a kind of affection for him. He was an Episcopalian, and had better principles far than one commonly meets with in England, and a docile mind. We are quite sorry to have lost sight of him. Is the American Church to serve any purpose in the Divine scheme ? I begin to inquire whether the Revelations do not relate to the European world only, or Roman Empire, so that as ages of time may be summed up in the first verses of Genesis, and the history commences only with the creation of man, so the prophecy may end with the history of Christianity in the Roman Empire, and its fortunes in America or China may be summed up obscurely in a few concluding sentences ; if so one would almost expect some fresh prophecy to be given when the end of the European period comes. I should add we afterwards found out that our good friend belonged to the Wesleyan Episcopalians. To return, doubtless there are God's saints here, and perhaps brighter ones than with us. We heard of one man—at Messina, I think—who, while bearing his witness against the profligacy of the priesthood, rigidly attends Mass, and, on being asked why, answered that the altar is above the priest, and that God can bless His own ordinances, in spite of the instruments being base. This seems very fine, but the majority of the laity who think, run into infidelity. The priests have lost influence exceedingly since the peace. The French Revolution and Empire seem to have generated a plague, which is slowly working its way everywhere. At Malta we heard the same, and at Corfu.

I have been asking myself what the especial beauty of Naples (that is the Bay) is, and why we are disappointed with it, which we continue to be. Now its fame seems to arise, first, from the mountains and high hills scattered round it, and next from the beauty of the colouring. Now, as to the second point, we have not seen this by reason of the season. I can fully believe that in fine weather the painting of the scene is enchanting, and am convinced that the colours are almost different in kind from anything we have in England. But this I believe is the case with Corfu too, and in fact I think that Corfu had spoilt us for Naples. As to the first point, the land outline is certainly fine, especially Vesuvius, a graceful object on the left, and the islands. Add to these a grand expanse of water, calm, and dark blue—what can be finer? Nothing, to those who have not seen Corfu. The panorama there is far grander and more varied. The town itself contains two picturesque rocks. Naples is surrounded by lumpish cliffs like bolsters. Vesuvius indeed is perfect in its way as a beautiful object, but cannot compare in grandeur with the San Salvadore range at Corfu, which is a long ridge as high as Vesuvius, and is taken up by the Albanian mountains, some of which, 100 miles off, are little inferior in height to the Alps. Whereas the Salerno range, striking as it is, is at the highest point not above 4,000 feet. Then at Corfu you have inland seas, and hills covered with olive-trees far finer in shape and size than anything I have found here or in Sicily, and the beautiful cypress, which I have seen nowhere else. So that we have come to the conclusion that Naples is a *watering-*

place with watering-place scenery, and will be admired chiefly by watering-place people; with a delightful climate in its season—a place for animal gratification and as such chosen by the luxurious Romans, who, tired with the heat of Rome, made Baiæ their Brighton. We have seen the villas of Lucullus, Cicero, Cæsar, &c., which skirted its coast; there are the ruins of numberless others all along from Misenum to Pozzuoli, to Pompeii, &c. But if we want real beauty, not mere luxury, we must cross to the other side of the Salerno range, and see Salerno itself, Vietri, Cetara, Minori, Maiori, Atrani, and Amalfi.

We have seen the Lake Avernus, the Sibyl's grotto, and Cumæ, and eaten oysters at Fusaro.

We have been to Pompeii and Herculaneum—wonderful sights!—and had a prosperous expedition to Pæstum, where the temple exceeded my expectation.

Rome: March 3.

We arrived here safe yesterday evening after a tiresome journey.

We have just heard Mr. B., the chaplain here, a perfect watering-place preacher, semi-evangelical. Mr. Bennett, at Naples, is an accomplished man; has travelled much, speaks various languages, and is liberal; he will be a great loss to the chapel there.

This is a wonderful place—the first city, mind, which I have ever much praised. We were at St. Peter's yesterday. It is of a prodigious size. Everything is so bright and clean, and the Sunday kept so decorously.

To HIS SISTER HARRIETT.

Rome: March 4, 1833.

I hope my plans are pretty well settled. Edward Neate, who is here, is well disposed to go with me to Sicily. Impatient as I am to return on every account, I feel it would be foolish, now that I am out, not to do as much as ever I can. I only wish I could have the satisfaction of hearing from you. It is now three months—thirteen weeks today—since I left Oxford, and I have only had my Mother's letter and yours of December 17. It would be a great satisfaction merely to know you had received my letters. I am always making conjectures of the dates at which you ought to get them.

Pompeii and Herculaneum are wonderful places, but they do not move me. They are curious and strange. Pompeii was destroyed by ashes, Herculaneum by lava. The lava must have been quite liquid, and in immense quantities. It has literally filled up every part of the theatre, as water might; every recess, every crevice is blocked up; it has got through the windows and doors, and run about everywhere. What a torrent it must have been! It was the first eruption of Vesuvius for centuries, though Pompeii is built upon lava, and there is evidence of a crater before the date of the destruction of the two cities. But it was a crater so seemingly spent that it was covered with vegetation, and something like the crater of the Solfatara now, which is a royal park [in Vesuvius it was that Spartacus and his followers took refuge]. Again, while Etna's eruptions are continually mentioned in history, there is a silence about those of Vesuvius. After its breaking out (A.D. 70–80) it continued in action till about A.D. 1100, when it ceased for nearly five centuries, and then the vegetation gradually returned. We have an account from writers who ventured down its crater; they went down a mile or two. The mountain is altogether the creation of volcanic action. Lava was thrown up from the level of the surface, hardened, and formed a cone; fresh lava was thrown up in time, and thus the mount gradually rose and increased. Even now its height is continually varying. The eruption of 1822 lowered it by breaking away the sides of the crater; then afterwards there was more lava, and it recovered its height.

To return: Pompeii, of course, is full of interest; the amphitheatre most of all. The people were at the games when the cinder clouds fell. You have the lions' den distinct; a lion's bones were found there, and the bones of the keeper. Excavations are going on in both cities, but very slowly. The royal palace of Portici is built over Herculaneum; not much will be done there. It is five miles from Naples; Pompeii, on the same road, fifteen.

We set off for Pæstum this day week (February 25), passing Pompeii to Nocera and La Cava, and so to Salerno. I have not seen such scenery since I was in Sicily. Salerno is a beautiful town, and the inn is very respectable. It set in to rain just after we arrived, so from 2 P.M. the day was lost. Next morning at five we set off for Pæstum. The country is highly cultivated, and the country people are well dressed.

They are strong, handsome, and pleasant-looking. They gave us a very favourable notion of the peasantry. I think the murder of Mr. and Mrs. Hunt some years back at Pæstum was hardly more [in intention] than what a petty theft would have been in England. The murderers were not bandits. Mr. and Mrs. Hunt took a good deal of plate with them, and showed it. Some labourers in a field near the road, without previous design, were seized with the temptation to plunder them; and Mr. Hunt stooping down as if to seize hold of a pistol, one of them at once fired. The shot went through him and his wife. The assassins made off. [The peasantry take their guns with them into the fields. This afterwards I saw on the eastern coast in 1847-8. Why is it allowed ?]

The roads are very well guarded now, and excellently made. There were five parties there, besides ourselves, the morning we went there.

There are ruins of two [Greek ?] temples, a basilica, a theatre, amphitheatre, Roman temple of peace, city walls, gates, the foundations of the greater part of the city, &c. The country is not striking, though the Apennines are fine; but the large temple far exceeded my expectation; it is as far superior to the temple at Egesta as its situation and the scene:y round are inferior. It is, indeed, magnificent. We got back to Salerno comfortably by six in the evening, and next morning went to Amalfi, and back by sea. This side of the Bay of Salerno contained such cliffs, ravines, caves, towns perched aloft, &c., that I am full of silent, not talkative, delight. How *can* people talk of the beauty of Naples with such true beauty in the neighbourhood? Amalfi is a town in one of these ravines. The mountains open, and a long, narrow, steep valley winds through their folds; two abundant streams run down it. On these streams there are fourteen paper mills, which pond up and then pour down the water from a number of precipitous heights. As you ascend, you are surrounded by cascades, and grots with green creepers. All is beautifully cool and sweet. The rocks above are 1,000 or 1,500 feet high. We were particularly pleased with the look of the population. All were so neat and clean. There was not a bad smell in the whole place, and they were handsome. We met, coming down the hill, a clerical school (such as we had often seen elsewhere); the boys were so bright and smiling and intelligent-looking. There were a great many of them—boys from fourteen to seventeen years old. We had hoped to get over the mountain to Castel-a-mare, but did not venture. We rowed back, and so to Naples, where we all arrived about half-past 8, very tired, not having eaten since 7 A.M. On Thursday we packed up. On Friday set out for Rome. I have no sort of affectionate feeling towards Naples.

We are settled here in very comfortable apartments—six rooms, kitchen, servants' room, and house-tops—for thirty scudi the month, *i.e.* about 1*l*. 11*s.* the week. They are clean and airy [in the Via Babuino], a few doors from the Wilberforces and E. Neate. And now what can I say of Rome, but that it is the first of cities, and that all I ever saw are but as dust (even dear Oxford inclusive) compared with its majesty and glory ? Is it possible that so serene and lofty a place is the cage of unclean creatures ? I will not believe it till I have evidence of it. In St. Peter's yesterday, in St. John Lateran to-day, I have felt quite abased, chiefly by their enormous size, added to the extreme accuracy and grace of their proportions, which make one feel little and contemptible. Fancy, I have been at the Coliseum, have stood in the Forum, have mounted the Capitol, have crossed the Tiber, and live in the Campus Martius, and yet I have scarcely begun to see the city. The approach to Rome from Naples is very striking. It is through ancient towns, full of ruin, along the Via Appia; then you come to the Pontine Marshes ; then, about fourteen miles from Rome, to a wild, woody, rocky region ; then through the Campagna—a desolate flat, the home of malaria. It is a fit approach to a city which has been the scene of Divine judgments. After a time isolated ruins come to view, of monuments, arches, aqueducts. The flat waste goes on ; you think it will never have done ; miles on miles the ruins continue. At length the walls of Rome appear ; you pass through them ; you find the city shrunk up into a third of the space enclosed. In the twilight you pass buildings about which you cannot guess wrongly. This must be the Coliseum ; there is the Arch of Constantine. You are landed at your inn ; night falls, and you know nothing more till next morning.

March 9.

Still no letters from you *via* Naples ; so I have learned to despair. I only want to know one thing—that you are all well, and that I am not wanted. I go on acting and planning with the notion that any moment I may be summoned back [by the Bishop], though to return without summons seems absurd ; so I must be content.

Rome grows more wonderful every day. The first thought one has of the place is awful—that you see the great enemy of God—the Fourth Monarchy, the Beast dreadful and terrible. We need no Tower of Babel ; the immense extent of the ruins ; the purposes to which, when in their glory, they were dedicated ; the arena where Ignatius suffered ; the Jewish candlestick on the Arch of Titus ; the columns, with the proud heathen inscriptions still visible, brand the place as the vile tool of God's wrath and Satan's malice.

Next, when you enter the museums, galleries, and libraries, a fresh world is opened to you—that of imagination and taste. You find there collected the various creations of Greek genius. The rooms are interminable ; and the marbles and mosaics astonishing for their costliness. The Apollo is quite unlike his casts. I never was moved by them at all, but at the first sight of the real statue I was subdued at once. I was not prepared for this at all. I had only been anxious to see it, and the celebrated pictures of Raffaelle. They are beyond praise : such expression ! What struck me most was the strange simplicity of look which he has the gift to bestow on the faces.

As to the third view of Rome, here pain and pleasure go together, as is obvious. It is strange to be standing in the city of the Apostles, and among the tombs of the martyrs and saints. We have visited St. Gregory's (the Great) Church. It is built on the site of his house ; and an inscription at the entrance records the names of some of our early Bishops, including the monk Augustine, as proceeding from the convent attached to it. The Roman clergy are said to be a decorous, orderly body, and certainly most things are very different from Naples. There are no trumpery ornaments or absurd inscriptions in the streets, profaning the most sacred subjects, and the look of the priests is superior. But there are (seemingly) timidity, indolence, and that secular spirit which creeps on established religion everywhere. It is said they got Mr. Spencer quickly out of Rome because his fastings shamed them [This is nonsense.—J. H. N.], and that no one thinks of fasting here—a curious contrast with the Greeks. The schools are neat and pleasant-looking. One I saw yesterday, of orphan girls, was very interesting : but the choristers at St. Peter's are as irreverent as at St. Paul's.

I conclude with some verses, the idea of which beset me as I walked along the Appian Way over the Pontine Marshes, while the horses were changing.

> Far sadder musing on the traveller falls
>   At sight of thee, O Rome !
> Than when he views the rough sea-beaten walls
>   Of Greece, thought's early home;
> For thou wast of the hateful four whose doom
>   Burdens the Prophet's scroll;
> But Greece was clean till in her history's gloom
>   Her name and sword a Macedonian stole.
>
> And next a mingled throng besets the breast
>   Of bitter thoughts and sweet ;
> How shall I name thee, Light of the wide West,
>   Or heinous error-seat ?
> O Mother, erst close tracing Jesus' feet,
>   Do not thy titles glow
> In those stern judgment-fires which shall complete
>   Earth's strife with Heaven, and ope the eternal woe?

REV. J. H. NEWMAN TO FREDERIC ROGERS, ESQ.

Rome: March 5, 1833.

I hope my friends have not measured my attachment to them by the punctuality of my correspondence, or I shall get into disgrace with many of them, and with you in the number. Indeed, my conscience has sometimes reproached me for my silence in your case, since you are the only person I have heard from in England since I left (except a chance letter of my Mother's, written a day or two after I went). You cannot imagine how wearisome it is to be without news of home. At the time I got your letter at Malta I was confined to my room with a bad cold, and, short as it was, it was most welcome. Thank you for all the trouble you and your Father and Mother took about the introductions. You know, now, I missed some of them in England ; but I availed myself of those you sent, though, unluckily, Sir H. Hotham was away. For other reasons, besides your letter, perhaps, you have claims upon my handwriting. I must seem strangely inconsistent to you in having determined not to return by the election at Easter ; though, if I recollect right, I hinted to you in the letter which first announced my plan that I might stop abroad a month or two later. But the state of the case was briefly this : Froude and I calculated, and found that *one* of us merely returning would have no effect whatever on the votes of the election, and as his Father had determined he should stay till June (and I think wisely), it was literally no manner of use my going back as far as my vote went; and I fully believe you have too many well-wishers among us to need me for anything else. And I found, too, that we were not to be at Rome till March; so that, had I returned, I should have seen nothing, hardly, and scarcely done more than wander about the wide sea. Still, I am extremely anxious, and at times annoyed almost with myself, lest I have been wrong. Were you not to succeed, I know I should reproach myself—yet I cannot doubt you will. I am so sorry about your eyes, and hope you have taken my advice not to say much publicly on the subject. This will get to you just as the election is coming on—all good fortune be with you. If you could send me just a line when it is over (and about Wood and Wilson too) addressed to me, 'Mrs. Oates, 70 Vicolo Freddo, Naples,' it will get to me on my return from Sicily, whither I suppose I shall go with Neate just after the Holy Week (but do not mention this idea of mine, for it is not settled). I long to be back, yet wish to make the most of being out of England, for I never wish to leave it again. Pleasures I have had in abundance, and most rapturous; yet somehow (as was natural) *aliquid desideravere oculi mei.* It might have been different were I younger; but when one's mode of life is formed, one is often more pained than interested by what is novel.

We arrived at this wonderful place only Saturday last (March 2) from Naples. It is the first city which I have been able to admire, and it has swallowed up, like Aaron's rod, all the admiration which, in the case of others, is often distributed among Naples, Valletta, and other places. It is scarcely with patience I hear people talking of Naples in comparison—nor will I degrade Rome by dwelling on the notion. Of course, I have seen very little of it; but the effect of every part is so vast and overpowering—there is such an air of greatness and repose cast over the whole, and, independent of what one knows from history, there are such traces of long sorrow and humiliation, suffering, punishment and decay, that one has a mixture of feelings, partly such as those with which one would approach a corpse, and partly those which would be excited by the sight of the spirit which had left it. It brings to my mind Jeremiah's words in the Lamentations, when Jerusalem, or (sometimes) the prophet, speaks as the smitten of God.

Oxford, of course, must ever be a sacred city to an Oxonian, and is to me. It would be a strange want of right pride to think of disloyalty to it, even if our creed were not purer than the Roman ; yet the lines of Virgil keenly and affectionately describe what I feel about this wonderful city. Repeat them in your memory every word, and dwell on each. ' *Urbem, quam dicunt Romam, Melibœe, putavi, stultus ego !* ' &c. And if you had seen the cypresses of Corfu, and the graceful, modest way in which they shoot straight up with a composed shape, yet boldly in their way, being landmarks almost for miles round, you would see the beauty of the comparison of the *inter viburna cupressi*. Since I have been abroad I have been taking in stores of pleasure for many years to come. It is impossible to enter into the full power of what one sees at once—the sights of celebrated places are like seeds sown in the mind. I have often felt the retrospect more delightful than the first enjoyment, great as that was. It is strange, too, the different kind of pleasure one has in different places. Only think, I have seen Ithaca—seen it for hours—coasting, in fact, all round it ; and then again Rhium and Antirrhium and Corcyra—and again Sicily—and the landmarks leading to Carthage. All these places had their own pleasure, and as different as Homer is from Thucydides. I have so often wished for you and others to share my gratification, but the plague is, one feels it *never* can be. In other cases one says, ' Well, some other day, perhaps' ; but, though you may see, I shall not—it is a thing past with me, not to return.

For two months we were without sight of English news. At Naples, even, it is difficult to get an English newspaper, but here there is a reading-room, where papers are regularly received. It has surprised us to see how far Ministers have gone in their Irish Church Reform Bill—abolishing sees, taxing benefices immediately, &c. ; not that we doubted their sacrilegious will, but thought them now too much of Conservatives. If it is any consolation to have partners in misfortune, we have abundance here ; for the clergy all through Italy and Sicily (as far as we have been) appear to be in a wretched state of destitution (*i.e.* more or less). In Sicily a great portion of their revenues is appropriated for the payment of Goverment pensions—in Naples, &c., their property seems to have been almost entirely confiscated, the French having completed and confirmed the spoliation. They subsist by their Masses in the most cowardly contemptible way possible, not having had spirit enough to resist, but keeping good friends with their robbers. They seem to have lost all hold on the people, and we learn (as at Malta and elsewhere) that there had been a considerable growth of avowed infidelity in the course of the last fifteen years. It strikes me the superb religious edifices with which Italy abounds are a great snare to the clergy—they are a property of theirs which the State holds as a bond for their servility. 'We will take your rich churches' is a virtual threat which persuades them to submit to any insult or injury. At least, I think most men would be exposed to the temptation had they such wonderful structures. I am alluding now to the churches of Rome chiefly—we have seen only a few, but the principal—and no words can describe them. They could not have been in any place but Rome, which has turned the materials and the buildings of the Empire to the purposes of religion. Some of them are literally ancient buildings—as the Pantheon, and the portion of the Baths of Diocletian which is turned into a church. And all—St. Peter's, St. John Lateran, &c. — are enriched with marbles, &c., which old Roman power alone could have collected. The first effect produced on the mind by these noble piles (and I can as yet speak of no other) arises from their gigantic dimensions—everything is proportioned to the size of the building. The statues of the Apostles (*e.g.*)—all that the Germans would call *insanæ molis*—produce quite a moral effect of humiliation on the *homunciones* who gaze on them. Thus we have all the richness of the latter ages of the arts added to the magnitude which is the peculiarity of the early Egyptian, Cyclopean, &c. It is a realisation of the skill and power of Dædalus, who was beautiful while he was stupendous (*posuitque immania templa*, &c.). Talking of great works, I have seen Pæstum, and the principal temple there far exceeded my expectations. It is, indeed, wonderful; but you know it so well from pictures that nothing can be said about it except that it is wonderful. The most exquisite treat we have had was a visit to Egesta, to see the ruins and the remaining temple. The contrast between the wildness and the richness of the country we went over with the utter desolation and loneliness of the spot itself and the miserable state of the population, and our own little sufferings in the way of indescribable filth and annoyance, combined to stamp quite a picture on the memory, which is every day more touching. The temple itself is *very* fine, but the situation—oh, the situation ! What strange fellows those old Trojans and Phœnicians were to place themselves in so wild a place ! When the city was in its splendour in Roman times it must have been very magnificent. It is perched on the top of a high hill (higher far, I should think, than the ἀκροπόλεις of Greece), and a long stair wound up to the city gate.

You have an unintelligible paragraph in your letter in which you seem to quote some words from my last. I quite forget what they were about, but suspect about verse-making. If so, I really think you should give it a trial, as you seem disposed to do. If *e.g.* you feel disposed to mathematise (as men do on the top of coaches) well and good. This may be a better employment; but, rather than none, attempt verses. One ought to make the most of one's talents, and may write useful lines (useful to others) without being a poet. Ten thousand obvious ideas become impressive when put into a metrical shape ; and many of them we should not dare to utter except metrically, for thus the responsibility (as it were) is shoved off of oneself, and one speaks ὡς παιδίζων, though serious. I am so convinced of the use of it, particularly in times of excitement, that I have begun to practise myself, which I never did before ; and since I have been abroad, have thrown off about sixty short copies, which may serve a certain purpose we have in view. Should you want a subject for conversation the next time you happen to see my Mother (if by yourself ; for pray be mum about this to *every* one), you may ask for such as I have sent home, or, at least, for the more lively ones, for many are sonnets, which are proverbially dull. At least the sight of them may stimulate you, and put you in good spirits, and suggest ideas and how to *begin*— which is the great difficulty in all things.

Pray remember me most kindly to all friends, though I hope to write to many of them in a day or two. Please to write my name in my Tillemont, for which you have observed, doubtless, I have as yet no fitting place in my library ; but I hope it is duly spread, as I ordered it to be, on the escritoire between the windows, that it may cut a figure. By-the-bye, I left one or two drawers of the said piece of furniture open for you (have you found them out ?) with some regret that I had closed so many. I often think of you, and fancy you in my rooms. Oxford is the first of cities. What does Telemachus say of Ithaca ? I read great part of the 'Odyssey' (beginning directly old Atlas was visible) while we wandered up and down the Mediterranean ; and have read more of Virgil, and sapped at it, than I have done since I was ten years old.

Ever yours affectionately,
J. H. NEWMAN.

REV. J. H. NEWMAN TO J. F. CHRISTIE, ESQ.

Rome: March 7, 1833.

. . . Now I am in for it the chance is I shall stop as long as I can, and see all that can be grasped in the time, for I sincerely hope never to go abroad again. I never loved home so well as now I am away from it—and the exquisite sights which foreign countries supply both to the imagination and the moral taste are most pleasurable in *memory*, but scarcely satisfactory as a present enjoyment. There is far too much of tumult in seeing the places one has read so much about all one's life, to make it desirable for it to continue. I did not know before, the mind could be excited in so many various ways ; but it is as much so as if it were literally pulled about, and had now a leg twitched and now one's head turned. The pleasure which the sight of the Morea gave me was different in kind from that which I gained from seeing Ithaca, or Sicily, or the Straits of Messina, or again Rome. This is a fine sentence ; for it seems as if I had travelled over the Morea, whereas we only landed on the coast for an hour or two at night at a miserable, whole-burnt, half re-built town. Yet our visit was sufficiently picturesque. In the first place, the town was Patras, *i.e.* Patræ, of which Oxford men hear in Thucydides ; and we saw in the dusk of the evening the wild mountains of both coasts, and in the distance, Rhium and Antirrhium. Next, the country was in a state of the wildest anarchy, swarming by land and sea with bandits and pirates. The former extended through the whole Morea, which was at that moment in a state of great excitement, King Otho being almost daily expected. Accordingly some were hastening to Napoli to make interest with him on his arrival ; others, secretly favoured by Russia, were keeping aloof, determining to watch the course of things before they committed themselves. A worthy of the latter class presided over the destinies of Patras at that moment, *nomine* Tzavellas, or Svellas, or Sbellas, or the like. He had taken possession of the citadel, and some time before, the French had summoned

him in vain. Three ships with the colours of the three great
Powers lay before the town. The English sloop was commanded by Sir J. Franklin, who for nine or (as some said)
eighteen months had been stationed there without anyone on
board having set foot upon land! that is, from fear of being
obliged to take part with one or other of the hostile parties.
We did not like to lose the opportunity of touching the Continent, and pushed off from the steamer in the boat. The
town, so to call it, is in a miserable condition, and we had
great difficulty in the dark in keeping our legs amid the
foundations and ruins of the houses; there had been rain,
and was much mud, and it was very dark. You will say this
was a curious way of seeing a town, especially as the town
was not yet built; but we walked through the high street,
which was in a tolerably forward state; we went into various
shops, we took coffee in the first coffee-house of the place,
which was full of Greek merchants, in their very picturesque
dresses, which were quite clean, since it was a feast. The
coffee was capital (we have got very little good since we have
been out of England), it is milled up in a strange way. Our
most respectable adventure was falling in with Zavellas' men-
at-arms, who were not a little surprised at seeing us, and
through whom we walked with as much silence and quiet
rapidity as you would expect. On our return there from
Corfu, we found there had been a mutiny in the garrison
owing to Zavellas' refusing to pay his troops the money he
had levied for that purpose from the merchants of the place.
The Russian consul had interfered and persuaded him, and
they were all engaged in putting the castle in a state of defence
against their neighbours, who were expected to march against
it. It seems quite a hopeless task to civilise the Morea—
otherwise *i.e.* than by exterminating vast numbers of the inhabitants. We were told by travellers who had lately
travelled through it that there is certainly a better sort of
persons, and that the present anarchy is rather owing to
the ascendency of the worst spirits than to the character of
the people. But even allowing this, how can you alter the
inveterate habit which the better class have got of *succumbing*
to the most violent? Nothing but great craft or great
tyranny will be able to manage them. It is curious that with
all their brutality these fellows observe most strictly the fasts
of the Church, which may be called the distinguishing feature
of the Greek Communion, as Masses, &c., is of the Latin,

and they both answer the same purpose, and are a substitute apparently for moral obedience and an opiate to the conscience. (The Greeks have two fasts of forty days in the course of the year, besides many others of days and seasons; during these times it seems to be scarcely possible, certainly not the custom, to get dispensations.) Meat of any kind is literally refrained from—nay, I believe eggs and milk; not that they are likely to consider their bandit-kind of life as requiring some make-up. But it is the cruelties accompanying it which must (more or less) revolt all but the most hardened mind. I believe robbery is not more thought of in these countries, even *at most*, than pilfering is with us. A bravo, adopts a *profession* indeed, and one in which murder *may* be added to plundering; but he is not in any sense more *habitually* disobedient to his conscience, or more pained or sensitive than a dishonest servant in England who picks up stray halfpence of his master's or purloins his tea and sugar. And sometimes the crimes which have been most talked about and were most shocking were the chance result of temptation. Thus in the case of the dreadful murder of Mr. and Mrs. Hunt, which took place at Pæstum some years since. . . . In the same way Lord Harrowby was attacked near Naples a year or two since. It was a rising of the country people—such an event very rarely happens—I was told nothing of the kind had happened between these two events. They had got a notion of Lord H. being a great English lord. It is said the English are less likely to be attacked than men of other nations; they make such a noise about it. Consuls and ambassadors remonstrate, and themselves and their friends offer large rewards, so that the guilty parties have no chance of escaping. The road from Salerno to Pæstum is well guarded, but it is with reluctance that one believes it necessary. The people are a fine-looking race, very well clad, and the ground is well cultivated. I wonder whether they make a distinction between heretics and Catholics? I suppose not. . . .

As to Rome, it is the most wonderful place in the world. We do not need Babylon to give us a specimen of the old exertions of our great enemy against Heaven (who now takes a more crafty way); it was an establishment of impiety. The Coliseum is quite a Tower of Babel; this is but one of a vast number of buildings which astonish one. Then when you go into the museums, &c., you get into a second world. . . . The collection of statuary is endless and quite enchanting. The

Apollo is indescribable ; its casts give one no notion of it; as an influence it is overpowering. And the great pictures of Raffaelle, though requiring a scientific taste to criticise, come home in a natural way even to the uninitiated. I never could fancy anything so unearthly as the expression of the faces. Their strange simplicity of expression and almost boyishness is their great charm.

Well then, again, after this, you have to view Rome as a place of religion ; and here what mingled feelings come upon one—you are in the place of martyrdom and burial of apostles and saints ; you have about you the buildings and the sights they saw, and you are in the city to which England owes the blessing of the Gospel. But then, on the other hand, the superstitions, or rather, what is far worse, the solemn reception of them as an essential part of Christianity. But then, again, the extreme beauty and costliness of the churches ; and then, on the contrary, the knowledge that the most famous was built (in part) by the sale of indulgences. Really this is a cruel place. There is more to be seen and thought of daily. It is a mine of all sorts of excellences.

The 'Lyra' goes on flourishingly. It will commence (I hope) in May ; but of course be silent. With best remembrances to the Common-Room.—Ever yours affectionately,

JOHN H. NEWMAN.

March 9.—P.S. On reading this over I am shocked at the slipslop it contains. Pray do not incautiously let anyone see it.

To REV. THOMAS MOZLEY.

Rome: March 9, 1833.

At first sight it would seem as if there were a great contrast between Morton Pinckney and Rome, our respective residences at present, but really there is not a great deal. I have learned thus much by travelling, to think all places about the same, which I had no notion of before. I never could believe that horses, dogs, men and houses were the same in other countries as at home, not that I exactly doubted it, but my imagination could not embrace the notion. But now I find that even the seasons are the same, which perhaps you are not aware of. I assure you cold in all its varieties is felt here as well as in England. We have had rawness and bleakness and sharpness and wet, and the wind has blown tempests. At Malta I had a cough such as I never had in my life before, and at Naples it rained incessantly and gave me a very uncomfortable cold. Really, I now come to think that the ancients went on as we do, which is a further step of philosophy. I have seen Herculaneum and Pompeii, and the museum at Naples thence enriched, and find that the ancients used portable stoves and ate cake; and at Rome there is a mule's head in marble, and a group of fighting dogs as like present nature as one dog is like another.

All this is gain, and I suppose is part of that *nil admirari* which one gets by travelling. It is astonishing how little it seems to have been at places when one has been at them. One walks about at Corfu or Rome, and having the same thoughts, feelings, and bodily sensations as at home, cannot believe for a time that it is foreign land. And then everyone about one is at home—if they would but seem strangers to the place, they might kindle a sympathy in us; but they take it very easy, and think it no great thing to be where they are. Nay if you fall in with those who have themselves travelled more to the east and south than you, the case is worse still. You feel actually little for having been as far and no further than you have, which is a pretty kind of reward for coming all the way to see them.

> Actum, inquit, nihil est nisi Pœno milite portas
> Frangimus et media vexillum pono Suburra.[1]

I do not know how this will operate upon me eventually, and when I am back again, but really it has a strange effect now. It has in a measure destroyed the romance which I threw around everything I had not myself witnessed. Yet perhaps it has taken away no pleasure, and may be profitable. I now do not wish to see Epaminondas or Cocles; I believe them to be ordinary mortals, *fruges consumere nati*. Now that I am at my confessions, it may be as well to add that I have (alas!) experienced none of that largeness and expansion of mind which one of my friends privately told me I should get from travelling. I cannot boast of any greater gifts of philosophic coolness than before, and on reading the papers of the beginning and middle of February I hate the Whigs (of course, as Rowena says, in a Christian way) more bitterly than ever. We do so wish to know what the Church in general, then Oxford, and then certain of our friends in particular, think of

---

[1] Juvenal, x. 155, 156.

the atrocious Irish sacrilege Bill. What Magister Præpositus, *e.g.*, says about it, and what poor Whately (*entre nous*).

We hope to be here a month or five weeks, and are busily employed every morning in seeing sights ; for as Rome was not built, assuredly it is not to be seen, in a day. I understand the meaning of this proverb now. This is a wonderful place ; you have in it remains sufficient to acquaint you with the *nature* of Roman magnificence and Grecian genius, which is all posterity can hope for ; and in its Christian monuments it affords a third and most abundant subject for contemplation. Neate is here, and very busy in learning all that is to be learned ; he is soon going to Dresden and Vienna to study German, and then he returns to England to keep terms at the Temple. The Andersons are here also, and the W. Wilberforces, so we have quite society enough, not much being wanted, when we have objects in the place itself to attend to. When I set out I expressed a wish that we should see one or two places thoroughly, and a great many hastily, just to say we had seen them, and this wish has hitherto been fully accomplished. The only thing I regret is having been so long at Malta (four weeks), but it could not be helped. . . . The only thing I did then worth mentioning was to get on with conversational Italian, and this I certainly did very considerably. I had learned the grammar and structure of the language some years ago, and could read it pretty well, so I got a master and made him do nothing but talk with me. But since I have left Malta I have gone back, for I have scarcely had any need to talk since (except using a few words), for one meets with English people, at least English talkers, everywhere. My only difficulty is when I attempt to talk French, for I am sure to mix a considerable infusion of my newly acquired Italian with it, and, considering how little I speak French at all, it is obvious how very little the balance is after the deduction. Italian is a very easy language. Were I to be here a few months, and threw myself into native society, I should easily master it, and it is provoking to be near an acquisition without acquiring it, yet qu. the use, did I acquire it ? Maltese itself is entirely or almost entirely Arabic ; the mixture of Italian is for the most part confined to the city. It is curious to trace the consequent connexion between it and Hebrew. I have seen tables of their correspondence, and nearly all the common words in both languages (*i.e.* the necessaries of life, &c.) are the same. The number of such agreements is very great. How remarkable it is that the Eastern nations should have so long remained the same, as in other things so in language.

Our plans for the future are quite unsettled. . . . I shall think of you all very anxiously as I go towards Sicily. You will be in the heat of the examination for Fellows : being at a distance, I may say without breach of decorum, that I am earnestly desirous that Rogers should succeed ; were I on the spot, to say this would be inconsistent with the impartiality of a judge. But I cannot doubt he will succeed, though it will be very annoying to be kept in suspense so long. Yet I am being inured to this—here I am above three months' time from England, and I have not yet heard from anyone there, *i.e.* except a few lines from Rogers and home a week or two after I set out. That wretched Naples keeps all the letters you direct to it ! you might as well direct to its bay as to its *poste restante.*

Naples is a disappointing place ; it has nothing to recommend it but its ices, which are capital, though here Palermo equals it—and, besides, fabricates a kind of cake called Spanish bread, which you get nowhere else ; it is superb and inimitable. You in England can have no idea of it ; it is eating ambrosia. If the maker imported himself to England he might make his fortune in no time. Palermo, by-the-bye, is a far finer city than Naples, and beats it in its own line, and the bay as far excels that of Naples *quantum viburna cupressi*. They are very extortionate at Naples. The wind ever blows, rain is always falling, the streets are most dangerously greasy (in spite of the rain)—you are sure to be run over—boys are ever picking your pocket, and the hills about the place are ugly and flat-topped. Vesuvius is graceful, and some distant heights have something of an outline ; but all this is nothing to Corfu.

By this time you are quite at home at Morton Pinckney. I wish I had any means of hearing how your Baptist chapel or other stumbling-blocks are going on ; there are no Baptist chapels here.

Pray give my best remembrances to the Provost and all the Common-Room.

REV. J. H. NEWMAN TO R. F. WILSON, ESQ.

Rome: March 18, 1833.

I have often thought since I left England that some of our friends must have addressed our steam-vessel with the *Sic te Diva potens*, &c., so exceedingly prosperous was our voyage from beginning to end. I do not mean to say we were exempted from sea-sickness, which indeed is not mentioned in that invocation ; nay, we had one or two tosses in the course of our expedition, but with these necessary exceptions our weather was perfect. . . .

Froude heard from Keble the day before yesterday, and so received news of Arnold's plan of Church Reform, which seems very comprehensive. If I understand it right, all sects (the Church inclusive) are to hold their meetings in the parish churches, though not at the same hour, of course. He excludes Quakers and Roman Catholics, yet even with this exclusion, surely there will be too many sects in some places for one day. This strikes me as a radical defect in his plan. If I might propose an amendment, I should say pass an Act to oblige some persuasions to *change* the Sunday. If you have two Sundays in the week, you could accommodate any probable number of sects, and in this way you would get over Whately's objection against the Evangelical party and others ; make *them* keep Sunday on Saturday. This would not interfere with the Jews (who would of course worship in the parish church), for they are too few to take up a whole day. Luckily the Mahommedan holiday is already on a Friday, so there will be no difficulty in that quarter.

Rome is one of the most delightful residences imaginable. The air is too soft perhaps to suit me for a permanence, otherwise I cannot conceive a more desirable refuge, did evil days drive one from England. But this is impossible of course, because one's duties bind one there, even were we cast out as evil ; and besides, I cannot quite divest myself of the notion that Rome Christian is somehow under a special shade, as Rome Pagan certainly was, though I have seen nothing here to confirm it. Not that one can tolerate for an instant the wretched perversion of the truth which is sanctioned here; but I do not see my way enough to say that there is anything peculiar to the condition of Rome ; and the clergy, though sleepy, are said to be a decorous set of men. They look so, except the canons at service, who laugh and talk. Far otherwise at Naples, which is a wretched place.

TO HIS SISTER JEMIMA.

Rome: March 20, 1833.

At length Froude has heard from Williams, and I have the comfort of knowing by implication that you are all well.[1] I have the satisfaction of stating that my first 100*l*. has barely gone even now. When we first came here we found bright weather, with cold mornings and evenings—that is, sun, and wind, and snow on the mountains; since, we have had rain. Rome is said to be a relaxing place. I think no place (to speak boldly) is good in winter for invalids without their own care. My friends have too great a notion that coming abroad is an *opus operatum*. There is an absence of frost and fog, but nothing is more common than sudden changes of temperature, and these are the chief occasion of catching cold. I wish I could say Froude's cough is gone.

The two special novelties which I find in Rome are the Fountains and the Mosaics. I had no notion of either before I came here—no notion at all of the mosaics, which are an exact imitation of painting, from the Transfiguration to a Lilliput St. Peter's upon a brooch. It is the mosaics which are the chief boast of St. Peter's: first, the huge pictures I have spoken of; next, the altars, which are adorned with the most delicate and softest scrolls and wreaths imaginable. As to the fountains, those which adorn the Piazza of St. Peter's are, I suppose, twenty feet high, and take the form of a graceful white lady, arrayed in the finest, most silvery of dresses. There are a number of others—an abundance of water, in an abundance of fountains. Water is found in almost every other street.

Have I noticed the astonishing abundance of Marbles in Rome? Churches are more numerous than the fountains; and a splendour and costliness of stones which would make

---

[1] It is scarcely necessary to say that letters had been duly and constantly written to the addresses left by Mr. Newman with his Mother. A letter from his sister Harriett, written on a sheet of large foolscap (filled by various hands), opens with the sentence, 'I begin all my letters with my vexation at the delay or loss of our letters, for that is always teasing me!' It almost amounts to sorrow, his Mother writes. His own letters home reached their destination with greater regularity and dispatch.

the city a wonder if it had only one church such. It is Herod's Temple repeated a hundred times over. I have sometimes been quite aghast when, thinking I had got through the churches here or there, I have gone into one I accidentally met with, and found a fresh world of wonders. I might enlarge, too, on the sculptures of the churches. They are splendid; but, if one must criticise, attitudinise too much for correct taste. As to the houses, I have seen little of them; but, fine as they are outside, the rooms are not near so fine as those at Naples, and still less than those at Malta.

We saw the Pope at St. Peter's last Friday.

We are in good spirits about the prospects of the Church. We find Keble is at length roused, and (if once up) he will prove a second St. Ambrose; and others too are moving. So that wicked spoliation Bill is already doing service; no thanks to it. We have encouraging accounts about Prussia from M. Bunsen, who has received us very kindly. There is every reason for expecting that the Prussian Communion will be applying to us for ordination in no long time. We hear, also, much about Germany, in the way of painters! which leads us to hope that a high reverential spirit is stirring among them. And the Wilberforces tell us that the recently ejected ministers of Geneva are applying to England for Episcopal ordination. Further, our friend the Yankee, whom we fell in with again here, gave us so promising an account of the state of things in America, that we mean, when turned out of St. Mary's, to go preaching through the churches of the United States!

As to poor Italy, it is mournful to think about it. Doubtless there are 7,000 in Israel. There are great appearances of piety in the churches, still, as a system, the corrupt religion— and it is very corrupt—must receive severe inflictions; and I fear I must look upon Rome, as a city, still under a curse, which will one day break out in more dreadful judgments than heretofore. Yet, doubtless, the Church will thereby be let loose from thraldom.

As to Greece, it does not teach Purgatory and the Mass— two chief practical delusions of Romanism. Its worst error is its Saint-worship, which is demoralising in the same sense Polytheism was; but this is not the Church's act (though it sanctions it in fact), but the people's corruption of what is good—the honour due to Saints; whereas the doctrines of the Mass and Purgatory are not perversions, but inventions.

I expect the 'Lyra' will commence in May. We have

heard of Arnold's pamphlet, the contents of which seem to be atrocious. I am very well; my Sicilian expedition will, I hope, complete the benefit. I look forward to it with great pleasure, but it will be far more delightful in retrospect than in actual performance. Spring in Sicily! It is the nearest approach to Paradise of which sinful man is capable. I set out on Easter Monday.

To his Mother.

Rome: Good Friday, April 5, 1833.

I have received to-day your letters five and six. Number four is still at Naples. As to Froude, whom Jemima blames, I cannot have fully stated how it was I was left alone at Malta. I had suffered much from being so much with strangers for five or six weeks, and I wished to be left alone, as the only remedy of my indisposition. In answer to Froude's many solicitations, and his offer to sit with me or read to me, I had assured him, all I wanted in order to recruit myself was perfect solitude—in fact, my solitude for ten days or a fortnight *had* surprising success; I was quite set up by it, and started from Malta with elastic spirits. The cough was an episode quite distinct from my other indisposition. In treating this, I *did* require assistance, but he was not in the way then to give it. You know I can be very earnest in entreating to be left alone. If I said anything else in my letter, it was the inconsistency of the moment.

I fear my letter pained you as if I had been very ill. I assure you I never will conceal anything from you. On my voyage to Sicily I shall take a servant with me, since I am alone. If a vessel *is* about to start from Palermo to England at the beginning of May, I may be at home by the 15th or 20th; but this is too good an anticipation to be fulfilled.

I am quite sure I shall be pleased with your proceedings about the change of house.[1] The only disadvantage I can think of is its loneliness; so you see I do not see many objections.

As to the *Roman* Catholic system, I have ever detested it so much that I cannot detest it more by seeing it; but to the Catholic system I am more attached than ever, and quite love the little monks [seminarists] of Rome; they look so innocent

[1] From Rose Hill, Iffley, to Rose Bank, Iffley.

and bright, poor boys! and we have fallen in, more or less, with a number of interesting Irish and English priests. I regret that we could form no intimate acquaintance with them. I fear there are very grave and far-spreading scandals among the Italian priesthood, and there is mummery in abundance; yet there is a deep substratum of true Christianity; and I think they may be as near truth at the least as that Mr. B., whom I like less and less every day.

To his Sister Harriett.

Rome: April 5, 1833

We have seen Tivoli, which is unlike the knowing of it, and Frascati (Tusculum), and the Lake of Albano; and we have seen pictures and statues without end. Canova is out of fashion as being affected. Thorwaldsen aims at simplicity and *is* in fashion. The original Roman stone was peperino; afterwards they used the travertino, *i.e.* tiburino, for it is made of the water about Tivoli, which you smell a mile off; it is of a blue milk colour, and quite hot. These sulphur rivers seem in ages past to have spread over the country and to have petrified whatever they met with. The process goes on now. We were at the Lake Tartarus, branches, reeds, roots, &c., all petrified. This stone was commonly used in Rome. I think the Coliseum is built of it. The most remarkable stone is that of the Temple at Pæstum, which is like a honeycomb; it is still found in the Silarus (Sele), the river which flows near it.

As to pictures, at the Palazzo Falconieri (Cardinal Fesch's) we have seen a picture of Raffaelle's when a boy of fourteen, which is the most grotesque thing I ever saw, curious as his —the passage of the Red Sea; one unfortunate horse has just his four legs visible in the air, all parallel to each other; his body being under water. Raffaelle degenerated, poor man! as life got on. At the Sciarra Palace was Guido's picture of the Cenci, which I admired extremely till I heard her story, which ends with her murdering her father. I wonder at the perversion of men's minds. It is worthily the subject of a tragedy by Shelley—I did not know this. Raffaelle's Violin-player is a beautiful picture, and Titian's Mistress, which is extremely striking. To go to a very different subject, a small picture of Albert Dürer's, the Death of the Virgin, is one of the most impressive, religious, and admirable pictures that I have seen. When you see Froude, which will be soon, ask him to give you some account of the pictures of Francesco Francia, to which he has taken a great fancy. At the Farnese we saw some frescoes of Caracci, and at Grotto Ferrata. On the whole, I am much offended by the picture galleries, and am amazed how men of any religious profession and clergymen can admire them.

What a delightful soothing place this is!

REV. J. H. NEWMAN TO REV. HENRY JENKYNS.

Rome: Easter Day, April 7, 1833.

. . . We are all of us charmed with Rome, where we have been five weeks, and are now going to leave it. This last week we have heard the celebrated Miserere, or rather the two Misereres, for there are two compositions by Allegri and Boii, so like each other that the performers themselves can scarcely tell the difference between them. One is performed on the Thursday, and the other on Good Friday. The voices are certainly very surprising; there is no instrument to support them, but they have the art of continuing their notes so long and equably, that the effect is as if an organ were playing, or rather an organ of violin strings, for the notes are clearer, more subtle and piercing, and more impassioned (so to say) than those of an organ. The music itself is doubtless very fine, as everyone says, but I found myself unable to understand all parts of it. Here and there it was extremely fine, but it is impossible to understand such a composition on once or twice hearing. In its style it is more like Corelli's music than any other I know (though very different too). And this is not wonderful, as Corelli was Master of the Pope's Chapel, and so educated in the school of Allegri, Palestrina, and the rest. These are the only services we have been to during the week.

We have this evening seen St. Peter's illuminated. It is a splendid sight, but so difficult and dangerous in execution that it is surprising they make it so much a matter of course. The men who are employed are let down by ropes outside the Dome. We went up the Dome the other day, which presents the most extraordinary sight of the kind I ever saw. Often as I had been in St. Peter's, I could never realise to myself its dimensions. I measured and measured, and though the problem *solvebatur ambulando*, as old Aldrich says, my imagination was unconvinced. But when you get aloft and look down inside the Dome, then you see what a mountain the building is. No words can do justice to the strange sight which everything below presents when you are only as high as the first gallery above the arches which support the cupola. The Tabernacle of bronze, which itself is 121 feet high, is shrunk and withered up, and seems to barely rise above the pavement. We went into the ball, but did not venture the cross, which is ascended by a ladder outside. We are not Dornfords—pardon us.

REV. JOHN KEBLE TO REV. J. H. NEWMAN.
Oxford: April 11, 1833.

My dear N.,—I am ashamed to scrawl in a paper so full of neat writing,[1] but I know you will be glad to hear that I never knew so smooth an election week. R. and M. [Rogers and Marriott] returned without a dissentient voice, and in the order in which you read their names; not that I think there is any comparison between the two; in strength of mind, indeed, I look on R.'s as one of the very best examinations I remember here, though I apprehend he has fallen very much below himself in apparent scholarship—everybody is here, Rudd and all.

Pray send me one letter if you have time, as I find it gives people consequence to receive such things, and let me know how Hurrell is. You would be very much pleased with the Duke's letter. I think I must send you some of it : 'Till I received your note of the 30th, I had not an idea that any body of H.M.'s subjects had thought proper to approve of the course which I followed upon the occasion referred to. I felt that my duty to the King required that I should make a great sacrifice of opinion to serve him, and to save H.M. and the country from what I considered a great evil. Others were not of the same opinion. I failed in performing the service I intended to perform, and I imagined that I had satisfied nobody but myself, and those of my friends who were aware of my motives and who knew what I was doing, and the course which I intended to follow. It is very gratifying to me to learn that several gentlemen of the University of Oxford observed and approved of my conduct upon the occasion

---

[1] The letter is the joint production of Mrs. Newman, his sisters Harriett and Jemima, Mr. J. F. Christie, Mr. Isaac Williams, Mr. Thomas Mozley, and Mr. Keble; the postage paid at Oxford 2*s.* 5*d.*

referred to ; and that they are desirous of testifying their sense of it in the manner stated in the letter addressed to your lordship. They may rely upon it that I will attend Mr. Chantry or anybody they please with the greatest satisfaction. I will do so not only because I am personally gratified by their approbation, but I am grateful to them as a public man and a faithful subject of the King, for the encouragement which they give to others to devote themselves to the King's service, by their applause of the course which I followed on the occasion referred to.'

Thus far his Grace. I hope you will like it as well as I do. Tell Hurrell I got his letter of the 17th in good time. I am very glad you are working so for Rose ; he pleases me more and more. I fear P. is not playing his part of a true champion in the House of Commons, and I fear the Bishops are disposed to concede about the Church rates. If they do, we must submit to the stifling and corrupting embraces of Whiggery for some time to come. Isaac is rather fagged, but not unwell I think. Here is Christie come for the letter, so God bless you.

Yours ever affectionately,
J. K.

P.S.—We have thrown out one of the Berkeleys from the city of Gloucester, which puts us in spirits.

REV. J. H. NEWMAN TO HIS SISTER JEMIMA.

Naples: April 11, 1833.

As I sat at table yesterday, solitary, just arrived from Rome at the Crocelli, with a variety of dishes before me after the Italian fashion, with a mincemeat of giblets, and a large dish of young green peas, I thought to myself how I should have been startled this time year had a glass been held up to me with the picture of what was to be in a twelvemonth. More novel and luxurious than pleasant. I was left to myself in a foreign land for the first time in my life.[1] How shall I describe the sadness with which I left the tombs of the Apostles ? Rome, not as a city, but as the scene of sacred history, has a part of my heart, and in going away from it I am as if tearing it in twain. I wandered about the place after the Froudes had gone with a blank face. I went to the Church of

---

[1] Archdeacon Froude and his son left Rome for France early in April.

S. Maria in Cosmedin, which Dionysius founded A.D. 260, and where Austin is said to have studied rhetoric. I mounted the height where St. Peter was martyred, and for the last time went through the vast spaces of his wonderful basilica, and looked at his place of burial, and then prepared for my departure. Also I have lost my companions, and I was going among strangers into a wild country to live a wild life, to travel in solitudes, and to sleep in dens of the earth—and all for what? for the gratification of an imagination, for the idea of a warm fancy which might be a deceit, drawn by a strange love of Sicily to gaze upon its cities and mountains. For half an hour I may be said to have repented of my choice of having thrown myself out of the society of others for a country which I had seen, though only in part, instead of going in their company to the South of France, where there was so much both interesting and new: and I was going to travel to Naples with one who was almost a stranger to me; who, civil and kind as he was, yet made it an obligation on me to talk and be agreeable, at a time when my heart was full, and when I would fain have enjoyed the only remedy of grief, the opportunity of grieving. So passed Tuesday, but on Wednesday morning, when I found myself travelling, as the light broke, through a beautiful country, which I had in March passed in the dark, I began to gain spirits. We had passed Terracina (Anxur) with its white rocks by moonlight; at dawn we had before us a circle of beautiful blue hills, inclosing a rich plain, covered with bright green corn, olives, and figs just bursting into leaf, in which Fondi lies. Then came Mola, where Cicero was murdered, and the country I saw was still more beautiful; and so at length we got to Naples in twenty-nine hours from Rome, including two hours stopping, the distance being about 148 miles.

By-the-bye, I was surprised how backward the spring is; the forest trees are not in leaf, scarcely in bud even yet. The weather is lovely. You will ask how I like Naples in a better season; I shall return substantially the same answer. The sea, to be sure, is exquisitely blue, and the mountains about the Bay are of a soft peach colour, tinged with slate, and the towns of Castel-a-mare, Sorrento, &c., are dotted on them in brilliant white specks; but the town is essentially a watering-place, and more like Brighton than any place I know; the same glare, the same keen brightness of the hills, the same disposition of houses opening upon the sea, the same boisterous wind, the same stimulating air, the same sparkling water, the same bustle, or rather tenfold, and the same apparent idleness of the people. Oh, what a change from the majestic pensiveness of the place I have left, where the Church sits in sackcloth calling on those who pass by to say if anyone's sorrow is like her sorrow!

I am interrupted by the thought that the decision of the Oriel election is at this very time taking place. The Provost is in the Common-Room, and the Fellows are sitting round. Would that I knew how it was to be ! . . . I shall not know for some weeks ; but please God I shall be much sooner with you than I could have supposed. Vessels go from Palermo to Marseilles almost daily, and the usual length of voyage is six days, sometimes only forty-eight hours, and sometimes ten days. If I get to Palermo by May 2, I shall be at Marseilles about the 10th, and in London by the 17th.

I have to-day made my preparations for my journey ; a set of cooking utensils and tea-service—curry-powder, spice, pepper, salt, sugar, tea, and ham ; cold cream, a straw hat, and a map of Sicily. I shall want nothing from the island but macaroni, honey, and eggs. I shall be sixteen days travelling. I shall take a servant and three mules—my servant finds his own food and lodgings. My whole expenses will be about 15s. a day—that is, for sixteen days 12l. Adding from Rome to Messina, from Palermo to Marseilles, the expense will be 17l. ; say 20l. more than had I gone with the Froudes.

I ought to tell you about the Miserere at Rome, my going up St. Peter's, and the Easter illumination, our conversations with Dr. Wiseman and with M. Bunsen, our search for the church of St. Thomas of Canterbury, my pilgrimage to the place of St. Paul's martyrdom, the Catacombs, and all the other sights which have stolen away half my heart, but I forbear till we meet. Oh that Rome were not Rome ! but I seem to see as clear as day that a union with her is *impossible*. She is the cruel Church asking of us impossibilities, excommunicating us for disobedience, and now watching and exulting over our approaching overthrow. A scirocco prevents the vessel sailing to-day and perhaps to-morrow (Sunday). It is half-past ten P.M. and I am busy writing a sermon for Mr. Bennett on the chance of its stopping. There is a fear I shall not get a place in it at all—it is so full.

I will give you some account of my going up Vesuvius yesterday. Mr. Bennett, Anderson and myself started about half-past eleven (just as the names of the new Fellows were given out). On arriving at Resina, five miles from Naples, we mounted mules and asses, which brought us up to the foot of the mountain. You go a long way between two walls, the boundaries of vineyards, then over the lava, which is like a ploughed field, in colour and shape, petrified. Properly I believe it is the scoriæ and the ashes which lie on the lava, or the substance into which the surface of the lava is converted —I forget which. On dismounting, you address yourself to the task of ascending the cone, which does not seem much too high to run up, though certainly steep ; however, it is eight hundred feet high. The material is fine ash with a few lumps of lava scattered about it, which fall upon your shins. Well, we set to, and a tug it was. The first ascent was six hundred feet, for they take you up by the lowest way, and when half up I confess I did for half a minute repent of beginning, though there was no sun and very little wind ; for my feet at each step slipped back about three-quarters of it. One's only consolation was that one must get to the top some time or other, and this I took to myself. At length we were landed on the first crater ; and, sitting down on the ashes at the top, which are so dry as not to dirt, we cooked some beef and drank some wine, most delicious wine, though it is the common wine of the place—so common as hardly to be drinkable anywhere else.

Then we began our rambles. First we went over some sulphur beds, which are of a bright greenish yellow in the midst of the black ash : then we commenced our ascent of the second cone, which is inside the first crater, and is above 150 feet high. It is the same loose ash. When we got to the top we found an awful sight ; the vast expanse of the true crater broken into many divisions and recesses, up and down, and resplendent with all manner of the most beautiful various colours from the sulphur, white clouds of which ever steaming and curling from holes in the crust, and almost unbearably strong for one's lungs. The utter silence increased the imposing effect, which became fearful when, on putting the ear to a small crevice, one heard a rushing sound, deep and hollow, partly of wind, partly of the internal trouble of the mountain.

Then we began to descend the crater [I think it was 300 feet deep], which is very steep and at times suffocating from the sulphur puffs. After various turnings and windings across its side, we saw before us the pit from which the chief eruption proceeds at present (for it varies year by year, and the *whole* of this second cone has been thrown up by the comparatively insignificant eruption of the past year), and we began to descend into it. Here I suffered from having foreign shoes on not sufficiently tight to my feet; they filled (as by-the-bye they filled both in ascending and descending the mountain) with the hot ashes, which were intolerable, so that I was obliged to cling by my hands. I can only say that I found both my hands and the soles of my feet blistered all over on my return to Naples, besides my hands being torn in various places. I assure you I quite cried out with the pain. At length I got to the bottom; there it is tolerably cool. A cold wind proceeds from the hole, which is not very large, and is blocked up with lava.

After ascending and then descending the inner cone we commenced our circuit of the outer cone, which is laborious, and is three miles round, the greater part of which we traversed. First, we ascended the remaining 200 feet of the 800, and then kept up and down an irregular ridge till we descended to where we had lunched. The view is very striking. The vast plain of Naples, which is covered with innumerable vines, was so distant as to look like a greenish marsh. We could see Pompeii and its amphitheatre very distinctly; and in the same direction various streams of lava, their age indicated by their shade of blackness, coursing down from the mountain's foot. It was grand to look down a sheer descent of 800 feet, which began at one's foot, the walking place being a narrow ledge almost perpendicular on each side. After getting to the luncheon place we commenced our descent, which is a regular tumble. The 600 feet ought to be done in three minutes, but my shoes obliged me to stop every twenty or thirty steps. It was very strange and amusing. At length we mounted our beasts, and then entered our carriage, getting home to dinner at half-past eight. The whole expedition only cost me a piastre (four shillings). I have given you a very tame account, but I am tired.

This is the most wonderful sight I have seen abroad.

REV. J. H. NEWMAN TO REV. S. RICKARDS.

Naples: April 14, 1833.

I hope you received, in due course, a letter I addressed tardily to you from Falmouth. I had intended, before this, to make up for its tardiness by inflicting upon you a second letter ; but again has my purpose been frustrated. So now you have tardy letter the second. . . . We were five weeks at Rome, and spent a most delightful time—its memory will ever be soothing to me. Jerusalem alone could impart a more exalted comfort and calm than that of being among the tombs and churches of the first Christian saints. Rome is a very difficult place to speak of, from the mixture of good and evil in it. The heathen state was accursed as one of the infidel monsters of Daniel's visions ; and the Christian system there is deplorably corrupt—yet the dust of the Apostles lies there, and the present clergy are their descendants. A notion has struck me, on reading the Revelation again and again, that the Rome there mentioned is Rome considered as a city or *place* without any reference to the question whether it be Christian or Pagan. As a seat of government, it was the first cruel persecutor of the Church ; and as such condemned to suffer God's judgments, which had not yet fully been poured out upon it, from the plain fact *that it still exists*. Babylon is gone. Rome is a city still, and judgments await her therefore. I have no intention of proving this here, but wish to state my view. When I had formed it I was surprised to find several confirmations of it in a book of Roman antiquities I happened to take up. Gregory the Great seems to have held the notion (three centuries after Rome became Christian) that still the spot was accursed. It was on this principle that he encouraged the demolition of the heathen edifices—such as the Coliseum— as monuments of sin ; and I own he seems to me to have a sounder Christian judgment than the moderns, who have affected a classical tenderness for what were the high places of impiety and the scenes of primitive martyrdoms. It seems, too, he especially considered Rome reserved for future superhuman judgments ; for he mentions with approbation the answer of some man, a servant of the Lord, to Alaric, that Rome was not to be destroyed by barbarians, but by earthquakes, tempests, &c. ; and he adds, ' which we have partly seen accomplished in our own times ' ; and certainly, from the very magnitude of the masses which lie in ruins, one should suppose nothing but elemental convulsions could have effected their overthrow. An Irish Bishop of the eleventh century states the same doctrine in a so-called prophecy which remains, of the series of Popes to their termination. With the authenticity of this document I am not concerned, much less with its inspired character (though it is remarkable that the list he gives is now within about nine of the end)—it is sufficient it was produced, A.D. 1600 about, in order to secure the election of a particular Pope. Thus its doctrine evidently has been acknowledged by a considerable party in the Church ; and, as a tradition, has a sort of authority of the opinion of the Church. It is contained in the concluding words, which are such as these—after filling up his list he says : ' Then shall she that sitteth upon the seven hills be destroyed when the Lord comes to judge the earth.' You will observe this document is written by an upholder of the Roman supremacy, who thus makes the *city and state* still accursed though God's Church be there. It may be said that it is impossible to distinguish between the State and the Church, since the Bishop of Rome has been the temporal sovereign. This is true, and accordingly (supposing this view to be correct) the question arises, *when* was he invested with the sovereignty, for that would be the period of apostasy. But, granting this, it does not follow that the Church is the woman of the Revelation any more than a man possessed with a devil is the devil. That the spirit of old Rome has possessed the Christian Church there is certain as a matter of fact ; that that spirit *lives* is most true, quite independent of this theory ; and, if it lives, must it not be led out to slaughter some day ? The revivification of ancient Rome in modern has often been noticed ; but it has been supposed that the Christian Church is that new form of the old evil, whereas it is really a sort of *genius loci*, which enthralls the Church which happens to be there. I am not so clear as I wish to be, but I think the distinction I make is important. Even were the old spirit dead, the city would be under the curse by which children suffer for their fathers' sins ; but the spirit lives to show they are the children of those who killed the Prophets. The Roman sway is still over its ancient territory even when the people disclaim its dominion (as in the territory of the Greek Church), it appoints its agents and representatives (bishops, patriarchs, &c.). Its language is still Latin, which is its bond of union as an empire. Its policy is still crafty, relentless and inflexible, and undeviating through a succession of rulers. It still sacrifices the good of its members to the splendour and strength of the Republic (what can be a greater instance of this than the custom of the forced celibacy of the clergy ?). The religion it upholds is still polytheistic, degrading, idolatrous ; and so strictly is all this connected with Rome as a local source, that its authorities lose their power if they quit

Rome. We were surprised to hear that the reason Bonaparte did not (as he wished) make Paris the seat of the Popedom was that he found the Romish authorities could not act out of Rome. I am a great believer in the existence of *genii locorum*. Rome has had one character for 2,500 years ; of late centuries the Christian Church has been the instrument by which it has acted—it is its slave. The day will come when the captive will be set free ; but how a distinction is to be drawn between two powers, spiritual and devilish, which are so strangely united, is as much beyond our imagination as it was beyond the power of the servants in the parable to pull up the tares from the wheat ; but that it is incomprehensible is no objection to the notion of God's doing it. Indeed, the more I have seen of Rome the more wonderful I have thought that parable, as if it had a directly prophetic character which was fulfilled in the Papacy. To the above may be added, as affording thought to the Christian mind, the remarkable confidence of the Romans in their safety—their *securitas*. They think nothing can harm Rome. When the insurgents two years since were at their gates, they were not at all excited. They said nothing could harm Rome, and went on just as usual—it is a certain insensibility to fear. This is not unlike the temper which may have existed in Babylon, though in individuals very likely there is much piety in it. Indeed, I am very far from thinking there are not many good men among them. I like the look of a great many of their priests—there is such simplicity, gentleness and innocence among the monks : I quite love them ; but I fear their system must cripple their $\tilde{\eta}\theta$ος.

Does it not seem strange that I who have been such a keeper at home should now be wandering among a people whose language I do not understand ? And yet it seems to come natural to one, so soon is the mind habituated to circumstances. Though I should have liked a companion I am not unwilling to rove by myself. Bad times are coming, and no one can tell whether one may not have to travel as Wesley and Whitfield. Harriett says you have been inquiring after my book. It will make its appearance next October as an independent work. I shall re-write nearly a third of it. I think this will be a great improvement, though I rather dread the labour. I am very well, thank God, and though I never (doubtless) shall be in strong health, yet I trust this expedition will set me up. I think I wish nothing else than to spend my strength, whatever it is, in God's service, and I suppose I shall never again in my life have a cessation from work, of this duration, nor can I wish it. Do you know that Keble has begun writing verses in the 'British Magazine'? I hear you are soon to see him. In point of interest I have seen nothing like Ithaca, the Straits of Messina, and Egesta (I put aside Rome), and in point of scenery nothing like Corfu. As to Rome, I cannot help talking of it. You have the tombs of St. Paul and St. Peter and St. Clement; churches founded by St. Peter, and Dionysius (A.D. 260), and others in the Catacombs used in the times of persecution; the house and table of St. Gregory; the place of martyrdom of St. Peter and St. Paul; but the catalogue is endless. O Rome! that thou were not Rome!

REV. J. H. NEWMAN TO HIS MOTHER.

Naples: April 17, 1833.

I write because I wish you to hear the last of me before you see me, and because you will not see me so soon as I said. Here I am at Naples on the 17th when I hoped to be at Syracuse. And I am going in a sailing vessel, and again in a sailing vessel from Palermo to Marseilles, so do not expect me till the very end of May. The steamer with 125 passengers went off yesterday morning, and I and my servant (who has been sixteen years in England in one family and is a trusty man) have got a passage in an English merchantman, the 'Serapis' of Yarmouth, which starts to-night or to-morrow morning.

Now all this seeming disappointment is a very good thing for me. First I avoid a very unpleasant passage in *rough weather* in a crowded vessel, for the sea was high yesterday. Next I escape what I always dreaded, the outpouring of passengers upon Sicily, who would make inn-room difficult, and raise the price of everything. My race against the Countess's people at Palermo is an experience of this evil. Lastly, I spend the bad weather here instead of at Messina, which is a great gain. Nor is my expense increased by waiting. By the sailing vessel I pay less than by the steamer. My only loss is that of time, which I grudge, first because I am impatient to get home, secondly because I had hoped to catch up Froude at Sens or Chartres. The season here is said to be most anomalous. Since Friday, when I went up Vesuvius, it has been very rainy, most of the days continual rain, and that accompanied with a boisterous wind, and a vehemence of pour which I have not seen since leaving Corfu.

Naples, then, has been unfortunate, supposing it was set on pleasing me. Indeed I believe I have been too hard upon it; not that I can ever call the outlines of the bay fine, or Vesuvius anything but graceful, or the grand range on the Salerno side near enough or distant enough for a picture, but the colours are certainly indescribably beautiful—the blues, the indigoes, the browns, and the siennas. And again the people are heathen, certainly. I am much offended at the very irreverent exhibitions of the Crucifix, and of the souls in Purgatory —these struck me more because here we first saw them— which are stuck about as puffs are on the London walls. But I have really found the people very civil and good-natured, though they are knaves, and the popular and exoteric religion as pagan as you can fancy. They are very clever, and humorous. They are quite Punches. Just now a ragged boy persecuted me with a miserable whining for coppers, following me for a minute or so. When he found that would not do, he suddenly began to play a tune on his chin, with great dash and effect. All the boys are full of tricks more harmless than that of filching pocket-handkerchiefs, in which they certainly excel. You see when we were here before we were simple strangers, and these fellows knew a stranger at once; it was bad weather; we had seen finer scenery; in consequence we were reasonably disappointed. So I think we have been hard on this poor place, which I begin to like, if it were only out of remorse for having abused it. I have made the most of my rainy time, having been to Virgil's tomb, up to St. Elmo, and to the library, pictures and museum.

And I find their living much better than before. Perhaps the hotels are better than the restaurants; certainly we were wretchedly off before. It is not so now; their onions are like fine-flavoured apples. They never introduce garlic; oil they are not afraid of, but I do not dislike it. I was tempted to take a bit of tempting cheese the day before yesterday, and had in consequence a nightmare in bed, as follows:

First a weight and horror fell on me, after which I found myself in the tower at Oriel. It was an audit, and the Fellows sat round. Jenkyns and the Provost had been quarrelling [what a shame! I suppose they never did in their lives], and the latter had left the room, and Jenkyns to expedite matters had skipt on in the accounts and entered some items without the Provost's sanction (the extreme vividness of all this was its merit; after waking I could hardly believe it was not true). I shook hands first with one Fellow then with another. At last I got a moment to shake hands with the gallant Dornford, who was on my right, with Denison, who stood next, and then Copleston [these were the new tutors in our place], who said: 'Newman, let me introduce you to our two new Fellows,' pointing to two men who stood on his right hand round the table. I saw two of the most clumsy, awkward-looking chaps I ever set eyes on, and they had awkward unintelligible names. With great grief of heart, but a most unembarrassed smiling manner, I shook hands with them and wished them joy, and then talked and chatted with the rest as if nothing had happened, yet longing to get away, and with a sickness of heart. When I got away at length, I could find no means of relief. I could not find Froude nor [J. F.] Christie. I wished to retire to the shrubberies, which were those of Ham [my Father had a house at Ham, near Richmond, from 1804 to 1807, and when I dreamed of heaven as a boy, it was always Ham]. 'There,' thought I to myself, 'on this seat or that arbour, which I recollect from a boy, I shall recover myself'; but it was not allowed me. I was in my rooms, or some rooms, and had continual interruptions. A father and son, the latter coming into residence, and intending to stand for some Sicilian scholarship. Then came in a brace of gentlemen commoners with hideous faces, though I was not a tutor, and, lastly, my companion with whom I travelled down here from Rome, with a lady under his arm (do what I will I cannot recollect who I thought it was—I saw him with a lady at St. Peter's on Good Friday). This was part of the dream, but only part, and all, I say, so vivid. What shall we say to a bit of cheese awaking the poetical faculty? I hope simply poetical, and not historical. Indeed I have grown calm out of spite, and am now so confident that Rogers has succeeded that I do not think about it.

I have letters of introduction to Messina, Catania, Syracuse, Palermo. I shall try at Messina for one for Girgenti, and then I shall be complete. But how I wish it was over—though I shall enjoy it much at the time—for I wish to get home.

Have I told you of the inconsistencies of these Southerners, of the delicacy and abundance of their table, and chamber linen so white, and the intolerable dirt of their carpets, so dirty that I dare not let my towel reach it? They have a fashion of spitting about, too, to an excess perfectly incredible to an Englishman. They are ever at it. I have seen an elegantly dressed lady on the Pincio spit manfully; nay, rather I heard her, which made me look round to be sure; afterwards I watched and saw her. In the churches this is quite a feature. I have seen a woman at her prayers spit about, and a priest at the most sacred part of the service.

April 18.—Another day, being the seventh of the scirocco. The day is somewhat clearing.

Weather mends, but wind immovable. Slight shock of earthquake last night. We look towards Vesuvius with expectation, but it is thick in mist to the base.

Friday, April 19.—Half-past 7 A.M., the wind is fair. I am off suddenly.

To his Sister Harriett.

Catania: April 25, 1833.

. . . I arrived at this place this morning, and should like to give you an account of my proceedings, but I am lazy from being tired.

I was hastily summoned on the 19th from Naples, just as I had domiciled myself there. Indeed, I was so content with the place that I was sorry to have to move. The pleasantest time I have had abroad has been at Rome, when I was stationary, and my habitual love of repose made me glad that my passage to Sicily was delayed from day to day; but at last, early on the 19th, news came that the wind was fair, and by nine o'clock we were off in the 'Serapis.'

There were three other passengers, Frenchmen, well behaved, very talkative, and, I thought, humorous; but I follow French far worse than Italian. Their conversation with the Captain, a thorough Englishman, was amusing, each party speaking his own language. 'Capitaine, quante miglie o'clock?' This, I believe, meant 'How many knots are we going an hour?' The Captain was a match for them. 'The other bâtiment' (speaking of a brig which had started with us) 'be aft this morning, gentlemen!' This sort of social intercourse sometimes went on for minutes. We did not arrive at Messina till 5 A.M. on Sunday. We were becalmed all Saturday near Stromboli; there had been a brisk breeze the day before, which made me very sick. On getting to Messina I attempted to achieve a service that day, but failed altogether. The Straits looked more beautiful even than before. I never saw anything equal to the colour of the sea and of the Calabrian coast. The steamboat went off for Catania between eleven and twelve. It was impossible to get passports till next day—Monday—and I did not start on my expedition till twelve o'clock; a loss of seven hours, which was a great inconvenience—but I am, in fact, tired; so I stop. [This was almost the beginning of my fever.]

On setting off from Messina I felt amused and almost ashamed of the figure I was cutting. I was chief of a cavalcade consisting of a servant, two mules, and several muleteers (though the latter were soon reduced to one, who was to go with us through), and when I happened to catch a sight of my shadow, the thought of my personal equipments, at least as regards my hat and my coat, was still more perplexing. My neckcloth was the only black thing about me, yet black without being clerical. Nor had I any such exuberance of spirits as would bear me up against the ridiculousness of my exterior. I was setting out on an expedition which would be pleasant in memory rather than in performance. I have been much annoyed at the delay of the passport, which threw me out of my projected itinerary. Inns are not to be found every mile here as in England; and, though I had been told I should certainly find accommodation at the twentieth mile from Messina, yet my muleteer, when questioned, contradicted himself. Nor was I satisfied with him; the baggage kept coming off, and we had frequent stoppages; and the weather, too, threatened, and I felt being alone—not because of the solitude, but because a tour is the best time for turning acquaintances into friends, and I was losing a great opportunity. Nor was there much in external objects to divert me from these depressing thoughts. The coast is beautiful, but is better seen from the sea than from a road. The lower hills were covered with vines and mulberries; those above them with corn and olives. We passed various fiumaras—dry, of course; one of them was about 250 paces, had two rapid brooks still alive in it. There were flags growing on the edge of the sea. At Ali the hills receded; and you saw Etna, looking very near and white. At length we ended the twenty miles. I never got through a walk so easily, and found an inn at San Paolo, and got a room and bed much better than I had expected, though there was no glass in the windows and plenty of fleas. So ends Canto the first.

Canto the second. Tuesday was a great success We set off between five and six, and had twelve miles to go to breakfast at Taormini. As we approached, the country got more and more striking.

Syracuse: April 27.

The two last miles we diverged from the road up a steep path, and soon came to the ancient stone ascent leading to Taurominium. I never saw anything more enchanting than this spot. It realised all one had read of in books about scenery—a deep valley, brawling streams, beautiful trees, the sea (heard) in the distance. But when, after breakfast, on a bright day, we mounted to the theatre, and saw the famous view, what shall I say ? I never knew that Nature could be so beautiful ; and to see that view was the nearest approach to seeing Eden. O happy I ! It was worth coming all the way, to endure sadness, loneliness, weariness, to see it. <u>I felt, for the first time in my life, that I should be a better and more religious man if I lived there.</u> This superb view, the most wonderful I can ever see, is but one of at least half a dozen, all beautiful, close at hand. One view is at the back of the theatre, with a view of Calabria and the Messina side of Sicily. Another is going out of Taormini on the descent. The landlady of the fondaco asked me if I was going to Paris, and begged me to take a letter to her daughter, which I have done.

And so I went off to Giarre. There first I went through the river-beds. The hills receded—Etna was magnificent. The scene was sombre with clouds, when suddenly, as the sun descended upon the cone, its rays shot out between the clouds and the snow, turning the clouds into royal curtains, while on one side there was a sort of Jacob's ladder. I understood why the poets made the abode of the gods on Mount Olympus.

And now I have told you nearly everything pleasant up to this date—the 27th (except that the frogs between Giardini and Giarre, which are louder even than those at Albano, are the most musical animals I have hitherto met with—they have a trill like a nightingale). I am hitherto disappointed in birds and flowers. I never thought this expedition was to be one of pleasure only, for I wished to see what it was to be a solitary and wanderer. On Monday night I had little sleep, and on Tuesday none, from the fleas. I counted quarter after quarter all through the night at Giarre, and there were noises in the next room which annoyed me. The fleas were innumerable, and they bite with a sting. In England we have no idea what a Sicilian flea is. On Wednesday I resolved to see the famous chestnut-trees, and so to go to Nicolosi under Etna. I went to see them as evidence of the wonderful fertility of the soil. From Nicolosi the ascent of Etna is made. The whole distance is not more than twenty-two miles, though very fatiguing. The distance from Giarre to the chestnuts is about six—a precipitous ascent over and along the beds of torrents. I was disappointed in them [they are nothing but roots, cut level with the ground]. We breakfasted in a house where was a sick man, who was attended by a village doctor. We were told it was three hours' march from thence to Nicolosi; it proved to be five; it is along fields of lava, very curious, certainly, but very hot with the sun on them—and curious conical hills, of the finest, richest light-brown earth, which seem dimpled by every breath of air, and lying in heaps as if turned out of a cart and left there.

At length we came to Nicolosi, where I had come in order to determine the possibility of going up Etna, as you never get right intelligence at a distance. I found every discouragement. The snow lay as it had lain two months before, and I was told I should have to walk for nine hours up and down, taking in the cone, half that time in the night, and all in the cold; and the leaves were not out, and there was nothing to see. And, on looking over the book of names of those who had ascended, everything was discouraging. One said, 'I have endured extreme fatigue, and advise no one to follow my example.' Another, 'Better be wise late than never. If you have been a fool in coming, do not be twice a fool in going up.' However, I think I should have attempted it, except that I had strained my leg in walking (but do not give this as the reason; the *season* is the straightforward reason), and my servant was tired.

The discomfort of the so-called inn was excessive; it was the most forlorn place I ever was in. It was a ground floor; one window and no glass; three doors with planks gaping to the external air; brick floor in pieces, and filthy walls. Mrs. Starke took me in by talking of 'reposing' before going up Etna. In addition, my spirits of wine failed, and I could not dress my dinner. I had lived on almost nothing for two days, and my servant had gone out to take care of himself. I lay down on my so-called bed, and thought of the sick-room at Ealing, and my mind felt very dry, and I thought, 'What if I should lose my reason?' and I was in dreadful irritation from the renewed attacks of the fleas. And I was altogether out of sorts. And the bed was on a board, and the bed things looked dirty, and I fancied it would all come to pieces in the night. But my servant came in and poached me some eggs, and threw down water under my bed against my enemies, and I lay down to sleep by eight or nine o'clock, and slept very soundly for eight hours, and got up on Thursday quite strong, with the happy prospect of walking in to breakfast to the comfortable town of Catania ; and the morning was fine, and the road (twelve miles) a pleasant descent the whole way ; and I lodged myself very happily there, and, though weak, I was recruited.

And now here I am at Syracuse, miserable again ; and I seem to think I shall never get home—that is, though quite well, I cannot realise it. I still think of the 121st Psalm.

To his Sister Jemima.

Syracuse: April 27, 1833.

My last letter (to Harriett), which I have just finished, left me safely disposed of at the Corona d'Oro at Catania ; there I subjected myself to a thorough wash and amused myself with looking over the travellers' names in the host's book, and their praises of himself. My knee and the blisters on my feet, and my considerable languor, hindered me moving about much ; but I called on Froude's friend, Signor C. Gemellaro, and he is to show me the medals of Sicily and Magna Græcia on my return to Catania from this place on the morrow (*i.e.* yesterday), Friday, by speronaro.

A speronaro is a large boat used in these seas running, *e.g.* from Malta to Sicily, from Sicily to Naples, &c. This was about thirty-five feet long, and in all had fourteen persons aboard. At the stern some hoops held up an awning some four feet high, the rest of the boat was open. Since our passports were made out for Syracuse ; we were not allowed to land at any other place. We could, indeed, have got to Syracuse that night, but not till after sunset, and then we should not have got pratique till next morning. We had no provisions with us, though luckily some wine, hearing the wine of Syracuse was inferior ; but the boatmen gave us a bit of bread apiece. Luckily I had taken my cloaks with me.

At six o'clock we pulled to the shore about six miles off Syracuse—a lonely spot ; and when for five minutes I got out upon the rocks, and saw the beautiful clearness of the water and felt the mildness of the evening, I quite congratulated myself on having an adventure with so little trouble. So we laid down, I wrapped up, and sleeping soundly a long while, very uncomfortable as everything was, including my companions —my next-door neighbour being the first vulgar Italian I have met with—and miserable as was my torment from fleas. At midnight we hoisted sail, and with some little wind slowly coasted on to Syracuse, where we arrived between three and four, but could not obtain pratique till between seven and eight this morning.

Archdeacon Froude had given me a letter to the Consul here—Syracuse—and he has been of essential service to me in all matters ; in seeing sights, getting passports, &c.; all which is a most tedious business here. The weather, however, has been against me. The scirocco has at length come down in profuse rain, and I can only be thankful that to-day was not yesterday, when I was in the speronaro ; indeed, there is no day on which I could have so well borne it since I set out. As it is, it has only had the effect of lowering my spirits and of making my visit here uncomfortable. I have seen the fountain of Arethusa, and rowed up the Anapus to gather the papyrus and to see the remains of the Temple of Minerva, which are indeed magnificent, and looked at the remaining columns of Jupiter Olympius. I have been conning over Thucydides, particularly yesterday, and this morning in the boat, and am at home with the whole place ; only I have not seen the theatre and amphitheatre, which, being Roman, I care little for. Glad to go back to Catania early to-morrow morning. My intention was to have remained here all Sunday, and, independent of my rule not to travel needlessly then, the inn is comfortable enough, and the place so interesting as to make one wish it ; but the wind is out of my power, and, since it may change on Monday, and is now fair for Catania, I ought not to run the risk of being detained here an indefinite time, or of another night adventure. I will here set down some verses which I composed last night in the boat. You will see that they want ease and spirit. Anxiety is the great enemy of poetry. In the 'Hermes' I had no foreboding care.

Well, it will be all over when you get this, and the time is not long. I do not mind saying all this to you, when you will read it as a dream of the night, if God so will. I often think of Cowper's two lines, 'Beware of desperate steps,' &c.

But for the verses, here they are :

> Say, hast thou tracked a traveller's round,
> Nor visions met thee there,
> Thou could'st but marvel to have found
> This blighted world so fair?
>
> And feel an awe within thee rise,
> That sinful man should see
> Glories far worthier Seraphs' eyes
> Than to be shared by thee?
>
> Store them in heart! thou shalt not faint
> 'Mid coming pains and fears;
> As the third heaven once nerved a Saint
> For fourteen trial-years.[1]

My servant taken from Naples is a very active, useful man, but he knows of course nothing of the ways and means of this country, and I am really roughing it. Yet I am not unwilling to do so; for I shall gain a lesson, so God does but sustain me. In retrospect all bodily pain vanishes, and mental impressions (which have been chiefly pleasant) endure. Taurominium will outlive Giarre, as Egesta Calatafimi. It follows, however, that I heartily wish it over; but this I have wished ever since I left England, as you know. I have great comfort in knowing I have your prayers, and of others at home; in this thought I seem to have a pledge of safe-conduct. I begin to dread the voyage from Palermo to Marseilles in a foolish way. The day makes me sad and stupid. The great harbour is now before my eyes, the Olympicium, the Anapus, Epipolæ, all drenched in wet; and here the Consul has just come to tell me that the passport people are laying their heads together to keep me here another day or extort money. So you see I am in strife and contention.

Catania: April 30.

Things improve with me this evening, but really I have gone through more fatigue and vexation since I last wrote than ever I did in my life.

I resume where I left off [April 27]. There were three

[1] *Lyra Apostolica*: 'Taurominium.'

Englishmen at the hotel at Syracuse, who had come from Malta on their way overland from India. They introduced themselves, and asked me join their dinner party, which I did, and went there in the evening to a great assembly for the celebration of the marriage of the son of a judge with a Russian Consul's daughter. The boudoir in which the ceremony was performed (we came too late for it) was splendidly fitted up. I went in traveller's dress, thinking, goose as I was, to be incognito, and merely a sightseer. You may fancy we were all lions. Though by no means a brilliant party, it was such a contrast to ancient Syracuse, that I thought of the Corfu ball. Somehow altogether Syracuse is more like Corfu and the Ionian towns than anything I have seen since: narrow streets, low houses, misery visible; and next morning when I went to catch a glimpse of the amphitheatre before starting, its being a garrisoned town reminded me still more forcibly of Corfu.

When we descended into the plain we had two rivers to ferry over, and the road was bad. To increase our perplexity we were told that the neighbourhood of the second river was infested with robbers; and to put the finishing stroke to our trouble, when we got near it (at half-past eight), with a moon, but a hazy one, we lost our way, our guide being quite at fault. However, by the good hand of God, we found it again, and got here safe by half-past ten (I use a strong expression), more dead than alive, from the jolting of the mule, which at one time I urged to between five and six miles an hour. I took some soup and went to bed, and had a remarkably good night. However, in the course of this day [April 30] some feverishness had come on; but now, thank God, it is gone away, and Signor Gemellaro tells me I shall have no roads like those I have traversed. So my spirits have risen, and I purpose to start for Girgenti, to reach it by Saturday.

If I may speak of what has happened as over, for I am not yet sure that I am what I ought to be, I would say I do not see how I have been injudicious, only unfortunate.

The only question is: whether I was right in going on a Sunday, and whether this wrong step has not brought all this upon me?

My servant is a treasure—very sharp-witted and ready— an old campaigner, having served through the Peninsula, a sailor in his earlier days, domesticated in England, yet a perfect Neapolitan in language. He cannot read or write. The place I slept at my first night was the ancient Thapsus.

Epipolæ is neither beautiful nor romantic, but striking as resembling huge human works, walls, &c. From Agosta we first passed over wild heath, then cornland, then wood, then we descended to the sand; and then the darkness came on. I cannot tell what. [We lost our way by getting between the river and the sea, and so crossing the former without knowing it, since it has no mouth, but is swallowed up by the sand. We got among shepherds' tents under Mount Etna, the dogs barking at us.] I like what I see of the people; dirt, with simplicity and contentment. This I found both at the creek and at Agosta. The English seem much thought of. We had a slight earthquake this morning—the day close and hazy, as at Naples on a similar event.

The tone of the last two letters to his sisters shows that Mr. Newman was already under the influence of the fever that prostrated him for many weeks in Sicily. The following letter of a much later date was valued by his correspondent as 'a particularly interesting' one, in which he gives the account of his Sicilian sickness.

To F. ROGERS, ESQ.

Palermo: June 5, 1833.

With what joy did I see in 'Galignani' yesterday that you were one of us. It was quite a chance I saw it. I had some days before looked over the papers of the last six weeks, having seen none during that time; and yesterday the person who lent them me said: 'There may be one or two yet which you have not taken—hunt over the heap again.' I took home four to read, and, as I was poring over some article on politics (I believe), the wind blew over the page, and I was arrested by the title of 'University Intelligence.' The first words were 'F. Rogers,' &c.

And now I suppose you are wondering what I do now at Palermo; and perhaps my friends at Oxford have been wondering, unless they have sat down in the comfortable conclusion that I am imprisoned here for want of a vessel. I only hope the Rose Hill people are not uneasy. I have *not* been weather-bound or shipless, taken by the Barbary pirates, or seized as a propagandist of Liberalism. No; but, you will be sorry to hear, confined with a very dangerous fever in the very centre of Sicily for three weeks. I will give you an account of it, if my hand and my head let me. Only do not mention it till you hear I am at home, which I trust will be in about a fortnight or three weeks. I sail, please God, in a Marseilles vessel on Saturday next, the 8th, whence I shall despatch this to you.

This season has been remarkable for rain in this part of the world, as Froude, if he is returned, has perhaps told you. At Catania, Dr. Gemellaro told me that there sometimes fell only seven inches of rain in the wet months, but that this year there had fallen thirty-four. In consequence, a bad fever, of the nature of the scarlet, was epidemic; which I did not know, nor should have thought of perhaps, if I had. The immediate cause of my illness seems to have been my expedition from Catania to Syracuse; but doubtless I was predisposed to take injury from any bad state of the atmosphere, by the sleepless nights and famished days (though few) which I had had immediately before. Sicilian couches abound in the most inveterate enemies of slumber, and my provisions—for you get none at the inns—though they ought not, were affected by the weather, or were in themselves bad. (I bought them at Naples.) And about Etna the transitions from heat to cold are very rapid and severe—in the same day I was almost cut in two, and exhausted with the scorching and dust of lava, though I believe I never got chilled. And in many places they have no glass in the windows, and the shutters do not fit tight, which is bad of a night. Now you will say, how was it *I* alone suffered all this of all Sicilian travellers? Why, to tell the truth, *the* way to avoid it would have been to have taken a Sicilian regular lionizer and purveyor, who would have avoided all difficulties; but this for *one* person is very expensive, and it falls light on several. I had a Neapolitan servant, a good cook (I had bought my provisions before I took him, and they *seemed* good), but knowing nothing of Sicily. I knew a great deal of Sicily from others—everyone was giving me advice to do things *they had not tried themselves*. It was from one of these plans I suffered. Now all this, that I have put down in the last half-page, sounds so *gauche*, that I beg you would keep it to yourself; for it is a gratuitous exposure on my part, and only takes up room in my letter, as you will see from what follows.

Everyone recommended me to go from Catania to Syracuse in a speronaro (by water). The distance by land and sea is forty miles—by land the road is indescribably bad, especially after rain—and the distance too long for mules in one day, and there is no inn on the road. The time by sea was unanimously declared by different persons to be seven hours—the boatman said five. Dr. Gemellaro so fully acquiesced in these statements as to allow of my making an engagement with him for the middle of the day on which I was to set out from Syracuse on my return. I set out for Syracuse by 7 or 8 A.M. Well, when we were about half-way, a scirocco sprang up, and by degrees it became evident we could not reach Syracuse that night. We made for *Thapsus*, and slept in the boat off the peninsula. On my return, which I made by sea from the probability of the scirocco continuing, and the probable state of the road, the same ill luck attended me. The wind changed, and I slept in the boat. Next morning we made for Agosta (all we could do), the ancient Hybla. (Megara Hyblæa—whence the honey.)—We arrived by 8 A.M. at Agosta. Delays of obtaining pratique, passport, &c. &c., kept us till 3 P.M., when we set forward on mules for Catania with the belief that the distance was twenty-two miles. By the time it grew dusk we had gone fourteen miles, and descended to the water's side; when to our dismay we learned we had eighteen miles before us, three rivers to ford or ferry, a deep sand to traverse for half the way, and the danger of being plundered. To complete the whole, when we got to the most suspicious part of our journey our guide lost his way. However, he found it again, and alarms are nothing when they are over, but half an hour was a substantial loss. We got to Catania between eleven and twelve at night. The sun had been broiling during the day—the night was damp. I must add, that the first day I was in the speronaro I had had no food for twenty-four hours—having of course taken no provision with me—that at Syracuse I had eaten very little, and only a breakfast on the day of this fatiguing journey; and, out of the three nights, I had slept only one, and that but a little. I am ashamed of the minuteness with which I am telling all this—but my head is not yet entirely my own.

From my return to Catania I sickened. When the idea of illness first came upon me I do not know, but I was obliged on May 1 to lie down for some time when I had got half through my day's journey; and the next morning I could not proceed. This was at Leonforte, above one hundred miles from Palermo. Three days I remained at the inn there with the fever increasing, and no medical aid. On the night of the third day I had a strange (but providential) notion that I was quite well. So on the next morning I ordered the mules, and set off towards Girgenti, my destination. I had not gone far when a distressing choking feeling (constriction?) of the throat and chest came on ; and at the end of seven miles I lay down exhausted in a cabin near the road. Here, as I lay on the ground, after a time, I felt a hand at my pulse ; it was a medical man who by chance was at hand, and he prescribed for me, and enabled me by the evening to get to Castro Giovanni (the ancient Enna). At first I had difficulty in getting a lodging – had it been known I had the fever I suppose it would have been impossible, for numbers were dying of it there, at Girgenti, and, I believe, everywhere. However, at last I got most comfortably housed. I did not then know what was the matter with me, I believe, but at Leonforte I had thought myself so bad that I gave my servant directions how to convey news of my death (should it be so) to England, at the same time expressing to him a clear and confident conviction that I should *not* die. The reason I gave was that 'I thought God had work for me.' I do not think there was anything wrong in this, on consideration.

At Castro Giovanni I was immediately bled—an essential service—but with this exception it seems as if nature recovered herself; but not till the eleventh day, during which time the fever was increasing, and my attendants thought I could not get over it. Since, I have gained strength in the most wonderful manner. My strength was so prostrated, I could not raise myself in bed or feed myself. The eighth after the crisis I began to walk about (with help). On the twelfth I began a journey of three days to Palermo, going one day sixty-two miles ; and here, where I have been these ten days, I have surprised everyone by my improvement (though I cannot run yet ; the weather is very relaxing). When I came here I could not read nor write, nor talk nor think. I had no memory, and very little of the reasoning faculty. My head had been quite clear (at least at intervals) during the early part of my illness, and I had all through the fever corresponded with the doctor in (really very good) Latin ; but a letter from home was brought me, containing letters from five persons, and I pored through it to find news of your election, you unworthy fellow, which it did not contain. This threw the blood into my head, which I have not yet quite recovered.

And now you will say my expedition to Sicily has been a failure. By no means. Do I repent of coming ? Why, certainly I should not have come had I known that it was at the danger of my life. I had two objects in coming—to see the antiquities and to see the country. In the former I have failed. I have lost Girgenti and Selinunti, and I have lost the series of perfumed gardens through which the mule track near Selinunti is carried. But I have seen Taormini, and the country from Advernò to Palermo, and can only say that I did not know before nature could be so beautiful. It *is* a country. It passes belief. It is like the Garden of Eden, and though it ran in the *line* of my anticipations (as I say), it far exceeded them.

I continually say *En unquam*,[1] being *very* homesick.

June 17.—At last our vessel is nearing Marseilles. I hope to send you a newspaper from London or Oxford to announce my arrival.

The day before this letter was finished, 'Lead, kindly Light' was written, and, however familiar to many, perhaps most, readers, it should have its place here.

> Lead, kindly Light, amid the encircling gloom,
>   Lead Thou me on!
> The night is dark, and I am far from home—
>   Lead Thou me on!
> Keep Thou my feet; I do not ask to see
> The distant scene,—one step enough for me.
>
> I was not ever thus, nor prayed that Thou
>   Shouldst lead me on.
> I loved to choose and see my path; but now
>   Lead Thou me on!
> I loved the garish day, and, spite of fears,
> Pride ruled my will: remember not past years.
>
> So long Thy power hath blest me, sure it still
>   Will lead me on
> O'er moor and fen, o'er crag and torrent, till
>   The night is gone;
> And with the morn those angel faces smile
> Which I have loved long since, and lost awhile.

June 16, 1833: *in the Straits of Bonifacio.*[2]

---

[1] Virg. *Ecl.* i. 68.

[2] 'I was aching to get home; yet for want of a vessel I was kept at Palermo for three weeks. ... At last I got off in an orange boat, bound for Marseilles. Then it was that I wrote the lines, "Lead, kindly light," which have since become well known. We were becalmed a whole week in the Straits of Bonifacio.'—*Apologia*, p. 35.

TO HIS MOTHER.

Palermo: June 9, 1833.

Here I am waiting day after day and week after week for a vessel, and very anxious lest you should be uneasy about me. Had I written to you *via* Naples when I first came here, though the letter would have been three weeks in getting to you, you would have heard in good time. I write now, though late, but I heartily hope I shall be at home before you read this. The captain of a Sicilian vessel promises to sail for Marseilles to-morrow.

Then, again, I am told that calms are common at this time of year—twelve or twenty days—but I run the chance. The average time is six days.

I have two letters written for H. and J., one of which I have destined for the post at Marseilles; the second is unintelligible without the first. [One went from Marseilles, the other from Lyons.] My further adventures when we meet, please God, by word of mouth – a more pleasant way. Excuse my scrawl; this place is very hot. I have enjoyed myself here very much, have been a good deal on the water. The breezes are most refreshing; there is a delightful public garden and terraces, and I know one or two of the merchants, who are very kind. From Catania to Palermo I passed through a country which baffles description. I never saw such a country before; it was a new thing.

I was very idle in verse-making till June, when I made a start, and have done one every day since June began, having done only three in April and May.

In much longing, for I am home-sick.

J. H. N.

P.S.—I have received the quinquipartite letter—you, H., J., Williams, and Christie.

On the address of this quinquipartite letter, which lies before the Editor, is written: 'This is the letter that came up to me at Castro Giovanni, and which I tried to read after the crisis of my fever, with the hope of learning about Rogers's election, till I threw the blood violently into my head, and it all seemed like a dream.—J. H. N.'

To his Mother.

Lyons: July 1.

I trust when you receive this I shall not be far from you. Really it seems as if some unseen power, good or bad, was resisting my return. The thought of home has brought tears in my eyes for the last two months. God is giving me a severe lesson of patience, and I trust I am not altogether wasting the opportunity of discipline. It is His will. I strive to think that, wherever I am, God is God and I am I. It is only forty-eight hours' journey from Marseilles here (200 miles), yet on arriving here last night I found my ankles so swollen and inflamed, that I have judged it prudent to remain here a day, though in a miserable dirty inn, yet the best in Lyons. I have the prospect of confinement in my bedroom all day, with the doubt whether I shall be able to proceed to-morrow, for at present it is with difficulty and pain that I hobble across the room. Rest is the great remedy, I suppose. So it is a simple trial of my patience. I am quite desolate. I am tempted to say, 'Lord, heal me, for my bones are vexed.' But really I am wonderfully calm, and I trust from right principles. Thwarting awaits me at every step. I have had much of this ever since I left Naples. I earnestly hope that to-morrow will end your doubts and anxieties about me by the receipt of my letter from Palermo on June 9.

I have said nothing about France, which is truly *la belle France* in all externals. I am enchanted with it.

[No letter was received in England from me between May 7 and July 1—eight weeks. In the letter dated April 15 and received in England on May 7, I said I was waiting at Naples for a wind to take me in a sailing vessel to Messina.—J. H. N.]

Mr. Newman arrived at his Mother's house at Iffley on July 9, 1833. On July 11 he wrote to Mr. Keble.

Rev. J. H. Newman to Rev. J. Keble.

Oriel: July 11, 1833.

I have come in a week from Lyons; I was up six nights out of the seven.

REV. ISAAC WILLIAMS TO REV. J. H. NEWMAN.

My dear Vicar,—Χαῖρε, πολὺ χαῖρε, and again πολὺ χαῖρε. How delightful it is to think of your being amongst us again, particularly after your being so long unheard of !

REV. H. W. WILBERFORCE TO REV. J. H. NEWMAN.

Bath: July 13, 1833.

I heard this morning, I need not say with how much thankfulness, that you have passed through London towards Oxford. Nor need I tell you how much I felt on hearing indirectly that you had been so dangerously ill in the heart of a nearly barbarous country, nor even the anxiety one could not but feel at your long absence. . . . I have thought much of Mrs. Newman and of your sisters, and of the suffering they must have undergone. . . . I shall think of you to-morrow, when, I suppose, you will be at St. Mary's. If you have judged me worthy, it will greatly delight me to hear something of what passed in your mind during all you have gone through. It is not curiosity—considering it the case of one so dear to me, and I think you will not fear from me that vulgar publication of feelings uttered in the confidence of friendship, which is one disgrace of our age.

It is not unlikely that this letter may have lived in Mr. Newman's mind, and put him upon writing at a later date what he could recall of his illness in Sicily. The following is a paper of recollections, dreamy and uncertain, of the incidents of his fever, written, as the reader must observe, at considerable intervals of time. There are breaks in the narrative, which may be understood as indicating passages too private for print or scrutiny of strange eyes.

A friend whose judgment may be relied upon, on being consulted by the Editor, has written on this remarkable paper, 'There is a great deal about his illness, and a good deal that goes into minutiæ and special feelings in illness. But he so plainly always looked on the fever in all its features as a *crisis in his life*, partly judgment on past self-will, partly a sign of special electing and directing favour, that the prominence given to it is quite accounted for by those who knew him, and explains why all these strange pictures of fever are given.'

My Illness in Sicily.

[*August* 31, 1834.]—I have wished for some time to write in this book an account of my illness in Sicily [in May 1833], for the remembrance is pleasant and profitable. I shall not be able to recollect everything in order, so my account may be confused, running to and fro. . . .

Again, I felt it was a punishment for my wilfulness in going to Sicily by myself. What is here to be noticed is its remarkable bearing on my history, so to call it. I had been released from College business and written a book which I felt on the whole was worth publishing Suddenly, I am led to go abroad ; the work being still in MS. When out, I could not but feel that something of service was in store for me. I recollect writing to [John F.] Christie to this effect, that, nevertheless, if God willed me a private life, the happier for me ; and I think I do feel this, O my God ! so that, if Thou wilt give me retirement, Thou wilt give me what I shall rejoice and prefer to receive, except that I should be vexed to see *no one* else doing what I could in a measure do myself. Well, in an unlooked-for way I come to Sicily. From that time everything went wrong : I could almost fancy it was on that day that I caught my fever. Certainly I was weak and low from that time forward, and had so many little troubles to bear that I kept asking almost impatiently why God so fought against me. Towards the end of the next day I was quite knocked up, and laid down at Nicolosi on the bed with the feeling that my reason perchance might fail me. Then followed my voyage from Catania to Syracuse and back, and then to Adernò, where the insects for the first time ceased to plague me. I had noticed feverish symptoms in me the foregoing day [*i.e.* I could not eat at Catania on April 30], and that night being almost choked with a feeling which at the time I attributed to having taken some ginger with my supper. However, I have got into the narrative here, without meaning it. What I wanted first to speak of was the providence and strange meaning of it. The fever was most dangerous ; for a week my attendants gave me up, and people were dying of it on all sides ; yet all through I had a confident feeling *I should recover*. I told my servant so, and gave as a reason (even when semi-delirious, and engaged in giving him my friends' direction at home, and so preparing externally for death) that ' I thought God had some work for me.' These, I believe, were exactly my words, and when, after the fever, I was on the road to Palermo, so weak I could not walk by myself, I sat on the bed on the morning of May 26 or May 27 profusely weeping, and only able to say that I could not help thinking God had something for me to do at home. This I repeated to my servant, to whom the words were unintelligible of course. Now it certainly is remarkable that a new and larger sphere of action had opened upon me from the very moment I returned. My book ['Arians'] indeed was not published for some months; but long before that I was busy. Immediately on my return I heard that Keble was going to preach an assize sermon on the times, and it was preached on the very first Sunday after my return; then it was printed. Close upon this—I suppose, within a fortnight of my return—I suggested to Palmer, Keble, and Froude an association for tracts. In August I wrote and printed four; then followed the address to the Archbishop, which with the tracts quite occupied me during Michaelmas Term, in the course of which (Nov. 5) my work was published. Then followed my sermons, published in February or March of this present year. Then, in Easter Term, the resistance of the Dissenters' University Admission Bill, in which I was much concerned.

Now for the particulars of my illness. On Thursday, May 2, I started from Adernò—the scene was most beautiful—hills thrown about on all sides, and covered with green corn, in all variety of shades, relieved by the light (raw sienna) stone of the hills. The whole day the scene was like the garden of Eden, most exquisitely beautiful, though varying, sometimes with deep valleys on the side and many trees, high hills with towns on the top as at S. Filippo d'Argirò, Etna behind us, and Castro Juan before in the distance. On the whole, I suppose I went forty-two miles that day on my mule, but with great pain. I set out walking, the mules coming after, and fell to tears thinking of dear Mary as I looked at the beautiful prospect. When I got to Regalbuto I was obliged to lie down for an hour or so. I cannot tell whether I thought myself ill or not. With much distress I proceeded, taking some wine at S. Filippo, and, I believe, elsewhere [I recollect with difficulty dismounting, and crawling with my servant's help to a wine-shop, and sitting on a stone], till in the evening I got to Leonforte.

Here [at Leonforte] I lay, I believe, without sleep, and next morning, when I attempted to get up, I fell back and was too ill to do so. (This is the best of my recollection.)

[*December* 28, 1834.]—I believe I must have been somewhat [not light-headed but] scarcely myself the day before on my journey, else surely my indisposition would have been forced upon my mind by my frequent stoppings and restings. I fancy I had but one wish—*to get on*; that my troubles at Syracuse had quite taken away my present enjoyment of what I saw, and that I looked at everything but as the matter for future retrospective pleasure, which indeed was my original view in coming here. Well, after some time, a great personage having gone from the other inn, I managed to dress and get down there. . . . I think it was Friday, May 3, that I began to think what I could take to do me good. . . . I thought and thought, till it struck me camomile would do me good [as being a tonic and stomachic.—March 8, 1840]. I had seen some growing wild at Corfu, and, remembering this, bade my servant inquire. There were no shops in the place, much less a chemist's; but it so happened that camomile was a familiar medicine with the common people, and each house had it, so he got some. At first he made me some tea of the leaves, which was very rough, and I had some comparison for it, I believe, at the time, but I forget what. Next he made me some with the flowers, which I thought beautiful, and was certainly very refreshing. I consider it was owing to this (under Providence) that I was enabled ultimately to proceed on my journey. I recollect thinking at last I had found out what was the matter with me, and the whole night I passed in that distressing way . . . which I used often to do at home before I went abroad. I told my servant so, and bade him feel my pulse. He said it was fever. I said, 'Oh no! I know myself better.' As I lay in bed the first day, many thoughts came over me. I felt God was fighting against me, and felt—at last I knew *why*—it was for self-will. I felt I had been very self-willed, that the Froudes had been against my coming; so also at Naples the Wilberforces, perhaps the Neates and Andersons. I said to myself, 'Why did no one speak out, say half a word? Why was I left now to interpret their meaning?' Then I tried to fancy where the Froudes were, and how happy I should have been with them in France, or perhaps in England. Yet I felt and kept saying to myself, 'I have not sinned against light,' and at one time I had a most consoling, overpowering thought of God's electing love, and seemed to feel I was His. But I believe all my feelings, painful and pleasant, were heightened by somewhat of delirium, though they still are from God in the way of Providence. Next day the self-reproaching feelings increased. I seemed to see more and more my utter hollowness. I began to think of all my professed principles, and felt they were mere intellectual deductions from one or two admitted truths. I compared myself with Keble, and felt that I was merely developing his, not my, convictions. I know I had *very* clear thoughts about this then, and I believe in the main true ones. Indeed, this is how I look on myself; very much (as the illustration goes) as a pane of glass, which transmits heat, being cold itself. I have a vivid perception of the consequences of certain admitted principles, have a considerable intellectual capacity of drawing them out, have the refinement to admire them, and a rhetorical or histrionic power to represent them ; and, having no great (*i.e.* no vivid) love of this world, whether riches, honours, or anything else, and some firmness and natural dignity of character, take the profession of them upon me, as I might sing a tune which I liked—loving the Truth, but not possessing it, for I believe myself at heart to be nearly hollow, *i.e.* with little love, little self-denial. I believe I have some faith, that is all ; and, as to my sins, they need my possessing no little amount of faith to set against them and gain their remission. By-the-bye, this statement will account for it, how I can preach the Truth without thinking much of myself. Arnold, in his letter to Grant about me, accuses me among others of identifying high excellence with certain peculiarities of my own—*i.e.* preaching myself. But to return. Still more serious thoughts came over me. I thought I had been very self-willed about the tutorship affair, and now I viewed my whole course as one of presumption. It struck me that the 5th of May was just at hand, which was a memorable day as being that on which (what we called) my Ultimatum was sent in to the Provost ; and that on the third anniversary I should be lying on a sick bed in a strange country. . . . I recollected, too, that my last act on leaving Oxford was to preach a University sermon against self-will. . . . Yet still I said to myself, 'I have not sinned against light.'

I cannot describe my full misery on this Saturday, May 4. My door would only *lock*, *i.e.* no mere clasp, but with a key ; my servant was a good deal away, and thus locked me in. My feelings were acute and nervous in a high degree. I forced myself up to keep my mind from thinking of itself, I kept counting the number of stars, flowers, &c., in the pattern of the paper on the walls to occupy me. Just at this time (before or after) the miserable whine of Sicilian beggars was heard outside my door, the staircase communicating with the street. Who can describe the wretchedness of that low, feeble, monotonous cry? which went on I cannot say how long (I unable to do anything) till my servant released me after a time. Now in my lowest distress I was relieved first by some music from some travelling performers, who were passing on (I believe) to Palermo. [N.B.—I had seen a *bagpipe*, to my surprise, between Catania and Palermo.] The music was, I believe, such as harp and clarionet. And now I think it was that my servant proposed a walk. He had talked much of some handsome fountain at the end of the town, but I put off seeing it, I believe now, and we walked out in the S. Filippo road, and then turned up a lane on the south (*i.e.* the left hand). There I sat down on a bank under a fig-tree (the leaves, I believe, were out), and wondered how it should be that I was there; it was the evening. I forget what else I thought of or saw. (I think this walk was on this day, yet somehow have sometimes a notion that the ride on the mule which is to come presently was to-day.) My servant wished to get on, I believe, naturally enough. [February 6, 1842, we had a speculation about having a *litter* made, in which I might be carried to Palermo.] He thought me dying, and told me a story about a sick officer he had attended on in Spain, who left him all his baggage, then got well. I did not see the drift of the story at the time. I gave him a direction to write to if I died (Froude), but I said, 'I do not think I shall. I have not sinned against the light,' or 'God has still work for me to do.' I think the latter.

[*Sunday, March* 1, 1835.] – During the Friday May 3 and Saturday May 4 I had eaten nothing or very little. I could not swallow. On the Sunday May 5 I was eating every half-hour all through the day. A fancy came upon me, either the Saturday or Sunday night, that I was quite well, and only wanted food; and I quite laughed with myself through the night at the news I should have to tell in England, how shameful it was and how ridiculous I had been to have missed seeing Girgenti from such a neglect. One of these nights, Saturday (I think), I was awake all night. (My servant slept in the room. I forget when first.) I recollect asking him whether he said prayers—he said, yes I had had a plan of reading to him on Sundays, and had hoped to do it on the

Sunday I supposed I should pass at Girgenti. I recollect [on the Saturday] the dreamy view I had of the room, with the wretched lamp. I dreamed of the buildings of Catania. Well, on the Sunday I kept eating all day. I do not think I knew it was Sunday. However, in the evening (if it was Saturday), we went out on our mules towards Palermo for a ride. It was very fine scenery. As we came back there was a Sicilian family of the upper rank with servants, &c., lounging outside the town near the steep parapet of the cliff. I recollect asking some questions about them, and somehow so strongly connecting them with the notion of its being Sunday that I certainly thought it was Sunday, whether it was or no. That evening I determined to set off next morning for Palermo. I had a strange feeling on my mind that God meets those who go on in *His way*, who remember Him in His way, in the paths of the Lord ; that I must put myself in His path, His way, that I must do my part, and that He met those who rejoice and worked righteousness, and remembered Him in His ways—some texts of this kind kept haunting me, and I determined to set out by daybreak.

Before setting out on Monday the 6th I drank some toast-and-water which my servant made. We set out almost before sunrise. Scarcely had we got half a mile, when I felt very *weak* (I believe), and said I must have something to eat. I said I must have some chicken (on which I had lived the day before). My servant remonstrated—the things were just packed up. I was peremptory, and he was obliged to undo the baggage and get it. I forget what was on my mind. As I went on again a great thirst came on. I began sucking some most delicious oranges which were on the wayside, very large and fine. I kept thinking what I should be able to say to my mother and sisters about the fineness of these oranges—not sweet or tart, but a fine aromatic bitter. (I believe they *were* very fine. My servant said so ; they were very large.) It was not thirst I felt, but a convulsive feeling of suffocation almost about my throat—very distressing. At last I took to eating the leaves of the trees as I went on. I said I must have *water*. I imputed it to the toast-and-water, which I was sure was bad. The bread had been harsh for some time and I said it was very *rough* bread. This I think was the notion which the feeling in my throat gave me. Several miles passed and no water—no house. At last a cottage to the right —but no means of getting anything. We were going through a level (high, I suppose), with Castro Giovanni before us. I recollect (then, I believe) debating whether it was worth while to turn aside thither ; it was four miles out of the way. We saw the outline of the buildings and a temple or castle. My servant was told by the muleteer it was Roman work, I think. There were few trees or beauty of scenery *near* the road. Caltanisetta, on the other side (the right), I forget whether I saw it now or in the afternoon, in my further progress.

This was seven miles from Leonforte. It might be between six and seven o'clock. I set off before five, and we went about three or four miles an hour. At length I was taken some little way to the right to a hut, I think it was a tent, where I got some water and rested. There was no floor, only the ground. Under Etna, where we lost ourselves, I noticed high black cones, like collections of hop-poles ; and I think shepherds were in them ; we heard dogs. This might be something of the same kind. My blue travelling cloak was spread under me, and I lay down at length. How long I lay—hours probably—I do not know. In the course of the day I recollect a man came in to the good people there, who were of different ages and sexes, and as far as I understood him, asked for money to pray souls out of purgatory. How in my then state I could understand his Sicilian I do not know. I recollect asking my servant whether a bad man had not come in ; and he said no, a very good man. As I lay when I opened my eyes, I saw the men and women, young and old, hanging over me with great interest, and apparently much rejoiced to see me a little better. At length, as I lay, I felt fingers on my pulse. [Sunday, September 6, 1835.] It was a medical man who was visiting persons ill of the fever (I believe), near, and some one had told him there was a sick person, a foreigner, close by, and he came. I forget what he said. I was almost stupid at times. I think he recommended to give me a drink of *camomile*, lemon, and sugar, every now and then, and to get to Castro Giovanni It was most refreshing. After a time, I do not know the time of day, someone said an English party was passing. It turned out to be a diligence on the way to Palermo. A thought came across me that if I were dying, I might let my friends know the last of me, and I insisted on speaking to them. My servant remonstrated. I was very earnest, commanded him, and could almost fancy I rose, or opened my travelling bag, or bade him carry it, or something or other. At length I got my way, and one of the party made his appearance. They were not English; but this man, a German, could speak English. I gave him the letter of introduction I had to Mr. Thomas (?) at Palermo, and begged him to say I forget what; and thanked him most fervently, and felt much relieved, though it was not much which I did, or he promised. After a time, I suppose towards the evening, I managed to be put sideways, and held on the mule, and so set off for Castro Giovanni or Juan. The parting with the poor people in the tent was very affectionate. I asked their name and said I would mention it in England. (I have forgotten it.) My servant burst into tears, though I should not have thought him especially tender. It was, I suppose, four miles to Castro Giovanni, and uphill, very steep. When we got there we could get no room; nothing appeared possible but some damp and dark place, which my servant would not consent to. Some friars (in brown?) passed by, and I entreated my servant to ask them to take me into a monastery. At length I got a very nice comfortable room in the house of a man of some property who let lodgings. I was put to bed; the medical man who had felt my pulse and was (they say) the chief in the place was out of the way, and they brought in another, who was said to be inferior, but I made much of him. He had moustaches and a harsh voice.

Now I do not know how to relate what comes. I shall recollect so irregularly, and medical and other circumstances so mingled together; and there were some things I do not like to put on paper. First, they determined to take blood from me. I preferred my instep to my arm, thinking they might not be skilful. They struck once, and I think again, and no blood came I thought myself going. (I cannot quite tell whether or not I am colouring this, so let me say once for all that any descriptions of my feelings should be attended all through with 'I believe,' for I have half-recollections—glimpses which vanish when I look right at them.) My servant was so distressed he fainted away. At last the blood came. I had three incisions. It was very like cupping. They took away four ounces – little enough. Mr. Babington, to whom I told it afterwards, said it could do me no good; but they said they were afraid to do more, I seemed so weak. I cannot tell whether I was myself the next morning. I have vague recollections of medicine being given me more than once, with an injunction to dose me with cold lemonade. My servant was for warm tea; I insisted on the lemonade, and made a formal complaint to the doctor that he (Gennaro) changed the prescriptions (and I would not see Gennaro for a while). I corresponded with the doctor in Latin. I have the papers still with me. He, I suppose, was no deep Latin scholar, and pretended my Latin was nonsense; but it is very good, particularly considering I was so ill. I was light-headed these days, and barely recollect things. I was not still a moment, my servant said afterwards, and was flushed in the face. They called it a gastric fever. It was very destructive there. Persons were dying daily, and at Girgenti and at Trapani (?) as I learned afterwards. It was attended commonly ... with what they called cholera, but not in my case. ... I don't know how long it lasted; perhaps from Catania to Adernò (May 1 or 2 to May 11 ?). ...

I have some notion that the other complaint lasted five days. I was in pain. ... They gave me over for a week, but my servant said he thought I should get well, from the avidity with which I always took my medicine. The fever came to a crisis in seven, nine, or eleven days—mine, I believe, in eleven. ... I had some miserable nights; the dreamy confusion of delirium—sitting on a staircase, wanting something, or with some difficulty, very wretched, and something about my Mother and sisters. How I dreaded the long nights, lying without sleep, as it seemed, all through the darkness. I wanted to get some one to sit up with me, but did not succeed. Indeed, it was with difficulty I got nurses. The principal one said to Gennaro (as he told me afterwards), and he to her, 'Well, we must go through with it, and if we catch the fever, we catch it.' Gennaro slept in the room. I got the muleteer to sit up with me. The heat, too, was miserable. I suspect I ought to have been kept quite cool. I was reduced to the lowest conceivable weakness, not being able to raise my hand to my head, nor to swallow. I had macaroni, &c., but nothing agreed; biscuits, some I liked. (When I first got there, there were some camomile flowers on the table near the bed, which were most refreshing, and I begged they might not be removed.) I continually had most oppressive almost faintings; I suspect the heat had much to do with it. They had nothing but vinegar to relieve me, which the muleteer with his great bullet tips of fingers (so I recollect I called them, while he administered it with them) applied to my nose in the middle of the night. When I got better I used to watch for the day, and when light appeared through the shutter, for there was no blind or curtain, I used to soliloquise : 'O sweet light ! God's best gift,' &c. By-the-bye, I discharged the muleteer after some days with a quarrel (he going before the magistrates) between him and me, through Gennaro, about wages depending on working and stopping days, in which I got somewhat the worse, as might be expected. My continual faintness was most distressing by day, afterwards. A continual snuffing up vinegar was the only thing which kept me up. I wanted cold water to my head, but this was long afterwards. The doctor and Gennaro would not let me. I managed to outwit Gennaro by pretending to dab my temples with vinegar, and so held a wet cloth to them. He used to bathe with vinegar temples, ears, nose, face, and neck (?).

A fair was held in Castro Giovanni after a few days, and [March 8, 1840, Littlemore] I think I was much annoyed with the great noise which this fair caused. It was under my window. It was a great fair, I believe, and there were to the best of my recollection lodgers in consequence, or guests, in the next room (through the folding doors)—three, according to my impression, who talked. What distressed me most was the daily Mass bell (I suppose it was in a neighbouring church). I used quite to writhe about, and put my head under the bed-clothes, and asked Gennaro if it could be stopped. He answered with a laugh of surprise that it should not annoy me, and of encouragement, as if making light of it. I have since thought they might suppose it was a heretic's misery under a holy bell. Gennaro ruled me most entirely. I was very submissive, and he authoritative. The master of the house was very civil. He heard I liked music, and he got some performers to play to me in the next room. It was very beautiful, but too much for me. What strange, dreamy reminiscences of feeling does this attempt at relation raise ! So the music was left off. When I was getting well, all sorts of maladies came upon me. One which came, or which I fancied, was determination of blood to the head. I had a notion it was mounting, mounting ; that it had got as high as my ears, &c. I got an idea that sleep would bring it on, that I ought not to sleep, and I did all I could to resist it. A cough came on, a wearisome continual cough, for some hours every day in the evening. I spit a good deal. At length they would not let me, saying it would hurt me. They made an issue in my arm for it, which took it off, I think.

Even at Lyons I had profuse cold sweats at night. I had a notion that I had got inflammation of the chest, and recollecting that at Brighton in 1829 Dr. Price had said he would not leave my Mother till she could draw a deep breath without pain, I was ever drawing deep breaths, and felt pain at the bottom of my chest.

When the doctor came in the early part of my illness, he used to shake his head on feeling my pulse and say, 'A-ah! a-ah! *debil, debil!*'

When I was getting better I walked about the room to gain my feet, first leaning on my servant and a stick. But even when I was come to Palermo I could not get out of the carriage by myself, and for some time walked with a stick; improving rapidly, so that one of the servants about the inn said—I think, in English—'Come, sir, cheer up; you will get quite young again.' After walking about the room a little of a day, my servant got me to walk a little in the next room, through the folding doors, partly to amuse me, for it was the time I thought I had inflammation of the chest, and at length he got me with great difficulty downstairs (down the stone steps) and took me out and seated me in a chair—I think under my window, looking across somewhat of a space, so I seem to think, to a pillar which he said was Roman. As I sat in the chair, I could not command myself, but cried profusely, the sight of the sky was so piercing. A number of poor collected about me to see me; I had made them a present already, at my servant's suggestion, as a thank-offering. The chief Lady Bountiful of the place had died of my fever during my illness. I heard of her state from day to day, and at last of her death. The bell at length went for her funeral. One day I was able, with Gennaro's help, to get as far as the Cathedral. I suppose it could not be far. I walked up the aisles. It was Norman, to the best of my recollection. I remember nothing but thick heavy capitals. The day before setting off for Palermo, for which I was very impatient, we went out a little in a close carriage.

When I was getting better, and lay in bed thinking, the events of my life came thick before me, I believe, but I could not recollect the state of things, *e.g.* I could not tell if Dr. Nicholas was alive or not. I had all sorts of schemes how I was to make money to pay my extra expenses from my illness. And I thought a good deal of my book on the Arians, and how it might be improved, and re-arranged parts—and I almost think I eventually adopted some of these suggestions. I think it was on one of these early days of my illness—no, it must be rather when I was getting well, for I fancy it connected with the rush of blood to my head—that I called for a pencil and paper, and, as it were, composed the verses (since in the 'Lyra') beginning ''Mid Balak's magic fires.' When I got to Palermo (I think it was) I found to my surprise that I had already composed them at Messina. The immediate cause of the rush of blood to my head was receiving a letter from home ; it came up from Palermo, and I think this was from five correspondents. I pored over it, small writing, without my glasses, with great avidity, hoping to see the news of the Oriel election, but it was not there. . . . It seemed like a dream or absurdity how I should ever get to England again. As to the Oriel election, I first saw the news of it in a 'Galignani' at Palermo, and on seeing that Rogers was elected, I kissed the paper rapturously.

[*March* 25, 1840 (*Littlemore*).]—I think I have forgotten to say that I had continual pains in the early part of my illness in a way which was very uncommon with me. Also I should mention some fantastic dreams I had when I was getting well, which I barely recollect now. One, that I was introduced to the Russian Court, and that I began talking to the Empress ; and then I bethought myself, ' How ill-mannerly ! In the case of great people, one should not speak, but be spoken to.' Another, that one army from Reggio was crossing the strait to another at Messina, and taking a town. I was in the one or the other, French or English, I think. Another was an army coming up heights to Castro Giovanni. These dreams about armies might be partly suggested by a visit of three magistrates to me, who talked about the quartering of the English at Castro Giovanni ; the occasion of their coming was a quarrel I had with my doctor. When I found myself getting well, I was greatly impressed with his skill and very grateful. I wished to make him presents over and above his pay. I gave him or the master of the house a pocket compass, thermometer, a Virgil and, I think, some other Latin books, and perhaps some other things. The doctor took a fancy to something which Gennaro thought too expensive to part with, or, as I fancy from the event, wished the master of the house to have. He took it away with him, and my servant took the matter before the magistrates, who accordingly, partly perhaps from curiosity, paid me a visit. I did not understand a word they said, though Gennaro interpreted some things. By-the-bye, on my falling ill, all my knowledge of Italian, such as it was, went, while Latin remained. One of the three was an ecclesiastic, and I do not know why, but I stared at him in a strange way, till my servant, thinking it would hurt me, forbade me briskly. I got my property back, and then Gennaro wished me to give it to Aloysio, the master of the house, but I would not. I was visited at the beginning of my illness by a priest ; and told my servant, when half light-headed, I wished to dispute with him. I was also visited by the brother of my landlord, who asked and obtained of me a yellow wash-leather, such as they rub plate with. There was some one else in the early part of my illness whom in my Latin with the doctor I called *probus homo* ; he might have been the husband of my inferior nurse.

And now I have said everything pretty nearly that I can recollect of this illness. I set off from Castro Juan on May 25, Whitsun Eve. I mistook, by-the-bye, and calculated it a week wrong. For at Palermo a week after, I fancied it was Whit Sunday, whereas it was Trinity. On the Sunday before, I was well enough to know that it was Jemima's birthday, and fancy that I revived about the 17th ; but the crisis must have been earlier. By-the-bye, I should have acknowledged the great honesty of all my attendants. Gennaro had charge of clothes, money—everything. I lost nothing. A large sum of money came to me from Palermo in dollars safe. He paid nothing without asking my leave ; and though he had coveted *all* my effects, if I died, yet even then he wished them formally bequeathed to him. My watch, and indeed everything I had, was at the mercy of a number of persons. No English consul was nearer, I suppose, than Girgenti. To proceed ; I set off on the 25th, and had great compunctions about travelling through the Sunday (next day), but at last overcame them. I travelled through an exquisitely beautiful country, part of it, however, by night. My joy was too great for me at first. I never saw such a country—the spring in its greatest luxuriance. All sorts of strange trees—very steep and high hills over which the road went ; mountains in the distance—a profusion of aloes along the road. Such bright colouring – all in tune with my reviving life. I had a great appetite, and was always coaxing (as I may call it) Gennaro for cakes. Here, by-the-bye, I should record my feelings of returning appetite after the illness. As I got better at Castro Giovanni he used to give me an egg baked in wood ashes and some tea for breakfast, and cakes. How I longed for it! And when I took the tea, I could not help crying out with delight. I used to say, 'It is life from the dead!' I never had such feelings. All through my illness I had depended on Gennaro so much I could not bear him from the room five minutes. I used always to be crying out, for I don't know how long together, 'Gen-na-ro-o-o-o-o-o!' They fed me on chicken broth. I did not take beef broth or beef tea till I got to Palermo, and that gave me something of the ecstatic feelings which the tea had given. I got to Palermo the third day, May 27, having (I think) on the 26th rested at a sort of inn where the landlord came and looked at me. I was very weak. When I got up the morning of the 26th or 27th I sat some time by the bedside, crying bitterly, and all I could say was that I was sure God had some work for me to do in England. This, indeed, I had said to Dr. Wiseman at Rome, but though sincerely said, the words were not pointedly said; but in answer to the question how long we stayed there, I said that we had work at home. I wish I could see my letter to Christie; I must ask him for it. But now my pulse was intense and overpowering, and my servant of course could not understand me at all. But to proceed to Palermo. I was lodged at Page's hotel—the hostess Ann Page, who had married, I think, an Italian or Sicilian. She was very eager to please me, and begged me to recommend her house at home. She was a motherly sort of person, and made me sago and tapioca, &c. The merchants (wine merchants) were very civil. At first they thought me dying. I was so very weak, and could not speak except drawling. I used to go on the water every day, and that set me up. I revived day by day wonderfully. I was there nearly three weeks, till June 13. It was a very trying time, yet perhaps I should not have been strong enough before that time—and to go by myself! I composed a Lyra a day, I think, from the day I got there. Hay-making was going on while I was there. I went up to the Monte Pellegrino; I went to the Hydra cave, &c.; but I made very little use of my time, expecting to sail almost daily, and home-sick and much disappointed at the delay. I went a great deal into the public garden, called, I think, the Villa Reale, and along the beach outside, sitting in the seats. However, they told me I must not go out in the middle of the day, though in the shade. Sometimes there were sciroccos and very trying, the wind like a furnace. The clouds were blue, the tawny mountains looking wondrous. I dined besides at the merchant's, at Mr. Thomas's, a merchant living two or three miles out on the Monreale road—a married man. The day before I sailed I met there Mr. Page of Ch. Ch. I called on the German who had passed and come out to me when I lay in the cabin on the road under Castel Juan. My conveyance in which I had come to Palermo came from Palermo. All this time I knew my friends in England were in a state of anxiety, but I had no means of communicating with them. My 'private diary' for 1833 gives many daily details.

I left Gennaro at Palermo; he was to go back to Naples to his wife and family. Since, I have heard he is in Lord Carrington's family in England. He was, humanly speaking, the preserver of my life, I think. What I should have done without him I cannot think. He nursed me as a child. An English servant never could do what he did. He had once been deranged, and was easily overset by liquor. I found him so at Palermo, though he denied it. He once or twice left me a whole day, or a long while.

When we parted, I fancy I gave him about 10l. over and above his wages and a character written. Before I had given him anything, he began to spell for something; but what he thought of was an old blue cloak of mine, which I had had since 1823; a little thing for him to set his services at – at the same time a great thing for me to give, for I had an affection for it. It had nursed me all through my illness; had ever been put on my bed, put on me when I rose to have my bed made, &c. I had nearly lost it at Corfu—it was stolen by a soldier, but recovered. I have it still. I have brought it up here to Littlemore, and on some cold nights I have had it on my bed. I have so few things to sympathise with me that I take to cloaks.—[March 25, 1840.]

[April 24, 1874.—I wonder I have not mentioned how I simply lost my memory as to *how* I came to be ill and in bed, and how strangely, by little and little, first one fact came back to me, then another, till at length I realised my journey and my illness in continuity.]

[*Littlemore: March* 25, 1840.]—The thought keeps pressing on me while I write this, what am I writing it for ? For myself I may look at it once or twice in my life, and what sympathy is there in *my* looking at it ? . . . Who will care to be told such details as I have put down above ? Shall I ever have in my old age spiritual children who will take an interest ?

How time is getting on! I seem to be reconciling myself to the idea of being old. It seems but yesterday that the Whigs came into power; another such to-morrow will make me almost fifty—an elderly man. What a dream is life! I used to regret festival days going so quick. They are come and they are gone; but so it is. <u>Time is nothing except as the seed of eternity</u>.

THE START OF THE MOVEMENT

From the long illness, fever, and consequent weakness in Sicily, the solitude of the sea, and the hurried journey, there followed at once the plunge into the Movement. On July 14 Mr. Keble preached his assize sermon, 'which,' Dr. Newman says in his 'Apologia,' 'I have ever thought the beginning of the Movement.'

The Editor is allowed to open what may be regarded as a history of the Movement, through the correspondence of its movers, with the following sentences from the pen best fitted to write upon it :—

'Mr. Newman landed in England at a critical moment. It was the moment when the fears for the Church, which had long been growing, and which arose, not merely from the designs, avowed or surmised, of her enemies, but from the helplessness of her friends, had led at length to the resolution in a few brave and zealous men to speak out and to act. Ten Irish bishoprics had been at a sweep suppressed, and Church people were told to be thankful that things were not worse. It was time to move if there was to be any moving at all. The month of July 1833 saw several things. The resolution was taken, Mr. Palmer has told us, in meetings chiefly in Oriel Common-Room, by himself, Mr. Froude, and Mr. Keble, "to unite and associate in defence of the Church." On July 14 Mr. Keble preached his famous sermon on National Apostasy. Between July 25 and 29 a meeting was held at Mr. Rose's rectory at Hadleigh, at which were present Mr. Palmer, Mr. Froude, Mr. Perceval, and Mr. Rose. Mr. Keble was to have been there, but there is evidence that he was not. Mr. Newman was not there. There appears to have been some division of opinion at the meeting, but two points were agreed on : to fight for the doctrine of the Apostolical Succession and for the integrity of the Prayer Book. And two things followed from it—the plan of associating for defence of the Church, and the "Tracts for the Times." Mr. Newman was not at the meeting, but he had already suggested the plan of association to Froude and Keble, with whom he was in close correspondence ; and, as soon as the determination was taken to move, he, with Mr. Palmer, took the labouring oars in the effort which followed it.'

It may be well to anticipate the rapid course of events in the last half of 1833 by giving here a fragmentary diary, written by Mr. Newman, the final words of which bear the date December 29, 1833. This manuscript seems to give the first suggestion of what issued in so memorable a stir and effort. Who the 'suggester' was, whom the writer 'will not name,' is not known to the Editor.

It was the habit of Mr. Newman in transcribing letters and records (as in this diary) to interpolate short notes, embodying them within brackets, in the narrative. This system will be retained. Whatever explanatory comment enclosed in brackets stands in the page itself, must be understood to be from the pen of J. H. N.—the only title which no change can put out of date.

FRAGMENTARY DIARY.

Oriel, December 6, 1833.—Keble preached his assize sermon July 14, and the Advertisement [1] prefixed to it was the first intimation of what was to follow on our part.

I was low-spirited about the state of things, and thought nothing could be done, when one, whom I will not name, suggested whether something could not be done in the way of a society, association, &c., for Church purposes, or at least so pressed me to do something that I thought of it. I forget which.

I wrote to Froude, I think, who was in Essex, and to Keble, urging on the latter the gift we had committed to us in being in Oxford, which was a kind of centre and traditionary source of good principles. On his doubting about it, I wrote him word he might join it or not, but the league was in existence. It was a fact, not a project. Froude and I were the only two members at that moment. I also wrote to

[1] That is, when published.

Palmer or spoke, and he liked the notion much. Rose, too, was written to, and he came into it. This was at the end of July.

I wrote to various friends in August, but cannot tell what was actually accomplished towards our object in that month. I thought I brought out the first Tract in the course of it, but the printer's bill dates it September 9.

Shortly after the first sheet and a half of tracts were out, Palmer went into Warwickshire, and excited a great interest there by the notion of an Association. By-the-bye, I should have said that in August Keble wrote his 'Declaration of Principles and Objects,' which we are now at length publishing. Palmer took it down to Coventry. It was thought not businesslike enough, and 'Suggestions for an Association' was written by Palmer, which on his return I re-wrote, and Ogilvie corrected. This paper was largely circulated; the tracts stopping which Palmer thought too violent.

By this time my views had much cleared on the whole subject of our proceedings. I was strongly against an association, *i.e.* any body in which a majority bound a minority, and liked Keble's way of putting it, 'we pledge ourselves one to another in our several stations, reserving our canonical obedience.' I found a great many people agree with me. Palmer went up to town at the end of October to Archdeacon Bailey, Mr. Norris, &c. I wrote out for him clearly my views, and he came into them.

Then I began reprinting my tracts most earnestly, and distributing them. I had before this written to Rose *how* we had best start agitating. He recommended an address to the Archbishop. When Palmer went to town the draught of the address from Keble ought to have gone with him. But there was a delay between Keble and Froude, who was going down on his way to Barbadoes, and I was obliged to send up to Palmer a draught of my own. This, in itself too moderate, since I wrote under the fear of Palmer's thinking me ultra, was further weakened by Palmer in London, who struck out all mention of 'extra-ecclesiastical interference,' and was still further diluted by our friends in London. Thus it came down to us, and written in a most wretched style. We polished it, struck out some offensive passages, and sent it back. It came down again as uncouth, and almost as offensive, as before. We amended it, and printed it; then circulated it far and wide.

Meanwhile the friends of the Church who in any sense listened to us split into two views of the subject—one party for a Society, the other for Tracts. The associationists abominated, or at least were offended at, the tracts ; the distributors of the tracts dreaded an association as being anti-episcopal, productive of party spirit, and open to secret influences, &c. In Oxford the unpopularity of the tracts was made a reason for denouncing the Association. Mr. Norris and his friends in London made Palmer abjure the Tract system. Rose was for the tracts. Pusey and Harrison of Christchurch took them up. Archdeacon Froude wanted a monthly supply of them—an idea of which I hope to take advantage, and get friends everywhere to let me send them to them periodically. Dr. Spry warmly approved the tracts. The Bishop of Winchester expressed approval. At Bowden's suggestion we made Turrill's our depôt.

At the end of November the questions became frequent, 'How are we to act?' and to myself, 'Do you approve an association or not?' So I wished to bring out Keble's original paper above alluded to. On going to Palmer I found Mr. Norris had almost cast off address, Association, and all, being frightened at the laxity of the address. Palmer seemed to assent to the proposal I came to him about. [This is expressed in P.'s letter without a date.—J. H. N.]

Wednesday, November 27.—E. Churton came down from London with the considerate desire of setting matters right between Mr. Norris and Palmer. He wanted the address altered, but found that impossible.

When I spoke to Palmer again about Keble's paper, he was most earnestly opposed to the notion of printing it [this is expressed in P.'s letter of November 29], but I determined to do so. He was to see it in proof. Accidents delayed the publication of it. Christie and Copeland had a talk with him, and his indisposition to it was lessened. Palmer seems to have thought that our joining the tracts to a project of Association in one paper interfered with his promise to Mr. Norris.

Tuesday, December 3.—Perceval called and made my acquaintance. Thinks the address weak ; assists the tracts. The 'Record' took notice of and quoted the tracts. Before this Rickards had written to me, strongly disapproving of parts of them. R. Wilberforce also.

December 5.—Letter from the editor of the 'Record,'

declining (or something like it) to receive any more communications from me, and expostulating about the tracts. I had sent him some letters on Church discipline.

December 6.—An attack upon us in the 'Record.' The 'Standard' began attacks on Dissenters in a series of letters. Letter from Rose approving of the tracts, urging their continuance, and mentioning his intention to insert them in the magazine; from Turrill, saying they were approved, sold well, and that he wanted more; and from the Librarian of the British Museum requesting copies.

December 15.—Since the last date the 'Record' has retracted the *violence* of its attack, apparently having been expostulated with by correspondents, who defended the doctrine of the Apostolical Succession while they gave us up. Thus it has, in fact, *advertised* us. I hear, too, that the 'Christian Observer' has attacked us—nay, Oriel by name. The Bishop of London has turned round, and advocates the signing of the address in his diocese, on the ground that it is the least of two evils. He has denied, moreover, that he had anything to do with a Ministerial Liturgical Reform. Stronger and stronger reports of the intention of ministers to introduce some sweeping measure, certainly ecclesiastical, if not liturgical.

December 29.—The 'Record' has taken up 'the Movement begun at Oxford' and the association, but has declared the tracts have been recalled and others substituted! I have seen the 'Christian Observer,' which does *not* mention Oriel by name, but is very vehement. The Bishop of London is said to have retracted his approval of the address, and again recalled his retractation. The ministers are said to be surprised and annoyed at our Movement.

[This diary did not get further than this.—J. H. N.]

The earliest correspondence connected with, but preceding, the start of the Movement relates to the little gathering of High Churchmen at Hadleigh, Mr. Rose's living in Suffolk. As Editor of the 'British Magazine' Mr. Rose had for some time been in communication with Mr. Newman and his friends. The previous July, 1832, he had visited Oxford as Mr. Palmer of Worcester's guest, and his impressions of Oxford and of the men to whom his host introduced him are given in a letter which the reader has already read in the order of its date.

The correspondence of 1833 must now be continued chronologically from page 362.

REV. J. KEBLE TO REV. J. H. NEWMAN.

July 1833.

I mean to send you on the other page some names of persons to whom I wish Parker and Rivington to send copies of my sermon [on National Apostasy—J. H. N.], otherwise, like many of its betters, it will surely pass away as a dream.

As you say [alluding to the 'Arians'] one's Opuscula do indeed seem miserable when one comes to look coolly over them; but I suppose one must put up with that, as with other unpleasant seemings or realities, for a chance of doing a halfpennyworth of good. I am much disposed to agree with you that very few of our brethren are yet in the right posture of mind for looking at this question; but I depend much on the illuminating power of a little wholesome persecution. Nothing in the world that we can write about is more likely to do good gradually than bringing forward such examples as St. Ambrose, &c. [allusion to my projected 'Church of the Fathers']. Pray do it with all your might. . . . I am very anxious that, whatever one does publicly, whether alone or in concert with others, should be somehow sanctioned episcopally; and I do hope Froude will bring us some facts or good opinions as to what their Lordships (of course I do not mean your Whatelys, &c.) would have us do.

Hurrell Froude, as has been said, was one of the party at Hadleigh. The following letter to Mr. Newman gives his report of proceedings and his impressions :

REV. R. H. FROUDE TO REV. J. H. NEWMAN.

Hadleigh: July 30, 1833.

I send you a line or two to say what we have been about. I don't think Rose likes the notion of putting 'Lyra' into the correspondence. [N.B.—*i.e.* that the 'British Magazine' should not be *answerable* for the 'Lyra Apostolica.'] I told him our notion of starting a separate concern, but he seemed to think that it would be a failure, though he did not say so. My own notion is that, with the assistance of Miller and others, we might start a purely religious periodical of prose as well as verse, with Keble's name, *Excubiæ Apostolicæ*, exactly on the plan of our present 'Lyra,' *i.e.* generally of personal religion and now and then ecclesiastical. I think, as in its nature it must exclude facts, it would take very little trouble, and I should not despair of a very great sale if we made a proper use of Keble's good fame among the Evangelicals. Let us start the first number about Advent. . . .

They [N.B.—*i.e.* the meeting at Hadleigh] think that no one will attend at present to anything one says about the appointment of bishops. I see that Rose has not abandoned Conservative hopes himself, and is in suspense. . . . His notion is, that the most important subject to which you can direct your reading at present is the meaning of Canonical Obedience, which we have all sworn to our bishops; for that this is likely to be the only support of Church government when the State refuses to support it. I myself have a most indistinct idea of what I am bound to; yet the oath must certainly contemplate something definite, and sufficient to preserve practical subordination.

Rose has many good notions, and I like him much, but he is not yet an Apostolical.

Perceval is a very delightful fellow in $\mathring{\eta}\theta o\varsigma$—a regular thoroughgoing Apostolical; but I think Keble should warn him against putting himself in the way of excitement. Some of the things he says and does make me feel rather odd. I am sure he should be set to work on something dull that would keep his thoughts from matters of present interest. I never saw a fellow that seemed more entirely absorbed heart and soul in the cause of the Church, and without the remotest approach to self-sufficiency, which his writing so often with his name made one suspect.

I have not heard from Rickards; so I have not ventured to go uninvited. I go to Round to-morrow, and shall pay Archdeacon Lyall a visit afterwards. He is a most agreeable man, and clever, and I should think not a mere Conservative at heart, though no Apostolical.

Rose has just been throwing out a notion that might be made something of; that is, that we should proceed to elect a Lay Synod, as $\delta\iota\acute{\alpha}\delta o\chi o\varsigma$ of the Church of England. . . .

REV. J. H. NEWMAN TO REV. J. KEBLE.

Oriel College: August 5, 1833.

. . . Palmer has returned from Rose, and I have heard from Froude, as you probably have. Froude wishes to break with Rose, which must not be, I think. Let us wait the course of events. Rose is hoping for a reaction: till we clearly see it [reaction] to be impossible, there is no reason we should talk of the repeal of the *Præmunire*—to say nothing of people not being prepared for it—and yet we may protest against measures we think unchristian. Rose has a notion of a Synod, lay and clerical, and to get it as an exchange for the Church rate being put on us, which he thinks inevitable. Is it lawful to compound in this way?

Do you not think we should act in concert, as nearly in the way of a Society as possible? *i.e.* to take measures for the circulation of tracts, pamphlets, &c., and to write systematically to stir up our friends. Would it be acceptable to the Archbishop (Howley) to know the feelings of people as to his speech on the second reading? Do not you think we could get many signatures under the heading of 'We, the undersigned members of the University of Oxford'? Does not the Duke's letter[1] show that public men do not hear of the approbation which quiet men give to their measures? And might not the Archbishop be cheered by it?

Do you know enough of the ecclesiastical law to decide what the clergy of Waterford should do? If you can show that they ought not to obey a Bishop of Cashel, ought we not to do our part in stirring them up, or in stirring up the bishops to consecrate a Bishop of Waterford?

A friend of mine is eager on this point, and has been writing to a clergyman in Ireland on the subject. Palmer, I hope, is preparing for Rose a digest of the Primitive Canons. I am anxious to see a paper in the Magazine from you on the subject of virtual excommunication, such as you gave us reason to look for. Really it would be of great use.

I have written one or two papers on St. Ambrose, but am diffident about them till Froude casts his eye over them. The subject is his dispute *about the Churches*. Perhaps I shall take his conduct towards Theodosius next. As to your proposal about the Discipline question, unless it turns out to be very

[1] See p. 335.

formidable, I should like to do it. I do not know Bishop Jebb's arguments, but it seems so open to common sense that a Church must have discipline (else, might a figure exist without outline) that it seems as if our business was rather to accustom the *imagination* of men to the notion than to convince their reason.

I fear they did not get on very well at Hadleigh. Froude wants you to give your friend Arthur Perceval a bit of advice, which I think Froude himself partly requires. We shall lose all our influence when times are worse, if we are prematurely violent. I heartily wish things may keep quiet for a year or two, that we may ascertain our position, get up precedents, and know our duty. Palmer thinks both Froude and Perceval very deficient in learning, and therefore rash.

I do not think we have yet made as much as we ought of our situation at Oxford, and of the deference paid to it through the country. Are not many eyes looking towards us everywhere, not as 'masters and scholars,' but as residents; so that all our acts, as coming from the University, might have the authority of a vote of Convocation almost, in such cases as when Convocation cannot be expected to speak out ? Now no party is likely to be active in Oxford but ourselves, so the field is before us. Do let us agree on some plan as to writing letters to our friends, just as if we were canvassing. Now, if I could say that other persons agreed with me in thinking it desirable to say and do all in our power to stir up the Church, and if I knew the points of agreement—*i.e.* if we were to settle on some uniform plan of talking as to principles, &c.—then I would not mind writing, as in an election, canvassing, to men I knew very little of. Pray think of this, and send me a sketch of principles—*e.g.* that by the Irish Bill the Church's liberties are invaded, &c. And should we not aim at getting up petitions next year to the King ? . . . What do you think of preaching about the state of things ? Of course no one should do so who is not conscious to himself that he is free from excitement, nay sick of all the nasty bustle. . . . If we leave our flocks in ignorance . . . will they not be surprised at a call to follow us *from* the Establishment, should it come to that ?

REV. J. KEBLE TO REV. J. H. NEWMAN.

[Few of his letters are dated, which has been a source of great trouble.—J. H. N.]

August 8, 1833.

Many thanks, my dear N., for your kind long letter. If I could answer half the questions in it I should be a much wiser man than I am. As concerning Mater Ecclesia, think if the Hadleighans could not agree [referring to the High Church Meeting at this time at Rose's living.—J. H. N.], where *inter quatuor muros* will you find six men to agree together? But I quite agree with you that Rose's Magazine must be supported — unless he actually rats, which I never will believe till I see it. As for Hurrell, he is so annoyed just now at his project not being accepted that I count his dissatisfaction for very little.

Now as to what shall be done, first and foremost will no bishop of them all give us a hint? It would be so *very* much better and more satisfactory to be acting under them, even though one might not always think they gave the wisest orders in the world. This I mentioned to Rose when I wrote to him last, and I hope he will be able to give us a hint. He need not name any names, as their Lordships are so *very* coy. Next as to my own feelings, I think my mind is made up thus far, that I cannot take the *Oath of Supremacy* in the sense which the Legislature clearly now puts upon it. I cannot *accept* any curacy or office in the Church of England; but I have not made up my mind that I am bound to resign what I have. Indeed, I rather think not, now that I have given public notice in what respect I differ from their construction. Also, I am convinced of the propriety of preaching and otherwise preparing one's flock for some trial of their Church principles. Indeed, I have already begun to do so; and I am meditating something of the kind in print. If for no other reason, it should be done to obtain the prayers of the well-disposed. Also, I am sure the thing can be made plain to them and interesting, too, without any kind of high political seasoning. I don't say without making them indignant; but if *we* are calm, that will not be *our* fault.

Then comes the question what line we should take in the 'British Magazine,' &c., and this is where I want, if possible, *authority* ; and if not, *very good advice.* I feel myself terribly unlearned ; but, with all deference to Palmer, is it so much a matter of learning ? . . . Saving, therefore, errors through ignorance, this is my feeling of what ought to be done. *If* there is any chance of such a reaction as shall lead the State to mend what has been done, re-establish the ten bishops in Ireland, and make the nation pay the church rates, by all means let us wait for it (I confess it seems to me as unlikely as the Duke of Bedford's restoring Tavistock Abbey) ; but if the *reaction* do not amount to a retractation of the anti-Church *principle,* I think we ought to be prepared to sacrifice any or all of our endowments sooner than sanction it. 'Take every pound, shilling, and penny, and the curse of sacrilege along with it ; only let us make our own bishops, and be governed by our own laws.' This is the length I am prepared to go ; but of course if we could get our liberty at an easier price, so much the better. Only I don't see what you gain by having a Synod, as long as the ruling members of that Synod are nominated by an infidel Government. This would make me hesitate about Rose's compromise ; but perhaps a greater sacrifice of property, in addition to the rates, would purchase the bishops' nomination for us ; and then the Synod would be worth having. I see old Whately and the 'Times' have both been broaching something of the sort (*par nobile*), and this you will say ought to make me suspect it ; but, however, it seems as if the thing were feasible. This may give you a rough notion of what I should like to be driving at in letters and the Magazine, &c., and perhaps in tracts and pamphlets. Your question about the bishopric of Waterford seems to me to involve it all ; but I fancied that Palmer had long ago thrown cold water on any notion of resistance there at present. The whole matter appears to me newly modified, and made infinitely more simple, and more within everybody's reach, by the notorious anti-Christianity of the House of Commons. *That* makes it a stronger case than St. Ambrose against Valentinian or Theodosius ; and I think should be dinned into people's ears in every safe way.

I like the notion of addresses to the Archbishop, but have had such ill-luck with the *many* which I have before now tried to get up, that I have little heart to originate one. When I have done my *Pastoral Letter,* perhaps I may try an appeal from the new to the old Churchmen, or some such thing, dwelling especially on the point of supremacy and the Coronation oath. I should like, too, to try the *Excommunicables*; but fear I ought to know my books better.

Perhaps I may run up to Oxford Monday evening, or Tuesday morning. How I should like to meet Palmer and you!

REV. H. J. ROSE TO REV. J. H. NEWMAN.

August 20, 1833.

Your packet is most acceptable. I shall begin your series ['Church of the Fathers'?] in October, and hope and trust that you may be able and willing to continue it very long. I deeply regret that I could not have the pleasure of seeing you at Hadleigh. I am, as you may well suppose, a good deal shattered and perplexed by the suspense and uncertainty which hang around my future movements. Rest is the only thing which I now crave, and for which I am fit; but there seems no prospect of that. . . .

I fervently hope that I may myself be spared from going to Durham, which under circumstances of health I should have coveted, as the duties of the Professor will so much lie in the formation of clergy. Pray forgive all this egotism. I am hardly equal to anything else.

REV. R. H. FROUDE TO REV. J. H. NEWMAN.

August 22.

. . . As to my preaching I have, on the whole, been successful. . . . I have written a sermon on the duty of contemplating a time when the law of the land shall cease to be the law of the Church; and I hope to get it preached by a friend of mine at the Bishop's visitation. My father thinks it most temperate and satisfactory. If I had strong lungs I should go about the country holding forth.

It has lately come into my head that the present state of things in England makes an opening for reviving the monastic system. Colleges of unmarried priests would be the cheapest possible way of providing effectually for the spiritual wants of a large population.

REV. J. H. NEWMAN TO REV. R. H. FROUDE.

August 22, 1833.

Read the enclosed nonsense ['Home Thoughts Abroad'] and send it back forthwith. I do not wish you to say it *is* nonsense, for I know it; but whether it is flippant, by which I mean what Keble blames in Arnold's writings, *conversational*. You will see there are few enough facts. If I go on there will be a chapter on the Gregorian Chants, if possible; and on painting, &c., in which Froude *loquitur*. Perhaps in another I may have a dialogue and bring in some good sentiments *à propos* of the Telegraph Bill or the Solfatara; and I want you to write a chapter on France, or at least to supply an account of Lamennais' system.

A friend of Mr. Newman's, admitted to the knowledge of the task imposed on the Editor, thus speaks of the papers published under the title of 'Home Thoughts Abroad.' Writing in 1885, he says:—

You should see some papers in the 'British Magazine,' 1835-6 (I should think), entitled (I also think) 'Home Thoughts Abroad,' which were the first to turn people's minds from the classical antiquities and fine arts of Rome to its Christian associations. It was a new idea to me when I read the paper, and I really think to everybody else. *Now any one would say it never was otherwise*; the fact was, however, that no one then thought of Rome in connexion with St. Peter and St. Paul, much less St. Leo and St. Gregory, or of sumptuous worship as anything but a kind of theatrical sight. So that the paper had an originality then which is now eclipsed by satellites of his satellites.[1]

REV. C. P. GOLIGHTLY TO REV. J. H. NEWMAN.

Penshurst: August 22, 1833.

You might safely have assumed that I would most gladly join your society—what do you call it? A Conservative Church Society?—and urge others to do the same. Of my neighbours, the Rev. G. B., a sharp intelligent little man,

[1] The paper enclosed to Froude did not really appear till 1836, afterwards reprinted in 'Discussions and Arguments' published by Dr. Newman in 1872. The opening advertisement says of the six portions of which it (the volume) consists:—'The first appeared in the *British Magazine* in the spring of 1836 under the title of "Home Thoughts Abroad."' As that title was intended for a series of papers which were never written, and is unsuitable for a single instalment of them, another heading has been selected for it answering more exactly to the particular subject of which it treats. The present title is, 'How to Accomplish it.'—ED.

has professed his readiness to become a member of it; and the Rev. W. G. to circulate its publications. One of your principles I own I do not like; you protest 'against doing anything directly to separate Church and State.' I would do the same perhaps in ordinary times; but, when the State takes upon herself to decide, and that without consulting the Church, how many bishops are necessary for the superintendence of the clergy, and the clergy are cowardly or ignorant enough to submit to her decisions, it appears to me that the time for separation is come. Again I am surprised that, among other views, you have not for your object the revival of Convocation. Further, I cannot but think that something may yet be done to rouse the Irish clergy. There are only 2,000 of them. I have had a letter from my Irish correspondent. 'If the clergy,' he says, 'will not now make a decided stand, the Church is gone, both in England and Ireland. I fear the bishops never will do so; and if not, we can do nothing. Though there is a noble spirit in the Church of Ireland, yet it is not easy to bring a body of men to act in a way that might interfere with their temporal interests. The step you mention would subject those engaged in it to a *Præmunire*; the whole body of bishops and clergy ought to brave it, and then let Government take their remedy!'

REV. J. H. NEWMAN TO REV. R. H. FROUDE.

August 23, 1833.

. . . I have got a most audacious scheme in my mind about myself, which will not bear to be put on paper; the ink would turn red. Perhaps before we meet I shall have forgotten it. [N.B.—This was to stand for the Moral Philosophy professorship.—J. H. N.]

REV. A. J. TROWER TO REV. J. H. NEWMAN.

August 26, 1833.

The intelligence you give me about your book [the 'Arians'] surprised me not a little [that it was rejected as one of the Theological Library Series.—J. H. N.], as Mr. Rose told me, when I met with him accidentally nine months ago, how highly he thought of it, how high an opinion it gave him of yourself, and that the public were not worthy of it. Your letter from Naples I received and was much interested in. I am glad the introductions were of use.

I do not deny I look upon you as an ultra. . . . I will not for a moment conceal that I look upon you as very extreme in your opinions . . . and I should say that I share the opinions, generally speaking, of those Evangelicals of whom you ask me whether 'I do not think there is great hope . . .' Golightly, I believe, has told you that my opinions are not quite 'satisfactory.'

REV. W. PALMER OF WORCESTER TO REV. J. H. NEWMAN.

August 31, 1833.

I received a letter from Rose to-day, which has given me great pleasure, as I am sure it will you. But I will copy a bit of it, written in reply to my letter to him about the Society. 'I have only just received your letter, and in reply can have no difficulty in saying that I enter warmly into your plan and feel that, as far as your description goes, no Churchman can entertain any objection to a Society the object of which is to disseminate right views as to the Church and the ministry among our less informed brethren. But I want more distinct accounts of your plans, and, if I had them, should not despair of getting sanction for them.'

I have written in reply to this, stating again our two objects of maintaining the doctrine of the Apostolical Succession, and the orthodoxy of the Prayer Book against Socinian innovations, and have informed him that our plans are to publish tracts, &c., on these subjects, and make use of the press, and that we should have a committee to revise, and pay great attention to the bishops, &c. But that on the details of our plans we wanted advice, and should be happy to take it. I also mentioned that we had many friends and supporters, and that branches could be formed, and begged him to speak to his friends, and especially to the bishops. I had a letter from Perceval a day or two ago in reply to one which I wrote, explaining the principles of the Association. He desires to be a member—so pray, Mr. Secretary, have the goodness to put him on your list of candidates.

REV. J. H. NEWMAN TO J. W. BOWDEN, ESQ.

Oriel College: August 31, 1833.

Most probably I shall be in London the second week in October. It would give me real pleasure to find myself with you ; and these are times when one's feelings and principles are tried so at every turn, that it is particularly needful to see one's friends often, to be sure how one is going on. I really often feel frightened at meeting friends after an interval, lest I should find they differ from myself about passing events—a judgment about which is no longer a matter of indifference. Your letter delighted me much ; there is not a word in it in which I do not quite agree with you, and this I do think rather wonderful and happy ; since in all political subjects there is such great room for variation of sentiment. But I suppose the time is coming when the bulk of serious persons will be on one side ; and this is a consolation among many annoyances.

As to the state of the Church, I suppose it was in a far worse condition in Arian times, except in the one point you mention—that there was the *possibility* of true-minded men becoming bishops, which is now almost out of the question. If we had *one* Athanasius or Basil, we could bear with twenty Eusebius's, though Eusebius was not at all the worst of the bad. The scandals of Arian times are far worse than any now. I wish the Archbishop had somewhat of the boldness of the old Catholic prelates ; no one can doubt he is a man of the highest principle, and would willingly die a martyr, but if he had but the little finger of Athanasius, he would do us all the good in the world. Things have come to a pretty pass when one must not speak as a Christian minister, for fear of pulling down the house over our heads. At the same time, I daresay, were I in high station, I should suddenly get very cautious from the feeling of responsibility. Well, it is a lucky thing to be able to talk ; and I think we who can should make the most of it.

Under this feeling, we are just setting up here Societies for the Defence of the Church. We do not like our names known, but we hope the plan will succeed. We have already got assistants in five or six counties. Our objects are ' to rouse the clergy, to inculcate the Apostolical Succession, and to defend the Liturgy.' We hope to publish tracts, &c.

I shall take great interest in seeing your Tract about Duelling. Do you ever see the ' British Magazine ' ? It is edited by Rose of Cambridge, and on the whole advocates good principles. Rose writes very cleverly, and there is a knot of persons here who support him,—Keble, Miller, Palmer of Worcester, and others. I have constituted myself editor (with another man)[1] of a poetical series which comes out in the Magazine, and which always contains some good things, though perhaps you may consider the September number somewhat violent.

But one gains nothing by sitting still. I am sure the Apostles did not sit still: and agitation is the order of the day. I do not at all fear for the result, were we thrown on the people, though for a while many of us would be distressed *in re pecuniaria*—not that I would advocate a separation of Church and State unless the nation does more tyrannical things against us; but I do feel I should be glad if it were done and over, much as the nation would lose by it; for I fear the Church is being corrupted by the union.

As to poor Whately, it is melancholy. Of course, to know him now is quite impossible, yet he has so many good qualities that it is impossible also not to feel for him. I fear his love of applause, popularity, &c., has been his snare; for a man more void of, what are commonly called, selfish ends does not exist.

My Mother and sisters desire me to send you their very kind remembrances. I found them quite well, after having almost despaired of ever seeing them again. I fell ill at Lyons again for two days, which frightened me, and made me travel fast (since I found I could) lest I should be laid up a second time in a foreign land. I am, thank God, remarkably well now.

REV. J. H. NEWMAN TO F. ROGERS, ESQ.

Oriel College: August 31, 1833.

... Thanks for the two letters, and the song, which will be the more acceptable because the present time is evil. A strange notion yours! as if we were not disposed more to cling to what was, on the ground of its being 'fuit.' Do you understand? Charles I. and his line are the more dear on account of the apostasy of others. Yet, I confess, Tory as I still am, theoretically and historically, I begin to be a Radical practically. Do not let me misrepresent myself. I, of course, think that the most natural and becoming state of things is for the aristocratical power to be the upholder of the Church; yet I cannot deny the plain fact that in most ages the latter has been based on a popular power. It was so in its rise, in the

[1] [N.B. This was Richard Hurrell Froude.]

days of Ambrose and in the days of Becket, and it will be so again. I am preparing myself for such a state of things, and for this simple reason, *because* the State has deserted us and we cannot help ourselves. You must not think, however, that I myself meant to hasten the downfall of the Monarchy by word or deed. I trust the Whigs and Radicals will reap their proper glory, and we but enjoy their fruit without committing ourselves. On this ground, I am against all measures on our part tending to the separation of Church and State, such as putting the bishops out of Parliament, &c., though, I confess, if the destructives go much further in their persecution of us —*e.g.* if they made Arnold a bishop—I might consider it wrong to maintain that position longer, much as I should wish to do so. *Entre nous*, we have set up Societies over the kingdom in defence of the Church. Certainly this is, you will say, a singular confidential communication, being shared by so many; but the *entre nous* relates to *we*. We do not like our names known. You may say as much as you will to any one about the fact of the Societies and their object. They are already started (in germ) in Oxfordshire, Devonshire, Gloucestershire, Berks, Suffolk and Kent—the object being 'to make the clergy alive to their situation, to enforce the Apostolical Succession, and to defend the Liturgy.' We mean to publish and circulate tracts. I have started with four. We think of a quarterly magazine. I wish I had more money (a respectable wish), but I have squandered mine in Sicily. All this plan of publication will not interfere with Rose's Magazine. Everything as yet promises well—but we are merely talking about it as yet, and have got no rules even. My work is passing through the press. Do you recollect how I was fussed about it this time two years, when I had not written a word? It has now been done the better part of a year and a half! I am somewhat in a stew with all sorts of indefinite fears—yet I hope I have committed no blunders.

We are bringing out a stinging 'Lyra' this September—moderate, well-judging men will be shocked at it. I am pleased to find we are called enthusiasts—pleased, for when did a cause which could be so designated fail of success? I have been writing a series of papers for Rose, called the 'Church of the Fathers,' which commences in October; I began another work besides, which is not known yet. You will be amused at this account about myself, but at present I have nothing else to talk or think about. Everyone is from Oxford, and nothing going on ; and your letter certainly did not contain materials for much comment or development. One would think that a man who uses his eyes and pen but seldom would abound in deep sayings when he put pen to paper. Every sentence ought to be a view.

I am surprisingly well, except that my hair has all deserted me, as is usual after fevers. It seems so astonishing to be in England after so many sad forebodings : *i.e.* I could not reconcile my imagination, only my reason, to the notion I should ever get back. The way seemed so very long. Yet now I am beginning to get very dissatisfied with not having done more in Sicily. It was most unlucky to be detained three weeks in Palermo, when I might have been roving over the island. How glad I shall be to see you as a Fellow. Everything went so against me in Sicily that I made up my mind you were unsuccessful. I am particularly obliged to you for your kind attentions to my Mother, according to my request. You have no notion how useful your Tillemont already is. The 'Church of the Fathers' is in great measure drawn up from it.

REV. J. H. NEWMAN TO REV. R. H. FROUDE.

September 2, 1833.

. . . As to your criticism on the doctrine [N.B. of 'Home Thoughts,' viz. as against the Church of Rome, which I have said was possessed with the local spirit of Pagan Rome] *absisto totus.* I never will cease to maintain that idolatry is wrong.

I have had most favourable answers hitherto, so much so that I have been obliged to print some tracts in self-defence : *i.e.* to save continual letter-writing. I send you two of them. Keble thinks them pompous, which I do not deny. I have not heard from Rickards, but hope to establish something in Suffolk through another. There is a clerical meeting in Berkshire on the 12th, which Cotton and John Marriott attend. The latter has taken it up warmly and will introduce the subject. Palmer, who was to have written to Cotton, is so ill as to have set off to Hastings. I fear Cotton thinks me hot something. Trower calls *me* an ultra and *you* an enthusiast. Marriott hopes through his uncle to set up a Society in Shropshire. Davison has sent his approval to Keble, but is silent as to his adhesion. Ogilvie approves also ! I walked to the consecration of Summers Town Chapel the other day with

Field [now Bishop of Newfoundland]. It is astonishing how we coalesce. He admitted that he feared the ministry, and I that bishops were no good in Parliament, though I would have nothing to do with removing them, in which he acquiesced.

James Mozley is circulating my tracts in Lincolnshire by post. I do hold a great deal may be made of this mode of circulation in the way of *agitation*. We hope to have a meeting here of Golightly, Blencowe, Marriott, and Mozley in a fortnight. Bramston was converted, *i.e.* is *at present*, by Keble's sermon. I have written to Rogers.

REV. JOHN KEBLE TO REV. J. H. NEWMAN.

September 1833.

I send you such as I can [his first tract "Adherence,"[1] &c.]: *rudis indigestaque moles* it has proved; but if it, or any part of it, is worthy of our friend King's press, you are hereby authorised to do what you will with it. The more I study your papers [the first tracts] the better I like them. I see Rose has taken Durham. Of course the Magazine must change hands.

I quite forgot when I saw you to speak to you about your kind thought of mentioning me at the beginning of your book [the 'Arians']. I *really* and *truly* think it had better not be done, as far as it goes, in respect of *the cause*. We have seen how ridiculous the Archbishop of Dublin and his set have become by their continual puffing and repuffing each other. It concerns us to avoid the *appearance* of anything of the sort. If we were not acting in a kind of set together, the objection would not be near so strong. Pray consider, and I really think you will agree with me. At all events, I thank you with all my heart, and hope by degrees to become more worthy of the intended compliment.

REV. S. RICKARDS TO REV. J. H. NEWMAN.

September 6, 1833.

It vexes me I have not been able to tell you how cordially I enter into the measure you propose for maintaining our proper position as Christ's ministers in these evil days. Everything ought to be done by us that can be done to show that

[1] 'Adherence to Apostolical Succession the safest course.'

we at least are in earnest when all around us seem in sport. The point to be maintained as to the Liturgy seems to me to be to admit of no changes, but such only as are made and sanctioned by the authority of the Church; they who are no Christians themselves must not legislate on matters of religion for those who are Christians. I would not stand forth and protest against alterations which were directed and approved by what might properly be called the *same* authority by which the same things have been done before among us.

As far as my opinion goes for anything, I disapprove of the concealment of names. 'I am small and of no reputation' is an old plea for shrinking, which the best servants of God have never liked, and I like it not any better than they did. The sooner the tracts are begun the better. Be so good as to advance a subscription for me, according as you may see fit

REV. J. H. NEWMAN TO R. F. WILSON, ESQ.

Oriel College: September 8, 1833.

... Your fears about my health are, I trust, as groundless as they are kind. True it is I had a fearful illness in Sicily and escaped as by fire, yet I have quite recovered, except weakness in my joints, and am now better than I have ever been these seventeen years—that is, through my whole Oxford life. Whether the blessing will last is another question, but there can be no harm in boasting of what is a fact, and what is a present, though it may be a transient, good. ...

If we look into history, whether in the age of the Apostles, St. Ambrose's, or St. Becket's, still the people were the fulcrum of the Church's power. So they may be again. Therefore, expect on your return to England to see us all cautious, long-headed, unfeeling, unflinching Radicals. We have set up Church Societies all over the kingdom, or at least mean to do so. Already the seeds of revolution are planted in Oxfordshire, Berkshire, Devonshire, Gloucestershire, Kent, and Suffolk. Our object is to maintain the doctrine of the Apostolical Succession and save the Liturgy from illegal alterations. Hitherto we have had great success; Rose and Davison, to say nothing of others, approve of our plan. And we have begun to print tracts. We intend to have nothing to do with party politics; *Tros Tyriusque mihi,* &c., and self-preservation, as Polignac said, is the first law of nature. ... If we succeed, you will see the consequences ; if we fail, we shall at least have the satisfaction of transmitting the sparks of truth, still living, to a happier age. It is no slight thing to be made the instrument of handing down the principles of Laud till the time comes. . . .

I was three weeks laid up at Castro Juan (the ancient Enna) without any proper advice. . . . I certainly roughed it ; not a bad seasoning for the life of a pilgrim at home, if times become bad, except that I was treated with vast respect as being an Englishman. The people are most kind ; the little experience I have had of them makes me quite love them. I would I could recompense the attentions I had as I lay by the roadside in a miserable hut. Those I received at Castro Juan I can acknowledge now I have got safe back ; but the poor peasants are quite unknown to me by name, though I shall try to get my frends at Castro Juan to find them out. Sicily is a superb country. It is not right to put life against any stake, but, as to my pain and anxiety, it is more than recompensed by what I saw there.

REV. R. H. FROUDE TO REV. J. H. NEWMAN.

September 8, 1833.

. . . I like your tracts much. My father thinks the generality of parsons here would not enter into the ἦθος of ' I am a Presbyter,' &c. I am astonished to see how much impression the march of events has made upon him. He says they [the Evangelicals] would all be pulling different ways with mare's-nests of their own. The High Church, he thinks, generally speaking, too apathetic to be worked upon. If we could get any good addresses to the poor written . . . he says he is sure he could circulate them among all the clergy of his archdeaconry, and that he could get the Archdeacon of Exeter to do the same. He has to preach a sermon for the National Schools at the Cathedral, and intends to speak in very plain terms about the apostasy, moral as well as religious, of the higher orders ; and the necessity of all serious people stirring themselves, especially with a view to instructing the lower orders in true Church principles, for that we must look to them, the poor, for our support.

What would be the effect of Phillpotts [Bishop of Exeter] bringing forward the *Præmunire* ? My father thinks it might take.

Why should not the Archbishop have Ignatius and Clement printed, and recommend the clergy to distribute? Ogilvie ought to be touched up about this. Without high authority the country clergy will never give a thought to the Fathers. They have got it in their heads that such matters are either out of date or Romish.

REV. J. H. NEWMAN TO REV. R. H. FROUDE.

September 9, 1833.

Our Conciliabulum [Golightly, Marriott, &c.] meets next Monday, and I want, if possible, the above ['An Association' and 'Considering, &c.'] printed by that time. No. 2 ['Considering that the only way, &c.'] is Keble's. No. 1 ['An Association has been formed by the friends of the Church, &c.'] mine. Keble has not seen No. 1. Criticise the whole very accurately in matter and style, and send it back by return of post.

You see I call the Association 'Friends of the Church,' *i.e.* by implication. Next about the Committee [Keble, Palmer, Newman, Froude, Williams (I.), Perceval, Prevost, Blencowe, Marriott, T. Keble]. As the meetings must be in Oxford, it is no matter what names we put in, yet I can find none but Oriel men. Nay I, without leave, printed Williams' name. Copeland I cannot put down without leave. Can you get any Devonshire names on the Committee? Keble has made Palmer and me secretaries. I am going to London in October, and hope to glean there; a most intimate friend of mine, a layman [N.B.—J. W. Bowden], has taken it up warmly, *i.e.* as far as the plan has been laid before him. I shall have a try at Benson [Preacher of Lincoln's Inn, Master of the Temple] and Hull [a barrister, W. W. Hull]. Rickards has written a most warm answer and begs to subscribe. A neighbour of his, an old contemporary of mine at Trinity, has done the same. . . . You must at once write a tract on 'the project of shortening Services.' Your knowledge of the breviary, &c., points you out as the man. Give a succinct view of the origin of our Services.

Keble is writing two tracts. I have written to Perceval for another. I have written four. I have proposed to Rickards to digest the opinions of Sanderson, Hammond, &c., on the Apostolical Succession.

I think I told you Rose joins; and, if we turn out well,

will get us high patronage. I am very anxious lest we should *enlarge our basis.* Not to get in bishops must we make any material alteration.

REV. R. H. FROUDE TO REV. J. H. NEWMAN.

September 15, 1833.

When I got home last night I found your letter. I should have had little to offer in the way of criticism. . . . Why don't you get Rose and Ogilvie to put their names on the Committee ? M. H. ought to be on, if it was only to give the thing an unintellectual character. We must not enlarge our basis even for Bishops. In short, I object to anyone whose ear we have not secured, so that our opinions may be the creed of the Association. I am quite surprised to find how easily I get on with people, now that one throws overboard the points about which prejudices are encrusted.

As to any conflict between ——'s views and ours, I apprehend no evil from him, however painful it may be. Anything that sets people agog is on our side. I deprecate a calm.

REV. J. H. NEWMAN TO REV. R. H. FROUDE.

September 18, 1833.

I doubt whether you will like the way we are going on. I myself am disappointed, and wish for your presence here. I will say a few words.

A difficulty has arisen about tracts. Your father's criticism on mine has been verified in the case of Cotton, who is offended at it. Then came the question : 'Do the tracts commit the Society ? ' No ; mine, for example, are designedly in the first person. Then Palmer says, ' No tracts must be issued without the Committee's approval, and we must have on it *men of different tastes, &c.* (always supposing they adopt our principles), that we may hit on the right thing for a sickly clergy, for such is the present generation.'

At present, then, I have agreed with Palmer on the following basis, which, however, perhaps will be modified : ' That the Society should put into its Committee men of the highest rank it can get ; that till it is more settled in its shape it should publish no tracts at all ; but that any individuals in it (of course) may publish what tracts they please.'

If, on the other hand, the higher powers will not join us,

we then may without immodesty take a bolder course. I am not satisfied with all this myself, but I do not see what else I could have done. I cannot but hope, on the whole, that this Society will be the first step towards bringing men of like minds together. We must not be impatient. Never mind, though our creed is not stamped on the body; we may single out from them those who agree with us, and form a second society out of the first.

I have many misgivings about the fate of 'Newman on Arianism.' The adventure with Cotton makes me think I shall offend and hurt men I would fain be straight with. Yet what can one do? Men are made of glass: the sooner we break them and get it over the better.

Is not Rose bold in this last number? I quote him against Palmer, when the latter preaches about moderation, since he has an especial notion of Rose's prudence.

Your father's question is quite out of my depth at present. Of late months the idea has broken on me, as it did a little before on yourself, that the Church is essentially a popular institution, and the past English union of it with the State has been a happy anomaly. It is odd this should be a discovery; for Gibbon, to go no further, is ever saying so. The Fathers seem to keep up as a constant principle the community of goods mentioned in the Acts—that is, a community *as far as food and raiment*, &c., go; the Church being the mere dispenser.

We have had our conference here—Golightly, Marriott, Stevens, Copeland, and Palmer—and it has been satisfactory. . . . Palmer is about to make a journey to Hook and others, and has sounded the Evangelicals of Liverpool.

REV. J. H. NEWMAN TO J. W. BOWDEN, ESQ.

Oriel College: September 23, 1833.

Our plan of a Society goes on hitherto very well, though of course we hear of objections; nor do I suppose any project was ever started against which real objections were not producible. As to your question of laymen belonging to it, we hail any co-operation as the greatest benefit to it. I send you one or two tracts which are not authorised by the Committee, but are written by individuals belonging to it. Indeed, our views are quite undecided as yet in what way, and with what degree of responsibility in the Society, we shall circulate them. Davison, Miller, Rose, Ogilvie, the Archbishop's Chaplain, Keble, Rickards, and others are more or less connected with us ; all have given their approbation and names at least.

In the following letter Mr. Newman's publisher writes of the difficulty of getting tracts, as such, into circulation. This, as will be seen, was a lasting difficulty.

MR. TURRILL TO REV. J. H. NEWMAN.

October 2, 1833.

. . . It is very difficult to obtain an extensive circulation for tracts without incurring a very considerable outlay, and, from the moderate price at which they must be sold, they rarely repay the capital invested. The best plan to get them into circulation would be to bring them out as weekly numbers, under some such title as 'The Churchman's Weekly Tract Magazine.'

REV. J. H. NEWMAN TO F. ROGERS, ESQ.

Oriel College: October 2, 1833.

. . . We are getting on famously with our Society, and are so prudent and temperate that Froude writes up to me we have made a hash of it, which I account to be praise. As to Gladstone, perhaps it would be wrong to ask a young man so to commit himself, but make a fuss we will sooner or later. . . .

My work is nearly finished, and I begin to get disgusted with it. I was out of sorts with it on taking it up on my return.

REV. ISAAC WILLIAMS TO REV. J. H. NEWMAN.

October 2, 1833.

I have been considering the subject of the weekly Sacrament, as you desired, and thinking over what objections there might be to it. . . . Likewise I want to say a word about our Society [N.B.—Association, which was to have accompanied the tracts]. We thought that it would be very desirable, as you say, to have a meeting, and some test, as soon as we conveniently could ; and that in the meantime, very desirable as it would be to set the matter before people, and to win their favourable hearing and concurrence, yet to be slow in increasing the number of our Society, as we very likely might have the adherence of some who would not like the tests we might think requisite. For instance, one, which I suppose would be most necessary, a concurrence with all the doctrines implied in our Prayer Book, in the most plain and obvious meaning. A subscription again, would, I suppose, be a great test of people's real heartiness in the cause. . . . Baptismal Regeneration seems a doctrine of such great importance, and the many practical consequences arising from the different ways of considering it so great, that it seems to me that in the Evangelicals we may find great impediments to that union which we must so much desire. But, however, hard times may do much ; and, *nil desperandum.*

I am very sorry to hear that you give but a poor account of Froude. If you hear of a few acres of land to be let at Littlemore, which would do to let out in small portions to the poor, I should be glad to rent them for that purpose.

REV. WM. WILSON,[1] WALTHAMSTOW, TO REV. J. H. NEWMAN.

October 3, 1833.

With the general purport of your letter I entirely agree. It must be beneficial that the attention of members of our national institutions should be more directly called to the authority on which the Church is established, and that combined effort should be made to preserve in its present form our truly scriptural Liturgy.

Whether the existence of an Association for the ends which you propose be desirable, without further information, I am not able to judge.

With those who sincerely love our Church I should be most happy to unite in resisting any and every alteration in the doctrinal and devotional parts of her Services. If we err, it is not in these respects, but in the want of discipline into which our National Establishment has fallen. The people have ceased to feel the value of our institutions, and therefore estimate no longer their importance. Will your Association do anything towards the renewal of a more efficient discipline ?

Pardon me, my dear sir, if I entreat you not to identify me in any exclusive manner with the class usually called Evan-

[1] [Mild Evangelical.—J. H. N.]

gelical. The duties of a parish containing nearly 5,000 souls leave me little time and less inclination to seek any association beyond its limits. I do indeed think that class to which I refer have been much and undeservedly misconceived. If a time of trial were to come on the Church of England, the last who would desert Episcopal order, and the last who would be faithless to her truly scriptural ordinances, would be the Evangelical clergy. But, being no Calvinist, I differ from those among them whose sentiments are extreme; and I think that those who are generally termed the High Church, on the other hand, err in their interpretation of the doctrine of the Sacraments, and therefore in their use of those effectual ordinances.

S. F. WOOD, ESQ., TO REV. J. H. NEWMAN.

Thursday, October 16, 1833.

I did write to you from Leghorn immediately after the Oriel election. I was sure, for many reasons, you would be rapturously pleased with the old classic countries; and I think your age (though it may seem a paradox) is the true one for going abroad. Many lose much pleasure by going too young.

I would willingly pass over what you say on the subject of the Church, because I think it almost presumptuous in me to deliver an opinion on the subject. But, as one is driven, as it were, by an external force, to think and judge about it, I will just say that I believe I differ with you a good deal as to the need the English Church has to be reformed; and also that I think it neither has the power nor the inclination to reform itself. And, therefore, though the spirit with which *some* men press on legislative interference is a very wicked one, I shall still rejoice that a furnace has been prepared, even in part by an enemy's hand, in passing through which the dross may be purged off. So far as the Society you allude to is a means of organising the friends of the Church to repel the organised assaults of her adversaries, I rejoice at its existence; so far as it may obstruct the plans of her friends, either from principle or custom, I am grieved at it.

In October 1833 Mr. Newman paid a six days' visit to Mr. Bowden. In the following letter his old friend remarks how soon his presence became a customary thing—an indirect testimony to the charm and ease of his society.

J. W. BOWDEN, ESQ., TO REV. J. H. NEWMAN.

October, 1833

It is absurd, considering the very short time you were with us, what hold the idea took of both our minds that your presence with us was a settled customary thing. Yesterday [Sunday], for instance, it seemed quite odd to go to Mr. B.'s chapel in the morning, or to Belgrave [Chapel] in the evening without you. And we felt both some difficulty in admitting the undeniable fact that you only passed one Sunday with us. [N.B.—This passage is so characteristic of dear B.'s feelings towards me.—J. H. N.]

REV. J. H. NEWMAN TO J. W. BOWDEN, ESQ.

Oriel: October 18, 1833.

Your tract on the Church has been revised by Keble and myself—that is, we have altered half a dozen words. It meets with great approbation, and we hail you as fellow-labourer with great satisfaction, especially as being a layman. . . . Rose has sent me two splendid letters since I saw you. He goes all our lengths. We talk of getting up at once a Declaration or address from the clergy to the Archbishop, against material alterations in doctrine and discipline, and against extra-ecclesiastical interference; at the same time granting improvements, if such, and the completion of our system. We have also instituted a bureau for newspaper influence. We have about twelve country newspapers already in our eye, which are open to our friends, and we hope to introduce tracts into them by their means. If you can do anything for us in the North in this way, it will be a service. Our papers are to appear in the 'British Magazine,' with a notice that all who please may reprint them cheaply, or have them from us. I have had a most interesting letter from Mr. Snow, who entirely agrees with the tracts, and gives some useful hints. We know Mr. Randolph only by name, but if you find him apt, we will find means to enter into correspondence with him : indeed, you can introduce us.

REV. J. H. NEWMAN TO REV. J. KEBLE.

Between August 5 *and November* 5, 1833.

. . . I had a swarm of intruders last week, Mozley, Golightly, Blencowe, Marriott and Stevens. We are getting on very well, but are anxious on the subject of tracts. Those hitherto published are not yet acknowledged as 'the Society's.' For myself, I doubt whether the Society ought to pledge itself to more than a *general* approval of the principles of *any* tracts. One thing strikes one reader, another another. If you correct them according to the wishes of a board, you will have nothing but tame, dull compositions, which will take no one; there will be no rhetoric in them, which is necessarily πρός τινα. But it is a subject of much difficulty. However, in giving away either yours or mine you must be cautious (please) not to involve the Committee. I say this especially about my own, because Cotton has signified his dissatisfaction with it. Not that I agree with his criticisms, but still let us make up our minds before we proceed. Palmer is gone off to exert himself in Staffordshire, &c.

I fear that Calvert, whom you may recollect here, and a physician now, has pronounced about Froude (not *to* him) a judgment so unfavourable that I cannot bear to dwell upon it, or to tell it. Pray exert your influence to get him sent to the West Indies. I know he has a great prejudice against it, but still what other place is hopeful? They say Madeira is not. He might take a cargo of books with him. N.B.—Could you not manage to send Isaac Williams too?

REV. JOHN KEBLE TO REV. J. H. NEWMAN.

October, 1833.

I like the new [Suggestions?] paper very well, and do not remember enough of my own to say whether I should have liked it better. The objection to this is, its being somewhat vague : nobody, I think, will know what it drives at without first inquiring the names of those who put it round. But on that very account I presume it is thought likely to attract signatures. At any rate, I am quite ready to sign it.

'The successive admission of Dissenters and Roman Catholics to the power of legislating for the Church' is mentioned in a way not unlikely to exclude people who, like Davison, are Churchmen on principle, yet concurred in these measures. And on the first of the three 'objects' I should like the word 'Prerogatives' to be somewhere introduced, as well as the words 'Order' and 'Succession.' Also, our friend [Palmer] must correct the Irishism on 'the objects of the

Association *shall* be,' &c., unless he wishes everybody to detect him. . . .

I am grieved to the heart with your account of him [Froude], and shall try all I can to send him off—perhaps Brazil might suit him.

[Froude came to Oxford October 5, and remained there till October 26, 1833. During these weeks the following letters passed between me and Palmer.—J. H. N.]

REV. J. H. NEWMAN TO REV. WM. PALMER.

October 24, 1833.

I put down my thoughts hastily for you, intending them rather as notes to remind you of what I mean than anything else.

I do not like the notion of forming a Society, or Association even, for many reasons.

First, there is an awkwardness in doing so without the sanction of the Bishops ; and, though it is enough for satisfying our conscience to know that really they are privately with us, yet the world cannot know this, and it goes out to the world as a bad precedent, and an inconsistency in the case of those who have (rightly) made the absence of episcopal sanction an objection to certain Societies hitherto.

2. Again, a Society is a formidable undertaking to start with. Many of us are inexperienced and have to learn how to conduct an important and difficult scheme. It is a dangerous thing to set up a large system at once. The London University started with an apparatus of professors, which first ensured ridicule, and then disappointment. Besides, a profession of something great excites jealousy and suspicion. There would be the notion abroad that we were taking too much upon ourselves, whereas no one can complain of *individual* exertion.

3. And further, if we profess an Association, we are under the necessity of bringing into the government of it men who do not agree with us. We feel our opinions are true ; we are sure that, few though we be, we shall be able to propagate them by the force of the truth ; we have no need, rather we cannot afford, to dilute them, which must be the consequence of joining those who do not go as far as we do. I am not denying (far from it) the inexpediency of obtruding at once

all we really hold ; but I consider it a loss of time and trouble to *unite* with those who differ with us—that is, with any who are not disposed to aim at obtaining the liberty of the Church and the restoration of discipline. And if any men think these objects chimerical, then I see no reason for stirring myself at all.

4. Moreover, there is a growing feeling that Societies are bad things, which is in my mind an objection to any such project, both as being a true feeling and as being held as true. The dissensions in the Bible Society and the present state of the Christian Knowledge Society make people feel that they are instruments of evil much more than of good ; or at least of a diluted meagre sort of good.

True it is, the Church is a Society, but it is a Society with a *head* ; in all other societies the real movers are secret and irresponsible ; and thus second-rate men with low views get the upper hand. Individuals who are seen and heard, who act and suffer, are the instruments of Providence in all great successes.

Again, there is an awkwardness in tracts coming from a Society. It is an assumption of teaching. And, further, they must in consequence be weighed and carefully corrected : and thus they become cold and formal, and (so to say) *im*personal. An address with much in it which others question, yet coming from an individual mind, has a life about it which is sure to make an impression.

Lastly, to form an Association, one ought to have a very definite object. Practical men shrink from engaging without knowing *what* is to be done ; but 'to defend the doctrine and discipline of the Church' is very vague ; vague for this reason —that we are on the defensive, and not knowing *when* and *how* we shall be attacked, we cannot say *how* we are to act.

For such reasons as these I would advocate a less formal scheme : not that I am not eventually for an Association, but not till the Bishop puts himself at our head in this or that diocese. I would merely exert myself in my own place, and with my own immediate friends, in declaring and teaching the half-forgotten truths of Church union and order to all within my influence. I address friends in other dioceses in turn, and urge them to do the same—in Keble's words, wishing them and ourselves to say to each other, 'We pledge ourselves to each other, reserving our canonical obedience.' We merely encourage and instruct each other : and, being able to say that others are doing elsewhere the same as we are, we have an excuse for being more bold : the circumstance that we have pledged ourselves allows us to introduce ourselves to strangers, &c. &c. We print and circulate tracts ; our friends in other dioceses read them, approve, and partly disapprove. We say, 'Make what use you will of them, and alter them in your own way : reprint them and circulate them in turn, and send us yours to do the same with.' We try to get a footing in our county newspapers ; and recommend our friends elsewhere to do the same. Thus gradually certain centres, in correspondence with each other and of a proselytising nature in their respective neighbourhoods, are formed.

But you will say that we are moving too slow, while external events are pressing upon us. 'Parliament will meet and settle matters while we are but forming.' Well then, here is a measure which will at once meet the danger and hasten the formation of the Association. Let us, for example, draw up a declaration or address to the Archbishop, an expression of our attachment to the doctrine and discipline of the Church. Rose recommends it, and it is evidently natural and seasonable. Let each of our centres, *i.e.* corresponding members, exert himself to get signatures in his own neighbourhood. This very attempt will lay the rudiments of a number of associations ; channels of communication will be opened with a most definite object ; and whether the attempt succeeds or not, the groundwork of a second future attempt will be laid, and this without any display of our real object, *i.e.* the organisation of the clergy. As this process is repeated again and again, being called for naturally by external events, an Association will gradually develop itself ; and when, in the course of events, the Bishop in this or that place puts himself at its head, then at length it may be avowed. Thus it will be formed as a habit by energising.

Another advantage of this plan is, that we need not formally adjust our opinions with each other. We have the same general views and aims, but one diocese may be more High Church than another, may modify the tracts of another, &c.

Do not suppose I am blind to the appearance of fancifulness and theorising in the above sketch ; but such must all anticipation of the future be. Doubtless many things would modify the plan in detail, when we came to put it in practice ; but its great advantage is, that it *may* be modified ; whereas, if we set up any Association at once, we commit ourselves.

You will see I am for no committee, secretaries, &c., but merely for certain individuals in every part of the country in correspondence with each other, instructing and encouraging each other, and acting with all their might in their respective circles.

Ever yours,
J. H. N.

[This letter seems to have determined Palmer to commence the address to the Archbishop, which was so successful. I say that it determined him; for, though the notion of an address was mooted, I think, at a Hadleigh meeting or soon after (*vide* Keble's letter of August 8, 1833), yet I don't find anything done towards it till the very day of the above letter of mine, viz. on October 24, when Palmer went to town to prosecute the matter.

It is remarkable that the day of his starting for London, October 24, is the very day that my long letter above is dated; also that I have the very copy I sent to him, with a notice on it in pencil. This Palmer had, and gave me back.

I infer that I sent up the letter to him to Beaumont Street in the forenoon; that he came down to me [and Froude] with it in his hand, and left it with me after we had a talk, and according to his prompt habits, started at once for London to carry out the plan of address, which we had agreed upon. P.S.—All this is confirmed by the fragmentary diary.

Another explanation is that my letter was a formal letter, the result of former conversations, which he was to take in his hand and show people in London; but it was far too confidential for that. And he does not allude to it in the following letter.—J. H. N.]

REV. W. PALMER TO REV. J. H. NEWMAN.

Bath Hotel, Piccadilly: Sunday Evening, October 27, 1833.

I have been so busy since I came, that I have not had a moment to myself until now. I write this to beg that you will, *without any delay*, send up whatever has been drawn up [Qy. by me and Froude] in the shape of an address to the Archbishop. Everyone approves of such an address, and it seems to be thought that it would strengthen the right cause very much.

I have seen Archdeacons Watson and Bayley (with whom

I have been in continual communication), Mr. Norris and Mr. Hook; and on Tuesday I am to dine with Mr. Norris at Hackney, where there will be men of the right sort collected from various parts, and I wish I had the address to submit to their inspection. [Extract from my Private Journal:—'Oct. 28, wrote sketch of address to Archbishop and sent to Palmer with 500 "Suggestions."'] Archdeacon Bayley is most active in the cause, and has been circulating the prospectus ['Suggestions'?] largely. Mr. Norris also has been writing to his friends in all parts. He is about writing to Archdeacon Froude, and has written to Archdeacon Oldershaw of Norfolk. I had a letter from Mr. Coddrington containing an accession of force from Cambridge, including Henry J. Rose, Mr. Isaacson, Mr. Wilson-Evans, Mr. Temple Chevallier and others; and they are going to work. In short, we are getting on at a tremendous rate. I wish you would send up 400 or 500 copies of the 'Suggestions' (or more, if you can spare them), by the same conveyance as the address comes by. Perceval wants them, so does Mr. Norris, and the Cambridge men, and Archdeacon Bayley.

I should tell you that this latter clergyman is a most leading man among the Church party, and in the closest communication with the highest dignitaries; and will take care that we do not give offence where we mean to support, and to express our sentiments of respect and approbation.

As far as I can see, it does not seem to be considered at all necessary that there should be at present anything of a more formal organisation, but probably by-and-bye we must have one committee in Oxford and another in London.

I am sorry to find the London clergy are generally quite of the Liberal school, and all under the Bishop of London. But the country clergy, I hope, are sound.

I wish you, and Froude, and Keble could have heard the Bishop of Limerick [Jebb] and Mr. Forster yesterday, talking of Church matters; it would have done your heart good.

Archdeacon Bayley is at the head of a clerical association in Hampshire, which he engages to aid us; and he has requested me to go to their meeting on November 21 to establish a communication.

Mr. Hook will come over to Oxford towards the end of the term, I believe.

I shall do what I can to get some good tracts written at Cambridge, or by Perceval and Hook.

I must now make an end ; and really, my dear Newman, I am so hurried, and such a number of things have occurred, that I have had no time for arranging my thoughts, but have just written what occurred to me. You must therefore make allowance for this.

Will you, then, send up, without any delay, the address and the 'Suggestions,' and if you can spare some tracts, especially that on the Liturgy, so much the better ?—Ever yours, &c.

P.S.—I intend to be in Oxford Wednesday afternoon. Will you send 100 prospectuses by the bearer, and the tracts ? If you can spare any more of the former it would be a good opportunity, as I shall probably see Norris, &c. Will you also make a list of *your friends and correspondents* in different counties as they occur to you, and as *full as you can*, that I may have my credentials complete, and be able to show our strength to our friends in London ?

REV. J. H. NEWMAN TO J. W. BOWDEN, ESQ.

October 31, 1833.

As to the depôt in town, I can scarcely do anything till Palmer returns. You do not know the plague that attends having to *consult* many persons, yet having all the execution upon myself. I have to write, correct press, distribute all the tracts. No one can help me : first, because one is apt to think no one can do so well as oneself ; secondly, because my friends are scattered, Palmer in town, Froude[1] gone to Barbadoes, Rogers's eyes bad, &c. Then, besides, I am Dean, and have a parish. As the man says in 'Ivanhoe,' 'a man cannot do more than he can.' I can only say I am busy from morning till night.

You shall hear more about our *centres* of communication, that is, living depôts, soon. *They* will print and reprint in their neighbourhoods. I wish H. Wilberforce could have called. I know he wished it particularly. But my friends are so stupidly bashful. Palmer is another of the same kind.

REV. R. H. FROUDE TO REV. J. H. NEWMAN.

October, 1833.

Tony Buller was here [Dartington] yesterday. He is a capital fellow, and is anxious to assist us with trouble and

[1] Froude had left *Oxford* for Barbadoes, but was still in England. He did not sail till the end of November.

money in any way he can. I told him it was better not to say anything about money till we had given people a longer trial of us.

REV. T. MOZLEY TO REV. J. H. NEWMAN.

November 1, 1833.

I and my brother James have had a long talk this morning with Smith and Bailey [of Edgcott]. Bailey has consented to send a circular to all the clergy within eight or nine miles, requesting them to meet at his house to consider the address to the Archbishop. He is anxious that you should come. He also wishes much for Lancaster's sanction and attendance. It occurs to me that you may feel some unpleasantness at coming over, from being the writer of this address, but Palmer or anyone would do as well. . . . It might be as well, perhaps, to send copies [of the address] round in the circular. Of course you will refer this to C. Marriott, who, I understand, is Registrar, &c., to the Society.

Some of the tracts I have given to Mrs. H., my new novel-writing neighbour, who has taken them to London, where they are to be exhibited in some literary soirées. . . .

The difficulty of getting the tracts into circulation—of selling them to those who wanted to buy them—was a standing one so long as they kept their original leaflet bulk, so great in fact as to make it hard to account for the noise they at once made. But the first idea was to distrubute; to sell became an after necessary consideration. Mr. Bowden is the first friend and ally to press this difficulty on the writers. In the 'Chronological Notes' there is this entry : 'November 1, 1833.—Sent parcels to Rickards, R. Wilberforce, Golightly, and Pope. [This is how we began scattering the tracts.]'

A few days after Mr. Bowden writes :—

J. W. BOWDEN, ESQ., TO REV. J. H. NEWMAN.

November 4, 1833.

I long to get your things in a distributable shape ; which in London is only to be done by selling them. Any tracts, of which you may send me a few copies, in a vendible shape, and with a *local reference*, I will push.

Those to whom I have shown the 'Suggestions' say, 'But where are the names? Who are they? Where are they?' For even the word Oxford does not appear thereon. For aught the 'Suggestions' say, the founders of the scheme might belong to the *operative* classes of Society, and their head-quarters might be in some alley in London. The year, too, should be put; a reader might, if he found a dirty copy, suppose the whole scheme ten years old.

REV. JOHN KEBLE TO REV. J. H. NEWMAN.

November 5, 1833.

With Mount I had a long conference; he willingly consented to be the agent for Bath; but as yet I have heard no more of him. I have had two long and sensible letters from Dr. Spry, who will be glad of some sets of the papers [tracts] . . . I conclude I am right in telling people that we are not so much forming one grand Association as little associations in various parts. Spry says he shall get Molesworth, Davison's old enemy, to act at Canterbury, and doubts not he will be a vigorous agent. But he (Spry) hopes you will (1) look very much to the position and probable wish of the Bishops; (2) admit and encourage the Laity as much as possible; (3) keep in view the formation of a grand Society out of the little ones.

Also I humbly suggest, that there is no need to let *quite* everybody make *quite* every alteration they please in our papers; and if any more of mine are printed, I shall bargain for the following words being added to the licence at the top: viz. 'it being, of course, understood that such alterations be not inconsistent with the general spirit and design of the papers.'

Now as to my memorial paper; I was rather daunted about it by Froude's criticisms, which I fancied convicted me of bad logic in it; so I have not yet revised it, but will try as soon as I have finished the Latin. However, I have good hope that John Miller is about it. I went down with Froude as far as Bath, put him into the coach in good plight on Tuesday morning last (Oct. 29) and proceeded to call on Mount.

Miller is full of 'cholers and tremplings of mind,' and seems to think he has committed himself farther than he thought. There is a sad hitch with him about the Athanasian Creed [the Anathema], but I will bring you his letters, and

I think you will say that such doubts as his are more profitable than a thousand unreflecting adherences.

Edward James, Prebendary of Winton, desires to have some papers sent to him, and says, 'Enroll me.' I will explain to him what 'enroll' means. If you have any new light to throw on the meaning of the word you will let me know. There is a very nice person near here [Fairford], Barton by name, of B. N. C., who called on me the other day and professed himself a hearty convert. He has sent to Ottley.

When I come up I hope to bring you some prose and verse, but you see I am growing old and stupid.

I want very much tracts for the poor now. The Layman's address is excellent, but hardly plain enough. It will do capitally for the middle classes.

I see by the 'British Magazine' that the clergy of Dromore and Carlow are making a stand, and calling on us for aid. Don't let us lose sight of that.

Rev. J. H. Newman to Rev. J. Keble.

Oriel: November, 1833.

I have heard so much criticism on my tracts that it is comfortable to have heard one or two things of a more pleasant kind: first, what you and Spry say; next, that the Bishop of London has asked to see them. The principal thing I fear is their being neglected, but if Bishops prick up their ears and D.D.s and Poetry Professors encourage, I care for nothing more. As to my anxiety for many tracts, it is simply on this account, because there are various classes to be addressed. We have scarcely any for the poor, and not many for the clergy, or (again) the middle classes.

Besides, one *improves by writing* : one hits off the thing better, and, at least, one offers a selection of styles to the reader, and tastes differ, so that this is no slight advantage. I have heard almost all of them abused, and again praised, by different readers. At the same time I fully agree with [John] Miller that we should not keep driving on one or two subjects, and that we should not press them on men. My notion was, when once we had done enough to make them known, to send merely one or two of each fresh tract to friends as a specimen and to refer them to Turrill's (where we have opened a depôt) for them.

It must be recollected, too, that it is quite necessary to go more into detail; our present tracts are vague and general, and too much in the way of *hints*, as you yourself observed. We have heard, on good authority from London, that the Marriage Service is to be altered to please the Dissenters. What this means I know not, but it is quite certain *you* must forthwith write a tract on that service. Do pray set Miller on some of his subjects. You must recollect there is another benefit of tracts; it engages staunch men in active warfare. Miller will kindle when he begins to write; and only think what authority it will bring to the cause and to the tracts to have his marked co-operation. Could you not set Spry to write? Finally, who knows we may have time to work six weeks hence? Let us write while we can.

Spry's letter is extremely valuable and encouraging. I am glad he approves of our doings as a whole. However, we must let no one control us. *You* shall be censor of the tracts, by your office as a University judge of compositions, prose as well as verse. But we will obey no one else, however thankful for suggestions from anyone. I will take down Mount's suggestions.

I have heard from dear Froude, who is certainly downcast. He left home to-day, and was to be with Canon Rogers till Saturday, when the packet sails. He is full of disappointment at the address; but then, say I, it effects two things—first, it addresses the Archbishop as the head of the anti-innovators, and it addresses him and not the King or Parliament; which has a doctrinal meaning and is a good precedent. However, Froude calls me names, and bids me stir you up into a fury if I can.

REV. J. H. NEWMAN TO REV. R. H. FROUDE.

November 7, 1833.

I miss you very much. You will be glad to hear that your articles on the *Præmunire*, &c., have done much good. Palmer brought word from town that you had effectually stopped the probability of certain promotions; in fact, that the Archbishop would be *afraid* to consecrate obnoxious persons; and at least you have given him a good pretence for refusing, as it was *known* that there was a party in the Church, 'and they not weak in talent,' &c. [Rose's words, in the 'British Magazine'], who would go all lengths rather than submit to State tyranny. Palmer is also delighted with your Hooker article in the last No.

The tracts are spreading and the Evangelicals of Cheltenham join us, but deprecate them. I received this morning 50*l*. from Thornton's brother [was not this ultimately paid back?].[1] Golightly has promised 50*l*. [he gave it and had it back ultimately], and 10*l*.'s, beginning with Rogers, are flowing in. Both Greswells (C. C. C. and Worcester) have joined. Pusey[2] circulates tracts, Harrison exerts influence. The Provost listens! Mr. Jeune of Pembroke joins heartily; he has been converted by Jeremy Taylor on Episcopacy. The Archdeacon [Clarke] joins; and recognises a plan of his own in our notion of an address to the Archbishop. You know Archdeacon Sheepshanks has joined? They say the Bishop [Blomfield] of London has a snug plan for reforming the Liturgy in preparation. I have left off being anti-aristocratical. I do not feel the time has come, in spite of your being right about the *Præmunire*. H. Wilberforce has been back here and working most vigorously; wherever he is he talks and distributes tracts with all his might.

November 8.—The address is done to-day. Such a composition I never saw; we have re-written each other's (London and Oxford) three times; but now we have made a few alterations *nostro periculo* and have printed it off. The word 'Bishops' at the close has been put in here and taken out there five times *sub silentio*. Dr. Spry has been the best London artist.

'We the undersigned,' &c.

'At a time when events,' &c.

'And while we most earnestly deprecate, &c. . . . Your Grace may rely upon the cheerful co-operation and dutiful support of the clergy in carrying into effect any measures that may tend to revive the discipline of ancient times; to strengthen the connexion between the bishops, clergy and people, and to promote the purity, the efficiency and the unity of the Church.' Southey is circulating the 'Suggestions' in Cumberland. Mr. Charnock, at Ripon, is reprinting our tracts. We are opening a depôt at Turrill's.

[1] Finally it was given to Cholderton Church, when in the course of building.
[2] First mention of Pusey's name in association with the Movement.

REV. H. W. WILBERFORCE TO REV. J. H. NEWMAN.

Farnham Castle: November 10, 1833.

I have brought with me a few copies of the tracts to show my Lord. . . . Sam proposes on his return [to the Island] to send round copies to the clergy, and ask them to express their notions thereon, that thus we may know how far we can reckon on their agreement with our principles.

I have shown the tracts to my Lord—that is, the 'Episcopal Church Apostolical,' the 'Primitive Practice,' the 'Liturgy,' and 'Shortening the Services.' He showed much more Church notions than I knew him to have. He approved all highly except the 'Sin of the Church,' and did not violently object to that; he particularly liked the 'Liturgy' and 'Episcopal Church Apostolical.' To sum up the whole, he said, 'Well, I think a copious and general distribution of these will do great good'; he then said, 'Why do they confine themselves so much to the one subject of the Apostolical commission? I wish they would treat other subjects.' I asked of what kind? 'Why, for example, Baptism. I think *much* too little is generally thought about it,' and from what he said more I think he quite agrees with us on that subject. He said that a private communication is always made to the Archbishop when it is contemplated to place any man on the bench, and if the Archbishop remonstrated, he has no doubt it would be dropped. But he approves the idea of petitioning the Archbishop if any man who seemed to the clergy very unfit was appointed. He spoke of Archdeacon Glover. He quite feels the want of intercourse among the clergy, and the good likely to arise from it.

I attacked Arnold. He had not seen his postscript, &c. I repeated the part about Ordination. And he seemed much shocked and immediately said, 'What can he make of the Ordination Service, "Receive the Holy Ghost," &c.?' This shows the sense in which *he* holds these words. I am sure you would like him if you knew his views and feelings.

REV. J. H. NEWMAN TO REV. R. H. FROUDE.

November 13, 1833.

I am in the midst of troubles and no one but such οὐτιδανοὶ [this is ironical] as Rogers to consult with. Palmer musters the Z.'s [Establishment men] in great force against the tracts, and some Evangelicals. He presses, and I am quite ready to admit, a disclaimer (in the shape of a circular) of the tracts. But he goes further, and wishes us to stop them. In these cases, success is the test of sagacity or rashness. The said tracts give offence, I know ; but they also do good ; and, I maintain, will *strengthen* the Association, by enabling it to take high ground, yet seem in the mean [μέσον]. I suggested to him that *we* were only doing *here* what *Rose* is doing *elsewhere*, who nevertheless is a member of the grand scheme. He said Rose was *known* as the editor of the Magazine. And so, I replied, I suppose Keble would have no objection to give his name to the tracts.

What will be done I know not ; but I want advice sadly. I have no confidence in anyone. If I could be sure of five or six vigorous co-operators in various parts, I would laugh at opposition ; but I fear being beaten from the field. Keble says we *must* be read, unless we grow stupid ; but I am not over-sure of our fertility even.

The tracts are certainly liked in many places ; among other persons, by the Bishop of Winchester. O that he would take us up ! I would go to the length of my tether to meet him. Henry Wilberforce is now there. I wonder whether, if one knew him, one might exert any influence over him. Evangelicals, as I anticipated, are struck with the 'Law of Liberty' and the 'Sin of the Church.' The subject of Discipline, too (I cannot doubt), will take them. Surely my game lies among them. I can make no hand of the Z.'s.

I am half out of spirits : but how one outgrows tenderness ! Several years back, to have known that half or all Oxford shook their heads at what I was doing (*e.g.* in the case of the Church Missionary Society) would have hurt me much, but somehow now I manage to exist. Do give me some advice and encouragement.

I do think our tracts, if we persist, will catch all the enthusiastic people among the Associated ; which will be wretched for the Z.'s.

One proposition is that we should cease the issue of the tracts till the address is happily got over ; but I say, 'Palmer, you delayed us five weeks with your scruples, which you yourself got over at last ; and now you are playing the same game again.' Yet I should shrink from spoiling the address, and I do not know what to do.

Tyler has at last plucked me, and sent back the sermons. He is dying for love of the Church, and most seraphic. I will give you the conclusion of his letter. I cannot find it. 'Salvam fac ecclesiam tuam, Domine,' is one of his *suspiria*. He gives no reason for not taking my sermons.

My dear Froude,—I do so fear I may be self-willed in this matter of the tracts. Pray do advise me according to your light.

P.S.—I have written to Palmer to say I will join his open Association if he wishes it, in spite of my dislike to it; but I will not cease my issue of tracts.

At Christmas I hope to make a missionary tour to Derby, Leicester, Huntingdonshire, Suffolk, Northamptonshire, &c.

Shuttleworth has, I believe, brought before the Hebdomadal Board the expediency of removing the Subscription to the Articles at entrance.

REV. R. H. FROUDE TO REV J. H. NEWMAN.

November 14, 1833.

'Αργείων ὄχ' ἄριστε, *i.e.* have you not been a spoon? to allow the Petition to have nothing about the 'system pre-supposed in the Rubrics,' and to leave out your key-words 'completing' and 'extra ecclesiastical'? The last word I would introduce thus: 'They take this opportunity of expressing their conviction that the powers with which God has entrusted the Spiritual Rulers of the Church are sufficient for its spiritual government, and that all extra-ecclesiastical interference in its spiritual concerns is both unnecessary and presumptuous.' My father is annoyed at its being such milk and water; do make a row about it.

I see already that I shall find in your book [the 'Arians'] sentences which I am sure stood when they were first written after some other sentence than that which affects to introduce them now, and seem conscious of being in the neighbourhood of a stranger—'buts' where there should have been 'ands' &c.—of which I shall make a catalogue and pay you off for all the *workings* you have given me before now. However, it looks very pretty; and when I puff it, and people turn over the pages, they have a very imposing effect. People say 'Ah! I dare say a very interesting work.'

In this correspondence R. H. Froude appears more as critic than originator or author. His more intimate friends required his criticisms and rested on his judgment. In his own person this faculty acted mainly as a check. He often speaks of trial and failure in his own attempts to bring out what was working in his mind, as, for instance : 'I have tried to write a criticism on the Apollo [Belvedere], but cannot bring out my meaning, which is abstruse and metaphysico-poetical. I always get bombastic, and am forced to scratch out.' His critical faculty was too masterful to be practised upon himself, but when exercised for the benefit of friends to whom he looked up, he could give free licence to a pungent pen, and yet leave the reader to understand how anxious those friends might well be to secure his comments as long as they were attainable. Keble, in his own simple way, sends his papers to his old pupil to be overlooked by him, and Mr. Newman was more at ease with Froude's imprimatur. Thus he sends him draughts of papers ; for example : 'No. 2 Keble,' 'No. 1 mine,' with the order, 'criticise the whole very accurately in matter and style, and send it back by return of post.' Of course the state of Froude's health made criticism more possible than authorship, but also different intellectual powers and functions are called into play.

REV. R. D. HAMPDEN, PRINCIPAL OF ST. MARY HALL, TO REV. J. H. NEWMAN.

November 15, 1833.

I am sorry to say that I have not had time as yet to give due consideration to the proposed Address from the Clergy, which you have been so kind as to send me. There are so many things before me just at present, which I am forced to attend to, that I readily pass over what is not equally imperative. I trust, therefore, that you will excuse my only acknowledging it with my thanks.

REV. J. H. NEWMAN TO J. W. BOWDEN, ESQ.

November 13, 1833.

We are full of difficulties. I have been strongly against an Association because it was awkward having one without Bishops, and because the High and Low Church parties would come into collision, and because it could hardly be responsible for tracts. You will see my scheme in the letter . . . however, I fear I shall be beaten. The consequence is, our tracts must be immediately disowned, as far as the responsibility of any Association is concerned. So circulars (I believe) are to be issued disclaiming them. We shall go on printing and circulating, however, through our own friends; though the High Church party wish us to stop them altogether. By 'we' I mean Keble, myself, Froude, and 'our friends' who are more or less the following (though not *associated* or bound together by any law; *i.e.* many people like naturally their own way) : Pusey and Harrison, Ch. Ch. (they *must* not be mentioned as of our party), Williams of Trinity; Christie, Rogers, Mozley and the Wilberforces, Oriel; T. Keble, Prevost, Rickards, Sale, of Magdalen; Rose, Perceval, Golightly, Dyson, &c. I am writing this in great confidence; to *say* these were with us would be quite unwarrantable, nor have we any wish to form a party, but I think they are persons who feel keenly, and would circulate our tracts.

On the other hand Palmer, backed by Mr. Norris, &c. &c., is afraid of the tracts, and wishes them stopped, and is aiming at an Association. I say, let everyone employ his talent in his own way. Let there be an Association, if they can do it, and we will be members of it, to avoid appearance of schism : though I confess I do not like joining in anything the Bishops have not publicly sanctioned. Still, nevertheless, why may we not go on with our tracts? Unless I see reason, I must. Perhaps we shall proclaim Keble editor, but this is uncertain.

We are very strong (I hope) in Leicestershire, Cheshire, Hants, Oxford, and Northamptonshire; but we may miscalculate our force here and there. Men fall off when they come to the scratch. The Duke of Newcastle has joined us 'in life and death, so that we are true to ourselves,' and Lord Arden, Lord Kenyon, Sir W. Heathcote, Joshua Watson, the Bishop of Winchester (I hope), Gladstone, &c. But I suppose these names must not be mentioned by anyone. Of course, there is much coldness and opposition here, for this is a criticising place; but never mind, we will beat them.

I will consider your objection about the leave to alter the tracts. Keble agrees with you, but I do not myself see the difficulty. Would a person go to the expense of reprinting a tract which he has made nonsense by inserting 'not,' &c., when he might write and print one of his own? I am very sleepy, so must leave off.

P.S.—We have no regular committee, but suppose we shall ultimately have one in Oxford or London. At present we aim at an indefinite number of local associations. For names of leaders take Rose, Archdeacon Bayley, Norris, Keble, Palmer, Hook, Rickards, Dean of Ripon, Archdeacon Froude, the Wilberforces, Greswell of C. C. C., author of the 'Harmony,' Lancaster, Miller, &c. We have agreed to make Turrill's house our depôt. I am the 'Churchman' of the 'Record.' I hope I have omitted no question of yours. Thanks for your criticisms, they are always valuable.

REV. J. H. NEWMAN TO J. W. BOWDEN, ESQ.

November 17, 1833.

... As to the indirect inculcation of the Apostolical doctrines, we have begun the records of the Church with that view. We are printing extracts from Eusebius, &c., giving little stories of the Apostles, Fathers, &c., to familiarise the imagination of the reader to an Apostolical state of the Church. It was with the same view that we projected our ballads. I had not forgotten Arius's, but his was the abuse of a lawful expedient. What is the 'Lyra Apostolica' but a ballad? It was undertaken with a view of catching people when unguarded. Besides, there is every difference between the especially sacred subject which Arius treated in a popular way and ours. However, I do not think you need be alarmed; probably the series will turn out to be composed of such passages as Dryden's (Chaucer's) description of a good parson, parts of Herbert's 'Country Parson.' ...

Whenever you talk of the tracts, mind and persist they are not connected with the Association, but the production of 'Residents in Oxford.' I wish them called the 'Oxford Tracts,' but I cannot myself so call them, for modesty's sake. So I think that soon I shall advertise them as 'Tracts for the Times, by Residents in Oxford,' which, of course, will soon be corrupted into Oxford Tracts.

If you had read the dissertations on Becket in the 'British,' you would be somewhat prepared for the kind of system we suppose Hildebrand to have set up. Now our notion is that things are returning so fast to a state of dissolution, that we ought to be prepared, and to prepare the public mind, for a restoration of the old Apostolic system.

The question of the Papal Apostasy is a long one. As to Prophecy, ought it to be the rule of our judgment about existing institutions? I am not quite clear.

REV. R. H. FROUDE TO REV. J. H. NEWMAN

November 17, 1833.

. . . As to giving up the tracts, the notion is odious. Norris writes to my father to announce that the tract system was (he was happy to say) abandoned. We must throw the Z.'s overboard; they are a small, and, as my father says, daily diminishing party. He is much inclined to them himself, but will take trouble to circulate the tracts. . . . I wish you could get to know something of S. and W., and unprotestantise and un-Miltonise them. I think they are our sort, enthusiasts of a sort there are not many of. A real genuine enthusiast is the rarest thing going; yet on Trower's authority we may aspire to that rank. . . . Do keep writing to Keble and stirring his rage; he is my fire, but I may be his poker. . . . I conclude with the emphatic words of Martinus Scriblerus: 'Ye Gods, annihilate both space and time,' and bring me back again with copious notes in my pocket on 'State of Religion in the United States.'

REV. JOHN KEBLE TO REV. J. H. NEWMAN.

November 19, 1833.

Spry's and Miller's letters put together seem to point out a definite mode of proceeding, which may be useful. Spry, you see, wants an Association, *quatenus* an avowal of principle, not *quatenus* tracts. Miller approves of our present notions, but wants some business-like statement to give effect to them in other quarters. I think it will be very hard to get anything like a distinct declaration, such as Spry wants, numerously signed enough; qy. whether the address will not answer the purpose sufficiently? If Mr. Norris, or any other weighty person or persons from afar, would meet my weighty self at Oxford next week, we might all lay our heads together to some purpose. Palmer will probably be back from Winton.

You will see in Miller's a hint touching the multiplication of tracts, which a little comforted me for having said what I afterwards feared might check or damp you in that line; you see what we mean—not to make things too cheap. The sooner we can set John Miller down to some of the tracts which he has got in his head, the better, don't you think?

I like your papers better and better, and so does my sister. Transubstantiation and all [this is a week-day lecture].

REV. SAMUEL RICKARDS TO REV. J. H. NEWMAN.

November 20, 1833.

I cannot let the day go by without doing what I can through you to enter my protest against the tract under the title 'Heads of a Week-day Lecture.' I do not dwell so much upon the points, which yet I think are objectionable, that it makes too rapid an advance upon events which may or may not be coming on, and that it is calculated to bring on the evils it alludes to rather than avert them; but what I most deplore is the language in which it speaks of some of the gifts bestowed upon the ministers of Christ, and especially the expression 'as intrusted with the awful and mysterious gift of making the bread and wine, Christ's Body and Blood.'

Of course I do not quarrel with the expression when I meet with it in writers who lived before the controversies introduced into the world upon the subject, through the errors of the Church of Rome; but to use it now, and moreover to use it in a set of tracts which at any rate will be read at first with a good deal of suspicion, and in most instances with a view to ascertain what sort of men write them, and what the real objects of the Association are, appears to me to be nothing less than tossing firebrands into our own work.

I do not at all like the supposition which this tract and some others also, too much encourage, that hitherto a very large share of the respect paid to clergymen has been because they were of the rank of gentlemen, &c. To my mind these allusions betray a soreness upon these matters much below and utterly unworthy of the parson of a parish; who, wherever he is really respected, stands upon ground quite his own, and with which his happening to be a gentleman has hardly anything to do.

I find great fault, also, that in an Association composed partly, and probably to a good extent, of persons who think that the point to be maintained is that no alteration should be made in the Liturgy, except under the competent authority by which it has been done before, the tracts (I think, rashly) take the higher station, and maintain that no changes should be so much as listened to—a line of proceeding which seems to me to betray an unwarrantable distrust of our bishops, as well as to treat the whole affair in the most provoking manner to those who are seeking for change.

There are other matters I could mention if I saw you, but I will not trouble you with more in writing ; but this in honesty I must add, that if the tracts are to be written in the same irritated and irritating spirit in which several of them have been written, I will belong to the Association no longer.

The 'Short Address' by a layman, and 'The Gospel a Law of Liberty,' appear to me to be models for our work, and calculated to do the greatest service to the cause. Indeed, there is not one of the whole set which does not please me a hundred times as much as it displeases me ; but there are ugly sentences in some of them. In my zeal for my own thoughts and feelings, and my efforts to blurt them out at all hazards, I have hardly left myself room to send my thanks for your book [the 'Arians']. I feel this is in appearance a very unkindly letter, and almost a fierce one, but it was never meant so.

[N.B.—Rickards would have liked tracts written in the style of Richard Hooker or Isaac Walton. They would have been classical, but would have failed of their purpose. As to the 'Short Address,' which is Bowden's, I remark that, suited as it is to minds like Rickards', it has by others been thought not only, on the one hand, *heavy*, but, on the other hand, '*provoking and irritating*.' As to its heaviness, Keble says (Nov. 5, '33), 'The layman's address is excellent, but hardly plain enough,' and I suspect that 'Richard Nelson' was written to do what the layman did not do. And, as to his style being irritating and provoking, I find from one of R. F. Wilson's letters, September 2, 1834, that Bowden's tract on Christian Liberty (No. 29) raised quite a storm at Bocking, and (I think) caused refusal of a church rate.—J. H. N.]

Mr. Rickards's pen was a rougher weapon than his tongue. In conversation with Mr. Newman his disagreement with the tract in question would have been perhaps as real, but personal contact would have softened, brightened, cleared the atmosphere. Mr. Rickards could not have spoken as he wrote, or, if he had, it would not have sounded quite the same. It would have been Mr. Rickards's way. Under his singular conversational gifts his censure would have fitted in with a certain quaintness of expression which gave character to all he said.

Mr. Newman answered this attack the next day. His letter has recently come into the Editor's hands (in 1889), being found in a packet of Mr. Newman's letters to Mr. Rickards, sent by his widow, many years after, to Mrs. J. Mozley. The letter told very strongly upon Mr. Newman's memory.

If Mr. Rickards's letter may be considered characteristic of its writer, the answer to it will be felt by the reader to be instinct with the spirit of the Movement and with Newman as its leader.

Rev. J. H. Newman to Rev. S. Rickards.

Oriel College: November 22, 1833.

Your letters are always acceptable; and do not fancy one is less so which happens to be objurgatory. Faithful are the blows of a friend, and surely I may be antecedently sure that I require them in many respects. As to our present doings, we are set off, and with God's speed we will go forward, through evil report and good report, through real and supposed blunders. We are as men climbing a rock, who tear clothes and flesh, and slip now and then, and yet make progress (so be it!), and are careless that bystanders criticise, so that their cause gains while they lose. We are set out, and we have funds for the present; we, like the widow's cruse, shall not fail. This then is our position: connected with no association, answerable to no one except God and His Church, committing no one, bearing the blame, doing the work. I trust I speak sincerely in saying, I am willing that it be said I go too far, so that I push on the cause of truth some little way. Surely it is energy that gives edge to any undertaking, and energy is ever incautious and exaggerated. I do not say this to excuse such defects, or as conscious of having them myself, but as a consolation and explanation to those who love me, but are sorry at some things I do. Be it so; it is well to fall if you kill your adversary. Nor can I wish anyone a happier lot than to be himself unfortunate, yet to urge on a triumphant cause; like Laud and Ken in their day, who left a name which after ages censure or pity, but whose works do follow them. Let it be the lot of those I love to live in the heart of one or two in each succeeding generation, or to be altogether forgotten, while they have helped forward the truth.

As to your particular criticisms, I have been so busy that I have failed to let my correspondence keep pace with work. *The Association has nothing to do with the tracts.* The latter are the work of Oxford men; Keble, myself, and others are answerable for them. This removes, I conceive, part of your objection. It would be highly indecorous in an *association* or *man in office*, or *of name*, to contemplate the downfall of the clergy; but the very use and meaning of anonymousness is that you say things worth saying in themselves, but not *fit* for you to say. Surely it is highly desirable that this topic should be present among other topics to the minds of the Church, as an element of bringing about certain results. I mean, stirring up the clergy; and if you say this is addressed not to the clergy, but to the people, I admit—but it was said *at* the clergy, and perhaps could not be decently addressed *to* them. The notion of the tract was to set the clergy upon preaching to their flocks; it only professes to be heads of a lecture, and the passage you object to was in matter of fact not delivered in the harsh form in which it stands. These remarks will explain, at least, that we do not act without thought and design, though of course you are quite at liberty to think that we err in judgment. The truth is there is an extreme difficulty in hitting the exact thing that will do. It is only attained by a series of experiments. Nor is it fair to look at each tract by itself: each is part of a whole intended to effect one or two great ends. Hence the different tone of them (which you notice), and which, be assured, does not arise from difference in the writers, but the same writer aiming (whether or not from error of judgment) at the same end in a different way. It is necessary to wake the clergy; if you get them even to criticise, it is no slight thing. Willingly would I (if I) be said to write in an irritating and irritated way, if in that way I rouse people. I maintain (whether rightly or wrongly, but I *maintain*) that by ways such as these alone can one move them. As to the *resisting alterations*, I am amused, though instructed, at the variety of opinions, as of criticisms (*e.g.* there is hardly one tract which in its turn has not been the best). Now it happens that, against my own judgment, I have been urged to drop the question of the 'Competent Authority' for altering the Liturgy (though it *is* noticed in some of the tracts), under the notion that people are not ripe for it (and it is matter of fact that the tract on alterations in the Liturgy has been more approved generally than any other), but all the while I quite agree with you it *is* a point to press ; and in matter of fact for the last six weeks a friend of mine has had a pamphlet on hand at my suggestion about it. I inserted a clause against ' extra-ecclesiastical alterations,' both in the ' Suggestions ' and the 'Address,' but each time it was cut out. Lastly, I must just touch upon the notice of the Lord's Supper. In confidence to a friend, I can only admit it was *imprudent*, for I do think we have most of us dreadfully low notions of the Blessed Sacrament. I expect to be called a Papist when my opinions are known. But (please God) I shall lead persons on a little way, while they fancy they are only taking the mean, and denounce me as the extreme. Thus all good is done (I do not say *kept up*) by going before people, and letting them fancy they are striking a balance. Let others be doctors of the Church. I do not aim at being such (though I think myself right); let me be thought extravagant, and yet be copied.

Here you have a sketch of views and feelings which, had I the happiness to be often with you, you at least would be more able to do justice to, as hearing them *vivâ voce*. We will take advice and thank you ; we will thank you for cuffs ; but we will take our own line according to the light given us by Almighty God and His Holy Church. We trust to be independent of all men, and to be liable to be stopped by none, and it is a weakness to be pained, which I hope to get over. Time was when to know the greater part of Oxford was against me would have saddened me. That I have got over, I think ; but still I suffer when criticised by friends. Never suppose I shall be 'over-praised.' I hear but the faults of what I do. It is good for me I should do so, but sometimes I am apt to despair, and with difficulty am kept up to my work. Nay, I am apt to go into the other extreme, and peevishly fancy men my enemies, as anticipating opposition as a matter of course. But enough of this.

The address goes on splendidly. Already we have two thousand clergy who will sign it. You do not state your view of it. Its object *entre nous* is threefold ; to rouse the clergy to think and combine, to strengthen the Archbishop against Whately, and to strengthen the Church as an independent power against the liberalisers in and out of Parliament. . . . Send me word if you will co-operate about the address, and I will tell you what to do.

Here this correspondence on the tracts appears to have ended. Letters continued to pass between the friends, as will be seen, showing kindly interchange of thought, but the conduct of the Movement does not seem to have been touched upon again. As time goes on, Mr. Newman confides to Mr. Rickards some doubts that pressed upon him, but there is no return to that happy freedom of intercourse on the subject that engrossed Mr. Newman's mind, which marks their early correspondence.[1]

REV. R. H. FROUDE TO REV. J. H. NEWMAN.

Pierce's Hotel, Falmouth: November 20, 1833.

The box we dined in last year with all the tricolours and trophies of the three days, but no Pedroites.

Friday.—I am to start to-morrow. I am at Archdeacon Sheepshanks'. First let me congratulate you on your letter

[1] It may be said that opinions, once formed deliberately, did seem with Mr. Rickards incapable of change, modification, or softening. His feelings towards the Church of Rome were such that nothing could prepare him, in the case of anyone he had once regarded with affection, for an actual conversion to her communion. These feelings were so well known to his friends that, as years passed by, they shrank from paining him by the reports that were familiar to the Oxford world, and were *more* than reports to those connected with Mr. Newman. It thus happened that in 1845, when at a social gathering of almost a public nature, the *fact* of Mr. Newman's reception into the Roman Church was spoken of as imminent, if not already accomplished, Mr. Rickards stood up and contradicted it. It was a blow that ought to have been spared him. A friend writing in 1878 described, or rather intimated, this scene to Dr. Newman. He wrote in answer: 'You could not have done a kinder thing to me than to tell me about Rickards. For it seemed to account for the conduct towards me of one whom I ever loved and whom in memory I ever look back upon with affection. No house was ever pleasanter to me than his, and I have him and Mrs. Rickards as in 1826, 1827 and 1832 vividly before me. But the tracts divided us from the very first. He protested against the earliest of them, and wrote me what he himself called a fierce letter. He made attempts to soften his words, but the "ugly passages" which he wished to cut out were just those which alone in my eyes were of any value. He wrote me a kind, or rather beautiful, letter after No. 90, and called once with Mrs. R. on me at Littlemore.'

Mr. Newman goes on to explain that he had wished those who knew his course of thought should report it to all friends who had, as he might suppose, a *right* to know. And when the act of separation from the Church of England came, he seems to have not been able to understand how any should be unprepared.

of yesterday. You have done it in style. [N.B.—I have not the letter ; it contained the correspondence between Arnold and me.] Polonius would give you most credit for the word 'respond.' 'Which of course has its praise' is capital.

This correspondence with Arnold is not in any of the papers that have been placed before the Editor.

VEN. ARCHDEACON FROUDE TO REV. J. H. NEWMAN.

November 25, 1833.

I had intended to have written to you this very day before Mr. Palmer's circular and your accompaniment were received. The address certainly is in itself a most unmeaning affair, but people who desire a movement will possibly give it some importance as a first step.

The fact may be that the great body of the clergy know so little of the actual state of things that they would hardly believe the near approach of an important crisis. . . . In this way I reconcile myself to the milk-and-water production that must go to Lambeth. Besides, a signature is looked upon as a sort of smart-money that in most cases will be acknowledged as a regular enlistment for future service. I can scarcely fix on an individual in my archdeaconry who is likely to make an objection ; but as the thing brings publicity, I dare say the Whigs will use all their influence to defeat us. My brother Archdeacons, Stephens and Barnes, are quite alive to the mischief that is brewing. They differ about the propriety of signing an address to our own Bishop. I think it had better be omitted ; for besides, as between a Bishop and his own clergy such a compliment goes for little, I should be sorry to have the main object mixed up with another measure. . . . Do desire Mr. S. Wilberforce to write to Mr. Lyte. My neighbour will be glad to find what his friend's views are. He is a capital speaker, very generally liked, and in times of difficulty will be sure to act an important part.

By the beginning of the year we shall be ripe for associations. Is it not advisable that you should be prepared to assist your country friends with forms, regulations, &c. . . .

The Rev. Saml. Rowe of Stonehouse will be a useful correspondent ; he is methodical, diligent, and right-minded, and has much influence with a respectable part of the yeomanry in the neighbourhood of Plymouth, as well as among a large population in his own parish.

J. W. BOWDEN, ESQ., TO REV. J. H. NEWMAN.

Capheaton: November 25, 1833.

With regard to the Chancellorship [1] I should be much obliged by a *single line*, as soon as the *day of election* is fixed. Why is not the Archbishop to be chosen ? Mind and let me know whom *you* and *yours* support, and, if there is any danger of a sharp contest, I will move southwards to be at my post. Were the Archbishop put up I would certainly come. I should like to see him returned by a sweeping majority, both with regard to its effect upon the country and on his own future conduct. It might tend to *athenaize* him.[2] But this, I am afraid, is a dream. I see the distinction you make between the apostasy *of* a Church and an apostasy *in* a Church ; but, as you say, the question is a long one.

I have heard of your correspondence with Arnold from Rogers. I shall make you show me, in confidence, the documents. I am getting out of the world of news. From some sneers which I saw in the 'Globe' against McGhee and others, I suppose that there have been some Apostolical proceedings in Ireland. I have got nearly half-way through the 'Arians,' which is what I expected it to be. I fear, though, that it is *too good* for extensive circulation at the present day ; but you do not write for *the day*.

I have never asked what Ogle thought of what was going on, partly, I believe, from a lurking fear that he was not with us.

The following letter shows that the Movement was beginning to tell and make a stir :

REV. J. A. STEPHENSON TO REV. J. H. NEWMAN.

Lympsham, Somerset: November 25, 1833.

Your name having been mentioned as that of an influential member of the Church Conservative Society at Oxford, I am requested by a society of clerical friends in this neighbourhood to solicit your kind attention and advice.

We have been informed on episcopal authority 'that the

---

[1] Chancellorship of the University of Oxford vacant by the death of Lord Grenville.

[2] Compare Justin Martyr, *Quæst. Gentil. ad Christianos* (III. ii. 350, ed. Otto): τὸν πάλαι ἀθηναΐζοντα φιλόσοφον Πλάτωνα.

ministerial plan of ecclesiastical and liturgical reform is intended to surprise the world by its extensiveness as much as the Commons Reform Bill did,' that it is designed to leave out of the amended Prayer Book everything that gives any offence to anybody, and that the Bishop of London and the Archbishop of Dublin have already 'come over' to the support of the alteration.

Under these circumstances we are fearful of the concession implied in the last paragraph of the now circulating address to the Archbishop of Canterbury being taken advantage of, and the condition attached to it being overlooked. We are fearful of the word 'correction' being construed as applied to the Liturgy.

The assault on that grand bastion, the Athanasian Creed (long since left out of the American Episcopal Liturgy), has been already opened by Canon Woodhouse. Feeling ourselves the inestimable value of that Creed, not only on account of its lucid, cautious, and most instructive explanations of the grand subjects of the Christian faith, but also on account of its forming, together with the Commination Service, the only remaining displays of the power of the Church to pronounce those excluded from its Communion, who do not adhere to its doctrines and its duties, we think that a determined stand should be made for its reservation.

Would it do to promote an address to the King or to the Bench of Bishops or to the two Houses of Convocation now adjourned, but not dissolved, to the following purpose?

We the undersigned. . . . beg to express our confidence in . . . . for the prevention of any alteration whatever affecting, directly or indirectly, the invaluable doctrines of the Church of England, or in any degree superseding the existing use of any of the three Creeds, the Hymn of Glory to the Father, &c., or any other standing formula of the faith. We are. . . . &c.

Lastly, if the idea met your approbation, would you originate it at Alma Mater? '*Dominus*' *est adhuc* '*illuminatio*' *ejus*. And from her the Light, scattering these dark clouds, ought, as in many former instances, first to radiate. God grant it may shine forth more and more brilliantly. We have no real reason for apprehension.

With much respect and gratitude for the exertions, of which some information has reached us, I am, &c. &c.

REV. THOS. MOZLEY TO REV. J. H. NEWMAN.

November 27, 1833.

You have had so many rubs and buffets that one looks on you as a person made to receive such things, with *robur et œs triplex* to bear any amount of vexation and annoyance one may inflict. Mr. S. has come to a complete standstill. He has been into Northampton, and among others seen a Mr. B., who entirely approved of the address, and was prepared to go any lengths; but, glancing his eye on the sheet, to his horror he found no printer's name, and immediately cast it away from him as a venomous thing. . . .

Now for your tracts. The one which has made you so very interesting a man to some of your readers—that is, 'The Gospel a Law of Liberty'—has not had the same effect here. Mr. Lloyd Crawley takes great exception to one or two passages: he underscores the *little* express command for public worship, and refers to Matthew xviii. 20; and having been engaged in various tithe suits and arguments with Quakers, in which he has always spoken of tithes as any other property, the result of individual grants, he is frightened at your founding the payment of tithes on imitation of the patriarchal and Jewish rule.

REV. E. B. PUSEY, D.D., TO REV. J. H. NEWMAN.

Monday evening: November 1833.

I shall have much pleasure in signing the address to the Archbishop, but I think it would be a great object not to make it the work of the Association, unless it were meant to express its loyalty and subordination. Many, I should think, would be glad to sign the address who would doubt about the consequences of an Association.

[N.B.—This was before Pusey had joined the Movement. Indeed, he was too ill to take part in it.—J. H. N.]

END OF THE FIRST VOLUME

www.ingramcontent.com/pod-product-compliance
Lightning Source LLC
Chambersburg PA
CBHW032137010526
44111CB00035B/604